Good
Writing

Good Writing

An Argument Rhetoric

Connie Snyder Mick

University of Notre Dame

New York   Oxford
Oxford University Press

Oxford University Press is a department of the University of Oxford.
It furthers the University's objective of excellence in research, scholarship,
and education by publishing worldwide. Oxford is a registered trade mark of
Oxford University Press in the UK and certain other countries.

Published in the United States of America by Oxford University Press
198 Madison Avenue, New York, NY 10016, United States of America.

© 2019 by Oxford University Press

Library of Congress Cataloging-in-Publication Data
CIP data is on file at the Library of Congress 9780199947256
Library of Congress Cataloging in Publication Control Number:
2018008308 (print)

9 8 7 6 5 4 3 2 1
Printed by LSC Communications, Inc., United States of America

brief contents

table of contents

preface

IN GOOD WRITING, an argument rhetoric for first-year writing courses, we propose that "good writers" persuade audiences to take action based on their presentation of facts, claims, evidence, and reasons. In addition, like many of us who teach writing, we are committed to the idea that "good writing" is in fact writing *for the common good*, ethical writing that persuades others to think and act in ways that advance humanity.

Good Writing: An Argument Rhetoric encourages emerging as well as experienced writers to discern their purpose and responsibility as writers, to acknowledge and inventory the choices available to them as writers, and to consider the ethics of those choices. We present argument as a powerful tool that comes with responsibilities, in academic as well as public contexts. As the primary way people lead others to change their mind, argument is the means by which academic exchange as well as social progress is animated—or thwarted.

The purpose of this textbook is not to teach that good writing *can* change the world, but rather to demonstrate how good writing *does* change the world. Good writing—and good writers—contribute to ongoing debates through clear and responsible representations of fact, evidence, and claims. Indeed, writers must have the courage to write with integrity—even when others do not. In this way, writing becomes an act of ethical leadership, and writing students are encouraged to imagine themselves in positions of academic, community, and workplace leadership.

APPROACH

Good Writing supports the teaching and learning objectives of first-year writing courses through its emphasis on linguistic and intellectual clarity in argument and research. Throughout, we have been both mindful of and guided by best practices in the teaching of writing, especially those set forth in two documents from the Council of Writing Program Administrators (WPA): the *Framework for Success in Postsecondary Writing*, and the *Outcomes Statement for First-Year Composition*.

The rhetorical instruction and diverse readings in this book advance the concept of writing for social change in a distinct yet accessible way. Interdisciplinary areas such as Futures Studies, Performance Studies, Poverty Studies, and Peace Studies inform strategies of creative yet practical inquiry, with an emphasis on temporal modes of thinking: knowledge of the past, awareness of the present, and vision for the future.

Acknowledging that writing skills and critical thinking skills are connected, *Good Writing* helps students work through arguments step-by-step to design *scalable, supportable,* and *significant* compositions. And it asks that those compositions relate to significant social concerns—not just what advertisers or pundits would have us attend to. This way, students develop the confidence that their writing matters, that through writing they have taught their readers—and themselves—something important. We teachers have an opportunity—even an obligation—to make those pages we assign each semester count, to encourage writing that contributes to critical thinking that advances the common good. In this approach, students can come to see skilled writing as a vehicle for positive expression in all domains—home, work, academic, and civic life—through published research, policy statements, letters to the editor, and the many ways we communicate daily.

Good Writing also teaches the principles of sound research—not only the practice of searching databases, but also the ethics of writing with integrity. Library resources evolve quickly. The research instruction that endures is that which emphasizes the ethics of sound research. As teachers, we cannot overemphasize the importance of writing with integrity—particularly when we encourage student writers to conduct field research with human subjects and engage in other ways of collecting information beyond the library walls. *Good Writing* analyzes the rhetorical situation with particular emphasis on understanding both audience and stakeholders, and therefore provides the foundation for writing with integrity in any domain.

Replete with readings and assignments class-tested on basic to advanced writers from across the disciplines, *Good Writing* focuses on the centrality of ethical research to meaningful discourse.

SERVICE-LEARNING, COMMUNITY ENGAGEMENT, AND *GOOD WRITING*

Good Writing provides a strong foundation for community-engaged writing and community-engaged composition courses. In addition to its alignment with WPA statements, *Good Writing* promotes the knowledge, skills, and attitudes that foster meaningful community engagement through writing as outlined by Campus Compact, the Carnegie Foundation Community Engagement classification, and the AAC&U emphasis on Civic Engagement and High-Impact Practices that includes writing intensive courses and service-learning/community-based learning.

Good Writing has ample support for instructors who wish to teach first-year writing as a course that fulfills a campus service-learning requirement, but it is in no way limited to community-engaged courses. Instructors who are not teaching a service-learning course will find in *Good Writing* an approach to deepen students' understanding and readiness to engage diverse communities in a way that is at once consonant with the principles of community engagement and transferable to other academic and professional writing situations. *Good Writing* encourages that deepening culture of engagement by helping students become more informed of current issues in local, national, and international communities; by introducing them to examples of engaged writing that have generated a positive impact; and by giving them opportunities to write for, with, and to those external communities. The assignments and readings in *Good Writing* reinforce those core principles of meaningful, respectful communication with others that are central both to the teaching of writing and to the development of authentic community engagement.

ORGANIZATION

Good Writing is organized to be both modular and flexible. The chapters can be assigned in a linear sequence or concurrently with each other. For example, a project from Part Three, "Writing with Purpose," could be assigned at the same time as chapters on research strategies (Part Five) and writing ethically (Part One).

Part One, "Foundations of Writing and Critical Thinking," introduces students to the importance of ethical argumentation in historical and current settings and lays the groundwork for critical writing and critical reading. Part Two, "The Writing Process," describes and models the writing process that scaffolds each major writing assignment in Part Three. The chapters represent the primary, recursive movements of composing—pre-writing, researching, writing, revising, proofreading—with specific steps within each that take writers from one point to the next in detail, illuminating their writing choices. The heart of the book is Part Three, "Arguing with Purpose." Here, seven chapters organized broadly by genre and purpose offer specific projects (traditional researched arguments, as well as more creative and multimodal compositions) that encourage students to practice the moves of academic and community rhetoric in increasingly complex, yet always personally meaningful, situations. Options are given for each writing project so that students and instructors can make choices that fit their interests and learning objectives. Each major writing assignment includes a detailed template that takes writers through the steps of completing a project detailed in Part Two. Each template is followed by authentic student as well as published writing from a diverse range of voices engaged with relevant topics. These compelling, evocative texts serve to model the learning objectives for that assignment, as well as encourage constructive in-class dialogue.

Part Four, "Writing Strategies," is a toolkit of writing fundamentals that offers useful guidance to emerging writers, as well as reinforcement for more confident students. Part Four offers expert yet accessible advice on employing classical and modern modes and refining style, including brief guides to Modern Language Association (MLA) 8th edition citation and formatting. In addition, Part Four includes detailed chapters on inclusive writing, as well as design and delivery of print, digital, and oral presentations; and it also considers ethical choices related to these topics. Part Five, "Doing Research," teaches students how to find, evaluate, and work with published and human sources that will support students' writing. Part Five emphasizes throughout not just the technical aspects of citation but also the ethical spirit of giving credit where credit is due.

Good Writing emphasizes the importance of achieving global goals through local means. Writers (especially emerging writers) who start with a personal connection to their subject, or who create a personal connection through direct engagement, typically write and research with greater passion, integrity, and impact. Many projects suggested in *Good Writing*, therefore, require writers to research widely but also give them the opportunity, with their instructor's permission, to create new information through fieldwork, interviews, surveys, and other kinds of research skills that invite direct contact with local experts and experiences.

Readings and *Good Writing*

Readings throughout *Good Writing* serve the multiple purposes of a writing classroom, including:

- Modeling student writing for class assignments in various stages, from invention to polished drafts, written by diverse students on a range of topics that show how they have used the assignment to explore their concerns
- Exploring information on current events that challenges students with provocative new ideas, facts, and points of view that motivate further exploration and inquiry
- Inspiring students through models of published writers who have made an impact on audiences in civic life

The three general purposes of readings, then, are to model (assignments and genres), inform (on social change historically and in current events), and inspire (through the writer's success in writing for social change). The emphasis in *Good Writing* on this last category is intended to encourage an emerging writer's development of *ethos*. Using a robust but focused theme enables students to accumulate knowledge on an issue that will inform and inspire their research and writing.

FEATURES

In addition to its consistent focus on applying an ethical lens to every element of writing, *Good Writing* includes the following distinct features:

Across the Chapters

- *Critical Questions*—Occasional questions provide pedagogical breathing points for instructors to assess students' understanding and engagement with the reading. Questions can be answered in writing by individuals or in groups as in-class activities. The questions may also function as pre-writing for major assignments.
- *Office Hours*—Beginning with each chapter in Part Two, this feature helps students navigate human help on campus: peers, professors, writing center consultants, librarians, and others. It reiterates the importance of testing writing on a live audience and guides writers through the best practices of getting good feedback.
- *In Process*—In each chapter of Part Three, major writing assignments are described in detail. Options are given so that students and instructors can make choices that fit their interests and learning objectives. Each major writing assignment includes a detailed template that takes writers through the steps of completing a project detailed in Part Two.

With Each Reading

- *Headnotes*—Each selection includes a headnote providing context about the author, publication, and rhetorical situation, modeling the advice *Good Writing* gives students on writing a rhetorical analysis.
- *"For Reflection"*—Questions that follow each reading help deepen conversations and make connections to content and concepts elsewhere in *Good Writing*.

ANCILLARIES

- *Instructor's Resource Manual*—Teaching materials offered through an Instructor's Manual and a robust website support instructors in helping writers define what counts as a significant social concern for that community of readers, offering probing questions for discussion or in-class writing. Through this process of inquiry, students define their interests, their self-interests, and ward off the feeling of disinterest in writing.
- *Website*—The website for *Good Writing* will be kept up-to-date with new readings and advice for instructors using the text. A social media presence for the book will provide an opportunity for community–to share each other's work, support each other's research, and examine current events through the lens of ethical argument.

about the author

CONNIE SNYDER MICK, PH.D., is Academic Director of the Center for Social Concerns and Co-director of the Poverty Studies Interdisciplinary Minor at the University of Notre Dame. At Notre Dame, Dr. Mick has taught a range of courses focused on writing and social action: Writing and Rhetoric (community-based learning and traditional); Multimedia Composition; Writing Center Theory and Practice; Graduate Practicum: Teaching Writing; Scientific Writing and Communication; Social Concerns Seminars; the Capstone for Poverty Studies; Introduction to Poverty Studies; Rhetorics of Gender and Poverty; Confronting Poverty: Bringing Service to Justice; Foresight in Business and Society (community-based research); Management Communication; and Ethical Leadership Through Service and Civic Engagement. She directed writing centers at Notre Dame and Loyola University, Chicago, for ten years. Dr. Mick seeks to advance the vision of the Center for Social Concerns as a "living well for social justice" by helping to deepen the culture of community-engaged teaching, research, and learning across the university. She supports the scholarship of engagement through consulting faculty on engaged teaching, awarding course development grants, and directing the community engagement Faculty Fellows program. Dr. Mick founded and directs the Community Engagement Faculty Institute, a three-day immersion into the theory and practice of community-engaged teaching, research, and scholarship. Dr. Mick's research addresses the impact of engagement on student learning and community development, the role of writing in social change, the rhetorics of poverty, the ethics of storytelling in engaged learning, and the pedagogies of community engagement. She published *Poverty/Privilege: A Reader for Writers*, Oxford University Press (2015). Recent work appears in the *Michigan Journal of Community Service Learning*; *Pedagogy: Critical Approaches to Teaching Literature, Language, Composition, and Culture*; *Service-Learning: Enhancing Inclusive Education*; *TESOL Journal*; *Advances in Service-Learning Research*; and *Foundational Practices in Online Writing Instruction*.

acknowledgments

THIS TEXTBOOK IS GOING PUBLIC AT A TIME when we need more attention to the ethics of civic discourse, and I am grateful to all the people who supported my vision to teach argument for the common good.

At Notre Dame, I thank Kasey Swanke for her tireless support as a research assistant early in the project, as well as undergraduate assistants Rachel Ganson and Elle Anteau. I thank Fr. Paul Kollman, Fr. Bill Lies, Fr. Kevin Sandberg, Jay Brandenberger, Mary Beckman, and all my colleagues at the Center for Social Concerns for supporting this work. Thanks to Danielle Wood, Darlene Hampton, and Jim Frabutt for insight on the ethics of human subjects work. Debbie Blasko and Patrena Kedik provided invaluable administrative support. Stuart Greene, John Duffy, Nicole MacLaughlin, Matthew Capdevielle, and Beth Capdevielle kept me close to and in awe of the University Writing Program at Notre Dame; in addition, Patrick Clauss and Erin McLaughlin provided critical feedback on multimodal composition. Colleagues in the dynamic field of Community Writing inspired and informed me along the way.

Thanks to Carrie Brandon for reeling me into this amazing work. At Oxford University Press, thanks to the magnificent Meg Botteon for making all my work better and to Garon Scott for making all the pieces pop. Thanks to Denise Phillip Grant, Chris Enman, Brad Rau, and Suzanne Copenhagen and their teams for support on permissions and editing.

Deepest thanks go to my Mick family who made this possible through their patience and encouragement—Brad, Sophia, and Harper. And thanks to my broader family—Mom, Elaine, and the whole Shafer crew who inspire my concern for the world and confirm my belief that change is possible.

Finally, the generous and in-depth feedback, suggestions, and critique from a group of outstanding reviewers helped me make significant improvements to *Good Writing: An Argument Rhetoric.* I thank James Allen, College of DuPage; Brigitte Anderson, University of Pikeville; Kathryn A. Baker, Santa Fe College; Erin Banks-Kirkham, Kettering College; Amy Barnickel, University of Central Florida; Marlo Marie Belschner, Monmouth College; Michael Bloomingburg, Somerset Community College; Rebecca Saulsbury Bravard, Florida Southern College; Laurie Buchholz, Austin Community College; Karen Campbell, Tarrant County College; Nick Capo, Illinois College; Lori Coffae, Rollins College; Kelly Concannon, Nova Southeastern University; Theresa Conefrey, Santa Clara University; Carolyn Cooper, Hartwick College; David R. DiSarro, Endicott College; Abby M. Dubisar, Iowa State University; Beth K. Eyres, Glendale Community College; Robert Ford, Houston Community College District, Central College; Clinton R. Gardner, Salt Lake Community College; Eli Goldblatt, Temple University; Lesley Graybeal, Wake Technical Community College; Ashley Horak, Kankakee Community College; Mary Husemann, Warren Wilson College; Lisa Ison, Hazard Community and Technical College; Tobi Jacobi, Colorado State University; Barbara Jaffe, El Camino College; Joseph Janangelo, Loyola University Chicago; Jeannine Johnson, Wellesley College; Greg Kemble, Yuba College; Pamela Kincheloe, Rochester Institute of Technology; A. Abby Knoblauch, Kansas State University; Kim Lacey, Saginaw Valley State University; Daniel Edward Lambert, California State University, Los Angeles; Christina Lovin, Eastern Kentucky University; Steven Lynn,

University of South Carolina; John Mauk, Northwestern Michigan College; John McKinnis, SUNY Buffalo State; Clyde Moneyhun, Boise State University; Seth Myers, University of Colorado Boulder; Margaret Oakes, Furman University; Amber Pagel, Eastfield College; Paul Patterson, Saint Joseph's University; Kara Poe Alexander, Baylor University; Kevin J. Porter, University of Texas at Arlington; Rufel Ramos, Eastfield College; Phoebe Reeves, University of Cincinnati, Clermont College; Brittany Roberts, Broward College; Elizabeth Rollins, Pima Community College; Elizabeth Shelley, Kendall College of Art and Design of Ferris State University; Megan Shepherd, University of Cincinnati Clermont College; Rachelle M. Smith, Emporia State University; Aimee N. Taylor, Ball State University; Michel M. Walker, Copper Mountain College; and Lavonne Weller, Spokane Falls Community College.

CHAPTER one

Why Write?

The objective of this textbook is to help you make good arguments and identify bad ones. As students, consumers, and citizens, you are barraged by arguments attempting to persuade you to think, buy, and act in particular ways. The presentation of information is rarely neutral: what is said, what isn't said, and how it is said reflects the author's understanding of an issue. When we communicate with others, we are often trying not just to inform but to persuade them to understand the information or issue just as we do. That's good in the hands of knowledgeable, ethical authors who care about their audience. It's bad in the hands of people who are uninformed or willing to deceive their audience intentionally.

Fortunately, although we are surrounded by all these types of persuasion, an understanding of rhetoric and the craft of argument can help us identify misguided arguments and construct sound ones. All writing exists in a specific context or rhetorical situation: time, place, and audience. A rhetorical analysis digs deeper to try to understand more qualitative measures of that situation, such as why and how that message was delivered at that time in that place to those people.

WHY WRITE? REASONS FOR WRITING

Writing allows us to share our experience across boundaries of time and place. We write to inform, entertain, and argue. We *inform* through the exchange of facts, data that represent knowledge we have learned firsthand or through research. We *entertain* through story, the telling of real or imagined events in such a way that readers get a rich sensory understanding of events and feel as if they have experienced them firsthand. We *argue* by stating or suggesting that others should think and act in a particular way based on examples and evidence. Writing that isn't purely informational, and most writing isn't, is a form of *advocacy*, calling others to new thinking and action.

In theory, writing is a neutral mode of communication. In practice, however, writing has aims and intentions. Our words become a representation of ourselves. The good writer writes with care and integrity. Good writing improves the world. Good writing is writing for the common good. Because writing is the means by which we come to clearer understanding of our own thinking, writers have an obligation to clearly represent facts, evidence, and claims. Writers must have the courage to write with integrity—even when others do not. Good writing is an act of ethical leadership.

In this textbook, we define good writing as writing that is both technically skillful and ethically guided. When writers lack the ethical intention and/or the skill to write with care and integrity, writing that should inform, entertain, and argue can misinform, weary, and confuse us.

Every word we write and send into the word either advances our knowledge and culture, or undermines it. Responsible writing should be routine, a habit of mind and practice that informs every sentence we write. Ethical writers understand that their words have the power to inform, entertain, and argue—and to shape the thinking that shapes the action that shapes the world.

WHO CARES? UNDERSTANDING AUDIENCE, UNDERSTANDING SELF

We have been arguing that good writers care about others, but what does that mean? Does it mean that we have to like them? Probably not. The most important audience might be the one you don't like or agree with.

In the broadest sense, there are two types of audience: private and public. The most *private* audience is one's self, writing that is only read by the author. In fact, you are an ideal *initial* audience because it's hard to communicate clearly with others when you haven't first sorted out your own thinking. Writing to and for yourself is a critical first step in discerning what matters to you—what's worth writing.

Public writing is writing that travels past that private boundary into the hands and minds of other readers. Audience is one of the three central points of the rhetorical triangle rhetoricians use to visualize the necessary components of communication in a given context—speaker, audience, and message (see Figure 1.1, "The Rhetorical Triangle"). Yet technology has expanded the ways we can reach an audience.

Aristotle (384 BC–322 BC), the Greek philosopher whose thinking on the elements of argument has shaped our understanding of

Figure 1.1
The Rhetorical Triangle

This diagram visualizes Aristotle's key points of rhetorical connection.

rhetoric, could never imagine these digital modes of communication. Yet the principles of rhetoric we derive from Aristotle's teaching hold up well today because they focus on communication philosophy, our process and motivation for exchanges.

You have probably experienced that sometimes dangerous crossing of boundaries into the public domain through social media. You post something in your space online, and it gets copied, liked, retweeted, and shared in spaces well beyond audiences you know or even anticipated. That speed and breadth of delivery can be good or bad. The speed of delivery could be bad if the message is uninformed or insensitive, or the author did not give permission to share the message with this extended audience. The speed of delivery could be good when urgent action is required, such as in the aftermath of a natural disaster when people need help immediately. At a time when audience can be extended into this hyper-public space, caring for our audience is both critical and complicated.

The anonymity afforded by online writing also challenges our understanding of self and audience. Some say the web allows democracy and community to flourish, as there are few filters on the voices and opinions posted online in the United States. Others argue that writing online can encourage writers to avoid careful thinking about audience. Once again, we argue that it's not the mode or the medium that determines the value of the writing. It is the values of the writer that determine the quality of the writing.

Becoming a good writer means learning to take responsibility for your writing. You take responsibility by identifying yourself as an author as well as by identifying and considering the needs of your readers. It is a privilege to write. It is a privilege to be read. We should honor the time that others spend reading our writing, whether it is a memo, a report for class, a letter home, or a letter to the editor. We should write as much to understand as to be understood.

WHERE ARE WE? RHETORICAL DOMAINS: SCOPE AND LIMITATIONS

In this book, we consider four major rhetorical domains: home, academic, work, and civic life. The *home domain* includes your personal connections, your family and close friends. The *academic domain* includes the academic connections and exchanges you form with teachers, school administrators, and other students. The *work domain* includes your professional contacts, your colleagues, supervisors, clients, and associates. The *civic domain* includes local, national, and international communities of people you are connected to through geographic, political, economic, religious, ethnic, or other connecting factors. The domain that inspires your writing typically shapes that writing in many ways, and it often determines your primary audience.

Audiences in all of these domains assess your writing based on the three major components Aristotle outlined: character or trustworthiness of the writer (*ethos*), soundness and relevance of the evidence and reasoning provided (*logos*), and emotional authenticity (*pathos*). See Figure 1.1 and chapter 4 for more on these concepts. Writing in private space serves an important purpose in clarifying our personal thinking, but for the writing to make a difference in the world, writing must be shared in the public domain with members of a specific audience.

The actual audience (the people who put eyes to words and read our writing) and the intended audience (the people we had in mind when we were writing) might be different. Writing that starts in one domain might flow into other domains. Our message might not ever make it to our intended audience, or it might be shared beyond our intended audience—perhaps with people who are less receptive to our ideas. If we commit ourselves to writing responsibly in every domain, that fluidity is less worrisome. And when we see the connections across these domains—when we see that what we care about in our home domain can inform what we care about in our academic, work, and civic domains as well—our lives become a little more coherent and our writing reflects our integrity.

HOW SHOULD I COMPOSE? MODE AND MEDIUM

How you transmit the message greatly affects its reception. Will you be handing your audience a piece of paper with typed writing? Will your audience visit a website you've composed that includes video and interactive text? A mode is the movement or connecting force of the text: printed alphabetic text, voices, video, visuals, or some combination of these. The medium is the specific type of material used: ink on paper, pixels in photos, paint on canvas, human voice through microphone, or some combination of these. How we write what we write matters. Different modes and media make different demands of our audience. It is our responsibility to determine whether we are delivering the sensory impact we desire.

WHEN SHOULD I SPEAK OUT? KAIROS, CONTEXT, AND LISTENING

The time when we write informs the content and reception of our message. Confronted daily by new evidence and personal experience, people can become hyper-aware of particular issues and open to new thinking. As a writer, it's your responsibility to recognize those moments and engage them ethically to guide readers through that new understanding.

The rhetorical term *kairos* refers to the ripeness of a moment in time when an issue aligns in such a way that a message meets a willing audience. Moments of extreme tragedy or triumph that directly affect the audience often make them more motivated listeners. Even then, not just any message will get through: a truly effective message is driven by the force of the moment, informed by fact, and tells the story of that moment in a way that is consistent with listeners' knowledge and experience. Such a message can become a catalyst for action.

Rhetorical exemplars of kairos include the speech by Reverend Dr. Martin Luther King known as the "I Have a Dream" speech, given at the Lincoln Memorial in Washington D.C. in 1963 during the Civil Rights Movement. Dr. King's speech has inspired generations of listeners (and readers of the transcript) to consider whether inaction is as immoral as immoral action, a claim King made to urge listeners to participate in civil disobedience against racism. President Ronald Reagan's imploring speech at Berlin's Brandenburg Gate in 1987, "Mr. Gorbachev, open this gate. Mr. Gorbachev, tear down this wall!" was soon followed by the sound of falling concrete as the people dismantled the wall that had stood steady since it was built in 1961. The series of demonstrations and uprisings collectively known as the Arab Spring, which began in December 2010, show how people in that region were ready for political change as changes in leadership and law spread across more than a dozen countries. In the United States, frustration with "Big Government" and "Big Business" led people to organize the Tea Party (2009) and Occupy Wall Street (2011) movements. The 2016 presidential election showed Americans' readiness to "Feel the Bern" with Bernie Sanders and to feel in a different way that they wanted to "Make America Great Again" with Donald Trump. To become a leading voice in times of change, writers must have a clear and compelling vision, as well as a powerful and articulate voice.

A word of caution about the type of iconic speeches we just mentioned: it's simplistic to say that all it takes are the right words at the right time to cause monumental change. It's more accurate to say that those speeches and slogans are successful because they capture existing ideas in such a way that they amplify and expedite that movement, thereby energizing existing impulses.

Of course, it can be a challenge when the call to write is not some independently identified moment that moves you to write in the public domain but is actually issued by the instructor of your required writing course in the academic domain and includes all kinds of restrictions about page length, sources, and maybe even fonts. Those requirements can crush that sense of kairos if you're not careful. Writing *as if* you're writing for the civic domain to address a pressing social issue within the actual domain of the classroom and for the actual audience of an instructor can feel artificial if you take an assignment only as an assignment and not as something that can have life within and outside the classroom.

You can't fake enthusiasm and expertise in writing. If you don't feel part of the kairotic moment, it will be hard to get others to get behind your ideas. What can you do to animate that kairotic groove? You can keep yourself current on news in the local, national, and international spheres to discern the signs of the times. By engaging current events as a curious and empathetic audience member yourself, you can begin to understand what issues have given others a reason to write. You begin to see what has aligned in their experience and understanding that makes a particular issue newsworthy, and in doing so, you can identify your own interests and passions worth writing about. So the first step is to analyze kairos in others through rhetorical analysis. The first step is to listen.

WHAT DO I THINK I KNOW? MESSAGE FROM DISCERNMENT

What you ultimately write about is a negotiation around the given assignment, the issues that seem kairotically vital at that time and place, and the original perspective you can contribute given your experience and research. Given your unique experience of the world, your voice has immense potential to say what hasn't been said, to notice what has gone overlooked, and to propose innovative solutions to ongoing problems.

Before you can change someone else's mind, you have to know your own. That knowledge comes through deliberate research and reflection. Research and reflection are the twin engines of critical thinking that lead to critical writing. The continued practice of research and reflection develop your capability for discernment, the process of identifying what motivates you not just to write about but to *be* about, to identify the issues you want to address in your life's work or vocation.

Critical Questions

1. How do you define "good"? Where have you heard this word used in the assessment process in your academic life (e.g., "I want to get good grades")?
2. Do you think grammar and ethics are equally important in writing? Why or why not? Have both been part of your assessment in previous writing assignments? In other words, do your teachers seem to care more about *what* you say or *how* you say it? What comments make you think that?
3. To what extent do you agree with this claim: "In some ways, we are what we write"? Support your answer.

CHAPTER two

Elements of Rhetoric

When we write for others—when we write for the public domains of college, work, or civic life—our message is shaped by what *we* want to say and by what we think others *expect* of us. Those expectations are socially constructed by the audience and the occasion for writing (the kairos). If our goal is to be heard and to have our writing taken seriously, then we have to think carefully, not just about what we think but about how we can be heard.

RHETORICAL SITUATION

In rhetoric, the basic elements of the rhetorical situation include the writer, the message, the audience, and the context. The Rhetorical Triangle (see Chapter 1, Figure 1.1) is one way of picturing how these elements interact to produce communication. The writer's role in this exchange is to reduce the risk of misunderstanding and to increase the potential for a full and fair reading.

Writers increase their chances for successful communication when they explore the rhetorical situation fully. The frame introduced in Chapter 1—Who? What? When? Where? Why? and How?—provides a useful structure to explore each element of the rhetorical situation and how each element impacts the other elements.

For example, writers have to think about their own knowledge and values before they can discern what they want to write about and what stance they want to take in their message. They also have to think about the knowledge, circumstances, and values of the audience who will receive their message so that the content and tone meet their expectations.

The following questions will help you analyze the rhetorical situation for your writing.

Why? Exigence and Ethics

Asking "why" helps you determine the rhetorical *context*, the reason for writing. As you prepare to write, think carefully about what calls you to do so. What exigence, or urgency, calls you to engage in this way? What could happen if you don't write? What could happen if you do? What ethical concerns call you to write to others? If this writing is assigned, why does your instructor think it is important?

Who? Author and Audience

Asking "who" helps you solidify the rhetorical roles of the author and audience. Before thinking about the audience, think about yourself. Who are you and what do you care about? How can those concerns shape your writing, either the topic or your approach to a given topic? Next, consider your audience. Who is your intended audience and what do they care about?

Where? Domain

Asking "where" helps illuminate the rhetorical domain. What domain are you primarily writing within: home, academic, work, or civic life? What are the expectations for such factors as tone, format, style, and content? Are those expectations codified somewhere or are they "unwritten rules" that you have to pick up on your own?

How? Mode and Medium

Your choice of medium should reflect not only what best suits your topic, but also the needs and preferences of your intended audience. As you plan your argument, be sure to consider the affordances (the actual and perceived characteristics) of the medium in which you choose to compose.

When? Kairos

Asking "when" helps describe the rhetorical context. How can you seize the moment when people are attuned to particular issues? How can you contribute fresh information or insights, and perhaps encourage people to take action?

What? Message

Asking "what" determines your written response to this audience in this rhetorical place. What needs to be said at this time in this place to these people? What *doesn't* need to be said? How does your voice fill a gap and contribute something meaningful to the conversation?

There is no correct order to these questions, but by researching and reflecting on answers to each one you get a fuller picture of your rhetorical situation, your reason to write.

AUDIENCE AND STAKEHOLDERS

Good writers think carefully about the audience they *want* to reach. In fact, they often do research to understand them better. The more writers know about the audience, the better able they are to deliver efficient and effective arguments.

Writers are more efficient if they understand what the audience already knows, as well as what they need to know. If writers spend time and space repeating information the audience already knows, the audience might lose interest, become annoyed, or just stop reading. If writers have a clear sense of what the audience needs to know, they can pitch the writing to meet those needs and interests.

How do you analyze your audience? You can investigate a range of factors that might help you understand them better, ranging from objective demographic data to more subjective attitudinal data. Each piece of information gives you another clue about their collective identity that will help you analyze how you can deliver an efficient, effective message.

Here are some objective, static demographic factors you might want to know about your audience:

- Age
- Gender
- Home address (or general area where they live)
- Household income level
- Marital status
- Highest level of education completed
- Religious affiliation
- Race
- Nationality
- Ethnicity

While demographic information is a fixed snapshot of the population at any given time, audience interests are dynamic—that is, they change based on new information and events. If your information or ideas stand to bolster or threaten the interests of your readers, then they will be listening keenly. You have to ask not just "What happens if things change?" and "What happens if things stay the same?"

You have to ask, "What happens to this person and to that person if things change or stay the same?" Even if not all of those stakeholders actually read your writing, your argument is strengthened by imagining their point of view. Here are subjective, dynamic factors to consider about your audience:

- **Concerns.** What do members of this audience worry about? Are their basic needs being met? If not, why not?
- **Aspirations.** What do members of this audience collectively want to do or become? How might those wants shape the way they hear your message?
- **Resources.** What financial, material, temporal, intellectual, or spiritual resources does this audience have the capacity to share on this issue? What would it take to get them to invest those resources in your ideas? What might cause them to withhold resources?
- **Local history and current events.** What historical or current events might be on the minds of this audience? How might those events shape their knowledge and receptiveness on certain issues?
- **Stakeholder interests.** Who exactly stands to gain and who stands to lose if things change or if things stay the same? Exactly what is gained or lost?

Audience interests might be easier to aggregate if you are writing to a more centralized local audience, such as the students in your dorm or members of your local city council. An audience that is more widely dispersed, however, might be more difficult to survey, so you have to think carefully about what brought that audience to your writing. The more you know about these factors, the better able you are to tailor your writing to audience interests and needs.

Sometimes, our writing ends up with an *actual audience* that's different from the *intended audience*. With digital writing, that's common. You can't and shouldn't write for every possible delivery of your writing, but if you write after carefully thinking about all potential stakeholders and taking their positions into consideration, a wider audience is more likely to be a receptive audience.

GENRES

Addressing these Who? What? When? Where? Why? and How? questions will help you determine the expectations of an audience at a given time. The more you understand, the better able you are to frame your writing in a way that will be informative, engaging, and persuasive. That writing frame is also known as its *genre*.

A genre is a recognizable format or pattern in writing. Before college, you might have learned about genres as types of writing that include fiction (imaginative writing), nonfiction (writing based on real people or events), and poetry, for example. You might also talk about movies, music, theater, and the arts in terms of genres (e.g., romantic comedy, horror, or action in movies, and jazz, hip-hop, and classical in music). We want to discuss genres as types of writing common in our four domains: home, academic, work, and civic. The domain helps set audience expectations. You can write more efficiently and effectively if you learn the general expectations of those common genres.

Writing within the home domain today is typically informal, fragmented, and fast: tweets, texts, chats, and social media posts often shape written exchanges in this domain.

Writing in the academic domain is shaped by the academic disciplines that define higher education, such as biology, economics, theology, English, sociology, anthropology, and psychology. Experts in these areas have particular ways of thinking and learning that are expressed in the conventions used in their writing.

Clear verbal and written communication skills are essential to your success in the work domain. Expectations will change depending on the sector of work that employs you, but in general, you will benefit from understanding the following writing genres commonly used in the work domain: reports, memos, summaries, letters, reviews, and proposals. Brevity and clarity are highly valued in business writing.

Writing for the civic domain is a critical part of participating fully in a democracy. When a public issue stirs you, knowing how to write your perspective into the conversation in that civic domain ensures that others can consider your experience as they make decisions affecting the community. Genres common to civic writing include letters, grants, posters, brochures, essays, poetry, and public service announcements.

The genre does not limit the aim of the writing to inform, entertain, or argue, but it does cue experienced readers that a particular type of writing will follow.

Interdisciplinary Writing

Academics read and write in genres that are specific to their disciplines. As you progress in your studies, expect to become familiar with the genres that reflect the values and conventions of these disciplines—lab reports in the sciences, memos and executive summaries in business, or ethnographies in sociology, for example. Becoming adept with a variety of academic genres as a student encourages interdisciplinary thinking and writing, an increasingly important skill in our complex workplaces and communities.

Why is interdisciplinary thinking and writing important? Because in the work and civic domains outside academics, we don't function in strictly segregated disciplines. The knowledge and skills from many disciplines are combined in new ways, depending on the situation. It's important to be able to listen to people whose perspectives and experiences (whether academic, professional, or personal) are different from our own, so that we can work together to understand and solve problems. Familiarity with the genres in which different communities and stakeholders communicate makes you a better-informed student and citizen.

AIMS

When we talk about the aim of writing, we are talking about its purpose: what is the writing trying to do? While there are many nuanced purposes to writing, we find it helpful to start with three main purposes: to inform, to entertain, and to argue.

Writing that primarily aims to inform attempts to teach us something fairly objective. In technical writing, that might be how to do a task. In scientific writing, that might be telling us what happened in an experiment. In journalistic news writing, that might be telling what happened in our community that day. Informative writing relies on facts and direct observation.

Writing that primarily aims to entertain attempts to reach readers on a more emotional level, reflecting on the world or human experience in some new way. In a memoir, we might be moved by a description of someone's childhood that was very different from our own.

Writing that primarily aims to persuade gets us to think or act differently based on relevant evidence and examples. An Op-Ed essay on a news website, for example, presents the opinion of a writer on a current issue debated in the community of that website's readership. The writer explains an opinion to get readers to agree.

Some writing falls exclusively into one of these three purposes. Technical writing about how to wire a circuit, for example, should not wander into entertainment or persuasion. Its purpose is to help readers accomplish a task quickly, correctly, and safely, so sharp focus is critical.

But writing can aim to do all three in one text, and when this is done well, the impact on readers can be profound. Katherine Boo's

2012 creative nonfiction book *Behind the Beautiful Forevers*, for example, informs us through firsthand observation about the dynamic and often devastating cycle of life in a Mumbai slum shaped by fiercely competitive political and work hierarchies that outside readers could not otherwise fathom. Boo entertains while informing readers by using narrative dialogue, descriptive language, and the technique of following specific individuals for several years. The book also persuades on many levels. For example, it challenges readers to take a critical look at the effectiveness of western-run nonprofits in areas of deep poverty as Boo informs us of the corruption and abuse in some organizations.

The genres we choose to write in are often closely connected to the rhetorical situation. Once you understand the reason for writing to this audience at this time, you can consider which of the rhetorical options suit your call to write and your audience's call to listen. For example, in different classes you are likely to be asked to write in different ways. At times, you will be asked to describe existing information to demonstrate your memorization of important facts and concepts. At other times, you will be asked to apply those concepts in new ways in order to demonstrate your ability to create new knowledge. Both types of intellectual work are valued across the domains; you just have to understand which action verb is activating that call.

Critical Questions

1. Which genres of writing have you been asked to do in your education so far? Discuss examples of those writing assignments with your peers. What seems to be the most common genre? Compare and contrast what's common in different disciplines. Why do you think those differences exist?

2. Which genres of writing do you encounter most frequently in civic life? Discuss examples of writing you read or avoid and explain why you do so.

3. Think of an issue in a community that needs to be solved. Who are the key stakeholders in that issue? What would it take to help community members come together and work on solutions? Profile at least three stakeholder perspectives on this issue. What are their desires and concerns? What solution might they propose? Is there any common ground across those solutions?

4. Read Michelle Alexander's essay "The New Jim Crow: How the War on Drugs Gave Birth to a Permanent American Undercaste" (in Chapter 18). What is the aim of her writing? Is the genre of the essay appropriate for this aim? Why or why not?

CHAPTER three

Reading and Listening for Writing

Good writers are good readers. They read a wide variety of writers and writing, and they pay attention to how that writing works. Good writers read rhetorically. In this chapter, we offer strategies that will help you sharpen those rhetorical reading skills.

THE RHETORICAL READING PROCESS

The following stages of reading outline the general actions an alert critical reader takes to learn from a text. This process works for written as well as visual and online texts. The stages are recursive, meaning that you might move back and forth based on the circumstances of your reading.

Stage 1: Pre-Read

Many basic elements of the rhetorical situation become clear as soon as you engage the text: author, intended audience, and clues about the context of the message. Careful attention to these contextual cues can inform your reading of the text itself.

These questions will help you gather data about the rhetorical situation of the writing through the information that surrounds the body before you even read the full text:

Author: What do you know about this author? What are his/her areas of expertise? Does he/she appear to be writing within that area of expertise?

Audience: Where is this writing published? What do you know about this publisher? Who is its typical audience?

Context:

Mode and Medium—Our first impression of a text is sensory. What does it look, sound, or feel like? What does the format suggest about the tone and style of the content?

Length/Size—We can quickly see and assess the scale of alphabetic text. While short or small creative works, such as poems and small artworks, have the capacity for great depth in meaning, brevity in non-fiction suggests limited data and a restricted scope. Longer works raise our expectations for depth and detail.

Publisher/Curator—Who has endorsed this writing by publishing it? What are the credentials and expertise of that publisher?

Publication Date—When was this published and how does that relate to world events, local events, and where the author was at that time?

Message: What does the title suggest about the message? Good titles engage readers and clue them in to the topic and author's position on it.

These steps can help you determine the most relevant and reliable sources to use in your research as well. See Chapter 27, "Working with Published Sources," for more on assessing sources for research.

Stage 2: Read

After pre-reading, it's time to give your full attention to the text. The keys to reading efficiently and effectively are to:

1. Control your reading environment. First, find a place where you can finish all the reading without face-to-face disruption from roommates, family members, or others. Second, minimize technological distractions such as audio and visual alerts. Reposition yourself if you start losing attention and retention of the reading.

2. Interact with the text frequently through passive (highlighting) and active (paraphrase and questions) note taking. Interaction with the text helps you remember it. Passive interactions include highlighting words, phrases, sentences, or (sparingly) whole paragraphs. Active interactions include note taking for more analytical tasks: paraphrase the author's point in your own words, ask a question of clarification, ask a question of challenge, make a connection to other readings in this class or elsewhere, or draw a visual map of a theoretical concept. Active notes begin the work of analysis you will share in class discussions or writing assignments. (For more on paraphrase, see Chapter 27, "Working with Published Sources.")

3. Read the text more than once, focusing the first read on understanding its message and the second read on challenging it. Do your best to read objectively and try to follow the logic and examples presented to understand how that author is attempting to inform, entertain, or persuade the readers. Note claims, facts, evidence, examples, and analogies used to construct the text and the ratio of each overall. On the second and subsequent readings, challenge both the writing and the writer. This move of first trying to understand how the argument might be valid and then switching to consider how it might not be so is what composition theorist Peter Elbow calls the "believing game" and the "doubting game"

(For more on assessing research, see Chapter 9, "Read: Strategies for Reading in Research").

4. Summarize and analyze the text after reading it, noting its strongest and weakest points in your own words. You don't have to choose one "side" or the other—either believing or doubting in the end. In most texts, you will have points when you do both. If you are going to write a rhetorical analysis of this text, you might want to shape that summary more formally. If this summary is just to aid your own discussion in class or for writings that involve other texts, those notes can be less formal but are best articulated in fully formed sentences that clearly differentiate the text's points from your own analysis to avoid unintentional plagiarism. (For more on plagiarism, see Chapter 5, "Writing Ethics, Responsibility, and Accountability.")

Stage 3: Research

After you have read, annotated, and responded to the text, consider doing external research to test the text even more comprehensively. As you look at your notes, you might find that you had questions of fact and questions of argument. If you put notes in the margin that said, "What does this mean?" or "Who is this?" or "What happened?" you know when to look up definitions and factual information from reputable sources.

As you sort through your notes, you should also find questions of argument that you want to address through further research, such as "What examples would counter this claim?" "What stakeholders are not represented here and what do they have to say about this?" "Is there another way to interpret this?"

Once again, you want to play the believing game and the doubting game. If the author cites sources in the text and/or in a works cited, you can follow those texts to see if the author represented them fully and fairly. You can also look for credible sources that challenge the author even further to help you assess the logos of the writing.

Stage 4: Revise

Revision is the word we use in the writing process to describe the act of literally "re-seeing" what we have drafted in order to re-think and re-write. "Re-seeing" in the reading process refers to the act of (1) literally re-reading the text for a second or subsequent time (described in Stage 2); (2) bringing new eyes, through new information gleaned in research (described in Stage 3); or (3) applying a new critical frame to the process, typically through rhetorical concepts that help open up the text in new ways.

The first two aspects of "re-seeing" are described in earlier stages of the reading process; the third aspect can be described as helping you deepen your reading of a text by giving you structured, rhetorical concepts through which you can review the writing anew. We have already discussed groupings that work well together for analysis—looking at *ethos*, *pathos*, and *logos*, for example, or analyzing aesthetic, practical, and ethical reasons. Considering other specific rhetorical concepts can help you analyze the reading in a new way as well.

Stage 5: Share

The final stage of the reading process is sharing what you've learned, perhaps through discussion with others in class or more informally with friends and family. If you intend to write a rhetorical analysis, then you are in good shape to do so now, although you still might dip back into the reading process as you progress in the writing process.

THE RHETORICAL LISTENING PROCESS

Verbal texts such as speeches and lectures are common in all domains. In civic life, debates among politicians and scholars are common. On campus, universities sponsor guest speakers to present their ideas and scholarship, and many of your professors present information orally in class. At work, you will probably hear presentations such as sales pitches, demonstrations of new technologies, or proposals for strategic planning. And who hasn't heard a lecture at home? This oral delivery requires attention to aural, which means "listening," reception. The rhetorical listening process shares many of the same strategies for success, but it differs in significant ways as well.

The following discussion of the stages of rhetorical listening will help you increase the retention and accuracy of your listening experiences.

Stage 1: Pre-Listening

Many basic elements of the rhetorical situation become clear as soon as you preview the listening situation: author, intended audience, and clues about the context of the message can be read through the environment, whether it is live (synchronous) or recorded (asynchronous). Careful attention to these contextual cues can inform your listening to the text itself.

These questions will help you gather data about the rhetorical situation of the verbal event through the information that surrounds the body of the text prior to listening:

Author: What do you know about this author? What are his/her areas of expertise? What has he/she been critiqued for? Does he/she appear to be speaking within that area of expertise? Should biographical data be considered in listening to this text?

Audience: Where is this event taking place? What do you know about the type of audience or messages attracted to this venue? If you are present in a live audience, what can you tell about them by looking around (e.g., gender, race, age)?

Context:

Mode and Medium—How is this verbal message being delivered to its audience? Has it been pre-recorded? Has that recording been edited in any way?

Formality/Tone—Is the author speaking from a stage with curtains and formal seating, or is he/she on ground level with the audience, speaking eye-to-eye?

Venue/Sponsor—Who has sponsored this event and why? What do they typically sponsor and what might that tell you about the content of this event?

Date—When is this event taking place and how does that information relate to world events, local events, and the author's relation to them?

Message: What does the title suggest about the message?

Stage 2: Listening

1. Control your listening environment and reposition yourself if you start losing attention and retention of the text. Acoustic control is especially important if you only get to hear the text one time. Make sure you can see the speaker clearly as well so that you can read his/her body language and the body language of other audience members listening to that message. Keeping visual focus will help you keep aural focus as well: when you make eye contact with the speaker, you know that he/she is paying attention to you and you are more likely to remain an alert listener.

2. Respond to the text immediately through note taking. Taking brief notes helps you underscore and retain key points while they

are fresh in your mind. Note key sources the speaker mentions so that you can research them later if you have questions—last name and key words from the title should be enough to find the source. Be sure to clearly distinguish direct quotes from paraphrase, and the author's points from your own points to avoid unintentional plagiarism.

3. Listen to the text more than once if possible, focusing the first listening on understanding its message and the second listening on challenging it. If the text is recorded or you have permission to record it and listen multiple times, then you can follow many of the same guidelines for attending to a written text outlined above.

4. Summarize and analyze the text after listening to it holistically, noting its strongest and weakest points in language that makes sense to you. This is where your believing and doubting reasons come together into a holistic assessment, as we described above.

Stage 3: Researching

Listening to a talk is likely to pique your interest about something you want to understand better, or perhaps you question some of the stated claims. If the talk is given by an academic or popular expert, it is often connected to a recent publication; if so, start your research with that text, which will probably point you to the author's sources of influence.

Stage 4: Re-Listening

While a recorded talk can be listened to after its original presentation (asynchronously), not all talks are recorded and thus must be absorbed and assessed live (synchronously). If re-listening is not possible, then it's a good idea to compare notes with others who attended the presentation.

It is also important to note that watching a recording of a live event is not the same as attending the event directly. Live events are shaped by the physical and emotional context of the place and people who attend. Downloading a recorded version of a talk or transcript will allow you to access the content more accurately, but it is important to note that you will not be able to speak definitively to the full rhetorical situation as you would have done, had you attended it in person.

Stage 5: Share What You Heard (and Start the Writing Process)

While reading a text is a solitary endeavor, listening to a live event constitutes a common experience with a group of people you might or might not know. How you respond to the talk is likely to be influenced by how those around you respond through applause, laughter, or even softly spoken affirmation or dissent. You are likely to have a "What did you think?" conversation with those around you immediately after the talk finishes. Those immediate thoughts might melt into a different impression over time as you talk to more people, exchange written impressions in social media, or do research to expand your understanding of the issue and the presenter's points, but do record your first impressions when that live performance is fresh.

Whether you have to write a formal rhetorical analysis or not, attending carefully to a text helps increase your knowledge, not just of content but also of successful writing strategies.

Critical Questions

1. Play the believing and the doubting game on this chapter. What does the chapter try to inform, entertain, or persuade you into believing or doing? What are its key points? What passive and active

notes did you take as you read? What rhetorical strategies does the chapter use to try to achieve those goals?

2. Think of an occasion when you had a very different impression than someone else of the rhetorical effect of a written text or live presentation. How did you discover that difference? How did you discuss it? Was anyone's perspective changed through discussion or additional research?

CHAPTER four

Argument

Academic argument is rhetoric that addresses an issue by making claims supported by relevant, credible evidence. The purpose of academic argument is to attempt to persuade the audience—through good, ethical writing—to think or act in a particular way. Through good writing characterized by a full and fair consideration of the issue, an academic argument offers compelling reasons for an audience to accept a premise and act upon its proposal.

ACADEMIC ARGUMENTS

Argument is essential to higher education because it helps students expand their knowledge by encountering new ideas and information. Through the encounter of research, they might find new evidence and examples that expand and change their minds. By writing and sharing an argument themselves, students offer ideas and information that can change the minds of others. Argument allows us to test and circulate knowledge to improve our lives.

Although types of academic argument vary across disciplines, the general outline of the academic argument provides a platform for demonstrating much of the knowledge (understanding of facts), skills (applied abilities), and dispositions (attitudes and habits of mind) valued at the university level:

- *Knowledge*—Writing academic arguments requires research to discover factual evidence and reasons within credible sources.
- *Skills*—Writing academic arguments requires the understanding and application of disciplinary methods such as interviews, surveys, and statistical regressions. Academic arguments require writers to do original research or to interpret existing research accurately.
- *Dispositions*—Writing academic arguments requires an ethical attention to opposing viewpoints and acknowledgment of sound evidence and reasons that challenge the author's position, defined by an intellectual ability to embrace contrary ideas rather than find one "right" answer.

Claims

A claim is an assertion the author declares to be true or right. A claim is an opinion informed by experience and research. There are three general categories of claims: claims of fact, claims of value, and claims of policy.

Of Fact

Claims of fact assert that something is true because it can be measured or verified objectively. Claims of fact rely on standards generally agreed upon around the world.

Some facts are considered hard or absolute. It would be unwise to center an argument on such facts because they are so thoroughly tested and universally accepted: scientific facts (carbon is a chemical element with symbol C and the atomic number 6); mathematical facts (3 is a prime number); historical facts (Rev. Martin Luther King, Jr. won the Nobel Peace Prize in 1964); or geographic facts (the country of Lesotho is entirely surrounded by the country of South Africa). If you were to state one of these facts, people could easily verify the information.

These types of facts are not the basis of a good academic argument because they are so universally accepted as true. However, you can get to arguable claims of fact when you move into interpretations of the significance of those facts, often related to causes. For example, you could write an academic argument with this thesis statement: "Lesotho's geographic location, completely surrounded by South Africa, makes it vulnerable to South African economic and political turmoil, contributing to its near 40% poverty rate." This is arguable because others might say that it is the legislative structure of Lesotho, its topography, or the influx of foreign aid itself that causes chronic poverty in Lesotho—not its geographic orientation.

Claims of fact generally refer to the past, assigning praise or blame for something that already occurred. The following examples show arguable claims of fact:

- Poverty makes us sick.
- The influx of foreign aid in Lesotho has created a culture of dependency that disrupted the development of sustainable infrastructures that would have helped citizens succeed financially on their own.
- "We can conclude that for adults living in the shelters, a future orientation may be most conducive to mental health and active coping behaviors." (See student writer Karmela Dalisay's "Motivating the Homeless," later in the chapter.)

Of course, as our knowledge increases, so do our tools for measurement. Facts can change over time as we discover new writings or materials from the past, revise definitions, or scientific experiments lead to new thinking. The claim, "Smoking is bad for your health," would have been arguable until researchers started studying the effects of smoking, leading to such public claims as the Surgeon General's 1957 warning of a causal connection between smoking and lung cancer. This is now considered a claim of fact.

Of Value
Claims of value assert that something is good or bad, right or wrong, based on specific criteria used for evaluation. The criteria used to assert claims of value are typically more subjective than those used to define facts.

Claims of value generally refer to the present, defining what we ought to believe today. The following examples show arguable claims of value:

- Good writing is linguistically and ethically sound.
- According to the United Nations Declaration of Human Rights, "All human beings are born free and equal in dignity and rights. They are endowed with reason and conscience and should act towards one another in a spirit of brotherhood."
- People in poverty deserve the most attention and resources. (Preferential option for the poor—a social justice principle.)
- Significant financial inequality causes greater volatility and unrest than more widespread poverty.
- "Motivation is key in helping anyone achieve independence and self-efficacy." (See student writer Karmela Dalisay's "Motivating the Homeless," later in the chapter.)

Beliefs are claims of value informed by religious or spiritual understandings that might not be verifiable as fact. Some claims of value are based on belief systems, so it's important to know whether your audience agrees or disagrees with all or part of those beliefs.

Of Policy

Claims of policy assert that a particular action should be taken. Claims of policy guide collective action and ideally advance the common good, declaring that an action, law, or rule is in the best interests of stakeholders.

Claims of policy generally refer to the future, identifying a specific collective action a community should take moving forward. The following examples show arguable claims of policy:

- The U.S. government should guarantee low-interest rate loans to any student who enrolls in a public university, regardless of citizenship status.

- The age to receive Social Security in the United States should be raised by two years to reduce costs.
- Eligibility for the Supplemental Nutrition Assistance Program (SNAP) should be adjusted to include more low-income people.
- "Perhaps TV time could be seen as a privilege or luxury gained after progressing within the SOSH program." (See student writer Karmela Dalisay's "Motivating the Homeless," later in the chapter.)

Claims of policy articulate practices to increase the well-being of a group of people. What's arguable is whether or not a particular policy will create the kind of well-being people value. To persuade others, you have to show that the outcome you propose is most likely to happen based on the reasons, evidence, and examples you provide.

We can make arguments of fact, value, and policy about any issue, and many arguments touch on all three types of claims. But as a writer, you should be clear on what you want to accomplish through your writing by balancing and framing your argument to set the right tone for that rhetorical situation.

Main Claim: Thesis Statement

In the United States, the main claim of an academic argument is typically announced in a thesis statement at the end of the first paragraph. By stating the primary point in the introduction, readers quickly learn the author's position, then read on to find out why the author has taken that position. This thesis statement focuses the writing on a primary claim of fact, value, or policy, which the rest of the writing will seek to explain and support through examples and evidence.

Readers of academic arguments in the United States generally don't expect surprises—they want to know what the writing is about and what stance the author is taking up front. Note that this is not the custom in some other countries where it is more typical to build up to a thesis statement delivered toward the end of the writing.

Explain the Claim: Substance, Support, Scale, and Significance

Academic arguments explain the claim through substance (details that connect ideas) and support (evidence and examples). After the introduction, the body of the argument focuses on supporting that claim to inform, entertain, and/or persuade readers to accept and act on that claim.

Academic arguments are detailed, taking readers through the writer's thinking step-by-step, but they are also scaled for the rhetorical situation. Many factors can be adjusted to fit the scale of the argument to the scale of the assignment. Here are some factors you can adjust, depending on the parameters of your rhetorical situation:

- Length of time analyzed in your argument: look at current situation instead of last 10 years, 100 years, or since the beginning of time
- Quantity and range of support: number of examples, testimonials, and facts used
- Geographic scope: look at the local rather than comprehensive national or international perspective

In addition to managing the breadth of the claim, we can also use scales to weigh the significance of a thesis, testing how it stands up to those critical questions, "So what?" and "Who cares?"

Measuring Argument Intensity

The "Measuring Issue Impact" (see Figure 4.1) and "Investment in the Ask" (see Figure 4.2) scales can help you think about the significance of the argument you're making by measuring who is affected and how critical the issue is to their lives. You can use these tools with your peers and instructor during the invention process to make sure your claim meets your instructor's expectations for significance.

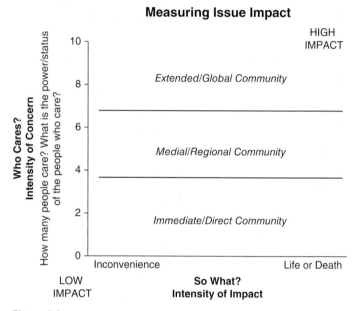

Figure 4.1
Measuring Issue Impact

This chart helps you think about the impact of your argument. You can use it as a talking tool with your peers and instructor to make sure you choose an argument that meets their expectations. For example, you can ask whether they are equally interested in high-impact arguments that would reach that upper right quadrant, such as whether or not the United States should put boots on the ground anytime they confirm the use of chemical weapons during conflicts, compared to more low-impact arguments, such as whether or not the university should reduce parking rates for low-emissions vehicles. These are both valid arguments, and there is a time and place for each in public discourse, but the scope and impact vary considerably. It's important to know what works for your assignments.

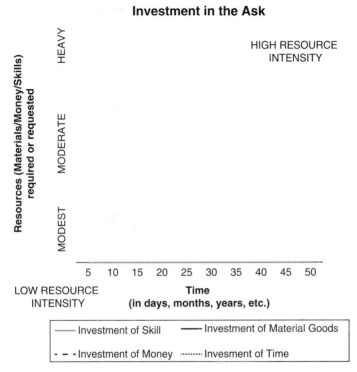

Figure 4.2
Investment in the "Ask"

This chart is designed to help you weigh how much you are asking for in your argument to address a problem. To tackle many problems, we have neither the collective will nor unlimited resources. Instead, we have limited resources, which others are competing for as well. We therefore have to temper our "ask" to be reasonable and have a chance of actually acquiring those resources from others. This chart, combined with the "Measuring the Impact" chart, helps you determine whether your "ask" is proportionate to the impact: we might call it the social impact ROI (return on investment).

ARGUABLE CLAIMS

Academic arguments need to be debatable and definable. A debatable thesis has a clear answer for the questions: "So what?" and "Who cares?" Reasonable people must currently disagree about this issue for it to be debatable and not considered factual or inconsequential. Is this issue making headlines somewhere, even if it's in a specialty field or a local source? If so, then it's potentially arguable.

To consider the difference between a debatable versus a non-debatable thesis, consider the following sentence: "U.S. President Bill Clinton signed the Personal Responsibility and Work Opportunity Act into law in 1996." Is that debatable? No, it is a well-documented fact. But start explaining why it happened or whether it was successful and you get into a debatable claim very quickly.

Now consider this sentence: "U.S. President Bill Clinton signed the Personal Responsibility and Work Opportunity Act into law in 1996 to 'end welfare as we have come to know it,' but 20 years later, it is clear that this Act only made it harder for low-income Americans to escape poverty." That's debatable. Some people will argue that the Act worked as planned, pointing to reduced spending on social services in the years that followed. Others will argue that even though many former welfare recipients went to work because their welfare benefits were restricted, that work was often at such a low wage that they became the working poor, no better off than they were before reform. The addition of that interpretation of the Act's success is what turns a factual statement into a debatable thesis.

The second test to see if you have an arguable thesis is to determine whether it is definable. Definition relates to scale and focus. The wording must be clear and accessible.

To compare an undefined versus a well-defined thesis statement, review the following sentence: "The media misrepresent the poor." In this sentence, both "the media" and "the poor" are too vague and expansive. By "the media," do you mean newspapers, television, and blogs? Do you mean local, national, and international news organizations? By "the poor" do you mean people who fall within an officially defined income bracket in the United States or internationally? And of course we'd also have to narrow down categories of "representation" to analyze. There's just too much to cover.

Now look at this sentence: "African American men have been over-represented in U.S. network news coverage of poverty in America compared to demographic statistics, leading Americans to misunderstand the causes and solutions to poverty." In this sentence, you know exactly where the writer is headed and you can even anticipate what types of evidence should be included to make this argument successful. If you were interested in this area of research, you could ask the same question on a smaller scale: How were poverty and race represented in my hometown newspaper in the past year? Do the photographs and descriptions map to the actual racial demographics? What can we learn about how these stories do or do not reflect statistical information?

When you are given the opportunity to create an argument, make the most of it. Compose an arguable thesis that can persuade people to think or act differently about an important issue.

QUALIFYING CLAIMS

A disposition or attitude of academic writers is that human knowledge is limited. We acknowledge those limitations by qualifying our claims with words that suggest there is room for uncertainty. Instead of using absolute language filled with utter certainty and assurance, such as *all, always, never, no, none, only,* we leave a little intellectual wiggle room. The following phrases, adjectives, and adverbs help qualify claims:

A bit	Generally
A little	Hardly ever
Few	Many

Most	Some
Occasionally	Sometimes
Often	Somewhat
Probably	Typically
Rarely	Usually

Here are some examples that demonstrate the difference between absolute and qualified claims:

1. *Absolute claim*: "Although some students who are homeless perform at the highest academic levels, experts agree that more needs to be done to stabilize the school experience for students who are homeless in order to reduce drop-out rates." *Qualified claim*: "Although some students who are homeless perform at the highest academic levels, *most* experts agree that more needs to be done to stabilize the school experience for students who are homeless in order to reduce drop-out rates." By inserting "most" to qualify this claim, the writer acknowledges that we could find some experts who think we are doing enough already or who would focus on other strategies to improve the academic performance of students who are homeless.

2. *Absolute claim*: "Airport security officers should *never* use profiling to make additional searches." *Qualified claim*: "Airport security officers should *rarely* use profiling to make additional searches." Just one word changes in this sentence, but the difference in ideology and worldview are quite significant. Some people would argue that there is absolutely no room for profiling, while others would accept this to varying degrees. The absolute claim might be what you intend, but you should be aware of the force of absolute claims.

3. *Absolute claim*: "Cable news shows contribute to the public impression that the media are biased because they *only* air commentary, not journalistic news reports." *Qualified claim*: "Cable news shows contribute to the public impression that the media are

biased because they *so often* air commentary, not journalistic news reports." In this case, the absolute claim is inaccurate and can be refuted with data from the Pew Research Center. This is, however, the kind of exaggerated claim we commonly hear in everyday conversations. In academic arguments, we have to be more precise, guided by research.

EVIDENCE

Your academic discipline, audience, and assignment description will help you determine what types of evidence to use in supporting your argument. Most arguments benefit from including multiple types of evidence so that the argument stands up from different perspectives. Familiarize yourself with the following types of evidence so you can recognize them in other people's arguments as well as use them skillfully in your own work.

Facts

Facts used as evidence should be those considered (1) common knowledge, (2) indisputable facts about history or physical nature that people around the world agree upon, and/or (3) data reported by neutral, widely respected sources. For example, in the essay later in this chapter, student writer Karmela Dalisay gives readers a sense of the local community through facts: "About 10% of the population of South Bend is in poverty and are homeless. Furthermore, many cities have reported a 12% increase in the number of homeless people since 2007." Don't confuse these with *arguments of fact* that challenge existing knowledge through new experiments or new interpretations of knowledge (see "Claims of Fact"). If you present facts as evidence and your readers dispute those facts, then you either have to explain yourself or risk losing their trust.

Good writers tell the truth, the whole truth, and nothing but the truth when it comes to representing facts. For example, a policy analyst using demographic data to support an argument would provide the details about how the statistics were generated, not present just one flattering snapshot of the truth that supports her position. In addition to putting that snapshot in a larger context, a good writer would also explain anything that does not seem to support her argument (see Chapter 21, "Rebuttal: Negotiating Opposing Viewpoints"). Scientists doing empirical research through experiments, for example, describe what they did in full detail as objectively as possible in the Methods and Results sections of their writing, and then offer conclusions based on their observations in the Discussion section. They also try to imagine what might make those conclusions untrue, posing questions for further research that could affirm or challenge their results.

Examples

Examples can be persuasive evidence when they are vivid and memorable. They show rather than tell readers what's meant. Effective examples can include:

1. Direct personal experience, something the author experienced or witnessed firsthand.
2. Anecdotes (stories) you have heard or read from reputable sources secondhand.
3. Hypothetical situations that you can reasonably imagine happening.

Any one of these types of examples could use analogy as a rhetorical strategy, suggesting to readers that what happened in one situation is similar to what could happen in this situation. For example, student writer Karmela Dalisay notes a personal observation that many guests of the Center spend a lot of time watching TV in the lobby, which sets her up to make an argument about policy in which administrators use TV as a reward.

Testimony

Quoting or paraphrasing authorities who have expertise on your topic helps build your own credibility and ethos. You can gather that expert testimony through library research, reading what others have written, or through field research in which you gather unique data firsthand through interviews or focus groups (we discuss the process of working with library sources in Chapter 27, "Working with Published Sources," and with human sources in Chapter 28, "Working with Human Sources"). Either way, the value of citing others lies in the relevance of their experience, and the value of quoting others lies in their ability to communicate that experience clearly.

When you find key experts whose work supports yours, mention those experts by name in the body of your essay and include their academic credentials or work affiliations to establish their credibility. For example, Karmela Dalisay identifies one source as "a renowned psychologist from Stanford," priming readers to trust his conclusions.

Of course, what counts as "credible" and "relevant" credentials depends on the issue. If you are analyzing the effectiveness of services for people who are homeless in your home town, you might want to quote the mayor, the executive director of the Center for the Homeless, and individuals who have been homeless in that town for various lengths of time. Each perspective is authoritative in its own way.

Finally, it is important to distinguish between types of expert testimony. Some people count as experts because they have academic credentials that signify how much they have studied an issue. Other people count as experts because they have firsthand experience of the issue and speak from the authority of their own lived observations. Firsthand experience is especially powerful from those who have been marginalized or victimized in some way because too often those voices are not heard. Human rights workers often take special care to record those voices by capturing the testimony of people who have had their human rights violated, building a body of voices that becomes evidence of that experience and, potentially, a route for action to prosecute offenders. In Latin America, for example, this body of narratives is called *testimonio*, a rhetorical genre in itself that collectively records and advocates against the crimes they embody, thus bearing witness to violations of human dignity.

While one person can never fully speak for another person, as a writer, you have the power to make room for voices that aren't always heard by carrying them into your argument to bear witness to life's atrocities and triumphs. That's a privilege. Including a variety of expert testimony is one way to demonstrate your care as a writer.

GOOD REASONS: AESTHETIC, PRACTICAL, AND ETHICAL

Reasons explain the justification, motivation, or cause for your conclusions. A reason articulates a premise that explains why, in your mind and in your argument, a claim is true. It is important to understand the basic underlying assumption of a premise in any argument and how that relates to the conclusion.

Common cues help identify premises and conclusions. Stay alert to these as you read, and use them in your own writing to help your readers follow your thinking.

- **Common cues for premises:** because, since, in light of, whereas, given that, for the reason that, for, in that, as indicated by, due to, furthermore

- **Common cues for conclusions:** therefore, consequently, hence, so, thus, in conclusion, accordingly, it follows that, as a result, it must be that

Understanding the different types of reasons will help you with rhetorical analysis and with expanding your own lines of reasoning. The three general types of reasons include:

1. **Aesthetic**—Aesthetic reasons speak to beauty, artistic quality, or taste.
2. **Practical**—Practical reasons speak to logical factors such as usefulness, efficiency, or cost.
3. **Ethical**—Ethical reasons speak to what is just, moral, and good for individuals and society based on a particular set of values, particularly those articulated by an institution such as a government, religious organization, or non-governmental organization.

With this framework in mind, you can check your arguments against each type of reasoning. Let's say you make an initial argument for buying shoes from an unlicensed vendor on the street based on the practical considerations of convenience and cost. You could reflect deeper on this issue by considering each type of reason in more depth.

Aesthetic reasons: Do the materials look sharp? Is this style appropriate for this season?

Practical reasons: Will the quality last or fade quickly? Will the shoes be worn often enough to justify the cost?

Ethical reasons: Were the shoes produced under fair labor conditions, including a safe working environment and a living wage? Is the unlicensed vendor hurting vendors who follow the rules?

How might those perspectives reinforce or challenge your argument and your action?

THE RHETORICAL APPEALS: *ETHOS, PATHOS, LOGOS*

Classical rhetoricians identified categories of appeals that provide a useful way of analyzing the effectiveness of a communication in reaching an audience. These three appeals connect with an audience in different ways.

Ethos

Ethos means the credibility, reputation, or trustworthiness of a writer. Ethos is built when a writer cites relevant, intelligent sources, even taking on the best voices of opposing viewpoints the way a boxer builds credibility by taking on the most worthy opponents. Academic writers also build credibility by publishing in highly respected, refereed journals and presenting at important conferences at which other highly credentialed speakers are presenting.

Developing a strong ethos is critical to the success of any argument. Readers need to trust writers to be persuaded by them. If the writer uses sophisticated technical language appropriately and nods to important voices on the issue right away—voices that agree and disagree with the writer's position—readers get the sense that the writer is offering a full and fair account of the issue.

If, on the other hand, the writing seems sloppy, unorganized, and uninformed by important sources, readers might wonder whether they should trust and follow what the writer suggests. Writers who are new to an audience (as you might be) have to prove and maintain their trustworthiness by faithfully following all the expectations of that rhetorical situation.

Pathos

Pathos refers to appeals with emotional resonance. This approach can be an important way to remind an audience to feel deeply about a subject. It can also be abused, causing people to feel rather than reason through an issue.

Writers need to be most careful in how they employ pathos in their arguments. Dramatic examples of pain and suffering can work readers into a frenzy, but good writers have an ethical responsibility to channel that energy appropriately. Provoking a frenzy is the nature of propaganda. Successful writers use pathos to direct the audience's emotions toward the common good, not to distract them.

Logos

Logos refers to appeals that rely on logic, reason, and informing through facts. This is typically the most salient appeal in academic arguments, the necessary backbone to organize and direct thinking. In "The White-Savior Industrial Complex," Teju Cole appeals to logos through a causal claim about what happens when some voices are silenced in public discourse: "Marginalized voices in America have fewer and fewer avenues to speak plainly about what they suffer; the effect of this enforced civility is that those voices are falsified or blocked entirely from the discourse." Good writing balances the three appeal types in a ratio that aligns with the rhetorical situation. If you were giving a speech on immigration in a course on legal issues you would attend to logos more than if you were at a march to Capitol Hill before a big Senate vote on this issue. If you were trying to organize and motivate a crowd, you might tell personal stories that pack an emotional punch to get people who already know the facts excited. Analyze the rhetorical situation to decide how to balance your appeals.

LOGICAL FALLACIES

Logical fallacies signal errors in reasoning: something has gone wrong between the premise and the conclusion. In the academic domain, good writers do not knowingly permit logical fallacies into their writing. However, advertisers and politicians are often accused of using logical fallacies. They are under pressure to persuade an audience in very little time—a 30-second commercial or sound bite on the news. That's not enough time to make a well-supported argument, so they often rely on shortcuts that evade reason and logic, such as using emotional appeals or irrelevant reasons and evidence to hook an audience quickly.

Fortunately for aspiring good writers, this faulty reasoning happens in predictable patterns of error that you can learn to recognize and challenge. Some of these patterns are known by different names in various fields, and some are so closely related that it can be difficult to put them in just one category. What's most important is that you can spot an error in reasoning in order to challenge the argument of others or to fix the error if you find it in your own writing.

Logical fallacies typically show one of these problems: (1) lack relevance or connection between premise and conclusion, (2) false premise, or (3) ambiguous or misleading language. Table 4.1 lists some of the most common logical fallacies:

Table 4.1 LOGICAL FALLACIES

	NAME	DEFINITION	EXAMPLE
1	Ad hominem	Attacks against the person (literally, "against the man" or person), not the issue. These attacks amount to name-calling and distract the audience from the real issue.	Of course your grandmother is advising you not to invest in technology stocks—she can't even figure out her TV remote.
2	Appeal to fear	An attempt to raise unrelated fears in order to scare an audience into accepting your argument.	How can we worry about protecting our own privacy when terrorists will do anything to kill us?

3	Bandwagon appeal	Equating popularity with sound judgment: everybody's doing it so it must be right.	All my friends text while driving and they've never been in an accident, so I might as well too.
4	Circular reasoning/ Begging the question	The conclusion merely repeats the premise. Appeals to tradition or novelty fall into this category.	We should have a Native American mascot at our school because we've always had that mascot.
5	False analogy	Compares one situation to another, but there are so many different factors that the comparison doesn't hold up. The comparison isn't necessarily "false" as the name suggests, but simply isn't a useful comparison. Sometimes relies on fear.	Arguing that civil disobedience causes violence is like saying that protestors commit suicide when they are killed by police who respond with violence to non-violent protests.
6	False authority	Deferring to the authority of a speaker when his/her credentials aren't relevant to the issue being discussed, or relying so fully on the person's credentials that you don't assess the support and reasoning of the argument yourself.	Professor Smith is a well-respected, award-winning expert on 19th century American poetry, so I trust him when he says that Americans shouldn't invest in early education programs.
7	False dilemma/ either/or	Suggests that options are more limited than they are. Thinking in terms of both/and helps open up those options: both this is possible and that is possible.	You're either a giver or a taker in society. You're either a patriot or a watchdog. You're either with us or against us.

(continued)

Table 4.1   LOGICAL FALLACIES (*continued*)

	NAME	DEFINITION	EXAMPLE
8	Hasty gen-eralization	Suggests that a limited example represents something broader.	Three women in Florida were caught getting public assistance they weren't eligible to receive, so all people on assistance are probably scamming the system as well.
9	Non sequitur	One point does not follow from the previous point.	She was incarcerated for years, so I'm sure she wouldn't be interested in attending college.
10	Oversimpli-fication	Addressing a complicated situation with a solution that doesn't acknowledge those details.	In the United States we have people out of work and we have jobs available: those unemployed people must not want to work.
11	Polarization	Exaggeration of other positions to make them seem extreme.	Those politicians must hate poor people because they want to reduce social services. Those politicians must hate military families because they want to reduce military spending.
12	Post hoc fallacy	Mistaking cause and effect relationships (literally meaning "because of this, therefore that"). Also called the Chanticleer fallacy after the rooster who thought that his crowing caused the sun to rise because it always appeared just after he sang.	Crime went down the day Mayor Perez took office, so she must be responsible for the decrease.

13	Rationaliza-tion	Excuses for why some-thing didn't succeed, often pointing to unre-lated reasons.	She didn't win the sci-ence fair because she's not religious and those pious judges wanted someone like them to win.
14	Red herring	A distraction onto another topic in order to take at-tention off the key issue.	Why would you blame me for misusing cam-paign funds when you're the one who was court marshaled for sexual harassment?
15	Slippery slope	Suggestion that if one thing happens then other—typically very bad things—will happen as a result of opening up that opportunity.	If we legalize gay mar-riage, then we have to legalize any type of marriage anyone wants.
16	Straw man	Setting up someone as if they represent an op-posing position in such a way that their position is easily knocked down.	If we allow charter schools to set the cur-riculum, then we could have schools that don't teach kids how to read, write, add, or subtract.

STUDENT READING

Researched Proposal Argument

The following essay, written by first-year student Karmela Dalisay, addresses a larger problem for the South Bend Center for the Home-less in its aim to "break the cycle of homelessness." Throughout her engaged learning work at the Center, Karmela recognized that moti-vation seemed to be lacking among some of the guests. When she was assigned to write a Researched Proposal Argument, Karmela needed to convince her audience— the staff at the Center— that motivation among the guests was a problem. She needed to further provide her au-dience with concrete solutions to this problem that they could feasibly

*implement. To do so, she weaves together scholarly literature and her
experiences at the Center. Her essay contains reasons why the Center
must motivate its guests and suggestions on how they could do so.*

Karmela Dalisay
Motivating the Homeless

"The hardest part of being on the street is that
it takes away your self-respect and confidence.
You're constantly lining up for a meal, sleeping
with your clothes on, trying to look decent."
This quote embodies the experience of homelessness. It illustrates a sense of failure that can
be overwhelming for those who try to escape
the vicious cycle. The Center for the Homeless
is trying to address the issue in South Bend,
Indiana, but they are facing obstacles such as
a decrease in the number of people attending
their programs, specifically those involving
education. The question is: How can program
leaders create the necessary conditions and
culture to motivate the adult guests to participate? Motivation is key in helping anyone
achieve independence and self-sufficiency.
Through research I have explored two of three
key factors to motivation: one's personal perspective, and the structure and culture of an
organization. In this researched proposal, I
will argue that the Center should continue
their Stepping Out and Stepping Higher
(SOSH) program, but make it more comprehensive in order to better motivate the guests.
In addition, I will argue that the staff at the

> Karmela provides the
> audience with a thesis,
> focusing the writing on
> a claim of policy, and
> limiting that policy claim
> to one homeless center in
> particular.

Center should make changes to create an environment that cultivates the guests' self-worth.

In a society driven by different needs, one must be able to establish why a particular issue requires more precedence than others. In South Bend, poverty is a pressing problem. According to the *2000 United States Census of Population and Housing Report*, St. Joseph County consists of approximately 266,000 persons, 26,200 of whom live below the poverty level ("Housing and Community Development Plan" 47). About 10% of the population of South Bend is in poverty and are homeless. Furthermore, many cities have reported a 12% increase in the number of homeless people since 2007 ("PBS"). Preventative measures should be taken in order to end generational homelessness, in which children who are raised in homeless shelters continue this life as adults. Albert Bandura, a prominent psychologist in behavioral learning, demonstrated that our behavior is powerfully shaped by observing others (Patterson, Grenny, Maxfield, McMillan, and Switzler 1–22). If the current guests at the Center can be motivated to participate in the programs, thereby gaining and maintaining their own housing, their children might learn how to avoid homelessness themselves.

A clear message is being sent that homelessness is a problem, but what could be a possible solution? Homelessness is a complex issue caused by various factors. I believe the

> Here, Karmela provides a claim that motivates the significance of the rest of the researched proposal.

> Karmela provides factual evidence that is both relevant and credible.

> Karmela provides credible testimony for her claim by inserting the name of a prominent scholar.

53

main factor is a lack of or need for motivation. Critics may argue that lack of housing is the main factor, and can be resolved simply through the provision of housing. This is supported by Maslow's theory of the hierarchy of needs which suggests that people who are homeless will give priority to lower-level physiological needs such as safety, food, and shelter rather than higher-level needs such as love, belonging, and esteem. However, some studies have suggested that higher-level needs play an important role in helping people escape homelessness (Patterson and Tweed). For example, researchers Diblasio and Belcher have found that high self-esteem is related to goal attainment among the homeless. Within any program, success requires the motivation of the individual. Whether individuals suffer from addiction, mental illness, or depression, they must want to help themselves; this is also true for those who are homeless. Exit strategizing for those who are homeless truly begins with the individual's decision to want to leave homelessness, and proceeds with the realization that they can (Ravenhill).

Karmela offers a claim, follows it with a debatable premise, and cites other credible sources to support her claim that motivation precedes the ability to achieve physiological needs.

The research I conducted adopts a psychological perspective on homelessness. Through various journals and articles, I found results of studies that can be applied to the Center for the Homeless. However, in order to understand the importance of these studies, it is essential for me to explain the fundamental

psychological theory that informs my recommendations. Self-determination theory
(SDT) is a theory that defines intrinsic
and varied extrinsic motivations, and it
provides a description of their respective
roles in cognitive and social development
("Self-Determination Theory"). One idea
of SDT is internalization, which is defined
as people adopting values or attitudes for
themselves so that the external regulation of
a behavior imposed by homeless center rules
becomes an internal regulation, no longer requiring the implementation from an external
force (Gegne and Deci). For example, when a
class of students continues to do homework
even when their teacher is not watching, they
have internalized the value of their homework beyond doing so simply for the sake of
avoiding punishment from the teacher. There
are three kinds of internalized regulation.
The first is introjected regulation, in which a
regulation has been taken in by the person,
but has not been accepted within his or her
cognitive schema. This includes contingent
self-esteem, which pressures one to behave
in order to feel worthy. Although introjected
regulation is within a person, it is a relatively
controlled form of internalized extrinsic
motivation. It would be better for individuals if they could identify with the value of a
behavior for their own self-selected goals. As
such, with identified self-regulation, people
feel greater freedom and volition because the

> Here Karmela uses a clear
> rhetorical statement to
> signpost what's happen-
> ing in her argument: she
> is pausing to explain a
> theory before moving on
> to cite the scholars who
> use those theories in their
> arguments.

behavior is more congruent with their personal goals and identities. They perceive the cause of their behavior to be a reflection of an aspect of themselves. The guests at the Center for the Homeless need to be fully aware that the steps they are taking now are in line with their future personal goals. The fullest type of internalization, which allows extrinsic motivation to be truly autonomous or volitional, involves the integration of identification with other aspects of oneself—that is, with other identifications, interests, and values. With integrated regulation, people have a full sense that the behavior is an integral part of who they are, that it emanates from their sense of self and is thus self-determined. Integrated regulation is often theorized to represent the most developmentally advanced form of extrinsic motivation, and it shares some qualities with the other type of autonomous motivation, namely, intrinsic motivation (Gegne and Deci). Integrated regulation does not, however, become intrinsic motivation but is still considered extrinsic motivation because the motivation is characterized not by the person being interested in the activity but rather by the activity being instrumentally important for personal goals. This is especially important at the Center, because if the staff can get the guests to internalize the importance of the SOSH program in helping them escape the cycle of homelessness, there

> Karmela indicates to her audience a concession that she and other researchers do not have full knowledge about her current concept by inserting qualifying words such as "often." In doing so, she advances her ethos as a fair writer.

could be an increase in the number of guests participating.

It is important to note that the SDT model of internalization is not a stage theory and does not suggest that people must move through these "stages" with respect to particular behaviors. Rather, the theory describes these types of regulation in order to index the extent to which people have integrated the regulation of a behavior or class of behaviors. As such, SDT proposes that, under the best conditions, people can, at any time, fully integrate a new regulation, or can integrate an existing regulation that had been only partially internalized. In summary, SDT is a self-determination continuum. It ranges from amotivation, which is a complete lack of self-determination, to intrinsic motivation, which is invariantly self-determined. Between amotivation and intrinsic motivation, along this descriptive continuum, are the four types of extrinsic motivation, with external being the most controlled type of extrinsic motivation, and introjected, identified, and integrated being progressively more self-determined.

Various scholarly studies on SDT measure the effects of self-determined behaviors on those who are homeless, and their conclusions can help inform programming at the Center for the Homeless. First, Philip Zimbardo, a renowned psychologist from

Karmela pauses to offer a summary of SDT, recognizing that its technical explanation might frustrate and lose readers. In doing so, she continues to build her ethos with her audience.

Stanford, and his colleagues studied the role of self-efficacy and time perspective in escaping homelessness. They assessed the activities that homeless families engaged in during their stays at a temporary shelter and their success in securing employment and stable housing upon their departure. Personal self-efficacy is defined as one's perceived competence to reach a goal. The results suggest that an individual with a strong sense of self-efficacy spent more time searching for both housing and employment, stayed at the shelter for a shorter duration, and was more productive. In contrast, those with low self-efficacy were more likely to stay longer at the shelter (Epel, Zimbardo, Bandura). Currently, the Center for the Homeless has the SOSH program, which is a five-week program that emphasizes personal development and awareness. The curriculum addresses the whole person: mental, emotional, physical, and spiritual functioning ("Housing and Community Development Plan"). In an interview conducted with a guest, the guest was asked: "What motivated you to be involved in those [programs]?" He responded, "I like to learn things...I could almost say that I was like the optimist" (Meyers). The problem is that the few individuals who do participate in the program already have a high self-efficacy. If the Center could add a brief assessment of self-efficacy beliefs at the

Karmela offers an anecdote with a vivid example to show that some residents are intrinsically motivated.

time of entry, they could target the individuals who need the most help. There could be a greater focus in shifting people from introjected regulation to integrated regulation. Increased self-efficacy has a reciprocal effect on integrated regulation. Consequently, more guests would participate in the program even though it is not mandatory.

This would be especially helpful in conjunction with the self-sufficiency plan that guests create with their coach. Perceived self-efficacy and the development of appropriate strategies have a reciprocal effect on each other. For example, in a study conducted by Epel, Zimbardo, and Bandura, setting proximate goals had a greater positive effect on school children's self-efficacy, persistence, and performance in a math course than did setting a distant goal or setting no goals (Patterson et al.). Though the study above involved math course outcomes, its results are likely generalizable to the Center. Guests at the Center who focus on increasing their senses of self-efficacy will likely have more confidence in being able to complete their goals. On a complex task, such as escaping homelessness, high self-efficacy is necessary for the ongoing search for effective strategies. Many of these individuals have experienced chronic failure, so step-by-step goals with a high self-efficacy is conducive. Failure is something that is experienced

> Here, Karmela deftly offers an argument by analogy, noting the possible limitation in the analogy, and qualifying her claim when she explains that the results are "likely" to produce positive outcomes.

every day, but it is a psychological hurdle that needs to be overcome (Ravenhill).

A possible goal could be to take responsibility for the issues that caused them to become homeless, striving to fulfill the responsibility of being a parent, and beginning to feel accountable for previous decisions and present conditions. Single-mother families with two or more children comprise a significant population at the Center. Coaches must affirm each mother's capabilities as a parent, and encourage responsibility as a parent. One employee at the Center who manages childcare is taking on some responsibilities such as filling in the medical forms of the children, when that should be on the mothers' agendas. Thus, other opportunities for improvement at the Center involve holding the mothers accountable for their actions, and providing a program that teaches mothers research-based best practices for raising their children.

Time perspective is defined as one's goal orientation. An individual can be either past, present, or future oriented. The function of a future time perspective is analogous to a searchlight, which helps to illuminate events ahead. The stronger the searchlight, the brighter and clearer the "goals," and the nearer and more real individuals perceive them. The results of the study showed that future orientation was associated with positive outcomes of enrollment in an educational program, learning valuable lessons from the experience of being homeless, and less passing time such as watching television. An interesting finding from the study is that time perspective may itself be influenced by personal crises. In stressful situations, it may be highly aversive to dwell on the present and emotionally adaptive to look to a brighter future. Thus, higher future orientation may in some respects be "stress-buffering" in such negative situations, such as homelessness. We can conclude that for adults living in shelters, a future orientation may be most conducive to mental health and active coping behaviors. In addition, one's sense of efficacy upon entering a homeless shelter can help predict some of the coping behaviors enacted while at the shelter (Epel, Zimbardo, Bandura).

> Karmela cues the reader that her concluding claim—a future orientation is beneficial to guests—follows from the premises she presented.

There is not an easy way to change one's time perspective, but the Center can influence guests' behavior. According to the book *The Influencer*, there are "some self-defeating behaviors that, if changed, could unlock a whole new level of performance" (Patterson et al. 1–22). For example, in the lobby of the Center is a television, and most often there are many individuals spending a large amount of their time in front of the television. A simple solution could be to limit the TV time that guests receive, or only allow certain channels. Perhaps TV time

> Karmela offers both an argument by analogy and a vivid example by direct experience.

could be seen as a privilege or luxury gained after progressing within the SOSH program. Some psychologists may argue that future orientation is a stable disposition, as opposed to a cognitive structure that is flexible and capable of modification. There is evidence that future time perspective is an outcome of the socialization process. Individuals learn that society as a whole, as well as the specific social class and groups to which they belong, provide an organized array of future events and goals, some of which are more specific than others. More socialized individuals have not only learned about these goals, but have also integrated them into their cognitive time structures (Seijts). However, homelessness pulls individuals out of that context and causes them to lose their sense of time perspective. This is why they may not even consider that the time spent watching TV could be spent in the programs at the Center. Furthermore, it is reasonable to posit that it is something that can be altered.

Another dimension of motivation is one's dignity: "Being homeless threatens the essential dignity of human beings, undermining or often destroying their ability to be seen, and to see themselves as worthwhile persons" (Seltser and Miller 93). The social stigma associated with homelessness can be degrading; however, dignity can also be renewed by improving one's sense

of self- or inner-worth. These are validated
both externality and internally, and they
are dependent on the interaction of individuals and their environments. A study
conducted by the Psychology Department at
the University of Illinois Chicago involved
interviews to assess what homeless persons
believed affected their dignity. Analyses of
the interview data revealed eight kinds of
events that validate dignity and eight kinds
of events that invalidate dignity. They also
identified two overarching categories that
seem to subsume the environmental events
that influence dignity. The categories include interpersonal events in which a homeless person interacts directly with others and
person–setting events in which a homeless
person interacts with the physical world
(Miller and Keys).

Results found that dignity is validated
through factors such as receiving care, being
recognized as an individual, personal service, and belonging to a community. Val-
idation led to an increase of self-worth and
being motivated to improve one's life. The
Center already supports anyone who enters
its doors, giving every individual hospitality
and respect. On the other hand, dignity was
violated by lack of individual identity, unfair
treatment, lack of care, arbitrary rules, negative association, and a negative physical
setting. The excessive use of these rules and

> Karmela appeals to her
> audience's emotions by
> discussing the dignity of
> people who are homeless.
> Her scholarly quote illus-
> trates the importance of
> discussing dignity. She
> quickly redirects this
> negative appeal to pathos
> by offering ways dignity
> can be restored.

limitations on choice-making constrict homeless persons' sense that they are trusted and that they possess the judgment to control their own lives. Thus, they may come to believe that they are not capable or worthy of self-determination (Miller and Keys). Consequently, the Center may need to reevaluate their current rules. A homeless person must first feel secure and trust others before he or she can begin to explore with an open mind other avenues for living beyond mere survival. For example, when guests arrive, they are presented with a set of rules that must be read or read to them and signed.

Much of my proposal involves instituting small changes, but these could likely go a long way in helping to increase the number of guests participating in the programs, while decreasing the rate of recidivism at the homeless shelter. The two factors I have examined are one's personal perspective and the structure/culture of an organization. According to the St. Joseph County Plan, "The second stage is to provide interventions to assist homeless individuals in dealing with the issues that caused them to become homeless. The final stage is to re-integrate these individuals back into the community by providing job training, counseling, and education" ("Housing and Community Development Plan"). In response to these stages, the Center should add a brief assessment of self-efficacy, provide more guidelines for mothers, and consider revising

> Karmela qualifies her general claim that her solutions will bring about change. She indicates to the reader that her knowledge and foresight are limited. Stating that her proposed solutions "could likely" impact homelessness suggests there is room for uncertainty.

64

their rules. The changes I suggest may help the Center for the Homeless achieve these goals to become a home for the homeless: "Home is far more than a roof; it is a physical, emotional, and psychological place and state" (Ravenhill). The Center for the Homeless can empower individuals to maintain the physical, emotional, and psychological health required to overcome the cycle of poverty.

> Karmela's conclusion, paired with the quote she provides at the beginning, serves as a frame for her essay in an appeal to pathos. Her opening quote signals a despair that motivates her proposed solutions, and her final sentences further motivate action while they also signal hope.

Works Cited

"About the Theory." *Self-Determination Theory*, www.selfdeterminationtheory.org/theory. Accessed 10 Dec 2011.

Epel, Elissa S., et al. "Escaping Homelessness: The Influences of Self-Efficacy and Time Perspective on Coping with Homelessness." www.des.emory.edu/mfp/Bandura1999JASP.pdf. Accessed 15 Nov 2011.

"Facts and Figures: The Homeless." *PBS*, 2010, www.pbs.org/now/shows/526/homeless-facts.html. Accessed 9 Dec 2011.

Gagne, Marylene, and Edward Deci. "Self-determination Theory and Motivation." *Journal of Organizational Behavior,* vol. 26, no. 4, 2005, pp. 331–362.

"Housing and Community Development Plan." *City of South Bend: Community,* www.southbendin.gov/docs/CED_HCD2010_14FinalPlanwithTables.pdf.

Meyers, Dale, Personal Interview. 19 Nov 2011.

Miller, Alison, and Christopher Keys. "Understanding Dignity in the Lives of Homeless Persons." *American Journal of Community Psychology*, vol. 29, no. 2, 2001, pp. 331–354.

Patterson, Allisha, and Roger Tweed. "Escaping Homelessness: Anticipated and Perceived facilitators." *Journal of Community Psychology*, vol. 37, no. 7, 2009, pp. 846–858. *Wiley Online Library,* doi: 10.1002/jcop.20335. Accessed 29 Nov. 2011.

Grenny, Joseph and Kerry Patterson. *Influencer: The Power to Change Anything.* Vital Smarts, 2005.

Ravenhill, Megan. *The Culture of Homelessness*, Burlington, Ashgate, 2008.

Seijts, Gerard H. "The Importance of Future Time Perspective in Theories of Work Motivation." *Journal of Psychology,* vol. 132, no. 2, 1998, pp. 154. Accessed 1 Dec. 2011.

Seltser, Barry J. and Donald E. Miller. *Homeless Families: The Struggle for Dignity*, University of Illinois Press, 1993.

In this chapter we explored what it means to construct an argument that is full and fair. Full arguments are appropriately scaled and supported. Fair arguments consider the strength of aesthetic, practical, and ethical reasons and make arguable, debatable claims based on relevant, credible evidence. When writers attend to these standards, they avoid errors in reasoning that constitute logical fallacies. When they also carefully consider the balance of appeals to ethos, pathos, and logos for the rhetorical situation, they are poised to present successful arguments. And if writers attend to these elements carefully, they can use the privilege of writing to address significant issues that warrant the time and attention of their audience.

Critical Questions

1. In your own words, explain why universities require students to study and practice argument the way we describe it here. How is argument important to the career you want to study?
2. Why is it important to include different types of evidence and reasons in an academic argument?
3. Describe a logical fallacy you heard recently. Was it challenged? Why do you think it was used?
4. Which of the three rhetorical appeals—ethos, pathos, or logos— are you most comfortable using now? On which appeal do you most want to improve your skill and why?

CHAPTER five

Writing Ethics, Responsibility, and Accountability

Good writing gives credit where credit is due. It correctly cites ideas and text from other people so that readers have a roadmap to the author's research and thinking. And it treats those sources as human beings with dignity, representing them fully and fairly. Good writing does not manipulate the words of others to suit the author's own agenda.

Citation is less about rules than it is about respect. While readers might forgive an error in your citation style, they won't easily forgive the omission of a citation that should have pointed to a source of information used in your writing, whether that omission was intentional or unintentional.

Always err on the side of acknowledging a source. When you write, your reputation rests on the accuracy and transparency of your argument. Strive to be known as someone with scholarly integrity whom readers can trust. Your ethos, or character, depends on your acting and writing ethically, from the initial invention process to the final product.

GUIDELINES FOR WRITING WITH INTEGRITY

While the principle of pointing to your sources is firm in all domains, the practice of citation differs across domains and genres (see Part Three: "Arguing with Purpose"). You are responsible for knowing and complying with those expectations. Citing your sources demonstrates your confidence: it illustrates your thought process and the rigor of your research, invites your readers to check your facts, and demonstrates your value as a contributor to a larger conversation. Correct citations demonstrate that you want to celebrate the sources you've discovered and curated in your research.

Here are some guidelines for responsible, accountable writing with integrity in all domains: home, academic, work, and civic life.

Home

The expectation in many homes is that families communicate to and about others both honestly and respectfully. Using a careful, calm tone and giving honest reasons for requests typically gets us further in family arguments than resorting to name-calling and ad hominem attacks—personal attacks against the author of the idea rather than a reasoned assessment of the idea itself (see "Logical Fallacies" in Chapter 4). Failure to do so might have a negative impact on your relationships.

Home should be a safe learning environment where principles of integrity are tested and reinforced. You might find that the way you were taught to communicate at home prepared you for a clear transfer to other domains, or you might find that the standards outlined here differ and require more of your attention.

Academic

In academic writing, the expectation for writing with integrity is high, and the consequences for not doing so are severe. In college, you are learning to act in a professional manner by exchanging ideas and information with maturity and dignity.

In terms of delivery, your written and verbal exchanges should use courteous and controlled language that allows your message to be clearly understood. Ad hominem attacks are unacceptable even in informal assignments.

In terms of content, academic writers must acknowledge all sources and avoid presenting any writing or ideas as their own that came in part or in whole from someone else. Representing an idea or text as your own that came from another source is called plagiarism. Plagiarism is a kind of intellectual theft and is considered a serious offense in college. The consequences for plagiarism vary. Familiarize yourself with your school's academic honor codes and policies towards plagiarism.

Intentional plagiarism is fraud. Intentional plagiarism includes a range of misrepresentations, from purposefully presenting someone else's writing as your own (whether that was from another student or a paper-writing service) to reusing all or part of something you wrote for another purpose but did not get permission to use again (called "self-plagiarism").

Consequences for intentional plagiarism in the academic domain range from a failing grade to expulsion. Such behavior is often perceived by faculty as contradicting the purpose and principles of higher education.

Unintentional plagiarism, however, suggests that the student is still in the process of learning how to demonstrate respect for scholarship by mastering the conventions of academic citation. This might happen when you try to paraphrase a text, for example, but end up using language that is too close to the original. In this case, if you have cited the source in your text, you have shown that you are trying to follow the expectations of academic writing. Your instructor will decide how to proceed if this happens.

The consequences of intentionally or unintentionally failing to treat your sources properly can be serious: your academic and/or professional reputation and career can be damaged permanently, and you erode the trust of your audience.

Your college writing, and your demonstration of academic integrity, will lay the foundation for success in the work and civic domains. If you attend to ethical writing carefully now, when you have the support of peers and instructors, you will be much more confident and competent when you are called to write ethically in the future.

Work

In the workplace, expectations for writing with integrity are also high, and the consequences for not doing so are severe. The tone of workplace writings must be both controlled and professional, whether in an internal email exchange or in an annual report. Examples abound of jobs lost over discourteous emails that suggest the sender cannot adapt her communication style to the expectations of respect and collegiality in the workplace.

Workplace communication rarely uses the citation styles and conventions (such as MLA and APA) used in academic writing. Your familiarity with the need for acknowledging sources and giving appropriate credit, however, will help you organize your research and determine—maybe even influence—the conventions of a particular workplace. In fact, collaborative team writing in which individual contributors are not equally recognized is common in the workplace; the sense of plagiarism and ownership of ideas in the work domain can be quite different from the academic setting. It is essential to understand the expectations for citation and recognition in the particular domain and unit you are working in: do not assume that the way writing works in your workplace will be acceptable in your classroom, or the other way around.

The consequences of using an unprofessional tone or presenting others' ideas as your own at work can be severe as well. Internally, such poor writing can make employers wonder if you are the kind of employee they want representing that company. Dishonesty in this area might suggest dishonesty in other areas.

Civic Life

In public discourse, the tone and quality of exchanges vary widely. You can easily find examples of completely uncensored and unsupported online posts, for example, that neither exhibit care for others nor demonstrate due diligence in fact checking. Or you can find examples of refereed, peer-reviewed forums that only publish writing that has been vetted by experts in the field and that demand respect for all participants and for the information they purvey to others.

All too often in the civic domain we see the disintegration of effective communication when people do not adhere to standards of ethical communication. In these forums, writers attack not just ideas but real people, and they frequently present myths and suspicions as confirmed fact. This kind of communication is most harmful when it comes from people who are perceived to have credentials that suggest both expertise and authority. Audience members who do not think critically about such sources might mistake the appearance of such credentials for actual integrity, and might mistake opinion for news, or conjecture for a well-researched and solidly supported argument.

The consequences for communicating without integrity in the public domain can be significant: both in positive and negative ways. Some media personalities who are particularly skilled at ad hominem attacks and spinning conjecture as fact have won fame and fortune as media sensations. Whether it's the entertainment value or the allure of wanting to follow people who seem so confident in their argument that we fail to check their evidence, we do sometimes rally behind people whose quick answers are mistaken for accurate and honest answers. This might be why it is sometimes a challenge for instructors to explain the importance of ethical discourse to students—it's often not what we see rewarded and celebrated in daily discourse.

But ethical writing and communication are present in public discourse, and we do also rally around exemplars of good writing. Reputable publications aim to fact-check every detail of every article they publish. They do not tolerate plagiarism. They publish retractions if they are found to have conveyed misinformation, and the authors who commit such errors move from reporting the news to becoming the news. That's integrity. Owning up to such errors and working to correct the record demonstrates accountability.

Who Is Hurt by Unethical Writing?

Finally, it's important to care about writing with integrity not just for the consequences you might suffer personally if you commit an offense in this area, but also for the hurt caused to others by such dishonesty. Writing without integrity risks hurting the readers who took time to review your work, and the people whose sources you stole or misrepresented. You also risk hurting, by association, people in your community or domain whose views and interests your writing might be perceived to represent.

The links of social media seem to make all of us interconnected. Whether we like it or not, individual writing and communication by one person is often taken as a proxy for the ideas and character of those close to us. How we treat others and represent our ideas reflects on our family, our peers, our colleagues, and our community. You may have noticed that the "disclaimer" is a frequent feature of workplace communication: "The views expressed here do not represent the views of . . ." We live in a litigious society (always on guard for the lawsuit) in which such protections seem to have become an inevitable part of engagement.

But this discussion isn't just advice on how not to get sued for expressing your views. It's about how we can successfully express our views fully and fairly, with care for other people, as well as the ideas guiding our writing. If we remember to respect both our audiences and those whose interests we claim to represent, the writing process is an occasion to celebrate the exchange of ideas, not a cause for concern.

QUESTIONS TO GUIDE ETHICAL WRITING

The following list of questions will help you examine your writing from an ethical perspective to help ensure scholarly integrity. You can ask these questions on your own, but it is ideal to have a peer or professor ask them of you during your writing process so that he or she can press you on the details if necessary. Review these questions before you begin each writing process to help prevent unethical behavior. Then review them again late in the process to ensure that you've meet these expectations:

1. Is every direct quote cited?
2. Is every paraphrase cited?
3. Is every summary cited?
4. Are both *texts* and *ideas* (including formative conversations with experts or peers) cited?
5. Do the citations follow the appropriate style? Have you double-checked that every source cited or noted in-text is listed in the proper order in the works cited or references?
6. Have you double-checked your sources to confirm that the facts, ideas, and information you convey in your writing are reliable and sound, verifiable across multiple trustworthy sources?
7. Is contrary evidence acknowledged fully and fairly, not avoided to seemingly strengthen your argument?
8. Would the authors cited read your writing and agree that their ideas have been represented fully, fairly, and courteously?
9. Are conflicts of interest acknowledged according to expectations in this genre? (This is more of a concern for advanced, professional researchers who might have to sign a legal disclaimer to this effect, but it's good to get in the habit of asking and being aware of this possibility in all domains.)
10. Have you self-plagiarized by using your own previous writing without getting permission from professors to do so and/or acknowledging that you've done so?

11. Have you dated and saved each new draft as a new file so that you have a record of your writing progress to show that you are writing with integrity, not using old work or work from others?

12. If you're doing scientific research, have you recorded all aspects of your methods such that others could independently verify your work?

13. Do you represent the significance of your findings and conclusions accurately, not overstating your contribution to the field?

14. If you ask people to act based on your writing, are you asking them to act responsibly?

Does the imperative to write with respect mean you have to write so cautiously that you can't say anything edgy or risky or provocative? Does it mean that your writing can only flatter and affirm? Absolutely not.

We wouldn't grow if we only endorsed the status quo. We *have* to move beyond praise and into blame—when that is warranted by a thorough review of evidence. The key here is to do due diligence in our research and to think of the people we write about and to as real human beings possessed of dignity and intelligence. Sometimes we lose sight of that principle when we are writing to and about people we might never meet in person. A valid claim or critique will get lost if it is delivered with dismissive language or peppered with inaccuracies.

As a college student and, eventually, college graduate, you have the opportunity as well as the responsibility to apply the lessons of scholarly integrity to your communications in all domains. Now that you know these principles, you cannot unlearn them: you can only ignore them. Embracing this call to hold yourself accountable to these high standards in all your communications will empower you as a writer in any situation.

OFFICE HOURS ➤ Understanding Common Knowledge

The only exception for citation is information considered common knowledge. Common knowledge is defined as information that most of your readers can be expected to know. If the information can easily be found in many reference texts, it's not necessary to cite it. For example, most readers in the American college setting know that the United States has a welfare system to help people in poverty, so you would not have to cite that general fact. However, they are less likely to know specifically that according to the 2011 American Community Survey, 25% of children under six years old live in poverty, and 12% of children under six years old live in extreme poverty. Most people don't know those numbers and probably don't know the difference between poverty and extreme poverty (extreme poverty means living at less than 50% of the federal poverty level), so you should cite your source when using this level of detailed information.

   If you have any question about whether something is considered common knowledge, check with your instructor. While you can always play it safe and cite something, citing too much can be disruptive to the reader, so you want to be sure citation is necessary.

Critical Questions

1. Is a lapse in scholarly integrity more critical in one of these domains than another? Why or why not?
2. What would be the hardest part about following these principles in each domain? What would make it easier to do so?
3. In what ways is fact-checking similar to the research process? Consult some of the following fact-checking sites to deepen your

understanding of this comparison: FactCheck.org, The Fact Checker, PolitiFact.com, OpenSecrets.org, Snopes.com, Pro-Publica.org, and TruthOrFiction.com. What did you learn about these sites? For what might you consult them?

4. Consider a time when you or someone you know was not given credit for something. Why do you think that happened? Was it intentional or unintentional? How did it make that person feel? How do you think writers would feel if they saw their work in another source without citation?

5. Describe a time in any one of the four domains when someone's tone got out of control. What ad hominem attacks did the person use? What specific words indicated that the tone was inappropriate? What were the consequences of that inappropriate expression? Try to think of extreme examples: ones with few consequences and ones with severe consequences. Explain why the consequences differed in scale.

6. Describe a situation in which someone in public life or in your personal experience was called to account for lacking scholarly integrity. What was the person accused of doing? Did he or she admit guilt or see the situation differently? What were the consequences? What did you learn from that situation about practicing your own scholarly integrity?

Analyze the Assignment

College writing prompts vary depending on the course, the instructor, and the objectives. In every case, plan to spend time making sure you understand what you are being asked to do. A single assignment might require you to argue, inform, and/or entertain, as we describe in Chapter 1. This chapter will help you learn to analyze your writing assignments to pave the pathway for success.

RHETORICAL ANALYSIS OF WRITING PROMPTS

You can use the six questions for inquiry we introduced in Chapter 1 to help you clarify the rhetorical situation of any writing assignment. Here are those six broad questions again, with more specific questions you might ask about your writing prompt:

- *Why (ethics)?* What specific ethical considerations should I weigh regarding the process and product of my response to this assignment? For example, is it clear whether I should seek out or avoid my peers' thoughts on this assignment? Is it clear how I should find and cite sources I consult or use directly? Is it clear how I should work with sensitive information or human subjects if those are part of this assignment? Is it clear whom I should consult if I have ethical questions about the process or product of this assignment?

- *Who (author and audience)*? What do I know about my instructor's objectives for this prompt based on the course content so far? What are the learning objectives of the course, and how might this prompt be testing my mastery and development related to those goals? What does the prompt suggest about my audience—the actual audience of the instructor and/or peers or some imagined audience?

- *Where (domain)*? Should I write this assignment only for the actual academic domain of this class, or am I intended to write for a different context?

- *How (mode and medium)*? What options or restrictions do I have on how I answer the question? Am I required to respond in a specific disciplinary genre or in a specific medium? Is experimentation with mode and medium allowed or even encouraged for this assignment?

- *When (kairos)*? What is happening in our class right now that warrants this assignment? What function does this assignment serve for our class? How will identifying the most urgent learning objectives and topics help me identify my most promising topics and approaches for this prompt?

- *What (message)*? What can I learn about the ideal scale and scope of my response to this prompt (see Chapter 4, Figures 4.1, "Measuring Issue Impact" and 4.2, "Investment in the Ask")? What do the parameters on word count/page length and number and type of sources indicate about appropriate topics and methods? What does the prompt allow me the chance to do and think, given my interests and aspirations? What can I do to make sure I own and enjoy this opportunity to write?

These questions will help you think deeply about the specific rhetorical situation created by this writing prompt in this class at this time.

The writing process begins as soon as you receive the assignment prompt. Think carefully about the prompt right away to encourage your mind to work in the right direction.

Because assignments are usually given in writing, you can do a rhetorical analysis of the actual prompt. Here are three ways to work towards a full understanding of the assignment:

1. Analyze the written prompt.
2. Consider assumptions inherent in the prompt (often related to the specific context of your class).
3. Call for clarification.

How you approach each part will depend on the rhetorical situation of your writing. By attending to these elements of analysis, you can be more confident that you are working in the right direction.

THREE ELEMENTS FOR RHETORICAL ANALYSIS OF A WRITING PROMPT
1. Analyze the Written Prompt

The first step in analyzing an assignment is to review carefully the written text of your assignment prompt. First, identify the verbs (e.g., *consider, argue, summarize, reflect*). The verbs tell you what to do, indicating the genre you're asked to use. If you see more than one verb, determine whether there is a sequence or sense of priority; for example, "first . . . then," or "after," or "you may also . . ." Think about how those verbs have been used and therefore defined in the specific context of your course. Here are some common writing verbs and definitions:

Table 6.1   COMMON VERBS USED IN WRITING PROMPTS

VERB	DEFINITION: THE TYPE OF WRITING YOU MIGHT DO IN RESPONSE TO THIS VERB
Analyze	Critique key texts and incidents carefully using your own insight and, if asked for specifically, the insight from outside sources.
Argue	Offer your own position on an issue and support it with reasons, evidence, and examples.
Clarify	Define and distinguish between ideas so that concepts are clearly articulated.
Classify	Give reasons and evidence to explain why an idea or event belongs within a clearly defined group and not in a different group.
Compare	Give reasons and evidence to explain how an idea or event is similar to another.
Consider	Think about this idea or event, then provide reasons or evidence to explain what comes to mind.
Contrast	Give reasons and evidence to explain how an idea or event is different from another.
Define	Explain the meaning of an idea or event based on your own consideration and common public thinking on this.
Describe	Use details, often drawing from the five senses, to show something in words.
Discuss	Write through your emerging thoughts on an issue, considering your own viewpoint and the ideas of others that both support and challenge your thinking.
Explain	Provide reasons and evidence to support an idea in detail, step-by-step, considering opposing viewpoints.
Explore	Thoroughly consider the causes, consequences, and/or solutions related to an idea or event in order to address a question or problem.

Identify	Name and list ideas or events according to explicit criteria.
Illustrate	Provide an example that helps explain an idea more concretely.
Interpret	Put an idea into your own words, staying true to what you think the original author intended to say but also adding your own insight.
Narrate	Tell a complete story in such a way that readers have the sense that they experienced the event as well.
Outline	Tell the highlights of a story or other original text in such a way that readers have a sense of what happened or what that text included even though they do not hear every detail.
Persuade	Write with the priority of gaining agreement from your readers.
Propose	Suggest appropriate thinking or action in response to new information.
Prove	Provide appropriate, convincing evidence in support of an argument or position.
Reflect	Think about an idea or experience, often a critical incident, in order to understand it more fully and connect it to other ideas and experiences.
State	Present an idea, claim, or information directly.
Summarize	Present the main ideas of another text in your own words.

After you have identified the verbs, consider cues that indicate the scope and scale of this assignment. The due date, page length, and percentage of course grade will collectively tell you a great deal about the significance of this assignment. Once you determine that time-frame, you can immediately schedule reviews with outside readers (see Chapter 14, "Review: By Peers and Experts").

2. Consider Assumptions Inherent in the Prompt

Rhetorical analysis of the written prompt can get you a long way in your understanding of the assignment, but it might not be enough. You must also consider the contexts for that written prompt, including the readings and discussions that have led up to the assignment. In some courses, the assignments might be sequenced to build upon previous assignments, taking you deeper into the course content and asking you to demonstrate increasing mastery of skills or experimenting with new content and skills.

As you read the assignment prompt, then, it's important to consider what it doesn't say but might assume. Here are some assumptions your instructor might have but not express in the actual writing prompt:

- You have read everything assigned for class and have a good grasp on the content.
- You have attended all classes or have caught up on missed discussion by talking with the instructor and/or classmates to make sure you understand all content, particularly as it pertains to discussion of the writing assignment (instructors often explain more about an assignment in class than they write in the prompt).
- You can learn writing techniques from published writers in various disciplines—even ones you do not intend to pursue—that will transfer to any type of writing you do. The readings you have done for class model, in some way, the writing your instructor wants you to do.

Exploring these assumptions will get you closer to understanding the full rhetorical context of that writing prompt.

3. Call for Clarification

If after analyzing the text and context of your writing prompt you still aren't clear on what is being asked of you, ask your instructor to clarify. Be prepared to explain what you think the prompt is asking and why (your rhetorical analysis). Also, be prepared to provide evidence that you've been trying to sort this out: the draft of a thesis, an outline, or proposal. Do not wait until you have a full draft written to make sure you're on track. This will help your instructor identify gaps in your understanding of the course material and methods, and/or it might also illuminate places where the instructor can clarify her teaching. Instructors want you to understand what to do so they can see how well you perform. They do not intend to confuse you with the prompt itself.

OFFICE HOURS ➤ Clarifying Cross-Cultural Assumptions

If your previous education happened outside the United States, you might find it difficult to spot those assumptions about what counts as good writing in an American academic setting. The writing prompt might outline details such as page length and number of sources required, but it might take a face-to-face or written exchange with your instructor to help clarify the ways those assumptions differ in cross-cultural settings. We will not generalize about those exact differences but instead offer a list of areas where you might encounter differences: use of personal stories, use of personal pronouns, use and placement of thesis statement, acceptable sources, stylistic preferences, and definition of academic argument.

Students educated in the United States need assistance in all these areas as well, but students educated outside the United States will sometimes find dramatically different expectations for writing. Having a conversation with your instructor when you receive the writing prompt is especially important so that you can locate those differences before you start to write. We recommend that you enter that conversation by describing the writing prompts and expectations you have experienced. Your instructor might be surprised to hear those experiences. By hearing your description, instructors can better explain how their expectations differ.

83

Critical Questions

1. Do you prefer writing prompts that are open-ended or highly specific? Explain.

2. Do instructors in different disciplines seem to have the same or different assumptions hidden in their writing prompts? Compare and contrast those assumptions.

3. Describe a time when you or someone else called for clarification from an instructor. What did the student say? How did the instructor respond? Did that experience encourage or discourage you from asking for clarification in the future?

4. What do you most like to be asked to do in your writing assignments? What verbs do you hope you'll find in those writing prompts? Which verbs do you least want to see in your writing prompts? Explain.

5. Do an inventory of the writing prompts you have received so far this year. What are the most and least common verbs used? Why do you think you see those trends? How do those trends compare with that of peers in other disciplines?

CHAPTER seven

Plan: Organizing the Process

After you analyze the assignment prompt, you can plan your writing process. Planning involves estimating what you have to do, how long each task will take, and who can help. Using a timeline to outline goals, resources, and deadlines will help you track your progress toward completion. Having a plan can reduce the stress that leads to writer's block, procrastination, and/or unreflective writing.

SCHEDULING TASKS AND RESOURCES FOR WRITING

Planning can help you write efficiently and effectively. Planning helps you set realistic goals and note the incremental measures of success that mark good writing and keep you motivated to continue. With your understanding of the writing prompt in mind, you create a plan by asking these key questions: What do you need to do? How long will it take to do that? Who can help? And when does it have to be done to meet a deadline? Table 7.1 shows how one student used a timeline to plan activities to write a narrative argument.

Tools to Organize Planning

As you begin to plan, consider the tools that can help you create, structure, and track that plan. Digital organizing tools range from free calendars to more robust fee-based apps. These tools allow you to enter all the deadlines you must meet to complete your assignment on time. Digital tools can help you visualize that information through such techniques as color-coding categories of information, flagging various priority levels, and displaying a satisfying checkmark next to a completed task. In addition, many digital tools support multiple media, letting you upload photos, videos, or voice memos.

To find such tools, explore the "Productivity" section of iTunes or Google Play to see what tools align with your work style. Or talk to friends, instructors, or advisors about what works for them.

What Do You Need to Do?

After you analyze the prompt and consult your syllabus for relevant in-class activities, you will have a sense of what your instructor expects you to do. Make a list of each *official* draft deadline and activity in chronological order (that is, mandatory deadlines assigned by your instructor). Now, enhance that official list with your *supplemental* list of additional drafts, reviews, and activities such as library visits that you think should be part of a successful writing process for this particular assignment. See Table 7.1 for an example of a thorough plan that includes both official and supplemental activities.

How Long Will It Take to Do That?

Now that you know what you need to do to create your ideal writing process, get specific. Think about past writing assignments you have completed successfully and estimate how long each task takes, erring on the longer side to be safe. Remember that you need time to step away from your writing to reflect and possibly do additional research. Prioritize and protect those critical thinking times when you are researching and drafting by reserving ample time to give yourself space.

Table 7.1 estimates how long one student thinks it will take her to complete each element of writing a narrative argument, and it names the exact times she put on her organizer to devote to each element. This student estimates that including time spent in class, at the writing center, with other reviewers, and on her own, she will spend about 25 hours over three weeks on her assignment.

You can follow this example to map out the appropriate time you need to complete your writing assignments as well. Schedule times to avoid work schedules, personal activities, and other school obligations (which should also be mapped onto your schedule). Account for travel time if you have to walk or drive someplace else to do research or find an appropriate writing space (see Table 7.2, "Writing Ritual Reflections," for help thinking about what's an appropriate space for you). Once those times are put on the organizer, protect them like any other mandatory responsibility. Hold yourself accountable to what you think it takes to achieve good writing. Scheduling reasonable times to accomplish each task will help you achieve those goals.

Who Can Help?

Now that you know what you need to do and roughly how long it will take to complete those tasks, think about who will help you complete them. If other stakeholders are involved—writing center tutors, peers, community partners, your instructor, and so on—your planning will have to account for their schedules as well. Chapter 14, "Review: By Peers and Experts," will help you think through all the ways these stakeholders can work with you. You might have to revise your schedule to reflect the actual availability of the people you will work with.

Note, for example, that writing center tutors often get busy around midterms and finals. However, by planning in advance, you can see when you will need to make that appointment, thus maximizing your chance to schedule an appointment before they fill up.

How Do You Meet Deadlines?

Start planning with the final deadline in mind. Your "writing window" is the amount of time between when you receive the writing assignment prompt and when the final draft is due. How much you can supplement your writing task list depends on the size of the writing window and your other obligations during that time. By planning ahead, you can set realistic goals for yourself, confident that you will continue to make progress on your writing.

Table 7.1   TIMELINE: PLANNING A NARRATIVE ARGUMENT

ELEMENTS OF THE WRITING PROCESS	OFFICIAL TASKS DUE FOR CLASS	SUPPLEMENTAL TASKS ON MY OWN	DUE DATE & TIME
WRITING WINDOW OPENS	Writing prompt received and discussed in class.		September 1 Time: Class time
Analyze the Assignment (Chapter 6)	Discuss writing assignment in class. Ask questions in class to clarify expectations. Look at successful models of student writing for this assignment in class.	Read the prompt several times after class and contact my instructor through email if anything is unclear.	September 1 Time: Class time plus 1–2 hours

Plan: Organizing the Process (Chapter 7)		Start to fill out this template and put dates on my calendar as review appointments are scheduled.	September 2 Time: 1–2 hours
Question: Exploring Issues (Chapter 8)		Use the library database to search with key terms.	September 5— 4:00–6:00 p.m. Time: 2 hours
	Working bibliography of 3–6 sources due in class		September 7 in class Time: Class time
Read: Strategies for Reading in Research (Chapter 9)		Do passive and active reading strategies: highlight, pull direct quotes, summarize, etc.	September 7— 4:00–5:30 p.m. Time: 1.5 hours
		Do more research based on peer feedback.	September 8— 4:00–5:00 p.m. Time: 1 hour
Invent: Take Note and Create (Chapter 10)		Brainstorm ideas. Create a concept map.	September 8— 5:00–6:00 p.m. Time: 1 hour
		Use concept map to generate an outline.	September 9— 7:00–10:00 p.m. Time: 3 hours
Arrange: Prioritize, Organize, Outline (Chapter 11)		Take notes on sources.	September 10— 4:00–5:00 p.m.

(continued)

Table 7.1   TIMELINE: PLANNING A NARRATIVE ARGUMENT (*continued*)

ELEMENTS OF THE WRITING PROCESS	OFFICIAL TASKS DUE FOR CLASS	SUPPLEMENTAL TASKS ON MY OWN	DUE DATE & TIME
Draft: Introduction, Body, Conclusion (Chapter 12)	Use outline to draft 3–4 pages; try to draft the whole paper if it's going well.		September 11— 4:00–5:30 p.m. Time: 1.5 hours
	Submit *first draft* for in class peer work-shop. Must be at least 3 pages long.		September 12 in class Time: Class time
Revise: Strategies for Re-seeing (Chapter 13)		Incorporate new research and peer comments into *second draft*.	September 14— 3:00–5:30 p.m. Time: 1.5 hours
Review: By Peers and Experts (Chapter 14)		Share complete draft with writing center tutor. Revise *third draft* based on comments while those notes are fresh in my mind.	September 17— 1:00–2:00 p.m., appointment confirmed; 2:00–3:30 p.m. revise Time: 2. 5 hours
Proofread and Submit (Chapter 15)		Look at lower-order concerns (i.e., punctua-tion, mechanics, style, grammar).	September 20— 5:00–6:30 p.m. polish on my own; 8:00–9:00 p.m. roommate helps with final proofread; 9:00–9:30 p.m. address room-mate's revision notes Time: 3 hours

WRITING WINDOW CLOSES	*Final Draft* Due uploaded to course dropbox		September 21 by 11:59 p.m. Total Time: about 25 hours

Sticking to the Plan

Once you complete your planning timeline, enter those activities in your calendar. Don't just put deadlines: actually block out the time you think it will take to do that particular activity at the time of day that works best for your writing style (see the next section, "Writer's Rituals: Know What Works for You"). Protect those writing and reviewing times as essential parts of your day, adjusting only if the outcomes of the writing itself cause you to do so—that is, add more research time if you are not finding the sources you need or change a review time based on a reviewer's request.

WRITER'S RITUALS: KNOW WHAT WORKS FOR YOU

Sometimes writing comes easier than other times. By reflecting on and analyzing the positive conditions that typically *enable* writing for you as well as the negative conditions that typically *block* writing, you can develop an effective writer's ritual. Table 7.2 lists questions to help you evaluate the conditions that encourage you to produce good writing—or good thinking and problem solving, if that's where you are in the process.

You can probably answer these questions easily, but you might not have thought of the combination of these elements as your writing ritual. Ask yourself: Does your writing ritual create the ideal conditions for writing, or do you need to make some adjustments? Because ideals are often unattainable, thus making it impossible to meet every factor on your list, it's also important to be flexible within an

Table 7.2   WRITING RITUAL REFLECTIONS

WRITING CONDITIONS	QUESTIONS
Sound	Do you write best with no background noise, or do you need music or other sounds?
Light	Do you write best with soft light that calms, or bright light that keeps you alert?
Company	Do you write best by yourself in isolation from others, by yourself but surrounded by people in a public setting, or in the company of friends who are also working?
Time of Day	Do you write best in the morning, during the afternoon, or at night?
Food/Drink	What food or drinks help energize you to write?
Level of Rest	Does it matter how rested you are when you write?

acceptable range. Plan ahead to consider when and where you will be writing so you can meet more of your ideal conditions.

CONFRONTING WRITER'S BLOCK

Even professional writers get "blocked." Writer's block is a sense that you just *can't* get the writing done and you find yourself sitting in front of a blank screen for long periods of time.

Here are two strategies for recognizing and working through writer's block. First, know the writing rituals that either enable or block your writing. Respond to Table 7.2, "Writing Ritual Reflections," and acknowledge what you know about your best writing conditions. Set yourself up for conditions that enable good writing, and reduce the conditions that tend to block your writing. Second, make a plan that gives you clear, manageable tasks that nudge your writing along.

Use the strategies from Chapter 10, "Invent: Take Note and Create," to restart in the areas where you were stuck:

- Brainstorm by talking with others about the assignment and your ideas—some people need to verbalize ideas before they write them
- Freewrite as quickly as possible, just getting ideas out in sentences or even lists for 5-10 minutes—try doing this from a specific quote or source
- Map your concepts visually to see how ideas relate to one another—use circles, arrows, images, and other visuals to picture your ideas
- Outline your ideas, giving the backbone not all the details of your argument
- Ask yourself the stasis questions regarding facts, definition, quality, and policy
- Ask yourself the journalist questions (Who? What? When? Where? Why? How?)

With these strategies in mind, you always have something to do. Pick a strategy and start writing. The writing will jump-start your thinking. This chapter should help you think strategically about what generally works and doesn't work to help get the writing done, and it should help you think specifically about *what* you can do *when* to keep writing.

OFFICE HOURS ➤ Resetting Your Writing Rituals

It's always a good idea to compare your best writing practices with what others do. You might find that what works well for others works well for you, too. Furthermore, if you are transitioning into the college writing environment as a first-year student, you might find that your routines have been disrupted. You might find it

---

(continued)

difficult to control the sound, light, and human distractions that swirl around you now. You might have to adjust or even invent your writing rituals anew, given your new circumstances.

To reset your writing ritual to a new environment, try talking to others about what works for them. If you responded to Table 7.2 in class, note the answers your peers gave. If you go to the writing center, ask the tutors what works for them. More experienced students might have the best tips on how to achieve the conditions that foster good writing—they might know the secret quiet spots in the library or the best times to visit a great coffee shop or how to write when you have kids at home. You should also talk to your instructors about their writing habits. They, too, continue to write while handling many other responsibilities, and they've been doing that successfully for years.

Gather those suggestions and start experimenting to see what works for you. And keep that list of suggestions because what works for you now might not work for you later—the coffee shop might get too popular or you just might need something different to energize your writing later on. Having that list of practical strategies for good writing should give you confidence that you have specific strategies you can draw on to help your writing succeed. Don't stare at a blank screen and wait for inspiration. Choose one of these strategies and take action.

Critical Questions

1. How might planning change across different types of writing? Give specific examples. How could planning your writing process help you avoid unethical writing?

2. Have you or anyone you know ever experienced writer's block as it is defined here? Describe what you felt or observed. What happened? Did the writing get done on time? Explain.

3. Have you ever had the opposite of writer's block, a time when you just couldn't stop writing? Describe that experience. Why do you think the writing came so easily in that situation?

CHAPTER eight

Question: Exploring Issues

After you have analyzed the assignment prompt (Chapter 6) and planned the tasks for each step of your writing process (Chapter 7), it's time to consider what you're writing about. Exploring initial resources will help you focus your topic and turn it into an issue. An issue is what people are arguing about within a topic. In this chapter, we give general guidelines on how to identify a topic, how to move from a topic to an issue, and how to explore initial resources. Part Three advises you on how to do this within specific genres and modes.

FINDING A TOPIC: WHO DECIDES?

Some writing assignments will tell you exactly what to write about—specifying both the topic and the genre. Other writing assignments will be specific about the genre but leave the choice of topic open for you to choose. Some people prefer to be given a specific topic; others enjoy the freedom of finding their own topic. You will probably encounter both types of assignments as you write in the academic domain. By analyzing the assignment prompt carefully, you will have a clear sense of guidelines for finding an acceptable topic for that specific assignment.

MOVING FROM A TOPIC TO AN ISSUE

In the academic domain, your instructors often expect you to move beyond *reporting* on a general topic and instead ask you to *analyze* a specific issue. It is also important to understand the difference between a *topic*, which is a broad category, and an *issue*, which is something contested within that category, something about which people actively disagree. See Figure 8.1, "Moving from a Topic to an Issue," for a visual of how these elements—primary topics, secondary subtopics, and issues—relate to one another and move from more general to increasingly

Primary Topic: Education

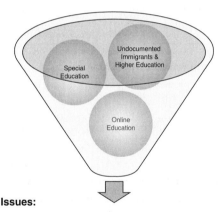

Potential Secondary Subtopics:

Undocumented Immigrants and Higher Education, Special Education, Online Education

Issues:

Issue Question: To what extent can technology replace K-12 classroom teachers?

Focused Issue Question: To what extent can technology replace classroom teachers in English as a second language elementary school programs?

Figure 8.1
Moving from a Topic to an Issue

specific questions for research and writing. Chapter 9, "Read: Strategies for Reading in Research," will help you plunge into that issue once you have done this initial discernment to find a strong issue.

STRATEGIES FOR FINDING ISSUES

In this chapter, we discuss strategies for exploring *initial* resources that will help you move from a topic to an issue that's appropriate for your assignment prompt. You will find a more detailed discussion of research strategies in Chapter 27, "Working with Published Sources," and Chapter 28, "Working with Human Sources." What we describe in this chapter will get your discovery process started but would not constitute a thorough research process for writing a paper.

Following are some strategies to help explore topics and issues if your assignment allows you room to choose your own path.

Listen to Peers, Family, Colleagues, and Instructors

One way to discover topics and issues is by listening carefully to what people around you are talking about. What frustrates your peers, neighbors, family, and workplace colleagues? If you are volunteering in the local community, what do the administrators and clients of that organization seem most concerned about?

Furthermore, listen carefully across your classes for your instructors to mention issues to pursue. Lectures and readings in other classes might raise issues you could address in your writing class.

Browse Websites that Aggregate Current Topics and Issues

Many online resources can prompt your thinking as you move from general topic to specific issue. Some are explicitly devoted to this purpose, offering a broad range of topics, subdivided into secondary subtopics, and then diving into current issues within those subtopics. Browsing through one of these websites early in your process can be an efficient way to focus and narrow your search for appropriate issues to write about.

Your campus or community library might have subscriptions for topic and issue aggregating websites. Many others are available free on the internet as well. One online resource that could help you at this early stage of the writing process is the *CQ Researcher* website (library.cqpress.com), which offers "in-depth reports on today's issues." Similarly, the website procon.org explores the "pros and cons of controversial issues." Each of these sources offers several main categories of topics with subtopics that then contain those controversial issues. Table 8.1, "Moving from Topics to Subtopics to Issue Questions," shows two examples from the *CQ Researcher* website, moving from broad topics to subtopics to issue-based questions.

Remember, though, that the topics and issues presented by such websites do not cover *every* possible issue you could or should explore. We do not mean to suggest that these websites offer the only or even the best topics for you to consider. Instead, we recommend them as a means of jump-starting your thinking. You will quickly see the difference between a topic and an issue, and you will see, too, how important it is to narrow topics down to very specific issues in order to write about them effectively.

Review Headlines

Another way to explore potential topics and issues for your writing is to review current news headlines in print or online. You can search for specific news websites online, go to the library to browse their print newspaper subscriptions, or subscribe to digital versions of the news to have headlines delivered to your email daily through most news sources (e.g., *The New York Times*, *The Washington Post*, the BBC). A quick review of the news section headlines will give you a sense of major events happening in civic life across a range of topics and

Table 8.1   MOVING FROM TOPICS TO SUBTOPICS TO ISSUE QUESTIONS

These examples from *CQ Researcher* show how this source organizes movement from broad topics to specific issue questions. You might narrow your thinking in different ways, but these examples offer some productive ways to explore topics.

Topics	Social Movements	Education
Subtopics	Civil Rights Movement Conservatism and Liberalism Environmentalism Feminism General Social Trends Hate Groups Prohibition Protest Movements Religious Movements Sexuality Student Movements	Bilingual and Multicultural Education College Financing and Funding Cost of Education and School Funding Diversity Issues Early Childhood Education Education Policy Education Standards and Testing Elementary and Secondary Education Libraries and Educational Media Online Education Private Schools and Home Schooling Research in Education Science and Mathematics Education Special Education Students and Social Life Teaching Undergraduate and Graduate Education Vocational and Adult Education
Issue Question	Police Tactics: Has U.S. law enforcement become militarized?	College Rankings: Do college rankings accurately reflect school quality?

locations. A quick review of the opinion section headlines will give you a sense of the issues being debated within those communities.

You might want to narrow your search to topics that interest you most or to the assigned topic of your course or assignment. You can filter your search in two ways: by setting alerts from news sources that will send you a message when a story appears on that topic, or by searching directly in a news source devoted to the specific topic you want to pursue. You can also set a Google alert for a specific topic, such as "poverty." This will return many non-scholarly reports, so remember that the alerts are for generating issue ideas, not necessarily for securing your final research sources.

To broaden your search to multiple news sources, you can search directly in a news source that aggregates stories on a topic. If you take this approach, make sure you start with an unbiased aggregating source so that certain topics and issues aren't filtered out. Visit your librarians to locate appropriate sources for your interests (see "Office Hours: Engaging Libraries and Librarians to Find Topics and Issues" later in this chapter).

GATHERING INITIAL RESOURCES

As you explore all these ways of discovering issues for your writing, capture what you find with accurate notes that identify your sources. You will save yourself time and prevent unintentional plagiarism—the act of accidentally representing someone else's ideas as your own without proper citation—by taking careful notes on sources (see Chapter 9, "Read: Strategies for Reading in Research").

Again, at this early stage in the writing process, you are researching ideas for issues, not conducting scholarly research for sources to support your writing. You are moving quickly through sources, skimming them for ideas that spark your interest and meet the expectations of the assignment. As you start to focus on that key idea, capture the full text of articles you encounter so that you can return to them later. Create a document file or web browser bookmark labeled "Topic Ideas" for this particular assignment and fill it with articles that seem most promising. These might not be the kind of scholarly sources you need for your final writing, but they might introduce you to the terms, experts, and additional sources that would be appropriate. These initial sources can outline the foundation for further scholarly research.

In the pre-writing stage of the writing process, your job is to narrow your focus onto a viable subject for your writing. Browsing external sources and listening carefully to the conversations around you will jump-start your thinking to find the topics and issues that will work best for your writing.

OFFICE HOURS ➤ Engaging Libraries and Librarians to Find Topics and Issues

Libraries and librarians are an excellent starting point in the pre-writing stage when you want to explore topics, issues, and ideas for your writing. Explore your library's website first to see how it can guide you through topics and current issues. Your library's website might include a guide to getting started on research that will take you step-by-step through the resources available to you, such as the databases to which it subscribes. A quick scan of those databases and their organizing structures will give you good insight on how topics and issues are framed in different disciplines and will alert you to strong starting points when you return to do your source research.

Ideally, you will be able to arrange a personal session with a librarian in which you discuss your assignment and ideas through email, chat, or (even better) face-to-face. A librarian can listen to you and guide you through the wealth of sometimes overwhelming resources available at your library.

As you plan your writing schedule, reserve time to visit a librarian. Investing time early in the writing process can help you find a promising issue for your assignment.

Critical Questions

1. In your own words, state the purpose of researching websites, headlines, and current conversations at the pre-writing stage of the writing process.
2. What is the value of saving full text of the most promising articles you find?
3. Why might the sources you encounter in searching for topics and issues not be the kind of sources you will cite in your final paper?

CHAPTER nine

Read: Strategies for Reading in Research

Different kinds of reading require different approaches from readers. When you read for leisure, you might not jot down notes or annotate the text. You might share an especially good passage with your friends through social media, but you are not reading with the specific purpose of incorporating that text into your own conversations and writing.

When you read essay drafts for peer review, your purpose is to advise the authors to help improve their text. You are likely to read more slowly, ready to mark anything that jumps out either as especially strong or in need of improvement. When you read for research, your purpose is to find reliable, relevant sources that support, challenge, and/or extend your main idea. Reading for research helps you deepen your knowledge and fine tune your position so that your writing is well informed and sensitive to the rhetorical situation of current conversations on that topic.

As we discussed in Chapter 3, there are three stages to the reading process: pre-reading, active reading, and re-reading. In pre-reading, you assess contextual cues, such as the text's mode and medium, length/size, publisher/curator, and publication date. In the active reading and re-reading stages, you interact with the text in ways we will discuss here. Active reading for research means applying the following critical reading methods, tools, and approaches to understand and evaluate the reading as a source for your writing.

ACTIVE READING FOR RESEARCH: METHODS AND TOOLS

Active reading for research means that you are interacting with the text, highlighting its main points, and questioning both its validity and its relevance to your research task. That interaction with the text typically takes the form of note-taking. There are two methods of note-taking in active reading: passive note-taking, which includes such activities as highlighting and underlining text, and active note-taking, which includes such activities as paraphrasing and asking questions (see Chapter 3, "Reading and Listening for Writing"). Good readers do both types of note-taking, choosing from a variety of tools from both types to interact fully with the reading. Here are some ways to do both active and passive note-taking.

The First Pass: Skimming and Scanning

In your first pass at a text, you read to make sure the content and quality of writing meet your needs for a specific assignment. Skimming is the process of reading the most informative sections of a text to see if the full text will yield information worth your time. Search engines are so powerful, and the databases available through campus and public libraries are so extensive, that your preliminary online research may turn up many more texts in your search results than you can—or should—read. Skimming means you are still exploring your topic, searching widely for relevant sources.

Effective readers learn to identify the most informative sections of a text, where key content is likely to be found. Those key content areas include:

- The abstract (not all texts have this summary up front, but articles from scholarly journals typically do)
- The table of contents (for a whole book)
- The introduction
- The first sentence of paragraphs (if the text is long, focus on the first paragraph of sections or chapters of the text)
- The conclusion
- Tables and charts
- Highlighted words
- The index (for a whole book)
- The works cited, references, or bibliography (to make sure your source is on track and to find other potential sources)

Skimming should take much less time than if you were reading every word. If you find that it's taking longer, that might mean you are finding useful information and are getting sucked into reading the text more fully. That's a good thing. It probably means you should go back to the beginning and read the text in full active reading mode, not skimming mode.

To scan a text is to read it specifically for a particular type of content. The information you are looking for could be a key word, phrase, concept, or name. If you are working with a digital text, use the "search" or "find" function to quickly locate what you need. That method is only as good as your search terms, however, so if your search yields no matches with several key words, you still might want to scan the text with your own eyes. You may discover different terms that are used to describe the same content that you are researching.

Passive Note-Taking

In passive note-taking, you identify the key sections of the primary text and draw attention to them. You flag points that seem to capture the main idea or that seem innovative, intriguing, or otherwise require more attention.

Highlight or Underline

Highlighting uses color to draw attention to key words, passages, or concepts. You can use different colors to represent different types of content, such as supporting evidence versus counter-evidence. The key is to be selective. If you highlight too much, you can get overwhelmed with information. The point of highlighting is to focus your attention. An advantage of highlighting is that you can see those quotes in context easily. That is especially helpful if you leave that text for some time and need some help remembering the nature of the quote.

Underlining offers essentially the same advantages as highlighting, except it lacks the advantage of color. However, some readers might prefer the more muted approach of underlining to the distraction of colored highlighting.

Pull Quotes

The term "pull quote" is an editing term for the feature common in publishing of pulling out key quotes from an article to visually emphasize that content. Here we use this term for the process of gathering together key quotes from the primary text in a separate document. Seeing those key quotes in isolation—as opposed to just highlighting or underlining them in text—can help you see what that source offers while also giving you room to develop your own voice around those key quotes.

A word of caution: You must cite those quotes as you gather them in your own document to prevent unintentional plagiarism. By the time you return to those quotes to consider using them in your actual draft, you could forget where they came from. To make sure you avoid unintentional plagiarism, cite each source clearly as you put it into your own document.

Active Note-Taking

In active note-taking, you have already outlined the text's critical points through passive note-taking strategies and now aim to interact with those critical points. This is where you voice your agreement, disagreement, or confusion. Those notes will outline how you use the text in your writing, helping shape your summary, paraphrase, or direct quotation.

Annotate

To annotate means to make notes on the text. These can be questions, brief summaries, challenges, or connections to other texts. The goal is to capture your thinking about a specific point in the text so that you can circle back to that section in the re-reading stage. The format of those notes can vary: written notes in the margin of the text, sticky notes on top of the text, or digital sticky notes layered on top of digital text. Many digital readers offer annotation options, and there are many apps to help you manage this task. For more information about digital options, consult your instructor or a reference librarian.

Reverse Outline

Reverse outlining is when you make an outline of a source text. Making a reverse outline of the text's key claims and supporting evidence will help you see the purpose, strengths, and weaknesses of its argument. In this process, you remain a neutral observer and simply reflect what that author appears to have constructed.

The format of this outline can be a more traditional numbered outline that shows subordinate levels of the text, or it could be more visual, using a concept map (see Chapter 10, "Invent: Take Note and Create").

Paraphrase

To paraphrase means to put an author's ideas in your own words. This strategy can help you better understand complex ideas and new concepts. In paraphrasing, you remain a neutral observer and do not interject your own ideas. A paraphrase can be formatted as a single block of text written to represent the full primary text, or it can be interspersed throughout the primary text. The interspersed approach is helpful, for example, after a particularly complicated paragraph. Paraphrasing while it's fresh in your mind can be an efficient way to read.

A word of caution: Remember that paraphrased ideas must still be cited in your writing. Even though you are putting the author's ideas in your own words, those ideas still belong to the author and must be correctly cited. If you write your paraphrase on a separate document, include the citation information for the original source with your paraphrase so that you do not plagiarize unintentionally.

Summarize

A summary is a comprehensive account of the source text. You can write a summary of any component part of a text—a whole book, a chapter, an article, even a single paragraph. Summaries often include direct quotation of key phrases or sentences. They are meant to be brief but accurate representations of the key points of the primary text. Summaries serve as an important exercise in making sure you have paid careful attention to the author's argument before moving to your own interpretations and reactions.

Believing and Doubting

Composition theorist Peter Elbow suggests a strategy for learning to read actively: the believing game and the doubting game. The believing game is the process of *welcoming* a writer's ideas. The doubting game is the process of *scrutinizing* a writer's ideas. By playing each game, readers find areas to believe and doubt in almost all texts, rather than fully accepting or rejecting texts entirely.

Readers who play these games challenge themselves to listen for and against a text in ways they might not otherwise have done due to their own bias or inattention. When our own values or beliefs seem to conflict with those of the author we read, we tend to hear what we want to hear to have our own thinking confirmed. The believing game and the doubting game can help us achieve more nuanced readings of a text.

Give it a try: Play the believing game and the doubting game on these very concepts. First, consider how this strategy could help you fine-tune your topic, locate gaps in current thinking, or even change your mind on an issue. Next, consider how this strategy might fall short of helping you reach those goals. Integrate those ideas into your own recommendation on whether your peers should use this strategy.

CHECKLIST: READING FOR RESEARCH

After reading a source carefully for your research, it is important to stop and reflect on what that source can contribute to your writing project. The following questions will help you determine if and how a source can contribute to your writing:

1. What is this source really about? Is it relevant to my writing?
2. How does this source support its claims? Is it reliable? Do I want my writing associated with this author, this article, and/or this publication or website?

3. How does this source support my writing?
4. How does this source counter my writing?
5. How does this source complicate or extend my writing?
6. How and where will I use this source in my writing?
7. What is this source's general contribution to the conversation I'm trying to enter into? Does it differ from other sources I have gathered?

If after reflecting on these questions you do not see how a source fits with your project, you should not use it. Good writers know when to cut their losses and not force a source into their writing just because they've spent time reading it.

Applying the methods and tools for active reading for research described in this chapter will help you foreground the most pertinent information and ideas in a text. After that work is done, though, active readers must determine if and how to use that information in their own writing. Doing a comprehensive rhetorical analysis with these methods will help you determine whether a text is worth time and attention in your writing.

OFFICE HOURS ➤ Surprises in Reading for Research

Reading for research can be surprising. The surprises happen because you are actively engaging with potential sources, not just thinking about the topic on your own. Here are some common surprises when reading for research that are worth further exploration with an instructor and/or a writing center tutor:

1. *Surprise! Someone already wrote that.* You discover that the argument you want to make or the research you want to do has already been done very well by someone else. As a result, you may be unsure if you should continue with the topic at all, or if there's

---

a way to adjust your approach so that you are able to contribute something new to the conversation. A talk with your instructor can help you determine the best tactic for your writing.

2. *Surprise! You changed your mind.* You discover in reading for opposing viewpoints that you actually agree with them. You want to flip your position and feel that you should check with your instructor to make sure that's okay.

3. *Surprise! You're just not that into this topic.* As you read for research, you discover that this topic no longer interests you and it feels like a chore to read further. It has, though, helped you realize what you might want to write about, and you want to see if this new topic is okay with your instructor.

While these surprises might feel a little unnerving to you, they are all part of the research and writing (and learning) process. Good writers respond to these surprises effectively by checking with their instructor to confirm that a change in direction is advisable given deadlines and assignment expectations.

Critical Questions

1. Complete this sentence in your own words: "Good readers _____." Explain your answer.

2. How might reading for research vary in different disciplines, such as reading for research for an English literature paper versus reading for research in a business case study? Explain.

3. For you, what's the hardest part of finding the right source to cite? Is it difficult for you to decide not to use a source you found? Explain.

CHAPTER ten

Invent: Take Note and Create

In chapters 1-9, we address the pre-writing stage of the writing process and the steps in research for assignments that require external sources for support. Now it's time to enter the active writing stage of the writing process, beginning with invention. In the invention process, you move from thinking broadly about how others have represented a topic or issue and start to try out your own thinking. You write notes, draw diagrams, and generally experiment with how you are going to enter the conversation on this issue. You also begin to organize those ideas, showing how they relate to one another. Strategies to visualize the relationship between ideas, such as concept mapping, can help show what you think *and* reveal gaps in your argument.

STRATEGIES FOR INVENTION

Invention takes place after you have worked through the pre-writing activities and, if your assignment calls for research, after you have done preliminary research. Each step in the process engages you deeper with your issue. The following strategies will help you see how far you've come, as well as help you consider your options for the next steps.

Brainstorming

Brainstorming refers to a range of idea-generating activities. Here we use it to identify the act of communicating with others—peers, writing center tutors, community partners, and so on—who listen to your ideas about your project and give you feedback. This works best if you share ideas without censoring yourself—just speak what comes to mind regarding the assignment. Your partner(s) can prompt you with questions that stretch your thinking. Instead of trying to take notes during a brainstorming session, which could distract you from the process, try recording your session (many apps are available for this). You can play it back later and summarize the key points.

Freewriting

In freewriting, you start with a blank screen or piece of paper and write nonstop about your topic or subject for a set amount of time. Don't worry about your grammar and don't censor yourself. You might freewrite in class when your instructor gives you a specific prompt or you can freewrite on your own. In both cases, it's important to set an alarm, usually 5–10 minutes, and write nonstop until it sounds. What you write won't be perfect, but it often uncovers some important ideas you can polish later.

Your freewriting can take different forms: complete paragraphs, full sentences, or even a simple list of ideas. Don't worry about punctuation or grammar or mechanics or citation or perfection, Just write without stopping. If you have to, write "I don't know what to write" over and over until you suddenly find something to write. The very act of writing often gets your mind in gear to translate ideas into increasingly significant writing.

Because freewriting requires so little time and therefore feels less intimidating, it's a good way to defend against writer's block. Just set the timer, focus, and write. You might be surprised by the good ideas that appear when you let go and write freely.

Freewriting from Sources

To freewrite from sources, choose a brief section that seems most interesting to you—maybe because you agree with, disagree with, or are confused by what the author says. Copy those sentences into a blank document and use them as your freewriting prompt. Ask questions about the specific words and phrases used. You might want to repeat this with all your key sources so that your writing says something meaningful about each source rather than just dropping in quotes from the primary text that seem disconnected from your own thinking.

If you do copy source text, be vigilant in distinguishing the source text from your own writing so that you do not unintentionally plagiarize later in the writing process. Put quotation marks around direct quotations and set them off further with highlighting, color coding, or a different font to remind yourself to cite the source if you use it in your final text.

Concept Mapping

Concept mapping is the process of visualizing the connections among ideas. Typically, mapping begins with the primary issue you were assigned or chose. That primary issue or concept is placed in the center of a document and is often circled or boxed. From that primary concept, secondary ideas or claims radiate out like the spokes of a wheel. From each secondary idea, you can spoke out further with related ideas (see Figure 10.1 for a concept map on student writer Karmela Dalisay's researched proposal argument "Motivating the Homeless" in Chapter 4, "Argument"). In the end, you can see where ideas flourish and where they flounder. Those flourishing clusters of ideas might be the heart of your writing. Those floundering spokes might point to places that need more thinking and/or research (or just need to be cut). Each cluster of ideas might represent a segment of your final writing, such as a paragraph or subsection.

Many digital tools and apps are available to help diagram concept maps. Those tools help you sequence ideas and easily rearrange them as your thinking develops so that you can start to outline your writing. Many apps allow you to include voice recordings, photographs, hyperlinks, and other media in your concept maps.

Outlining

An outline is the backbone of your argument. It shows primary, secondary, and tertiary points in short phrases. Instead of just listing or grouping, you are starting to think deliberately about the order and hierarchy of your points. Outlines use a formal order of numbers and letters to indicate this hierarchy, as shown here by student writer Karmela

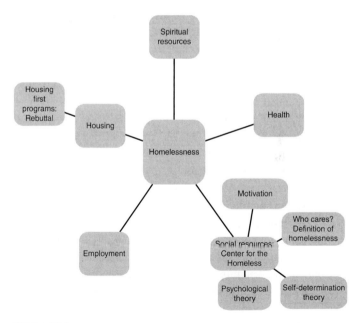

Figure 10.1

This concept map on homelessness and motivation was created using Microsoft Word's SmartArt.

Dalisay's outline of her researched proposal argument "Motivating the Homeless" in Chapter 4, "Argument." Many word processors have a function for outlining, and many tools exist online to guide you as well.

Motivating the Homeless: Outline
by Karmela Dalisay

1) Introduction
    a) Anecdote: Effect of homelessness on motivation
    b) Main question: How can the Center for the Homeless increase guests' motivation?
    c) Causes of motivation
    d) Thesis: The Center for the Homeless should expand SOSH and focus on increasing each guest's sense of self-worth.
2) Who cares? Definition of the problem of homelessness/poverty
    a) Statistics: Poverty demographics
    b) Reducing poverty/homelessness disrupts generational cycles
3) How can we reduce homelessness? Increase motivation
    a) Counterargument: Affordable housing fills basic need (Maslow's Hierarchy of Needs)
    b) My rebuttal: Address higher-level psychological needs first
4) Psychological theory that explains my argument: Self-determination theory
    a) Internalization
    b) Amotivation
    c) Extrinsic motivation and its four types
    d) Intrinsic motivation
5) Applying self-determination theory to research on homelessness
    a) Self-efficacy decreases time spent in temporary shelters
    b) Self-selection bias issue
    c) Center should assess self-efficacy early to prioritize interventions
    d) Guests should set reachable goals, then set higher goals
        i) Parenting goals

ii) Help guests set future-oriented goals that focus on positive outcomes
  (1) Limit TV time and/or make it a reward
iii) Increase guests' sense of dignity through improving inner-worth
  (1) Center should keep offering hospitality and respect
  (2) Avoid use of arbitrary rules
  (3) Allow guests to make some decisions on their own

6) Conclusion
  a) Summary of my argument
    i) Reduce homelessness via programs that strengthen self-efficacy
    ii) Means to achieve this goal include:
      (1) Increase guests' personal perspectives
      (2) Address the structure and culture of the Center
    iii) Action steps for Center:
      (1) Assess new guests' level of self-efficacy
      (2) Provide more guidelines to parents
      (3) Revisit and revise rules

Stasis Questions

Stasis questions guide people through careful thinking about an issue. You can write your answers to the following questions on your own or work through them with a peer or writing center tutor.

The stasis categories of questions include:

1. **Facts:** What is the problem? What happened? What are the facts? What is the issue? What is the cause? Can it be changed?
2. **Definition:** What is the nature of the problem or issue? How can it be categorized or counted?
3. **Quality:** Is this good or bad? How serious is it? Who is affected by it and how are they affected? What would it take to

address this? What happens if nothing is done? What are the
consequences?

4. **Policy:** What, if anything, should be done? Who should do it?
How should it happen? What does a successful proposal for this
look like? Should this be local, national, or international?

Journalist Questions

News stories are designed to deliver information efficiently to readers. Journalists therefore typically present the key elements of a story
up front, addressing the 5 Ws and 1 H: *Who? What? When? Where?
Why?* and *How?* Table 10.1 shows a few of the possible questions each
single word could ignite for invention.

Table 10.1   LINES OF QUESTIONING ALIGNED TO THE 5 WS AND 1 H

5 Ws, 1 H	Lines of Questioning
Who?	Who are the stakeholders in this issue? Who caused the problem? Who stands to lose or gain if things stay the same or if they change? Are all the people who should be at the table actually there? Why or why not?
What?	What is the nature of this problem/event/activity? Would everyone agree on that description? What can each stakeholder do to understand and/or improve her or his relationship to this?
When?	Does this relate to the past, present, and/or future? Does this require an urgent response? When will we know more?
Where?	Where does this happen or not happen? What differ-ence does location make?
Why?	Why did/does this happen? What are the possible causes or correlations?
How?	How does this happen? How should we respond to make things better?

Try using these one-word questions to brainstorm ideas. You will find that some are more useful than others for particular writing assignments. That's fine and might actually help you see whether your ideas suit the genre you've selected. For example, if you have a lot to say about "how" something should happen, you're probably writing a proposal argument (Chapter 22). If you find yourself exploring "what" happened and/or "why" it happened, you're probably writing an argument of causation (Chapter 18).

INVENTION AFTER DOING PRELIMINARY RESEARCH

If your assignment calls for researched writing and you have worked through Chapter 9, "Read: Strategies in Reading for Research," then your invention will be informed by the research you have done so far. Remember that finding sources and thinking inventively about how you will integrate them into your writing are two different steps in the writing process. The activities described in this chapter ask you to think with and yet *beyond* those sources to find your own approach to the issue.

To invent after doing research, set your sources aside and engage the activities described in this chapter without those sources in front of you (except for the activities that explicitly call you to look at source material). Setting aside sources you have read as you apply different invention strategies will help you locate what you want to say about an issue.

Invention is about capturing those foggy ideas that form in your mind so that you can see what you think. Once they are captured and represented in writing or images, you can step back and see what you have to work with. You can locate the strongest and weakest points of your thinking, places where you might need to do more research, places where you get off track, or places where content seems missing. The very process of capturing and representing those ideas engages and sharpens your critical thinking. After you invent, the fog begins to lift. You see those ideas develop into the main claims of your writing. You can return to these invention strategies at any point in the writing process when you need to reinvent your approach.

OFFICE HOURS ➤   Inventing at the Writing Center

If you have a campus writing center, you have a critical opportunity to invent with other skilled writers who can accompany you throughout the writing process. All the strategies we discuss in this chapter can be done with writing center tutors who will support you and give you feedback, helping you invent and reinvent to reach readers effectively.

Schedule an appointment either at the start of your writing process when you need to invent ideas and/or during the revision process when you need to revisit and perhaps reinvent your writing. A writing center tutor can brainstorm with you, ask you the stasis and/or journalistic prompts, and act as a conversation partner in all the activities listed here. You remain the writer and primary thinker and decision maker (see Chapter 5 "Writing Ethics, Responsibility, and Accountability"). When you invite writing center tutors into your invention process, you honor the social purpose of writing by engaging them as conversation partners to develop and deepen your thinking.

Critical Questions

1. Which of the activities described in this chapter would you do alone and in which would you engage others? Who specifically would you engage in these activities and why?

2. Do you think invention activities will focus your thinking or broaden it? Which do you think *should* happen at this point in your writing process?

3. This section claims that writing helps you see what you think. Describe a time when writing helped you clarify your thinking about an important issue. Or describe a time when you now think that writing might have helped you clarify your thinking about an issue.

CHAPTER **eleven**

Arrange: Prioritize, Organize, Outline

When you are satisfied with the results of your invention work, it is time to evaluate the main points that emerge. This chapter demonstrates the process of arranging the information and ideas you generated during invention to *prioritize* what is most important, to *organize* the remaining ideas into the most effective order for your rhetorical situation, and then to *outline* the foundation of your argument. From this process, you will develop your thesis statement or main claim.

STRATEGIES FOR PRIORITIZING IDEAS

Prioritizing ideas means deciding which ones are most important to your argument and which you could do without. The following questions prompt you to consider which points generated during invention should take priority in your writing:

- Are some points mentioned more frequently than others?
- Do some points take longer to explain?
- Are some points more critical to understanding the issue than others?

- Are some points clearer and stronger than others?
- Do some points rely on your sharing other ideas first?
- Do some points seem interesting but off-topic?

Next, rank these points into four categories:

1. **Essential** Your argument would not be successful without this point.
2. **Secondary** Your argument should definitely make this point, but it supports a major point and should therefore be subordinated or secondary to another point.
3. **Questionable** This is a good or interesting point, but it might not be as necessary or relevant once the other higher priority points are made. This might get cut.
4. **Unnecessary** Compared to the other points, this should be cut due to lack of relevance, weak support, etc.

Keep this ranking in mind as you start to organize your ideas. Make sure those high-priority ideas are placed in positions of emphasis, such as the beginning or end of the argument, or as topic sentences for individual paragraphs. Resist the temptation to go back to those "unnecessary" category four points, even if you think you are short on content. If you are struggling for ideas or examples, use invention strategies instead to generate more evidence and support for secondary points.

Drafting the Thesis Statement/Main Claim

The highest priority point is your thesis statement. The thesis statement is a sentence that expresses the main claim or controlling idea of your writing (see Chapter 8, "Question: Exploring Issues"). That sentence should give your audience a good idea of the issue and your stance on it. The purpose of the rest of the essay is to provide compelling support for that claim through reasons, examples, and evidence. As you prioritize, organize, and outline, your thesis should become increasingly clear. See Part Three, "Writing With Purpose" for thesis templates and models specific to different types of writing.

STRATEGIES FOR ORGANIZING IDEAS

All types of arguments share the same basic organizational foundation: an introduction, body, and conclusion. There are many options for building on that basic foundation. The placement of the thesis statement or main claim and the order of supporting points can be organized to emphasize different elements and control the pace of the audience's engagement with your topic.

Consider the following options for organization. Note that the tables show *possible* numbers of points and paragraphs in the body, not a script for exact numbers. The actual number of paragraphs you use to make a point (and the number of points you make per argument) depend on such factors as the assignment length, the complexity of the point, and the type of support you use to make that point. The tables below show you what an argument using each organizational format *could* look like. Analyze the rhetorical situation of your writing task (Chapter 6, "Analyze the Assignment") for further help determining which organizational strategies can work for your project and what they should look like in practice.

Order of Importance or Complexity

Identify your most important and persuasive point—the one you want to make sure no one misses. You can emphasize that point by *leading from your strength*, placing it in your opening paragraph. Or, you can close with your strongest point, *building up* to it so that your readers have an increasingly firm foundation before you make your most important point. Arguments that make especially effective use of this structure include evaluation, rebuttal, and proposal arguments.

If your topic is complex and your audience needs to be educated on the issue before they can understand your position, you might want to take the build-up approach. For example, in this chapter, we discuss the more complex types of organization, Toulmin and Classical, toward the end so that you get a sense of simpler types of organization before learning about more complex types.

If you worry that you might lose the audience's attention or that they might resist the content of your argument, then you might want to reveal your strongest, most important point first. Table 11.1 shows an organization moving from most to least important or complex points. Simply reverse the order if you want to take the build-up approach instead.

Table 11.1   ARRANGEMENT BY ORDER OF IMPORTANCE OR COMPLEXITY

FOUNDATION	ELEMENTS	PARAGRAPHS
Introduction		Paragraph 1
Body	Point 1: Most important or complex	Paragraph 2
		Paragraph 3
	Point 2: Second most important or complex	Paragraph 4
		Paragraph 5
	Point 3: Third most important or complex	Paragraph 6
		Paragraph 7
	Point 4: Fourth most important or complex	Paragraph 8
Conclusion		Paragraph 9

Chronological Order

Following a chronological timeline from earliest to most recent events can be an effective organizational strategy, especially if you want to emphasize cause and effect or narrate a sequence of activities. This linear approach moves the audience in a straight line rather than taking them into and out of events and action. This makes the narrative or the essential events that undergird your argument easier to follow.

Compare and Contrast

A compare and contrast organization moves thoughtfully between competing ideas and/or examples. That movement can happen within a paragraph, where you present one idea and its opposition together within that paragraph. Or the movement can happen

Table 11.2   ARRANGEMENT BY CHRONOLOGICAL ORDER

FOUNDATION	ELEMENTS	PARAGRAPHS
Introduction		Paragraph 1
Body	Point 1: Earliest event	Paragraph 2
		Paragraph 3
	Point 2: Next event	Paragraph 4
	Point 3: Later event	Paragraph 5
		Paragraph 6
	Point 4: Most recent event	Paragraph 7
		Paragraph 8
		Paragraph 9
Conclusion		Paragraph 10

at the end of a paragraph, where you only present one side per paragraph, then transition to present the opposition in the next paragraph.

For example, if you wanted to compare the benefits and weaknesses of solar and wind energy, you might organize your points based on four units of comparison, including cost of initial infrastructure, reliability, return on investment, and viability by geographic region. You could compare how each form of energy fares in each category point-by-point, then move to the next category (see Table 11.3, "Arrangement by Compare and Contrast: Point-by-Point Organization"), or you could explore these in the same order all the way through the full subject (see Table 11.4, "Arrangement by Compare and Contrast: Full Subject Organization"), first for one energy type (Subject 1), then the other (Subject 2).

Table 11.3 ARRANGEMENT BY COMPARE AND CONTRAST: POINT-BY-POINT ORGANIZATION

FOUNDATION	ELEMENTS	PARAGRAPHS
Introduction		Paragraph 1
Body	Point 1: Cost of initial infrastructure	Paragraph 2: Solar Paragraph 3: Wind
	Point 2: Reliability	Paragraph 4: Solar Paragraph 5: Wind
	Point 3: Return on investment	Paragraph 6: Solar Paragraph 7: Wind
	Point 4: Viability by geographic region	Paragraph 8: Solar Paragraph 9: Wind
Conclusion		Paragraph 10

Table 11.4   ARRANGEMENT BY COMPARE AND CONTRAST: FULL SUBJECT ORGANIZATION

FOUNDATION	ELEMENTS	PARAGRAPHS
Introduction		Paragraph 1
Body	Subject 1: Solar	Paragraph 2: Point 1 Cost of infrastructure
		Paragraph 3: Point 2 Reliability
		Paragraph 4: Point 3 Return on investment
		Paragraph 5: Point 4 Viability by geographic region
	Subject 2: Wind	Paragraph 6: Point 1 Cost of infrastructure
		Paragraph 7: Point 2 Reliability
		Paragraph 8: Point 3 Return on investment
		Paragraph 9: Point 4 Viability by geographic region
Conclusion		Paragraph 10

Chunking: Themes, Types, Classes

Chunking means organizing ideas around key elements of your argument. Those elements might be named for you in your assignment description, or you might identify them yourself. For example, you might want to divide a broad category of something into classes that more clearly explain what it is, such as explaining sustainable food practices through the following points: how food is produced, transported, packaged, and prepared (Chapter 23, "Multimodal Composition," explains classification in more detail).

Chunks can organize a single paragraph or sets of paragraphs that work through an aspect of that category (thus Table 11.5 shows various numbers of paragraphs per chunk).

Toulmin Method

This approach, named for its creator, philosopher Stephen Toulmin, emphasizes the construction of logical arguments. The Toulmin method is a process by which you can break an argument into its parts—claims, reasons, evidence, warrant, premise—to assess its strengths and weaknesses or to guide the construction of your own argument.

The Toulmin method can work particularly well for proposal and causation arguments. Arguments following the Toulmin method of analysis might follow the structure shown in Table 11.6, although the number of paragraphs per part may vary.

Table 11.5   ARRANGEMENT BY CHUNKING: THEMES, TYPES, CLASSES

FOUNDATION	ELEMENTS	PARAGRAPHS
Introduction		Paragraph 1
Body	Theme/Type/Class Point 1: How food is produced sustainably	Paragraph 2 Paragraph 3
	Theme/Type/Class Point 2: How food is transported sustainably	Paragraph 4 Paragraph 5 Paragraph 6
	Theme/Type/Class Point 3: How food is packaged sustainably	Paragraph 7 Paragraph 8
	Theme/Type/Class Point 4: How food is prepared sustainably	Paragraph 9 Paragraph 10 Paragraph 11
Conclusion		Paragraph 12

Table 11.6   ARRANGEMENT BY THE TOULMIN METHOD

FOUNDATION	ELEMENTS	PURPOSE	PARAGRAPHS
Introduction	*Claim*	Expression of main idea or thesis	Paragraph 1
Body	*Data*	Support or evidence for that main idea	Paragraph 2 Paragraph 3
	Warrant	Bridging assumptions or concepts that connect the data to the claim	Paragraph 4
	Backing	Further explanation and reasoning to support the warrant	Paragraph 5 Paragraph 6
	Counterclaim	A claim from an opposing viewpoint directly related to your claim	Paragraph 7
	Rebuttal	Your response to that counterclaim explaining why your claim is stronger	Paragraph 8 Paragraph 9
Conclusion		In contemporary argument, the audience expects some type of deliberate wrapping up that signals the end of your argument	Paragraph 10

Classical Argument

In classical rhetoric, rhetoricians followed a specific roadmap in constructing arguments (Chapter 1, "Why Write?"). In Table 11.7, the terms in the middle column show the elements used in arranging a classical argument—the Latin name is italicized and the translation of that concept is in English. On the right side is a brief description of the purpose of those elements. Contemporary arguments allow for more flexibility in the order and attention given to those elements. Those elements nonetheless still guide expectations for contemporary

readers and writers. Contemporary writers can use these elements as a
script or as a rough guide for core components in argument, particularly when composing proposal and rebuttal arguments.

Table 11.7   ARRANGEMENT BY THE CLASSICAL ARGUMENT METHOD

FOUNDATION	ELEMENTS	PURPOSE	PARAGRAPHS
Introduction	Introduction (*exordium*)	Invite the audience into the issue you will argue, get them interested and eager to hear more. Establish the urgency or kairotic importance of this issue at this time.	Paragraph 1
	Statement of facts (*narratio*)	Narrate the context, provide background, and offer examples or key facts.	
	Division (*divisio* or *partitio*)	Announce the thesis and elements of your argument, step-by-step.	
Body	Proofs (*confirmatio*)	Support claims with specific examples and evidence that "confirm" or back up the secondary claims you make to support your primary claim, your thesis.	Paragraph 2 Paragraph 3
	Refutation (*refutatio*)	Acknowledge and address opposing viewpoints, explaining how your position is stronger than others.	Paragraph 4 Paragraph 5 Paragraph 6
Conclusion	Conclusion (*peroratio*)	Synthesize the argument in a final statement that could include a call to action.	Paragraph 7

STRATEGIES FOR SELECTING A STRUCTURE

To choose an appropriate organizational structure, analyze the rhetorical situation. Organizational structures set a tone and relate to audiences in different ways. The following questions will help you analyze the rhetorical situation to decide which organizational structure or structures could work for your project.

Why? Exigence and Ethics

Understanding the context of why you are writing—to inform, to entertain, and/or to argue—will help you narrow down your choices for organizational structure. If you are writing to argue, for example, then it makes sense to consider the Toulmin method and classical argument. If you are writing to inform about a historical event, then chronological order could be effective. If you are writing to inform about a new species of plants, then chunking might help you explain your categorization. If you are writing to entertain, you might organize by compare and contrast to satirize two things that do not warrant comparison. The goal is to choose an organizational structure that clarifies and advances your argument.

Who? Author and Audience

As the author, consider which organizational structures you most enjoy using. If you are not a linear thinker, then chronological order might not be the most effective structure for you. Likewise, consider the preferences of your audience. How much do they know about your argument and which structure will help them best process what you share? For example, if you expect them to disagree with your argument, you might want to lead from your strength in the order of complexity structure so that you improve your chances of persuading them to agree with your position.

Where? Domain

Are you writing for home, academic, work, or civic life? What expectations are set for how arguments are organized in those domains? Will it matter if you break those expectations or does it behoove you to structure your project according to guidelines familiar there? For example, if your philosophy instructor expects you to use the Toulmin method, then even the classical argument structure might not be sufficient to meet those expectations.

How? Mode and Medium

Consider how your message will be received. Some structures could be easier to read than hear, for example, and vice versa. Using a compare and contrast structure might work well for an argument delivered orally because a listening audience can follow the back and forth pattern between two subjects being compared. The intricate organization of the Toulmin method, however, might make that structure difficult for a listening audience to follow.

When? Kairos

What's happening in the world around you might cue you in to an appropriate organizational structure. Are certain styles trending? If so, using or rejecting those styles will immediately tell your audience something about how you align yourself in relation to those who do follow that trend.

What? Message

How can what does and doesn't need to be said to this audience at this time in this place inform the organizational structure you choose? Again, consider your purpose. For example, does this audience need an argument or do they need basic information about this issue? How does that different purpose suggest which structures would and wouldn't work well for this project?

STRATEGIES FOR OUTLINING ARGUMENTS

Once you determine the most effective organization structure for your argument, you can start to outline the argument. Outlining means writing a brief sketch of your thesis, main claims, support, and examples in the order you intend to use them. Outlines are most effective if you use a parallel structure: each entry has the same grammatical structure and order, and roughly the same length, so that you can easily compare entries to follow the logic of the argument.

If your instructor does not have a preferred format for outlining, use the outline template (shown next) as a guide, adapting it to match the specific organizing structure you want to use. Add or subtract main points, increase and/or reduce support for each main point: the goal is clarity, not exact symmetry. The purpose of creating an outline is to clarify your thinking. If you see, for example, that you have no supporting points for one main idea and ten for another, then you know where to add and where to cut in your revision. You might need to do more research or rearrange what you already have so that it is distributed in a way that advances your argument clearly. Creating an outline highlights gaps, redundancies, and errors in order. Chapter 10, "Invent: Take Note and Create," includes an example of a student's full outline using elements of the classical argument organizational structure.

Outline Template

  I. INTRODUCTION
    A. Overview of the issue (includes attention-grabbing reason, evidence, example, etc.)
    B. Thesis statement (main idea)

II. BODY

A. Point 1

  1. Supporting Reason, Evidence, or Example 1
  2. Supporting Reason, Evidence, or Example 2
  3. Supporting Reason, Evidence, or Example 3

B. Point 2

  1. Supporting Reason, Evidence, or Example 1
  2. Supporting Reason, Evidence, or Example 2
  3. Supporting Reason, Evidence, or Example 3

C. Point 3

  1. Supporting Reason, Evidence, or Example 1
  2. Supporting Reason, Evidence, or Example 2
  3. Supporting Reason, Evidence, or Example 3

D. Point 4

  1. Supporting Reason, Evidence, or Example 1
  2. Supporting Reason, Evidence, or Example 2
  3. Supporting Reason, Evidence, or Example 3

E. Point 5

  1. Supporting Reason, Evidence, or Example 1
  2. Supporting Reason, Evidence, or Example 2
  3. Supporting Reason, Evidence, or Example 3

III. CONCLUSION

A. Synthesis of what you want the audience to do or think differently based on what you shared

B. Supporting Reasons, Evidence, or Example

IV. WORKS CITED or REFERENCES (if required)

Good writers learn from experience that taking time to organize, prioritize, and arrange their ideas not only saves time in the long run but also helps improve the quality of their arguments. By stepping back to see the big picture of the writing at an early stage of the writing process, writers have more freedom to make adjustments. Plan to take time to arrange, and protect that time as vital to the writing process.

OFFICE HOURS ➤ Take Time to Test the Thesis

During the process of arranging your ideas, take time to test your thesis or main claim by making an appointment with your instructor or a tutor at your writing center. At this stage, make sure you have the most promising and productive point at the top of your text, set to guide your drafting thereafter. A conversation with your instructor or tutor can help you fine-tune your existing thesis, help you realize that one of the supporting points in your outline should really be your thesis instead, or even lead you to draft a new thesis entirely. The purpose of writing an outline is to make the organization of your argument clear to yourself and others. If it is not clear, refine what you have or go back to invention. Don't be afraid of having this conversation. Be afraid of not having it and realizing later that you have even more rearranging to do.

Critical Questions

1. Do you create an outline even when you are not required to do so? Why or why not? What does your outline look like—formal (like the Outline Template just presented), more of a visual cluster, or something else?

2. Does arranging ideas come easily to you or is this difficult? Does arranging ideas seem similar to arranging physical items, such as organizing your room? Explain.

3. The work of arranging encourages writers to slow down and step back from the ideas they generate early in the process. If you skip this step and just write from introduction to conclusion, what could happen to the organization of your writing? Share hypothetical examples or examples from personal experience.

CHAPTER twelve

Draft: Introduction, Body, Conclusion

In Chapter 11, "Arrange: Prioritize, Organize, Outline," we encourage you to step back to look at the ideas you have generated during invention. Now it's time to write something that responds to your rhetorical situation. Gain confidence by reminding yourself that this is a *draft*, not the final version. In addition, remember that your writing process is already well under way. As the novelist E. M. Forster asked, "How do I know what I think until I see what I say?" The process of writing your thoughts out in full sentences, logically connected in paragraphs, does more than just transfer fully formed thoughts from your mind into written words. The process of writing itself promotes critical thinking. This chapter helps you develop strategies to create a successful draft through preparing your writing space, consulting your outline, writing, citing, and avoiding writer's block to sketch your introduction, body, and conclusion.

STRATEGIES FOR DRAFTING

In drafting, you see and sharpen what you have to say. You expand on, develop, and challenge the ideas you presented in your outline. Be comfortable and careful in this part of the process so that your draft is as thorough as possible. While you should plan to write as many drafts as needed to achieve good writing, put your best effort forward each time.

Prepare Your Writing Space

In Chapter 7, "Plan: Organizing the Process," we discuss the importance of knowing what *enables* your writing and what *blocks* your writing. Revisit our advice on "Writer's Rituals: Know What Works for You" in Chapter 7 to create your most productive writing environment. Consider such elements as sound, light, company, time of day, food and drink, and level of rest. This consideration will boost your confidence and help prevent writer's block. At this point, your writing is well under way if you have followed the writing process steps we discuss in this book. Your mind has been actively engaged with this assignment, and you probably have much more to write than you realize. Let your writing environment enhance your writing, not distract you from your focus.

Consult Your Outline

Next, review your outline. Make sure all the terms you use and the sequence of your ideas still make sense to you as you begin. Some people like to work directly from the outline, copying it into a new document and working through each section. Others just keep it visible nearby as a signpost. At this point, the purpose of the outline is to guide and inspire your writing, not to restrict it.

As you start to write, you are likely to think of new ideas, reasons, evidence, and examples that did not make it into your outline. When that happens, write through the idea as it comes to you and then see how it fits into the outline. Sometimes that new thinking develops and enhances your writing for the assignment; other times it takes you off track. The challenge is to stay open to new ideas that can improve your outline and yet to make sure those new ideas belong in your text.

As you draft, keep checking the outline to make sure you're on track, but err on the side of writing through those new ideas. In the revision stage, you can continue to refine your draft through peer review and techniques such as reverse outlining that help you see the actual structure of your writing. Once you see what you have written, you can add, rewrite, rearrange, and cut (see Chapter 13, "Revise: Strategies for Re-seeing").

Write! Write! Write!

Another advantage of drafting from an outline is that you can start writing from any point in the text. You probably feel more prepared to write certain sections than others, so start there. For example, it is often easier to write the introduction after you have written the body and conclusion. At that point, you have a clear sense of the key words and phrases that represent your thinking. The outline frees you to write out of order because you know where each piece belongs in your vision of the argument.

Once you start writing, just keep going. Don't be too critical of the first draft as you write. Each writing assignment presents a new rhetorical situation that you must address anew. With the right techniques, you can decrease your anxiety and increase your productivity. Drafting itself is progress, so just keep writing.

Cite! Cite! Cite!

Remember to cite throughout the drafting process. As you get into the groove and start writing, insert your citations as you go. Citation is not a job for "later." Citation needs to be done as you work so that you do not accidentally plagiarize by forgetting to return and insert the citation. If you have to, insert a placeholder to make sure you return to complete the citation. Use your writing software's comment feature or insert an all-caps message (such as INSERT CITATION) to make sure you finish this critical job (see Chapter 8, "Question: Exploring Issues,"

Chapter 9, "Read: Strategies for Reading in Research," and Chapter 26, "Design and Delivery: Print, Digital, and Oral Presentations").

Control Writer's Block

Review the advice in Chapter 7, "Plan: Organizing the Process," on preventing writer's block. It's much better to *prevent* than *manage* writer's block—that feeling that you do not have anything to write. If you have worked through the writing process as recommended so far, you have already thought through your argument and considered what you have to say. Your outline should prompt you to write through your ideas.

If you get stuck as you start to draft, however, you might need to return to the idea-generating techniques we describe in Chapter 10, "Invent: Take Note and Create." That is a normal part of the writing process. Don't panic and abandon your topic. Instead, push forward to see where this critical thinking takes you.

LAYING THE FOUNDATION

While the introduction, body, and conclusion each serve the same purpose in any writing, they are executed in different ways according to the purpose and goals of the writing. Consider the following guidelines as you draft each element.

Introduction

Your introduction sets the tone, gives your readers some context for the issue, and often reveals your position on the issue in a thesis statement (although the thesis statement or main idea can come in succeeding paragraphs). You can capture or lose readers with your introduction, so plan to draft and revise it several times.

The success of an introduction depends on its alignment with the rhetorical situation. You establish your ethos in the introduction, so you want the audience to trust that you have researched the issue, listened to people on all sides of the issue, and have something thoughtful to contribute to the conversation. The tone you use in the introduction should be generally consistent with the tone throughout your argument.

The rhetorical situation also impacts the genre of your message and that, in turn, can help you determine the most effective mode for your introduction (see Chapter 23, "Multimodal Composition"). If you were writing a researched argument for a history class, for example, your introduction might use the mode of description to take readers into an event you intend to analyze. If you were writing a business letter, you might use the mode of explication in your introduction to quickly name the critical incident you are addressing.

Here are some approaches to writing an introduction that will help you establish your credibility on the issue and articulate your main idea in a way that captures readers' interest and encourages them to care and read on:

- *Anecdote/Example*—Describe a relevant event that will show, rather than tell, readers what you want them to think about.
- *Background/History/Timeline*—Set the scene by narrating, perhaps in chronological order, a brief overview of key events.
- *Call to Action*—Help readers feel engaged in responding to this issue by showing how the issue relates to them. Then call on them to do something about it based on what you share.
- *Common Ground*—Establish what readers are likely to have in common on an issue before digging into an aspect of that issue on which they might disagree.
- *Direct Quotation*—Include a direct quotation from a relevant expert or witness about the issue you address. Avoid quotation in your first sentence.
- *Humor*—Make people laugh in a way that also exposes some truth or hypocrisy or irrational behavior you explore. Do not make fun

of your readers—make sure they are laughing *with* you. Ask reviewers to check the tone to be sure.

- *Key Definition*—Define in your own words key terms your reader might not know, or redefine terms in a new way. Avoid using common reference materials such as Webster's Dictionary or Wikipedia to give definitions.
- *Key Question*—Directly ask the question that drives your writing and research. Take the audience on the journey from question to answer as you have experienced it.
- *Personal Experience*—If the genre and assignment allow for you to express your own voice, include a personal story, an experience that led you to discuss this issue.
- *Prediction*—Get readers wondering "What if?" by speculating about something that could happen in the future.
- *Shocking Statistic or Fact*—Grab readers' attention with information about your issue that you think will surprise them.
- *Surprise/Mystery*—Drop your readers into the middle of the action by narrating an interesting event, but do not explain until later what that story means for the issue you address.
- *Survey/Overview*—Establish the significance of the issue and your authority on it by briefly surveying or summarizing the issue. Avoid clichéd phrases like "since the beginning of time" or "from this time forward," which disappoint readers by promising too much and saying too little.

Body

Organize the body of your argument according to the genre required for your rhetorical situation. The domain you write in might limit the genres available to you or, if writing in the academic domain, might tell you exactly what genre pattern you must follow. See Chapter 11, "Arrange: Prioritize, Organize, Outline," along with the description of writing purposes in Part Three.

Conclusion

The conclusion, or ending, of your text is your final chance to convince your audience to think or act differently based on your argument. Make it easy for them. Endings, like beginnings, are points of emphasis, meaning that an audience tends to tune in more closely. Synthesize your most important points and clearly state what your audience should take away from your argument. Use your key words and phrases to repeat and therefore emphasize the concepts that should stick with your audience (see Chapter 8, "Question: Exploring Issues"). Finally, consider using some of the same approaches we recommend for introductions, such as quotation, examples, and/or an explicit call to action.

The work of drafting moves you from fragments of ideas to a coherent expression of what you want to say. If you have worked through the writing process we describe, that transition from outline to full draft should be fairly smooth. That does not mean, however, that your first draft will become a final draft. Even the strongest first draft can be improved through revision, by sharing it with others and looking at it anew. We will describe these revision strategies in the following chapters.

OFFICE HOURS ➤ Writer's Block, Writer's Bloat, and Writer's Bleh

Writing is always a challenge. Sometimes you just can't write anything—writer's block. Sometimes you write way too much—writer's bloat—and it's all bad. *Really* bad—bleh! How do you get to good writing?

There's no simple answer to this, but one thing is true: you have to let readers in. It can be so intimidating that you might not want to write anything at first, but the end goal is to use writing as a means of connecting with the world. You write to teach others and to learn from their response.

(continued)

If the idea of sharing your writing with peers in class is intimidating, start by sharing your writing with a tutor at your campus writing center or a friend or family member who is a good reader (see Chapter 14, "Review: By Peers and Experts"). Expect to hear some critique—the feedback wouldn't be much help if you didn't hear critique—but know that responding to this feedback will make your writing better and your argument stronger.

Critical Questions

1. Which approaches to writing an introduction do you prefer to use in your own writing? Which do you prefer as a reader?
2. The body is the largest part of a text, but the structure varies the most. What is your preference for the organizational style of the body of an argument? Describe the length of paragraphs and order that are most appealing to you as a reader. What writers do you most admire for using this structure in their writing?
3. What do you think makes a weak conclusion? Describe a specific example.

CHAPTER thirteen

Revise: Strategies for Re-Seeing

As you finish your first draft of an assignment, reflect on these two questions: Have you done what you were *asked* to do? Have you done what you *wanted* to do? A quick review of Chapter 6, "Analyze the Assignment," will help you make sure you have met your instructor's expectations. If you're confident you have met your instructor's expectations, then it's time to consider whether your own expectations have been met. You should feel satisfied that you have risen to the assignment's challenge, that you have shown what you know, and that you have written something worth reading. Revision is the process of making sure you have met the expectations of your readers and yourself.

While there are no shortcuts around writing multiple drafts to achieve your best outcome, there are strategies to help you make that process successful. To see your own writing anew, you need to create a sense of distance from it. Use these three strategies to distance yourself from your writing, enabling you to see how you can strengthen your draft:

1. Separate yourself from the draft.
2. Research further.
3. Seek feedback from a good reader.

We will explore each approach in greater depth. First, though, let's consider how to ask good questions about your work in process.

ARTICULATING QUESTIONS FOR REVISION

If you have questions about your draft, write them down. Create a list with two categories of concerns: (1) concerns about meeting assignment expectations, and (2) concerns about meeting your own expectations for what you can do with this opportunity. List those concerns as questions, as shown in Table 13.1.

As you make those lists, you are likely to see two levels of questions emerge: higher-order concerns, which are related to the big picture content questions of argument, audience, evidence, and arrangement; and lower-order concerns, including questions about style, mechanics, and format. Address higher-order concerns about content and purpose first, then address lower-order concerns. Higher-order concerns might require substantial changes, such as deleting or adding content. It would be a waste of time to address lower-order concerns in content that you are likely to revise substantially or even delete. (See Chapter 14, "Review: By Peers and Experts," for more on higher-order concerns and Chapter 15, "Proofread and Submit," for more on lower-order concerns.)

Finally, if your revision process includes peer reviewers in class or writing center tutors, capture those questions during your discussion. The questions they ask will reveal much about where you should focus your attention. Completing a chart like the one in Table 13.1 will help you determine how to proceed.

Table 13.1   REVISION QUESTIONS BY ORDER AND AUDIENCE

	ASSIGNMENT EXPECTATIONS Have I done what I was *asked* to do?	PERSONAL EXPECTATIONS Have I done what I *wanted* to do?	GOOD READER EXPECTATIONS What does an external reader want to know about your writing?
HIGHER-ORDER CONCERNS	Have I responded to each element of the assignment prompt in ways the prompt's verbs suggest I should?	Does my paper say something interesting and important that represents my thinking accurately?	What was the purpose of the assignment?
	Have I delivered information or analysis consistent with each element of the prompt?	Is my writing coherent, moving in a logical order with clear transitions?	What is your thesis? Where in the paper do you say that?
	Have I used sources in the way the prompt directs me to?	Will my audience—even people who disagree with me—listen to what I've said and respect the way I've said it?	What do you think is strongest about your draft?
	Have I been ethical in how I collected and represented my sources?	Am I clear and organized?	What do you think is weakest about your draft?
	Does my response correspond to the scope and scale indicated by the prompt?	Did I support my claims?	What can the audience learn by reading this?
LOWER-ORDER CONCERNS	Did I follow the expectations for style, mechanics, and format particular to this course and assignment?	Does my writing follow style, mechanics, and format rules consistently? Have I checked for my usual errors in these areas?	What concerns do you have about style, mechanics, and format? Were you given specific directions on these issues?

CREATING NEW PERSPECTIVES IN REVISION: THREE APPROACHS

Creating a new perspective on your writing is about returning to the invention stage of writing, trying to generate new ideas that will deepen, sharpen, and support your writing. Three effective strategies to achieve that new perspective include distancing yourself from the text, researching further, and consulting good readers.

Distance Yourself from the Text

It might sound like contradictory advice to distance yourself from your writing when you're trying to dig deeper into your topic, but getting some distance can actually help you dig deeper.

To get a fresh perspective from which you can see gaps and redundancies in your writing, create some distance between yourself and your writing. We offer three strategies here to help you see your writing anew.

Take Time Away

Effective revision begins with taking time away from your finished draft. As with other kinds of problem-solving, your mind will continue to explore your topic even when you're not actively writing. Engaging your mind in a different activity will help you reset and refresh your perspective when you return to your writing.

Read Aloud

When you return to your draft, try reading it aloud. Reading aloud slows you down and helps you focus on each word. Sentences that are difficult to read aloud or that simply don't "sound right" will probably be hard for your audience to understand as well. Reading aloud also helps you hear overused words, phrases, and sources. You will hear both your confidence and your uncertainty. Note those places as you read so that you can attend to each.

Create a Reverse Outline

An outline (see Chapter 11, "Arrange: Prioritize, Organize, Outline") is the sketch you make before you write to note your thesis and key points. A reverse outline is the sketch you make after you write, noting what actually appears as your thesis and key points. We discuss reverse outlining as a *reading* strategy in Chapter 9, "Read: Strategies for Reading in Research," but here we discuss it as a *writing* strategy. It's important to do this objectively, moving paragraph-by-paragraph as a reader, not as the author. Create an outline based on what's actually there. Write a sentence or phrase that represents the main point of each paragraph. Review that outline and see if it represents both the writing you were asked to do and wanted to do. Note the structure and logic of what you've actually written. From there, you can see where content should be developed, added, or removed. Compare this reverse outline to your original outline to see where they align and where they differ. Decide whether those divergences make sense or whether they point to areas where you got off track and need to return to the original organization presented in your outline.

Research Further

Another way to approach your own writing with a fresh perspective is by learning more about your topic. Identify areas where your content seems less developed or where your citations all seem to come from the same source. Read additional sources, particularly ones that challenge your position.

One way to decide where to start this next round of research is by looking first at your Works Cited or References page as well as any in-text citations. Readers notice and are troubled by papers that are overly dependent on a single source. They might see such dependence as a sign that you did not read all your sources thoroughly or did not try to develop your own thinking. Finding new sources or taking time to reread existing sources more thoroughly can help you generate fresh thinking.

Once you have gathered additional information, try using a reverse outline or a concept map to see how those new ideas fit into your existing draft. Do they strengthen an existing point or introduce a new claim? You can add supporting evidence or examples to existing paragraphs if they don't get too long. If, however, you introduce a new claim or concept, review your outline carefully to see where it belongs.

Consult a Good Reader

To get a fresh perspective on your writing, share it with good readers who will give you honest, detailed feedback (see Chapter 14, "Review: By Peers and Experts" for additional advice on this topic). Share your writing prompt so they can consider your instructor's expectations, then listen carefully. Tutors trained to provide feedback to student writers can model highly effective techniques for helping strengthen your writing. Some gaps in knowledge or gaffes in tone can only be caught by other readers. Pay attention not just to what the other person has to say, but also to how you yourself explain and justify your argument or writing. Note the order of your discussion, the amount of time you spend on certain topics, places where you struggle to find the right words or evidence, and your audience's reaction.

DOING REVISION

After you have done your own thinking and thinking with others on your draft, it's time to do the work of revision. That work happens in four moves: adding, cutting, rewriting, and rearranging.

Add

Add content when you have new insight, new ideas, and/or new information. Just because something wasn't in your first draft, doesn't mean it can't appear in your final draft. It takes time to think, talk, and research through a concept. Often, our best ideas come toward the end of the writing process. Make room for those revelations whenever they arrive.

Rewrite

Rewriting means changing what you have in substantive ways. As you researched further, for example, you might have discovered new terms more suited to your topic. If so, upgrade your vocabulary to reflect your new knowledge. You might also discover in rereading your writing that your tone is not right for this rhetorical situation. Adjusting your word choice to move from an angry to a more professional tone, for example, would be a substantive rewrite.

Rearrange

Rearranging means organizing sentences or paragraphs or sections of writing into an order that tells your story more effectively. For example, you might discover that an example in the middle of your writing would have greater impact as an introduction. Or your readers might have told you that they need more information early in the paper, enabling you to work up to more complex ideas. Rearranging involves shifting existing elements into the most effective sequence.

Cut

It's hard, but sometimes you have to let your writing go. As your writing evolves, you might find that some of your earlier points are not clear or are not relevant. Cut weak writing. Cut wandering writing.

REVISER'S BLOCK

Writer's block describes the feeling writers sometimes get when they sit down to write and can't figure out how to start (see Chapter 7, "Plan: Organizing the Process"). Reviser's block is when writers sit down with a draft and don't know how to start revising. It can be just as hard to think about pulling a completed draft apart as it is to stare at a blank screen when you first start writing. It might be overwhelming to consider all that good feedback you gathered when it's time to address it in your writing. Here are some practical strategies for overcoming reviser's block.

Inventory Your Revision

First, take inventory of all the ideas and feedback you've generated in looking at your draft anew. Prioritize and categorize that list. What are the most important, higher-order items on your to-do list? Which of the four acts of revision does that feedback ask you to do: add, rewrite, rearrange, or cut? Assign an act to each note of feedback, then rank the actions from most critical to least critical. Now you know exactly *what* you have to do. To think about *how* to do it, think about sequencing those actions in a logical order.

Revise in a Logical Order

Next think about the logical order of implementing those revisions. The following order typically works best: add, rewrite, rearrange, cut. First, add, which is the act of expanding your ideas to see what you can express most successfully. Second, rewrite. Refine your thinking and your language to make sure it is precise and effective. Third, rearrange. With all of your ideas in writing, reorder your content, adjusting transitions to reflect the new order. Finally, cut. Let go of what no longer belongs in this argument.

You can deviate from this order, but having a template for *what* to do *when* will help you dig in and do it. Just as your draft came together when you first started to write, so too will it come together again when you address your revisions one step at a time.

Revision is a going back—back to your writing, back to your research, back to your readers—in order to go forward with stronger writing. Good writers plan to revise, allowing ample time in their writing process to do the work of revision described in this chapter. Advanced thinking requires advanced writing that gets tested, refined, and improved. The strategies in this chapter will help you revise successfully, overcoming any blocks.

OFFICE HOURS ➤ Converting Comments into Acts of Revision

After a great conversation about your writing during peer review in a writing center session or in a conference with your instructor, it can be hard to translate that feedback into specific actions.

When you enter a peer or expert review session, listen for places to add, rewrite, rearrange, and cut. With those four categories in mind, you can inventory actions as you go. You can see right away if those comments will help you make robust revisions.

For example, if all the comments you receive seem to fall into the *add* category and your draft is already at the maximum word limit, be sure to talk about what to *cut* as well. Or, reviewers might be confused about something. You can then explore with your reviewer whether your revision should *add* more content and/or *rearrange* the order of existing information to prevent that confusion.

Keep these four revision categories in mind as you work with reviewers to create a clear, well-prioritized revision task list. You might extend that list as you revise and your writing evolves, but having that list will help prevent reviser's block.

Critical Questions

1. Describe a time when you or someone you know experienced reviser's block. What did you (or the other person) do to get through it?
2. Inventory the types of feedback you typically get in the writing process. Which types of comments do you get most, which do you get least?

3. Explain in your own words why this order of revision moves seems logical: add, rewrite, rearrange, cut.
4. How do you feel when you delete your own writing because it doesn't meet the expectations of the assignment or meet your own goals? Do those feeling last or fade?
5. Have you ever panicked when you reviewed a draft of your writing because you realized that it did not meet expectations? How did you manage that panic? What worked? What didn't?
6. What other types of activities require a type of revision, a going back to go forward with more success? Explain.

CHAPTER fourteen

Review: By Peers and Experts

Good writers need good readers. Consulting good readers early and often in the writing process will improve your writing. We write for others, so hearing what some of those readers think before you finalize your writing improves your chances of creating a successful message. In this chapter, we explore the purpose and process of getting expert and peer review, asking *why*, *when*, *who*, *where*, and *how* this review succeeds. We also explore reasons why some people might resist such exploration.

WHY? THE PURPOSE OF REVIEWS

In a writing class, we focus on the *process* of writing, not just the final *product*. A critical part of that process is seeking feedback from different kinds of readers, and then responding to that feedback by thoughtfully revising your work.

Reader feedback is especially useful to help writers revise higher-order concerns such as argument, audience, evidence, and arrangement. Here, reader feedback can offer new perspectives, counterarguments, and evidence that challenges writers to reconsider their thesis and strengthen claims. The more opportunities you take to see how someone with a different worldview interprets your message, the more likely you are to write and think in a way that connects with a wider audience and therefore has the greatest potential for impact and change.

WHEN? TIMING AND FREQUENCY OF REVIEWS

Ideally, you would get feedback through review early and often. But the reality is that both you and your potential reviewers have limited time, so you have to think strategically about how to schedule those reviews. Your strategy should take into account your writing process style, availability of preferred reviewers, and your deadlines.

Early Review

By communicating with your audience early in the writing process, you can test and refine your ideas so that you start writing with a more focused idea of what you will write about. If you prefer to process ideas verbally, this is probably a good strategy for you. And by getting review early in the writing process you should have ample time to address that feedback in your drafting.

A disadvantage of *only* getting feedback early in the process is that your ideas might evolve significantly as you write, so reviewers cannot speak to more developed higher-order concerns. Nor can they speak to lower-order concerns, because you did not yet have a written text to share.

Later Review

Seeking review later in the writing process means you have a complete or nearly complete draft. The advantage of this approach is that your reviewers can address higher-order and lower-order concerns. Good readers will keep those responses in balance and in order of priority: higher-order concerns should constitute the bulk of their response.

A potential disadvantage of *only* getting feedback late in the process is that you might be advised to make significant changes. Writers are sometimes reluctant to make changes on full drafts, or they might run out of time to do the work that needs to be done.

If possible, schedule both early and later reviews so that you benefit from both. Look at your deadline, consider who will review for you, and plan to get as much feedback as possible.

WHO? PEOPLE WHO CAN HELP

People inside and outside your class might be able to give you feedback. To decide who should review your writing, consider two questions: Is it ethical for that person to review your writing? And, what could that person contribute to your writing process? The following discussion will help you answer those questions.

Ethical Review

Before you approach anyone for feedback on your work, be sure that you know the honor code rules that inform ethical collaboration on academic work. Ask questions if you are unsure about what is acceptable collaboration or how you should acknowledge or cite that collaboration. Talk to your instructor, and see Chapter 5, "Writing Ethics, Responsibility, and Accountability," for more on the ethics of working with others.

What Readers Contribute

Some readers might be more helpful than others based on (1) their rhetorical situation in relation to your writing assignment, and (2) their level of training in reader response. Table 14.1 helps you consider which type of readers you should consult in your revision process.

After considering the strengths and limitations of each type of reader, arrange your appointments as your schedule allows.

Table 14.1   QUICK GUIDE TO READERS

TYPE OF READER	STRENGTHS	LIMITATIONS
In-Class Peer Reviewers	• Know the assignment expectations • Know all the course materials • Can work together in class—saves external work time.	• Around the same learning point as you in this writing assignment; might share your questions. • Might only advise on how to improve that writing, not how to become a better writer overall. • Might not know how to distinguish higher-order from lower-order concerns, or how to prioritize comments.
Out-of-Class Peer Reviewers (e.g., the roommate, the go-to English major, the approachable upperclassman)	• Peers who have taken this course before can share strategies for success. • Peers who haven't taken this course provide a genuine outsider's perspective. • They already have a rapport with you that lets you give and take feedback in good spirit.	• Peers who haven't done this assignment must rely on your knowledge of the expectations for the assignment • Might not know the code of academic honesty in that class, or might even feel exempt from it. • Might not be skilled in showing clear options for revision. • Might not know how to distinguish higher-order from lower-order concerns, or how to prioritize comments.

Campus Writing Center Tutors	• Trained both in writing *and* in the art of effective tutoring. • Skilled at addressing both higher-order and lower-order concerns *and* know when to address each. • Work in Centers with access to writing resources. • Have reliable schedules so you can count on them to be there. • You can work with various tutors to get different input. • Your tutor is likely to have training in ethical writing and can support your ethical practice.	• Only work at scheduled times and places. Availability might not meet yours; hard to get an appointment at busy times. • Might not know your assignment, so they must trust your interpretation. Might not have inside knowledge of course content.
Instructors	• Know course content and what counts as a successful response to their own writing assignment. • Use language and terms you know from class. • Can point you toward additional research and materials that will help your revision.	• Instructors are busy; their office hours might not align with your needs.

(continued)

159

Table 14.1   QUICK GUIDE TO READERS (*continued*)

TYPE OF READER	STRENGTHS	LIMITATIONS
Instructors (***Continued***)	• Skilled at addressing both higher-order and lower-order concerns *and* know when to address each.	
Local Community Experts	• Know what's happening in the local community. Can introduce you to sources of local significance. • Care about making change and welcome interested students who want to engage local issues.	• Limited time and availability. • Might not use the same language and concepts used in your course. • Might not know the expectations for academic honesty and ethical argumentation in your class. • Might have a bias or agenda related to their work. • Might not know how to distinguish higher-order from lower-order concerns, or how to prioritize each type of comment.
Librarians	• Can locate relevant sources that meet assignment expectations. • Might be familiar with your assignment from working with your instructor or other students. • Can provide an objective external view on the strength of your sources. • Understand ethics of writing.	• Might not understand the expectations of your assignment. • Might not have time to read and respond to an actual draft. • Might not know how to distinguish higher-order from lower-order concerns, or how to prioritize each type of comment.

WHERE? FACE-TO-FACE AND DIGITAL EXCHANGES

Following are some situations and places in which you can share your writing with a real audience, either face-to-face or through online exchanges. These descriptions will help you prioritize your time and weigh which kinds of feedback you need and when you need to schedule them.

In-Class Peer Workshops

Take advantage of class time scheduled for peer review. Follow your instructor's guidelines on how to prepare and what to bring. It is to your advantage to bring more rather than less, as long as you are willing to revise based on the feedback you receive.

Campus Writing Center

Campus writing center tutors work with writers one-on-one at any stage in the writing process. They do not write papers for students. And they do not grade your work, so you can learn how to accept constructive critique with less anxiety. Tutors can offer considerable help with higher-order concerns. Writing centers generally offer both face-to-face and online sessions. Your writing instructor can tell you more about what's offered on your campus.

Your Neighborhood

Look outside of your immediate writing classroom for other students, friends, or family members with demonstrated writing competence. Such writers are often willing to review drafts of work, offering feedback on both higher-order concerns (argument, audience, evidence, and arrangement) and lower-order concerns (style, mechanics, and format). However, without training, these consultants might become too directive or simply "correct" a paper for you rather than have a conversation in which you deepen your thinking.

Library

Librarians navigate the ever-evolving expanse of information to help you find the strongest possible sources in the least amount of time. While you are responsible for understanding the assignment questions, librarians can guide you along paths that will answer those questions efficiently and effectively.

Full-Class Workshops

Some instructors offer the opportunity to do a full-class workshop on one writer's draft. While this can be intimidating, it can also be incredibly helpful to gain the insight of such a robust audience. Just as in smaller peer workshop groups, you might find that consensus about what works and does not work will shift as peers respond.

The Local Community

If you are in a service-learning course or writing about something of interest to the local community, don't just write *about* them, talk *with* them. Test your ideas on local stakeholders, community experts who would be affected by your topic. They might recommend further resources to revise your work, possibly adding relevance for a local audience. Cite those community experts as a source if your talk turns into an interview and you get permission to include their thoughts (see Chapter 28, "Working with Human Sources").

Instructor Conferences

 If instructors are willing to talk through your ideas or writing, take them up on the offer (without taking advantage of their time by *overusing* this privilege). Come prepared with specific questions and easy access to relevant texts. Be prepared as well to respond to their suggestions in your revision. Instructors want to see the ideas they recommend implemented or at least addressed in future drafts. See "Office Hours: Instructor Writing Conferences" at the end of this chapter for guidance on how to get the most from an instructor conference.

Grades and Instructors' Comments

In some classes, particularly "writing intensive" classes, you might be allowed or even required to submit a draft for instructor comments prior to receiving a final grade. This is a remarkable opportunity to hear from a key stakeholder in your audience, and an excellent time to schedule a conference with your instructor to clarify his or her feedback and discuss your revision plans. Instructors' comments personalize the writing assignment specifically for you. From the comments, you should be able to determine what the instructor now thinks you can accomplish with this assignment.

 Your instructor's comments on your draft might be directive, telling you exactly what steps to take, or they might more broadly suggest your options going forward. On the other hand, the comments might only tell you what's wrong or praise what's right, and leave you to decide how those observations should inform your revisions. While the job of responding to those comments is yours, approach your instructor if you have any questions about the comments. You are essentially performing a rhetorical analysis of your instructors' comments, and if you can get clarification directly from the author, you have a distinct advantage in interpreting the text successfully (see Chapter 13, "Office Hours: Converting Comments into Acts of Revision").

Some instructors allow students to revise and resubmit an assignment that has already received a grade. If you have such an opportunity, carefully consider not just the letter grade but all of the comments and feedback your instructor gave you. Instructors who allow students to revise and resubmit an assignment have high expectations for the scope and quality of that revision. It is not enough to simply correct mistakes in grammar or citation styles—you are unlikely to receive a higher grade simply for addressing lower-order concerns. Likewise, in the workplace, you will face situations where your projects need significant revision based on new information or stakeholder feedback. Set aside personal feelings of disappointment or defensiveness. Approach the opportunity to revise and resubmit your work as a valuable chance to practice responding constructively to criticism.

Where you seek revision is connected to questions of who, when, and why. Consider the range of places you can seek feedback and whether face-to-face or digital responses would be most effective for you given your own communication style preferences.

HOW? WAYS OF RECEIVING REVIEW

Feedback can be delivered verbally or in writing. Good writers will try to make sure that feedback is clear and organized by asking good questions. Writers can come up with their own questions, or they might use some type of rubric that prompts those good questions to make sure readers respond effectively. Then, they think carefully about how to respond to all that feedback.

Use an Argument Review Guide

The "Checklist: Argument Review Guide" (Table 14.2) outlines higher-order concerns that a peer reviewer (or you) should consider first in responding to your draft. (Chapter 15, "Proofread and

Submit," includes a complementary "Checklist: Proofreading Guide" to address lower-order concerns.) This guide can be adapted to meet the expectations of any writing assignment. You can use this guide for discussions about your work with any reviewer, such as a writing center tutor, to prompt the responses you need for revision.

Table 14.2   CHECKLIST: ARGUMENT REVIEW GUIDE

Reader: _____

Writer: _____

CHECKLIST ➤ Argument Review Guide	
ARGUMENT: **Thesis,** **Position,** **Proposal,** **Opposition,** **Stakes,** **Appeals** *Main claim should argue strength of this position among opposing viewpoints.*	☐ *Thesis* is arguable, specific, manageable, and interesting. ☐ Presents a provocative argument that contains a *position* on and/or a *proposal* concerning a critical issue currently disputed by reasonable people. ☐ *Differing viewpoints* are respectfully engaged or refuted. ☐ Explains the *stakes* of the argument—what happens if things stay the same, what happens if they change as proposed? ☐ Rhetorical appeals of *ethos, pathos*, and *logos* are developed and balanced appropriately for the genre and aims.
AUDIENCE: **Interest,** **Cooperation,** **Credibility** *Appeals should interest audience and build ethos.*	☐ Argument fully engages its target audience by focusing on a compelling issue of *shared interest* to this audience at this time. ☐ Tone respectfully asks for the audience's *cooperation* in understanding an issue and/or resolving a problem. ☐ Author speaks confidently in her own voice, establishing her *credibility* and expertise.

(continued)

Table 14.2   CHECKLIST: ARGUMENT REVIEW GUIDE (*continued*)

EVIDENCE: **Reasons, Facts, Examples, Support** *Evidence should give audience new insight on issue.*	☐ Claims link to *good reasons, sufficient facts*, and/or *strong examples* from reliable research. ☐ *Support* is relevant, varied, and valid.
ARRANGEMENT: **Title, Thesis, Introduction, Conclusion, Paragraphs, Transitions** *Order should cue readers to follow the argument.*	☐ *Title* accurately and engagingly reflects the author's argument, giving a clear and positive first impression. ☐ *Thesis* is clear quickly. ☐ *Introduction* maintains readers' attention and compels them to read on whether they agree or disagree with the author's position. Introduction connects the audience with the issue, employing appropriate rhetorical strategies to establish the need for analyzing this issue at this time with this audience (kairos). ☐ *Conclusion* reflects on the preceding argument, offering a substantial contribution rather than merely summarizing. Leaves the audience with a clear, memorable, and motivating sense of what they should think and do based on this argument. ☐ Each paragraph is clearly constructed: *paragraph introduction* opens with a topic sentence in the author's words (not quotation) that makes a claim pointing back to the thesis statement while transitioning from previous paragraph; *paragraph body* follows with varied, relevant, and valid support for that particular claim; and *paragraph conclusion* uses the author's words to synthesize and bring the idea into focus rather than ending with quotation. ☐ *Transitions* are varied and move the argument forward by highlighting the relationship between ideas.

Readers—Focusing on argument, audience, evidence, and arrangement complete the following lists citing the page and paragraph to which your *specific* comments are directed, or make it clear that you are providing general comments.

Cite three specific aspects of the text that are working well:

1)

2)

3)

Cite three aspects of the text that can be improved, then offer suggestions for improvement:

1)

Suggestions for improvement:

2)

Suggestions for improvement:

3)

Suggestions for improvement:

Assignment Goals. Reader checks appropriate box after full review.

- ☐ Meets the assignment criteria for word count, outside sources, argument type, deadline, and/or necessary revisions at this draft stage.
- ☐ Does not meet the assignment criteria for this draft stage in the following ways:

Respond to Feedback

After you have gathered constructive feedback from reviewers, what do you do with all that information? Sometimes the process of review raises more questions than it answers.

You will either get written comments from your reviewer (possibly on a reader response sheet like the one in Table 14.2, and/or on the draft of your paper itself), or you will take notes as you have a conversation with that reviewer. The real work starts when you look at those notes to determine what to do next. Good readers give reasons for their claims supported by evidence from the text, and they suggest multiple ways you can respond to their assessment. If you understand why something did not meet a reader's expectations, you can consider which solutions might solve that problem.

All the comments you receive represent valid reader responses. If, however, you carefully consider a reader's comment and have reason for resisting it—for example, the reader does not understand the expectations of the assignment—then you can choose not to make the changes suggested by that reader. But you should only reject suggested revisions after you have considered your writing from that reader's perspective.

When Reader Responses Conflict

Sometimes, you will receive conflicting feedback from different readers. What do you do when that happens?

The more information you have about why readers made specific suggestions, the better able you will be to reconcile apparently conflicting points of view. As Table 14.1 shows, different readers have different strengths and limitations, so you have to determine what to do based on the strength of their reasoning, not their unsupported claims.

In the end, you are the author of your own writing, and that writing will have integrity and coherence as long as *you* control it, informed by the good readers you aim to reach.

RESISTING REVIEW

Writers may resist consulting others for two key reasons: they feel pressured by time, and they fear negative feedback. While careful planning of a writing assignment allows time for peer feedback, the fear of negative reactions to your work is likely to diminish with time and practice. Here are some tips for overcoming resistance to review:

- **Plan ahead.** Set early draft deadlines for yourself and arrange time with good readers so that you will have enough time to address their feedback before the assignment is due. You also want your readers to have enough time to give constructive feedback.
- **Put responses in perspective**. The fear of negative feedback can be managed by putting readers' responses into perspective. Feedback from the final audience, whether it is your instructor or a workplace colleague, can seem less intimidating if you have shared your writing with another audience first. If they are good readers skilled in giving productive feedback, they will not only tell you what is not working for them in the writing, they will explain *why* and give you options for revision. The "Quick Guide to Readers" (Table 14.1) helps you consider the strengths and limitations of various types of readers so that you can choose readers and help create the conditions for effective feedback.

Writing is a social act. Although we might resist including readers in our writing process due to time constraints or the fear of what they might tell us, this is a critical part of revision. Different types of readers will bring different perspectives on our writing, and it's important to consider what they can and cannot see from their perspective. Reviewer feedback is only meaningful when writers use it to reflect on and revise their work. Your role as a writer is not simply to either fully accept or completely reject reviewer feedback. Rather, it is about understanding where those comments come from and seeing if you can revise your message to meet your readers' needs.

When you inventory all the ways you give and receive feedback in every domain—academic, home, civic, and work—you will see that this is a common practice. That doesn't mean it is easy to ask for feedback or to give it. There are, however, strategies for creating conditions for successful review in academic writing. By scheduling reviews at the right time, with a thoughtful reviewer, in a place that supports your process, with the questions and tools that will equip you for a productive exchange, you create the conditions for successful review of your writing.

OFFICE HOURS ➤ Instructor Writing Conferences

Instructors generally welcome the opportunity to discuss drafts of your writing outside class. When seeking additional feedback from your instructor during the writing process, be respectful and be prepared.

Respectful contact with your instructor begins with reading and following the guidelines for contact in the syllabus. Be polite in requesting a meeting or asking for assistance. While you are not graded on this correspondence, consider it a useful opportunity to practice respectful communication skills that will be useful in the workplace as well as the community. Third, it is important to respect instructors' busy schedules by giving your instructor enough time to arrange an appointment. While instructors expect you to learn and practice good time management skills, they also want to help you manage the stress of your assignments.

You will get the most out of a conference with your instructor if you come prepared. This does not mean you have to have a full, polished draft. You might be stuck -- and that's okay. Here are four steps to prepare for your conference:

1. Do a rhetorical analysis of the writing prompt (see Chapter 6, "Analyze the Assignment").
2. Do as much reading connected to this assignment as possible.
3. Draft at least an outline and thesis.
4. Have specific questions ready to ask.

Here are some general writing conference questions you can adapt for your purposes. They move from higher-order concerns to lower-order concerns. Higher-order concerns should be addressed early in your writing process; lower-order concerns should be addressed when you are closer to a final draft. An instructor conference is probably most effective at an early stage of your work.

1. Am I following the expectations of this genre?
2. Does my thesis meet the expectations of the assignment?
3. Does my use of sources meet the expectations of the assignment? What advice do you have for finding different sources if that seems necessary?
4. Is my tone appropriate for the assignment? If it's not appropriate, what specific words or phrases would you address?
5. Do you see any major issues with my grammar or format? (It is unlikely that you will have time to discuss these lower-order concerns if you fully engage higher-order concerns.)

Critical Questions

1. Describe your attitude about review and give reasons for it. Do you ever sabotage your chance to get feedback by procrastinating or psyching yourself out about what reviewers might say?
2. Name specific things readers can do to motivate writers and things they can do to discourage writers. In what aspects of reader response are you strongest and what aspects do you need improvement? What can you do to develop your skills as a good reader?
3. What can you learn about yourself as a writer by listening carefully to good readers? Give examples.
4. What might you learn about yourself by the way you approach reader responses? How would you describe your current style and your ideal style of receiving feedback?
5. Explain the connection between the claims that writing is a social act and that reader response is critical to good writing.

CHAPTER fifteen

Proofread and Submit

In Chapter 14, "Review: By Peers and Experts," we discussed the importance of getting feedback from good readers who address higher-order concerns—argument, audience, evidence, and arrangement. By now, you should have considered that advice and revised accordingly. As a result, you should be confident in the strength of your assignment's content. Before you share your assignment with its final audience, however, it's time to address lower-order concerns—style, mechanics, and format. This chapter shows you how to use a proofreading checklist to address those concerns. A checklist helps you consistently address issues of style, mechanics, and format. This chapter also helps you consider how to submit your final draft appropriately.

AIMS OF PROOFREADING

In the revision process, reviewers gave you feedback on the higher-order concerns that could help your argument succeed. While they might also have noted some lower-order concerns, good readers attend to big picture issues related to content first, knowing that their time is limited and that higher-order concerns are top priority. Those lower-order concerns do matter in your writing, however, and once your revising is finished, it is time to proofread.

Proofreading means reviewing your writing specifically for lower-order concerns such as style, mechanics, and format. Problems with lower-order concerns risk distracting readers and diminishing their engagement with your writing. The good news is that you can take steps to avoid those distractions. The longer and more complex the project, the more time you need to devote to proofreading, but the strategies we recommend in the next section can help you prevent these problems.

STRATEGIES FOR PROOFREADING

Some of the strategies for proofreading are similar to the strategies for revising we discussed in Chapter 13, "Revise: Strategies for Re-Seeing." Some, however, are different in that they focus on fine details that can be overlooked, especially if you have read your own work many times. We recommend you do all of the following.

Distance Yourself from the Text

Just as in revising for higher-order concerns, it is important to distance yourself from the text so that you can see it anew. It is easy to read over missing words or spelling errors when you have reviewed the writing so many times that you gloss over the text rather than reading what is actually written. Along with two strategies discussed in Chapter 13—taking time away and reading aloud—we also recommend that you try *reading backwards*. Reading sentence-by-sentence backwards from the end of the writing to the beginning forces you to slow down your pace and focus more on style, mechanics, and format than on content. This is not, however, an effective way to proofread for style, nor is it practical for lengthy writings.

Keep a Writing Handbook Handy

The purpose of a writing handbook or reference guide is to give you the answers when lower-order concerns get confusing. You do not have to memorize every grammar and punctuation rule, just make sure you have access to a clear, comprehensive, easily searchable print or online reference guide when you sit down to proofread. You will be less likely to let a possible error go if you make it easy to double check. Your instructor can recommend a reliable print or online handbook.

Focus on One Concern at a Time

Lower-order concerns cover everything from apostrophes to MLA style. It would be overwhelming to review all those concerns at once. Instead, plan to read your draft several times, targeting a specific lower-order concern each time. For example, you might want to check the format of your in-text citations first, then go through again to check usage of semi-colons, and yet again to check agreement in verb tenses. By using a word processor's search feature, you can quickly identify and check your target concern (although technology can miss some things—see cautions in the following section "Use Technology, But Don't Trust Technology").

Know *Your* Common Errors and Target Them

Expanding on our advice to focus on one concern at a time, we recommend that you know which lower-order concern errors are most likely to appear in your own writing and target those first. Most people—even experienced writers—tend to make the same few errors over and over again. The same is true for spelling—we all have a few words that get us every time. Know your own personal common errors and search specifically for those among all the possible lower-order concerns you could search for.

Use Technology, But Don't Trust Technology

Most word processors can do helpful tasks such as search for words, phrases, or punctuation. Many also provide reference materials, such as a dictionary and thesaurus, so you can check usage of a word and find synonyms. They can also highlight spelling and grammar errors.

While all of these are helpful tools, it takes an attentive human to make them work correctly. For example, a search feature cannot find the absence of an apostrophe that should be present—you have to find that on your own. And it cannot always detect a homonym error such as mixing up *they're, there,* and *their* because these words are spelled correctly. Nor does it always catch extra words or misuses of prepositions. You have to search for errors beyond what the computer identifies because it will not catch them all.

As a general rule, pay attention to your word processor if it flags something as incorrect. In most cases, something could be improved. But look up the rule it suggests you are breaking in your handbook to confirm that the computer is correct. Humans know much that computers cannot catch or correct.

Enlist an Outside Reader

To counter the fatigue and familiarity that might cause you to miss some lower-order errors, we recommend that you work through the strategies we present here on your own first, then enlist help from an outside reader if possible. Each additional set of eyes that review a text increases the chance that you will catch an error and prevent interruptions to your connection with the audience.

Use a Proofreading Guide

Polishing your work through proofreading covers many possible issues, and it comes at the end of your writing process when it can be hard to focus. The following Checklist: Proofreading Guide (Table 15.1) can help you present your writing as the clearest, strongest representation of your thinking.

Table 15.1   CHECKLIST: PROOFREADING GUIDE

CHECKLIST ➤	Proofreading Guide
STYLE: **Clarity, Simplicity, Voice, Visualization** *Style should be appropriate for the rhetorical situation and reflect the author's character and sensibility with original expressions and images.*	*Clarity* ☐ Paragraph structure (topic sentences, mode) ☐ Sentence structure (parallelism, variety of grammar patterns and sentence length) ☐ Word choice (formality, precision, vividness) ☐ Emphasis (beginnings and endings, repetition) ☐ Format (headings, italics/dashes/all caps/bold) *Simplicity* ☐ Sentence structure (transitions, coordination) ☐ Effective words (vivid verbs, specific nouns, no zombie nouns) ☐ Unnecessary words (redundancy, intensifiers, clauses) *Voice* ☐ Formality (common words, contractions, first/second/third person) ☐ Ethos (respect, ethics) ☐ Tone (attitude balances pathos and logos) ☐ Active and passive voice (present/absent author) ☐ Positivity/kindness (respect opposing views) *Visualization* ☐ Analogies (comparison) ☐ Metaphors (one thing is like another thing) ☐ Similes ("like" or "as,"; avoids clichés and euphemisms)

MECHANICS:	☐ Sentence fragments
Grammar, Punctuation, Spelling	☐ Run-on (also called fused) sentences
	☐ Overused commas
Mechanics should be error-free, consistent with guidelines for this rhetorical situation.	☐ Pronouns
	☐ Modifiers
	☐ Mixed sentences
	☐ Verb forms, tenses, mood, voice, subject-verb agreement
	☐ Semicolons
	☐ Colons
	☐ Exclamation points
	☐ Apostrophes (possessiveness)
	☐ Parentheses
	☐ Ellipsis mark
	☐ Brackets
	☐ Hyphens
	☐ Dashes
	☐ Spelling (homonyms, foreign words, accents)
	☐ Other _____
FORMAT: MLA/ APA/Other Style Guide	☐ Quotation marks (double/single, placement, etc.)
	☐ Signal/introductory phrases before every quotation followed by correct punctuation
In-text and bibliographical citations should follow expected format; elements of style related to format, such as	☐ Page layout (font, margins, page numbering)
	☐ Parenthetical citation
	☐ Works cited page format
	☐ Text title format
	☐ Capitalization
	☐ Underlining/italics/quotation marks applied to titles of works

(*continued*)

Table 15.1   CHECKLIST: PROOFREADING GUIDE (*continued*)

capitalization, should be consistent with guidelines for this rhetorical situation.	☐ Abbreviations ☐ Numbers (numerical or spelled out) ☐ Other _____

SUBMITTING WORK WITH CARE AND CONFIDENCE

After you complete the writing process, you are ready to submit your final draft, your best response to the rhetorical situation. If you have followed these guidelines carefully, your work should be thorough, thoughtful, and polished.

If you have worked that hard, make sure you go the "last mile" to submit your work with care. Following are some hallmarks of such care.

Timeliness

Avoid marring your audience's first impression of your final draft by submitting it late, by even a short time. Know the exact deadline and give yourself a cushion of time to account for technical difficulties or traffic delays or printer problems or whatever might stand between you and that finish line. Don't cut it close. Plan ahead so that you cross the finish line calmly and in control, not making excuses or asking for more time.

Delivery Format

Review the guidelines for where and how your writing should be delivered, and respect those expectations. For example, if you are asked to put the printed paper in your instructor's mailbox, don't slip it under her door or email it to her. Respect the reasons behind that request even if you don't understand them. Your instructor or other audience members shouldn't have to contact you to ask you to re-deliver your work. Pay attention and submit it correctly the first time.

Good writers show they care by attending to detail in their writing, including proofreading it well. They know that format, mechanical, and style errors make the audience wonder what other errors lurk inside the content, where else the author might have stopped short in reasoning or research. Proofreading errors give the impression that the author has not been a careful writer. Good writers therefore reserve ample time to work through the Proofreading Checklist to minimize errors and increase the audience's trust and engagement in their work. When writers design and deliver their work with the kind of care outlined in this book, they can submit their writing with confidence.

OFFICE HOURS ➤ Proofreading for Non-Native Speakers of English

Both native and non-native speakers of English (also called English as a Second Language [ESL] or Language 2 [L2]) make mistakes with lower-order concerns and need to spend focused time on polishing. Like native speakers of English, these students do not make *every* error; they make a few errors over and over again. Students who are non-native speakers of English, however, might still be developing that ear for English that enables native speakers to catch some of their own mistakes when they listen to their own writing. By identifying those patterns of errors and understanding how to fix them, students who are non-native speakers of English gradually become better at preventing them.

Consult a handbook for comprehensive discussions and examples of additional common mistakes. Here are some common errors among students who speak English as an additional language:

Table 15.2   COMMON ERRORS AMONG NON-NATIVE SPEAKERS OF ENGLISH

Articles: a, an, the	Use an indefinite article ("a" or "an") in the first reference to something and if something is not known to both the reader and writer. Use a definite article ("the") when this is not the case.
Adjective order	When listing multiple adjectives to describe something, American English follows this order: (1) Quantity/Number/Article, (2) Quality/Opinion/Observation, (3) Size, (4) Age, (5) Shape, (6) Color, (7) Proper Adjective/Origin, (8) Material, (9) Purpose or Qualifier.
Capitalization	*Do Capitalize*: The personal pronoun "I"; proper names of people, institutions, and major events; the first word in a new sentence; nations and national nouns and adjectives; weekdays, holidays, and months; etc. *Do Not Capitalize*: Common nouns
Change in tense	Present tense is the default tense. Use past tense when something took place fully in the past and is now over. Use future tense for events that have not yet taken place. Use conditional tense for events that could happen.
Plural and possessive	Plural: Add "s" or "es." Possessive: Add "'s" or "s'."
To make or to do	Make: Use for building and creating. Do: Use for activities and ideas.
Me, Myself, and I	Me: Use when the speaker is the person receiving. Myself: Use when the speaker acts and the action comes back to him or her. I: Use when the speaker is the actor.
Run-On Sentences	If a sentence has two or more main clauses that could stand as their own sentence, you must either connect them with a coordinating conjunction (and, but, or, for, so, nor, yet) or stop them with a period or semicolon.

Remember that most audience members, including instructors, care more about the higher-order concerns of audience, argument, evidence, and arrangement than they do about lower-order concerns. A perfectly polished text that lacks a clear argument, compelling evidence, or connection with the audience does not qualify as good writing for any author.

Critical Questions

1. Which of the proofreading strategies do you use regularly? Which do you find most helpful? What other strategies do you use?
2. Name your top five most challenging areas on the Checklist: Proofreading Guide.
3. How would you proofread for style? Would you use the same strategies to proofread for style on your own writing and for others? What might you do differently?

CHAPTER sixteen

Rhetorical Analysis: Getting the Message

Rhetorical analysis is the process of thinking critically about a text to understand both *what* it means and *how* it means. After reading, viewing, listening to, and/or interacting with a written or multimodal text for the first time, we respond immediately with agreement, disagreement, or mixed feelings. A word, phrase, image, or reference often strikes a chord of agreement, or upsets us. After reading a text just once, however, it is often difficult to explain how the text led us to that interpretation.

In a rhetorical analysis, you consider every unit of meaning—from words in alphabetic text to pixels in visual texts—to help understand how those individual elements work together to create an effective argument. In rhetorical analysis, you review the primary text many times, from as many different points of view as possible, in order to understand what it says and how it works.

After examining the primary text using the "Strategies for Rhetorical Analysis" described in the next section, you can then construct your own analytical text, which consists of two main parts:

1. A summary of the main argument of the primary text
2. An examination and assessment of how that argument was constructed in order to show its key strengths and weaknesses

A rhetorical analysis does not typically include a writer's thoughts about the issue being discussed. It only includes the writer's thoughts on how successful the text's author was in furthering his or her own thoughts about the issue. When writing your own rhetorical analysis for the assignment described in this chapter, be careful not to get sidetracked by asserting your own views on the issue.

Rhetorical analysis is an essential step in critical reading, forming the basis for most critical writing. When we understand what works and does not work in how others construct an argument, we gain insight into how to construct our own arguments more successfully.

STRATEGIES FOR RHETORICAL ANALYSIS ARGUMENTS

The following strategies for rhetorical analysis offer a menu of approaches. Writers often pick just a few approaches to highlight in a written rhetorical analysis. But you will quickly see a relationship among all these strategies, which depend on each other to convey the desired effect. Rhetorical analysis is a method of taking a close look at how the parts function within the whole organism of the text.

Strategy 1: Analyze Context

Context includes such factors as the time, place, audience, and mood particular to that rhetorical situation. Contextual analysis focuses on the author's rhetorical strategies. This type of project identifies the main claim, the most important reasons the author uses to support that claim, and the most important rhetorical moves the author makes to convince his or her audience of this claim. Equally important, it introduces specific textual evidence, quotes and examples from the text, to support its claim. Your entire project might just focus on ethos, for example, as long as you justify why ethos is the most crucial appeal given the purpose and audience.

Strategy 2: Analyze Written Text

Analysis of the written text addresses the author's choice and arrangement of words, sentences, paragraphs, and sources. When reading critically to analyze the rhetorical construction of a text, you could note any or all of the following:

- How appeals to ethos, pathos, and logos are used
- How the text is organized on the level of sentences, paragraphs, and overall structure
- How word choice and phrasing contribute to tone
- How embedded visual appeals (photos, drawings, metaphors, similes, etc.) expand, underscore, or distract from messages in alphabetic text
- How logical fallacies are used intentionally or unintentionally
- How emphasis is constructed through such strategies as repetition, omission, signposting, and loaded language
- How beginnings and endings are used strategically as focal points
- How sources and casual references build or erode credibility through direct quotation, paraphrases, and allusions

Strategy 3: Analyze Performative Text

The performative text refers to the interaction between the writer, speaker, or performer; the text; and the audience. This interaction can be synchronous (same time), such as a live speech, or it can be asynchronous (different time), such as a website that allows the audience to interact freely. To analyze the performative text of a speech, consider both how the speaker delivers the text and how the audience responds to that delivery.

From the speaker, you could analyze physical expressions, such as:

- Gestures
- Eye contact
- Vocal control: intonation, volume, pace, silence

From the audience, you could analyze the intensity of vocal and physical expressions, such as:

- Applause
- Laughter
- Shouts of dissent or agreement
- Gestures of dissent or agreement

Classical rhetoricians who taught the art of oratory identified categories of appeals (see Chapter 4, "Argument") that provide a useful way of analyzing the primary pulse of a communication or its key ways of getting through to an audience.

ELEMENTS OF RHETORICAL ANALYSIS ARGUMENTS

A strong rhetorical analysis includes the following elements: (1) a clear explanation of the rhetorical situation, and (2) a clear explanation of how the text is constructed to convey its meaning.

Element 1: Context

A strong rhetorical analysis typically opens by situating the text in its context. The rhetorical situation sets the stage for the text, and a rhetorical analysis often addresses those contextual cues up front.

Element 2: Meaning-making

A rhetorical analysis focuses on *how* a text conveys meaning, not on what it argues. The goal is not to agree or disagree with the author but to break down how the author constructed the text to make that meaning. Your goal is to make an argument about how well the text was constructed using specific examples from the text to support your assessment.

IN PROCESS: RHETORICAL ANALYSIS
Project: Rhetorical Analysis of a Speech

Objectives

- Demonstrate your ability to analyze a primary target text carefully in order to see how its rhetorical construction is connected to its argument.
- Demonstrate your ability to construct a persuasive argument about what works and does not work in the target text offering good reasons supported by specific examples from the text.

Description

Write a rhetorical analysis of a speech that has had significant influence on society. To determine whether a speech rises to this level (as it can be difficult to establish a clear causal connection between a speech and a specific social change), consider the general knowledge of the speech among key stakeholders and the extent to which specific ideas or phrases first introduced in that speech have become part of a community's collective knowledge. Note that this is an evaluative process in which you determine whether or not a given speech should be defined as "significant." (See Chapter 20, "Evaluation: Considering Criteria," to learn more about constructing arguments that are primarily evaluative.)

Speeches that stand the test of time combine a foundation of good writing delivered with added meaning through the poise and presence of a rhetor (the "speaker") who connects fully with the audience. The most successful speeches connect not only with the people who were present for the original delivery of the speech but also with those who read, watch, or listen to it much later.

To complete this assignment successfully, your rhetorical analysis will first consider and address the *context* of the speech (its purpose, audience, and social moment of delivery). Next, you will consider that context as you analyze the *written text*, attending to its main claim and support. Finally, you will analyze the *performative text* by watching or listening to the speech as it was delivered, attending to the ways vocal tone (emphasis and silence) and physical gestures add meaning.

In the writing models that follow, you will see two approaches to the rhetorical analysis of a speech. In the published reading, Ta-Nehisi Coates analyzes selected excerpts of speeches given by Michelle and Barack Obama to find a larger pattern of themes related to race and social mobility. In the student reading, Dan Jacobs responds to the assignment description you see in this chapter, analyzing critical elements of a speech he selected.

Thesis Template

Here is a template that demonstrates one way you might construct a thesis statement for your rhetorical analysis of a speech:

> [Name of person giving speech] effectively uses [ethos, pathos, logos, kairos] to achieve [describe purpose of speech] by [insert specific examples that will become main topics in your argument]. By addressing [insert key focal point], [name of person giving speech] led [name of affected audience] to [description of change ignited by speech].

Model Thesis

Here is an example of a thesis statement based on the template. This thesis statement would be part of the introduction to a rhetorical analysis of Martin Luther King's "I Have A Dream" speech:

> "While Martin Luther King, Jr.'s 1963 'I have a Dream' speech given at the Lincoln Memorial before thousands of people is memorable for its emotional appeals to pathos, such as the image of black and white children holding hands, it was the carefully framed appeals through logos that offered compelling reasons that helped change the minds of white segregationists."

Published Reading

How the Obama Administration Talks to Black America

Ta-Nehisi Coates

> *Ta-Nehisi Coates is an American journalist who serves as the Senior Editor and blogger for* The Atlantic *magazine. His book* Between the World and Me, *framed as a letter to his 14-year-old son explaining what it means to be black in the United States, won the 2015 National Book Award for Nonfiction, among other prestigious recognitions. He frequently offers argumentative analyses on political rhetoric, including the following piece, originally published in* The Atlantic *on May 20, 2013. In this piece, he synthesizes public quotes from both Michelle and Barack Obama in order to craft a larger argument about the effects of presidential rhetoric on race.*

The first lady went to Bowie State and addressed the graduating class. Her speech was a mix of black history and a salute to the graduates. There was also this:

> But today, more than 150 years after the Emancipation Proclamation, more than 50 years after the end of "separate but equal," when it comes to getting an education, too many of our young people just can't be bothered. Today, instead of walking miles every day to school, they're sitting on couches for hours playing video games, watching TV. Instead of dreaming of being a teacher or a lawyer or a business leader, they're fantasizing about being a baller or a rapper.

And then this:

> If the school in your neighborhood isn't any good, don't just accept it. Get in there, fix it. Talk to the parents. Talk to the

teachers. Get business and community leaders involved as well, because we all have a stake in building schools worthy of our children's promise....

And as my husband has said often, please stand up and reject the slander that says a black child with a book is trying to act white. Reject that.

There's a lot wrong here.

At the most basic level, there's nothing any more wrong with aspiring to be a rapper than there is with aspiring to be a painter, or an actor, or a sculptor. Hip-hop has produced some of the most penetrating art of our time, and inspired much more. My path to this space began with me aspiring to be rapper. Hip-hop taught me to love literature. I am not alone. Perhaps you should not aspire to be a rapper because it generally does not provide a stable income. By that standard you should not aspire to be a writer, either.

At a higher level, there is the time-honored pattern of looking at the rather normal behaviors of black children and pathologizing them. My son wants to play for Bayern Munich. Failing that, he has assured me he will be Kendrick Lamar. When I was kid I wanted to be Tony Dorsett—or Rakim, whichever came first. Perhaps there is some corner of the world where white kids desire to be Timothy Geithner instead of Tom Brady. But I doubt it. What is specific to black kids is that their dreams often don't extend past entertainment and athletics. That is a direct result of the kind of limited cultural exposure you find in impoverished, segregated neighborhoods. Those neighborhoods are the direct result of American policy.

Enacting and enforcing policy is the job of the Obama White House. When asked about policy for African Americans, the president has said, "I'm not the president of black America. I'm the president of all America." An examination of the Obama

Part III   Arguing with Purpose

administration's policy record toward black people clearly bears this out. An examination of the Obama administration's rhetoric, as directed at black people, tells us something different.

Yesterday, the president addressed Morehouse College's graduating class, and said this:

> We know that too many young men in our community continue to make bad choices. Growing up, I made a few myself. And I have to confess, sometimes I wrote off my own failings as just another example of the world trying to keep a black man down. But one of the things you've learned over the last four years is that there's no longer any room for excuses. I understand that there's a common fraternity creed here at Morehouse: "excuses are tools of the incompetent, used to build bridges to nowhere and monuments of nothingness."
>
> We've got no time for excuses—not because the bitter legacies of slavery and segregation have vanished entirely; they haven't. Not because racism and discrimination no longer exist; that's still out there. It's just that in today's hyper-connected, hyper-competitive world, with a billion young people from China and India and Brazil entering the global workforce alongside you, nobody is going to give you anything you haven't earned. And whatever hardships you may experience because of your race, they pale in comparison to the hardships previous generations endured—and overcame.

This clearly is a message that only a particular president can offer. Perhaps not the "president of black America," but certainly a president who sees holding African Americans to a standard of individual responsibility as part of his job. This is not a role Barack Obama undertakes with other communities.

Taking the full measure of the Obama presidency thus far, it is hard to avoid the conclusion that this White House

190

has one way of addressing the social ills that afflict black people—and particularly black youth—and another way of addressing everyone else. I would have a hard time imagining the president telling the women of Barnard that "there's no longer room for any excuses"—as though they were in the business of making them. Barack Obama is, indeed, the president of "all America," but he also is singularly the scold of "black America."

It's worth revisiting the president's comments over the past year in reference to gun violence. Visiting his grieving adopted hometown of Chicago, in the wake of the murder of Hadiya Pendleton, the president said this:

> For a lot of young boys and young men in particular, they don't see an example of fathers or grandfathers, uncles, who are in a position to support families and be held up in respect. And so that means that this is not just a gun issue; it's also an issue of the kinds of communities that we're building. When a child opens fire on another child, there is a hole in that child's heart that government can't fill. Only community and parents and teachers and clergy can fill that hole.

Two months earlier Obama visited Newtown. The killer, Adam Lanza, was estranged from his father and reportedly devastated by his parents' divorce. But Obama did not speak to Newtown about the kind of community they were building, or speculate on the hole in Adam Lanza's heart.

When Barack Obama says that he is "the president of all America," he is exactly right. When he visits black communities, he visits as the American president, bearing with him all our history, all our good works, and all our sins. Among recent sins, the creation of the ghettos of Chicago—accomplished by 20th-century American social policy—rank relatively high.

191

Leaving aside the vague connection between fatherhood and the murder of Hadiya Pendleton. Certainly the South Side could use more responsible fathers. Why aren't there more? Do those communities simply lack men of ambition or will? Are the men there genetically inferior?

No president has ever been better read on the intersection of racism and American history than our current one. I strongly suspect that he would point to policy. As the president of "all America," Barack Obama inherited that policy. I would not suggest that it is in his power to singlehandedly repair history. But I would say that, in his role as American president, it is wrong for him to handwave at history, to speak as though the government he represents is somehow only partly to blame. Moreover, I would say that to tout your ties to your community when it is convenient, and downplay them when it isn't, runs counter to any notion of individual responsibility.

I think the stature of the Obama family—the most visible black family in American history—is a great blow in the war against racism. I am filled with pride whenever I see them: there is simply no other way to say that. I think Barack Obama, specifically, is a remarkable human being—wise, self-aware, genuinely curious and patient. It takes a man of particular vision to know, as Obama did, that the country really was ready to send an African American to the White House.

But I also think that some day historians will pore over his many speeches to black audiences. They will see a president who sought to hold black people accountable for their communities, but was disdainful of those who looked at him and sought the same. They will match his rhetoric of individual responsibility, with the aggression the administration showed to bail out the banks, and the timidity they showed in addressing a foreclosure crisis which devastated black America (again.) They will weigh the rhetoric against an administration whose efforts against

housing segregation have been run of the mill. And they will
match the talk of the importance of black fathers with the
paradox of a president who smoked marijuana in his youth but
continued a drug-war which daily wrecks the lives of black men
and their families. In all of this, those historians will see a dis-
comfiting pattern of convenient race-talk.

I think the president owes black people more than this.
In the 2012 election, the black community voted at a higher
rate than any other ethnic community in the country. Their
vote went almost entirely to Barack Obama. They did this
despite a concerted effort to keep them from voting, and they
deserve more than a sermon. Perhaps they cannot practically
receive targeted policy. But surely they have earned something
more than targeted scorn.

For Reflection

1. Why do you think Coates puts two phrases in quotation marks in
   the following sentence: "Barack Obama is, indeed, the president of
   'all America,' but he also is singularly the scold of 'black America.'"?
2. Why does Coates claim, "I think the stature of the Obama
   family—the most visible black family in American history—is a
   great blow in the war against racism"? How does this high "visibil-
   ity" work to change the rhetoric around race?
3. What does Coates mean when he says that Obama uses "convenient race-talk"?
4. Coates offers a rhetorical analysis of the Obamas' quotes in order
   to construct a larger argument about the effects of their rhetoric on
   America in general. In doing so, how does Coates succeed in meeting the goals of a rhetorical analysis? How does he demonstrate
   his ability to construct a persuasive argument about what works
   and does not work in the Obamas' messages, offering good reasons
   supported by specific examples from the text?

Student Reading

Dan Jacobs wrote the following rhetorical analysis as a first-year college student, analyzing president Lyndon B. Johnson's "We Shall Overcome" speech about racial equality because it significantly influenced his immediate audience (members of Congress) and the American public.

Dan Jacobs

"We Shall Overcome": Passion, Freedom, and Triumph as Americans

United States president Lyndon B. Johnson's 1965 speech to Congress titled "We Shall Overcome" came at a pivotal point in the formation of what the word "freedom" truly stands for in America. The 1960's played host to the driving forces of the civil rights movement: the protests, clashes, and dialogs, the end of segregation, and the enforcement of voting rights for blacks. Thousands took a stand against police, government officials, and their fellow citizens in making sure that their rights were protected.

Johnson's speech was a special address to a joint session of congress on March 15, 1965, following violence that occurred in clashes between police and protest marchers in Selma, Alabama a week previous. In his address he announces the introduction of a bill protecting these rights and appeals to congress to expedite the bill's progress and to join with him in his cause. Many in congress and many in the general public differed in opinion in regards to the situation, but Johnson uses the Selma events as a platform and starting point for his cause to protect the right to vote for blacks and all citizens of America. Johnson appeals to his audience's identity as Americans through patriotism to create a rhetorically successful argument.

Throughout the duration of the 90 minute speech, Johnson thoroughly utilizes the tool of engaging his audience's pathos, their emotions. By approaching the listeners through their emotions towards patriotism and liberty, he is able to find one thing in common which everyone in his audience shares, furthering his push towards greater unity. By comparing the revolutionary battlegrounds of Lexington and Concord, to a more modern place of battle—Selma, Alabama—Johnson also makes a historical connection, evoking emotions of the hurdles America has overcome in the past to become the nation it is now in the present. The obvious point of comparison here is the goal towards which they fight: "the values, and the purposes, and the meaning of our beloved nation." He quotes phrases used in the development of the United States as a union, such as "all men are created equal" and "government by consent of the governed" to further place the modern fight into perspective. He makes sure his audience understands that they reside in a unique point in history, a point where they as a body have been given exclusive power to make great change and that they must use that power wisely.

Johnson then states the facts about what America has produced and proved itself to stand for, thus appealing to the logos, the logical conviction of the listener. Every citizen, no matter their race or origin, is still a citizen to the full extent. Each citizen should have the same rights, with the right to vote pivotal among them. He appeals here not only to congress, but to the entire American people—no matter what laws he passes, if Americans cannot accept this fact, there is nothing even he, their elected president, can do to stop them.

He once again appeals to the patriotism of his audience—addressing this time the unity that we all share with one another. As we are all Americans, it is our duty to support one another. He presents the fight of blacks in America, not only as their fight, but the fight of all Americans. Instead of being an isolated movement, the goal of defining the rights of the citizen is a growing topic. He further says, "It is the effort of American Negros to secure for themselves the full blessings of American life. Their cause must be our cause too. Because it's not just Negros, but really all of us, who must overcome the crippling legacy of bigotry and injustice." He moves on to say, "How many white children have gone uneducated? How many white families have lived in stark poverty? How many white lives have been scarred by fear, because we've wasted our energy and our substance to maintain the barriers of hatred and terror?" Once again, the subject is unity. We all are suffering together and together we as Americans must join and fight, just as in the revolutionary war, just as the blacks marched in Alabama. The questions have been raised, but still wait to be answered.

Johnson begins his address by saying, "I speak tonight for the dignity of man and the destiny of democracy," Johnson does his job well, and accurately presents to Americans exactly what position in history they reside in, and the importance of the events taking place in their towns, their states, their country, and the world. Rhetorically, President Johnson's argument conveys its purpose quite successfully, addressing his audience's concerns, trust, and conviction towards the matter at hand. As this is a speech, however, the presentation is equally as important as the words themselves. Though he speaks slowly, his voice resounds heavily throughout the chamber with a deep passion for what he speaks of. Johnson shows his audience that he has taken this cause as his own and extends his passion for his argument to each and every person whether actually in attendance or simply listening to the audio of his speech.

Today we are once again contemplating the same question that America has fought to promote dialog of for decades—what is our definition of freedom? This portion of American history was one pivotal step in the right direction. Johnson tells congress that it is their duty to carry out this work, and that passing this bill will be one of the most, if not the most important decision they will make in their career. Soon after, this bill was in fact passed and its influence has redefined the last half century of American life. As Johnson says in closing, "God will not favor everything that we do. It is rather our duty to divine his will. But I cannot help believing that he truly understands and that He really favors the undertaking that we begin here to-night." Though his audience consists of hundreds of representatives from all across the diverse regions of the United States, Johnson knows that the one identity they all share is that they can all call themselves an American. While not all Americans may share the same morals, beliefs or views, we all agree by attributing ourselves Americans that we and all of humankind are granted certain inalienable rights which cannot be taken away and are entitled to our rights of life, liberty, and the pursuit of happiness. By appealing

to that shared patriotism Johnson is able to
access the emotions of the listener and thus
create a successful rhetorical argument.

Works Cited

Johnson, Lyndon B. "We Shall Overcome." United States Congress.
    United States Capitol Building, Washington, D.C. 15 Mar. 1965.

For Reflection

1. How would you go about determining whether or not this speech
   is significant enough for this assignment? For example, how would
   you judge whether it impacted members of Congress at the time?
2. If you were reviewing this as a draft, what rhetorical elements would
   you suggest the author address in addition to what you see here?
3. To what extent does Dan focus on the rhetorical construction of
   the text and not the content itself?
4. What about the speech and the rhetorical context makes it seem
   relevant to audiences today?

RHETORICAL ANALYSIS: THE WRITING PROCESS

In the following section, we use Dan's notes and drafts to examine his
thinking about the writing process.

Analyze the Assignment

The title of this assignment, "Rhetorical Analysis of a Speech," gives
you some important clues about it: you are to *analyze* the *rhetoric* of
a text. So the object of your analysis is the rhetoric of the text; that
is, how it was put together and delivered. This is not the same as

analyzing the issue the text discusses. Your opinion about that isn't part of this assignment. Here, you are asked to look instead at how the text makes meaning and whether or not it was successful in its attempt. A strong rhetorical analysis will show that you've looked at the primary text carefully to see how it works.

Dan created a new folder on his computer for this project, labeling the folder "Rhetorical Analysis of a Speech." Next, he created a new document in that folder, named it "Assignment journal," and recorded his preliminary ideas and questions this way:

Assignment Analysis

- The action verbs in the assignment are
  1. "Determine" a "significant" speech
  2. "Consider," "address," and "analyze" the elements of the text
  3. "Identify" the main claim
  4. "Introduce" evidence and examples
  5. "Focus" on certain rhetorical pieces
  6. "Acknowledge" sources in my argument
  7. "Cite" sources in works cited page
- The audience is my instructor and classmates as we do peer review. If I choose a speech they have likely heard before, I'll need to find an interesting angle to tell them something original.
- I'd like to go to the library and research the context of the speech I choose. The assignment says I don't have to do that, but I like knowing the history around an event. I will have to keep track of the sources for my works cited.
- I'm going to ask for a model of this assignment so I know what it looks like in the end. I'm clear on the "quantifiable" criteria—word count, MLA style, and those details—but I'd like to read another student's rhetorical analysis before I do my own so I have a better sense of the "qualitative" criteria. How do I make sure it's not boring or too report-y?

Plan: Organizing the Process

Your instructor will set your deadlines and paper length for this assignment. Once you know those two critical pieces of information, you can map your schedule, giving yourself plenty of time to read and annotate the text thoroughly early in the process as that primary text is the engine for your work in this assignment. Dan opened up his project folder and added the following text to his assignment journal:

Schedule

I have 3 weeks total from the day we were given the assignment to the day it's due. A "complete draft" is due in the second week for in-class peer review. I want to work with a Writing Center tutor before the peer review so I can get more feedback. If my peer review tells me I have a lot of work to do, I can go back to the Writing Center after, early week 3 before the final draft is due. So my plan is:

WEEK 1: Make an appointment at the Writing Center for Week 2. Use the "American Rhetoric" website to explore possible speeches and select one quickly that meets the criteria of being "significant" in history. Read the primary text at least twice and take notes. Start brainstorming: list possible ideas and draft a paragraph on most promising ideas. Go to the library to find historical materials that will help me understand why this speech was given.

WEEK 2: Take brainstorming ideas to session at the Writing Center to narrow my focus. Draft entire paper for peer review in class. Draft questions to ask my peers.

WEEK 3: Revise based on peer review comments and advice from the instructor in class. Have instructor read my introduction if possible to make sure my thesis statement meets the assignment expectations. Reread the primary text and do more research if necessary. Turn paper in!

Question: Exploring Issues

One of the first items on your plan to write the rhetorical analysis of a speech should be to find a good primary source to analyze, one that has enough depth to give you fodder for analysis, one that stirs you in some way, one that has had significant influence on society.

The following databases of compelling speeches are excellent resources:

- TED Talks—TED talks generally focus on technology, entertainment, and design (TED). Presenters are challenged to "give the talk of their lives" in under 18 minutes. You will find a wide range of dynamic talks from renowned "thinkers" (scholars) and "doers" (practitioners) and from young people in a variety of fields. Many talks are multimodal, incorporating video, visuals, and audio.
- *American Rhetoric*—This website archives hundreds of memorable speeches from American history, and from political and popular events worldwide presented in English. It also includes significant speeches from entertainment, including movies. The site offers video, audio, and text when available.

There is no formula for selecting the perfect speech to analyze. Different types of texts will simply require a different approach to your analysis. After Dan explored the resources at TED and *American Rhetoric*, he added both his initial responses as well as ideas for how to proceed to his assignment journal:

- I got totally caught up watching different speeches on TED and American Rhetoric. I was all over the place listening to new talks on science and old talks from history. I emailed five of them to my dad. I made myself stop and sleep on it. When I woke up the next morning, the speech that stayed with me wasn't one of the new ones, it was one I had heard before: Lyndon B. Johnson's "We Shall

Overcome." Some of his lines were still ringing in my ears and that means he made a strong impression on me. I want to know why, so that's the primary text I will use.

- I don't have to use other sources for this assignment, but I want to make sure I have all my historical facts right. I know I'm a visual learner, so I think it will help me to see pictures of the crowds and to know more about the event surrounding this speech. There has to be a lot out there and I better find it if I'm going to write about such a popular speech.

Read: Strategies for Reading in Research

Critical reading means trying to understand what the rhetor (the author and deliverer of the speech) is attempting to communicate by asking key questions about the text's weaknesses. What does it fail to say? Does it use the strongest reasons and evidence? Does it address opposing viewpoints adequately? You know you have done a good job of reading critically if you can agree with an author's thesis but still thoroughly critique the argument as it is written. Critical reading is the basis for rhetorical analysis. Dan saved a transcript of Johnson's "We Shall Overcome" speech as a Word document and used Track Changes tools to annotate the speech with his responses.

I speak tonight for the dignity of man and the destiny of Democracy. I urge every member of both parties, Americans of all religions and of all colors, from every section of this country, to join me in that cause. At times, history and fate meet at a single time in a single place to shape a turning point in man's unending search for freedom. So it was at Lexington and Concord.

Powerful opening line, uses alliteration and strong adjectives.

203

So it was a century ago at Appomattox. So it was last week in Selma, Alabama. There, long suffering men and women peacefully protested the denial of their rights as Americans. Many of them were brutally assaulted. One good man—a man of God—was killed.

> Repetition of phrase: "So it was" shows that he is creating an analogy from history to show that what was happening then is like what happened before.

There is no cause for pride in what has happened in Selma. There is no cause for self-satisfaction in the long denial of equal rights of millions of Americans. But there is cause for hope and for faith in our Democracy in what is happening here tonight. For the cries of pain and the hymns and protests of oppressed people have summoned into convocation all the majesty of this great government—the government of the greatest nation on earth. Our mission is at once the oldest and the most basic of this country--to right wrong, to do justice, to serve man. In our time we have come to live with the moments of great crises. Our lives have been marked with debate about great issues, issues of war and peace, issues of prosperity and depression.

> This phrase would have been hard to follow if you were just listening to the speech, and the word "majesty" seems too royal to me.

> Language excludes women.

I printed out the speech and took notes right on the text, underlining the lines that I thought were strong and the ones I thought people in his audience might have had a problem with at that time. It's a long speech, so I thought it was important to find a couple of really important lines, find patterns in the words and themes he used, and then think about the overall feeling I got from the text. I kept track of important points by flagging them in the margins as I read. Hearing the speech also helped me know what Johnson thought was important, where his voice told the audience to pay attention through things like pauses and increased volume or a change in pace.

I played the "believing game" to see what works, and I played the "doubting game" to really question the text. I was glad to have to do that because Johnson is known to be such a strong communicator that I probably wouldn't have thought about criticizing his work if I hadn't been asked to look at it from both of these angles. I'm going to use that strategy in the future—it reminds me that even good writers can be better. They don't always make it easy on their audience.

Invent: Take Note and Create

Watch or listen to the speech, read it, then listen and read again. Record your reactions using both close textual annotation and open note taking techniques. What surprises you? What angers you? What seems off-track or irrelevant? Where did the text lose your interest? Dan opened his marked-up critical reading of "We Shall Overcome," scrolled to the bottom, and created a chart to record his thoughts about what worked especially well (or not so well) in the speech:

I created a chart to help organize my thoughts around both positive and negative reactions to the speech.

TABLE 16.1   WORKS, DOESN'T WORK, NOT SURE CHART

Works	Doesn't Work	Not Sure
Powerful opening line, uses alliteration and strong adjectives: "I speak tonight for the dignity of man and the destiny of democracy."	This phrase would have been hard to follow if you were just listening to the speech, and the word "majesty" seems too royal to me: "For the cries of pain and the hymns and protests of oppressed people have summoned into convocation all the majesty of this great government."	I hear the biblical reference here. Today, a President has to be careful about religious references, but maybe that was more acceptable to the audience then: "For with a country as with a person, 'What is a man profited, if he shall gain the whole world, and lose his own soul?'"
Second paragraph: Repetition of phrase: "So it was" shows that he is creating an analogy from history to show that what was happening then is like what happened before.	I don't agree with this claim, and others at that time might not have either, so that challenges his ethos: "This was the first nation in the history of the world to be founded with a purpose."	I had to read this a couple times before I understood what it meant, but the examples that follow do help clarify: "Every device of which human ingenuity is capable has been used to deny this right."
This repetition [parallelism] builds perfectly to that important claim: "There is no Negro problem. There is no Southern problem. There is no Northern problem. There is only an American problem."	This repetition makes it more about Johnson than anyone else—that could have offended politicians who also wanted to be credited for these successes: "I want to be the President who helped to feed the hungry and to prepare them to be tax-payers instead of tax-eaters. I want to be the President who helped the poor to find their own way and who protected the right of every citizen to vote in every election."	Gendered language. He has been referring only to men until this line, when he also mentions women. It made me wonder if he should have been talking about the specific challenges for women all along: "Allow men and women to register and vote whatever the color of their skin."

Arrange: Prioritize, Organize, Outline

In writing a rhetorical analysis, your paragraphs are likely to be organized around individual examples or clusters of related examples from the text. For example, if you wanted to argue as your thesis that in his "I Have a Dream" speech Martin Luther King, Jr. develops a sense of kairotic urgency through his reference to time, you might find several places in his speech where he refers to time and explore each one in detail in separate paragraphs. If this were instead one of three ways you were going to establish urgency, then you might explore them all more briefly in one paragraph. The accumulation of so many examples would provide compelling evidence. (See Chapter 11, "Arrange: Prioritize, Organize, Outline.")

Dan opened his assignment journal and wrote:

Right now, these are the key ideas that stand out to me and can become an outline for the paper:

- The recent violence in Selma is important to the rhetorical context—Johnson highlights this and I should too.
- Patriotism and freedom are common American values—Johnson wants to emphasize things everyone can agree on.
- Americans are also united by history and by the wars they have fought to protect those values. That is similar to the violence—not a war, but comparable—happening in the South at this time.
- Again, the idea of unity is important, so Johnson even talks about whites who live in poverty and need support from their government as well.
- Pathos is strong when he draws on historical and current examples. Logos comes out when he talks about sticking to what our constitution says we value but in practice we aren't supporting. Ethos seems less important for me to discuss because it's so obvious that his voice is important: he's the President of the United States talking to a joint session of Congress.

Draft: Introduction, Body, Conclusion

With so many options available on how to do a rhetorical analysis of a speech, it's important to let readers know right away which approach you're taking. Let readers know to what extent you'll analyze the context, the written text, and the performative text of the speech. Introduce key rhetorical terms you're using and give us a sense of your approach—are you looking at the whole speech or narrowing your focus to a specific theme or area of the text?

It is also important to establish early on that the speech you've chosen fits the criteria of the assignment. It asks that you look at a "significant" speech—give evidence that this speech fits that expectation. (See Chapter 12, "Draft: Introduction, Body, Conclusion.")

Introduction

Do not assume that the importance of the text you have chosen is self-evident. Readers need to get a sense of why you care about this in the first paragraph so that they can care too. By the end of the first paragraph, readers should know your answer to the questions, "So what?" and "Who cares?" And they should care enough to want to read on. In the "Outline Ideas" section of his assignment journal, Dan noted:

How do I summarize the Civil Rights Movement? That's hard, but I think I have to come right out and explain the context for this speech in the introduction to show how it was given at such a critical time. I also need to assume that my readers know enough about this that I don't have to give a lot of details.

Body

A key consideration for the body of the text of a rhetorical analysis is the ratio of summary to analysis. You want to set up the text and explain its context and reception to some extent, but you must leave ample room for analysis so that summary doesn't overtake the argument. In an argument such as a rhetorical analysis that does not require outside sources (other than the text you're analyzing), support comes from relevant, specific examples in the text. If you find yourself making claims without support from examples that demonstrate your point exactly, then you must return to the text to find supporting examples. If you cannot find worthy examples from the text, it might be time to concede that your claim is unwarranted and must be revised. In the "Outline ideas" section of his assignment journal, Dan jotted down some preliminary thoughts about the body of his analysis:

This is such a long speech that I can't summarize the whole thing and I don't want to get caught in any one part of it either. I'm going to stick with those key points I outlined and go into detail in just a few spots of the speech. I think I'll organize my points in the order they come up in the speech. We are allowed to use some outside sources if we want, but I don't think it's necessary. I think my readers and I have enough common knowledge about the historical context that I don't need to pull in other sources. This speech is also so long and so full that I think it would detract from the close analysis I want to do.

Conclusion

In this assignment, you are analyzing the construction of the text, including the strength of its support. You are not analyzing the issue of the text from your own perspective. Remember, you are assessing the success of the argument the author actually makes. Dan also recorded a possible approach to his conclusion:

To show how important this speech is, I want to show how even though we aren't still in a violent fight for Civil Rights in the United States, we do still fight for "freedom" and struggle for unity. Johnson's words about remembering what unites us still ring true today, so I want to show that as I pull things together in the conclusion.

Revise: Strategies for Re-seeing

Rethinking the rhetorical analysis will happen when you talk to others, when you learn more about the context of the speech, and when you just keep reading that primary text carefully. Imagine yourself in that original audience. What might have been on your mind? How might you have reacted then compared to now? Dan returned to his assignment journal to update his progress:

I took my outline of key points and chart on "What Works" to the Writing Center and the tutor there helped me prioritize my points. Actually, she first made me explain the assignment and summarize the speech because she hadn't heard it. At first, I thought that was a little annoying because I just wanted to start writing, but it was actually pretty helpful to make sure I remembered what I should do. I hadn't thought about what rhetorical terms I might use until I told her I had to include some.

Review: By Peers and Experts

Solicit as much input from others as possible on this assignment to get perspectives you might not see on your own. For example, some people notice tone right away given specific word choices while others are more cued in to such aspects as authority of sources cited. Dan returned to his assignment journal to update his progress:

> The peer review in class was helpful in get-
> ting other perspectives. They confirmed that
> I shouldn't do any more on the historical
> context—I should get to the text since it has
> so many good lines and ideas to explore. They
> said I should talk more about ethos, though,
> and feel like I shouldn't talk about that just
> to talk about it. You should only look at the
> terms that really give you something inter-
> esting to analyze. My group members had all
> chosen more recent speeches, so they asked
> why I wanted to do this one. That made me
> think I should definitely use the conclusion to
> explain why this speech is still relevant today.

Proofread and Submit

Your rhetorical analysis is likely to use many examples from the primary text, so make sure that all the direct quotations are properly
cited in text and in your works cited page. When Dan updated his
assignment journal, he noted:

> I know I have a problem with run-on sen-
> tences, so I'm going to look for those. I'm also
> going back to the Writing Center because
> I've looked at this so many times I don't

211

think I can pick out the errors anymore—
they can look at the main points and help me
with some of those grammar issues now that
I'm in the polishing stage.

WHAT HAPPENS NEXT?

Rhetorical analysis gets you started on most writing about current
issues because it helps you understand where other stakeholders
stand on these issues and why. Once you have read widely (through
research) and deeply (through rhetorical analysis), you can consider
addressing those conversations in the civic domain, perhaps writing
letters to a local news website, or writing as service on behalf of nonprofits. Rhetorical analysis will lead you to skills in producing your
own persuasive texts.

OFFICE HOURS ➤ Honor Codes

When you begin collaborating in the university environment, you
should first know the rules of engagement. You probably discussed
the honor code and maybe even signed a pledge at orientation.
Now that you're writing, all those details about academic honesty
become real. *Who* can you talk to and *how* can you work with them
regarding assignments for class? We can't learn in isolation, so
what's an acceptable level of communication and collaboration on
your writing and research?

   Each university makes its own statement on these issues and
it is essential that you follow—*exactly*—the guidelines outlined at
your institution. Your honor code is likely to address the following
issues: plagiarism, reuse of your own work, presenting someone
else's work as your own, and cheating. Your honor code is likely
to outline the role of students and faculty when a violation of the

---

code is suspected, taking you step-by-step through the process and consequences.

To understand more fully what it means to write with academic honesty as you work with others, conduct a rhetorical analysis of the honor code for your university. How are ethos, pathos, and logos at work in this document? What aesthetic, practical, and ethical reasons does it give in its argument? What does the document tell you about the knowledge, skills, and disposition the university wants to instill in you? How do you see the honor code referenced in all your classes? Is there any variation across different classes about how this is addressed and what is acceptable? Doing this rhetorical analysis of such a key document will help you understand the motives and purpose behind your school's academic honor code.

CHAPTER seventeen

Narration: Composing from Personal Experience

Storytelling is the heart of narrative argument. Narrative arguments provide a detailed picture of a few representative people or events. By zooming in to understand a singular personal experience, readers get a visceral sense of the author's argument. They understand the author's message not through the quantity of objective points but through the detailed quality of specific examples. If those specific examples are reliable and relevant, readers can infer meaning that extends well beyond that specific example. Good narrative arguments inform and persuade by providing a vivid example we can trust.

While narrative argument can be the primary frame of an argument—often propelling the genre of creative non-fiction, for example—it is also a common strategy used to support other argument types, such as definition argument. Imagine, for example, an argument defining food insecurity in which narration is used to follow a single child through one volatile week of finding food. Narrative arguments help connect with the audience through the depth of specific examples.

STRATEGIES FOR NARRATIVE ARGUMENTS

A narrative argument can use many of the same literary techniques used by novelists, short story writers, or poets to help others experience an event and its actors, but both its context and content are factual and true. Consider the following strategies when writing a narrative argument.

Strategy 1: Acknowledge Point-of-View

Narration happens in first-person (e.g., "*I* will never forget the smell of the Toyota Corolla station wagon *my* daughters and *I* lived in for 16 months") or third-person (e.g., "*Carla* said *she* hoped that *her* children would remember life before *they* lost *their* home"). A story's point-of-view immediately signals something about its reliability to readers. That something, though, is different for different readers. Some readers find first-person narrative the most reliable form of storytelling because the person who had the experience is sharing it directly. Others argue that we have a limited perspective on our own experiences and therefore external witnesses bring more objectivity to understanding critical events. This raises tensions: Who is entitled to tell a story? How does the story change when told from different points of view? Chapter 28, "Working with Human Sources," will help you think further about the ethics of telling other people's stories.

Good writers acknowledge the bias readers might have about the point-of-view used in a narrative and adjust accordingly. For example, to bolster your ethos and credibility when writing a first-person narrative, you can include the voice of others in paraphrases or direct quotation to help validate your storytelling. If you are writing in third-person, you can include first-person direct quotes to help validate your storytelling. Including multiple perspectives is one way to increase reader confidence in the reliability of your narrative.

Strategy 2: Expand the Scale: Allegory and Empathy

Many narratives work as allegory. In an allegory, one story is taken to represent and/or mean something larger. The value is not only in understanding that one experience but in understanding how that one experience stands for a larger body of experiences and meaning. In "Measuring the Immeasurable," for example, Phil Garrity narrates the example of a sick, impoverished man sharing his meager meal with Garrity. The lesson is not just about that one man but is allegorical in the sense that it teaches us about the dignity of all people who want the right not just to be served but also to serve others from what little they have. We might expect Garrity, the medical expert, to heal, but it is the patient who is most powerful in this narrative.

Empathy is an exchange of human experience from the one who experienced it directly to the one who wants to receive and understand the experience of others. Some say empathy is what sets humans apart from species that do not transfer knowledge and emotions through story. Others say empathy can be overstated, causing some people to claim others' experience as their own in ways that exploit or manipulate the original narrator. See Chapter 28, "Working with Human Sources," for more on the ethics of narrating other people's stories. Good writers care for the people they represent in their writing, striving to separate fact from interpretation in their storytelling.

Strategy 3: Get Dramatic: Organize the Plot Creatively

Texts written primarily as narrative argument can use a creative organizational structure. The organizing elements might revolve around dramatic plot pivots that make the story's action rise and fall: exposition (explaining the setting), conflict, turning point, and resolution. The point of the narrative argument—its thesis—might not be clear until the resolution offered in the final paragraphs of the argument. Or the thesis might never be stated but only inferred through close reading.

Strategy 4: Appeal to the Senses

Readers connect with narrative arguments when they get a glimpse of the experience you narrate. Descriptive writing that animates the senses can help readers see, hear, taste, touch, and feel the experience as it unfolded. If readers feel as you might have felt during that experience, they might better understand your response to it—and your argument will be more effective

ELEMENTS OF NARRATIVE ARGUMENTS

The two core elements of good narrative arguments are reliability and relevance. For a story to be more than entertainment—for it to inform and persuade us through the entertainment of narrative style—readers must trust the story and see how it relates to them and to the world.

Element 1: Reliability

Good narrative arguments tell stories that readers trust as authentic. Authenticity is connected to ethos. If the author seems trustworthy, readers will allow themselves to be transported into the story and mindset of the writer despite the distance of time, geography, gender, or other factors that could prevent connection. Likewise, if the narrative is all claims and interpretation about the experience without tangible, more objective descriptions of the people or events being analyzed, readers have no touchstone of truth from which to consider the writer's representation of events.

Element 2: Relevance

For a narrative argument to transcend its particular story, the narrative must resonate with readers and allow them to connect this story with their own stories. This connection both validates the story's reliability and shows that it has meaning beyond the individual. In this case, story is at the service of the argument. It serves to show that this is perhaps allegorical, an individual story that represents a larger narrative that teaches us something important.

IN PROCESS: NARRATION

Project: Autoethnography

Objectives

- Understand when narrative argument is an appropriate persuasive strategy.
- Practice selecting events that are relevant, compelling, and scalable to further a specific claim or argument.
- Study literary techniques and tropes that can be employed in narrative argument storytelling.
- Develop descriptive writing skills through careful word choice and attention to sensory appeal.
- Practice writing in which the main point of the argument might be more implied through how an event is recounted rather than delivered overtly in a thesis statement.

Description

We all have different values, experiences, and practices that express our culture. This becomes exceedingly clear when cultures collide in the college setting. Practices that seem natural to you in the home domain might seem contested in the academic domain. College is a place where students can explore and engage those different cultures. It is also a place to articulate your own cultural experiences as a mode of self-examination and discovery. The autoethnography assignment is designed to help you describe, analyze, and share an aspect of your own culture with others.

An autoethnography is a story you tell to explain an aspect of your own culture to others. Think of culture in a broad sense, including any group with a common goal, interest, and/or background. Some groups to consider include sports, religion, recreation, hobbies, family, work, arts, music, race, gender, nationality, disease, housing, or criminal record. Identify an aspect of your life that connects you with one group of people but separates you from others. Your explanation should include objective narration describing an aspect of your culture as well as analysis about that cultural practice that makes an argument about it through rhetorics of praise or blame, celebration or critique. You might be proud of this cultural practice and/or you might see problems with the expression of that culture in society. Good autoethnographies are thorough and honest in their depiction and assessment. In the academic domain, autoethnography is an increasingly important tool of inquiry in sociology, communication, education, and health sciences, among other disciplines.

This narration should move beyond reporting fact-by-fact about your culture. Instead, it should try to *show* that culture through storytelling. Storytelling in narrative argument borrows techniques from storytelling in fiction, but it is different in that it relies on factual, true events and people rather than imagined ones.

The narration in your ethnography should demonstrate both reliability and relevance. Readers must trust that your descriptions and explanations are authentic, and they must learn something more than the particular from your narration—they must see that it is representative of others and has bearing and meaning beyond your individual reflection.

Here are some possible ways to approach this assignment:

- Show a scene or scenes of your culture in contact with others, with either a positive or negative outcome (see student writer Geraldine Mukumbi's "The Elephant Ear Memory," in this chapter).
- Explore common stereotypes about your culture by countering them with specific examples that challenge those perspectives.
- Show your culture through the eyes of an outsider.

Thesis Template

Writers have considerable latitude on how they convey the main point of the argument in this genre, but here is one possible approach:

> While this *[event/incident/example]* is common in my *[family/club/team/church/city]* it might surprise others because *[insert reason for surprise by outsiders]*. By describing this practice, I intend to *[insert reason for sharing this story at this time to this audience—what you want them to understand or do based on your narrative argument]*.

Model Thesis

Here is an example of a thesis that uses first person point of view while also introducing a skeptical character who might represent the audience. It also uses imagery to get the audience thinking metaphorically about the "world's weeds":

> "My friend Brad kept asking why I get up at 7:00 a.m. every Saturday instead of sleeping in or playing sports, so I finally convinced him to join me at the community garden so that he could see how the people and plants energize me, make me feel part of the world, make me feel that the world's weeds can be conquered if we all just commit to showing up."

Published Reading

Measuring the Immeasurable

Phil Garrity

> *Phil Garrity, 25, joined the Partners In Health staff in Boston in 2011 after volunteering with Socios En Salud, PIH's sister organization in Peru. As program coordinator on the Monitoring, Evaluation, and Quality (MEQ) team, he helps measure and*

220

evaluate PIH programs to improve quality of care and demon-strate the success of the PIH model.

In August 2012, Garrity was unexpectedly diagnosed with osteosarcoma, an aggressive and rare bone cancer, and began an eight-month treatment program that included surgery and chemotherapy. As he transformed from a servant of the sick to a patient himself, he learned to value an underappreciated aspect of service, which he terms "non-doing."

Garrity wrote the following reflection, which he read aloud to Partners In Health staff on May 15, 2013, the day his medical team declared him cancer-free, as a message of thanks for their accompaniment throughout his journey.

Over the past two years volunteering and working for PIH, I've been lucky enough to take part in a movement to integrate data-driven quality improvement into our operations. Much of my team's work involves distilling an often nebulous web of people and activities down into a conceptual framework that reflects what is actually happening on the ground. We map out work protocols and data flows, we select process and outcome indicators, we create systems to collect, analyze, and visualize the information—all to gauge three simple but key aspects of our programs: What are we doing? How well are we doing it? How can we make it better?

But without drowning in the details, I'll synthesize all this by saying that much of our work and my role here at PIH con-tinues to place particular emphasis (as it rightly should) on an intrinsic part of serving the poor: the doing. My mind is often focused on what protocols our staff are implementing, how many home visits our community health workers have com-pleted this month, how often our HIV patients have been seen in clinic. You may preoccupy yourself with such questions as how many letters have been sent, web pages designed, meetings scheduled, donors courted, supplies procured, services delivered, money raised. And, logically, we can't know what's being done unless we measure it. Because, as one MEQ site leader once remarked, "If it's not documented, it didn't happen."

But this is where we reach a dilemma. To simply measure the value and quality of our work by the numbers, the performance levels, or the concrete investments of time, energy, and resources seems to neglect another invaluable, but often hidden, dimension of this work: the non-doing. This concept may baffle those of us more accustomed to the rational side of life, for so much of our culture values and rewards the practical and pragmatic, the logical and analytical. The idea of "non-doing" is easily equated to "not doing anything"—nothing more than a futile exercise and utter waste of time. But allow me to reflect on a few personal experiences that have transformed this irrational concept into a mysterious truth, one that I've come to find resonates less with my mind and perhaps more with my spirit.

I'm drawn back to my time volunteering with a local nonprofit in Cusco, Peru, in the months preceding my internship with Socios En Salud. A few days each week, I'd help out at a nursing home for the destitute run by an order of kind yet stern nuns who led by rigid example and hardly ever by word. Feigning competence, I'd be handed a pot and ladle and I would feed the ancianos; handed a bottle of ointment, I'd rub it on their itchy legs; handed a pair of clippers, I'd trim their overgrown toenails—all of this often done in total silence, even lathering and shaving the old men's faces, eight of whom were blind. Their quiet gratitude for something so simple and seemingly trivial astounded me then and perhaps more so today as I look back and wonder what it all meant.

At the time, I was beginning to delve into questions that would serve me well in Lima and later in Boston: What were we really trying to achieve here? What were our goals and how close or far were we from reaching them? The long hours of just sitting with these old people, hearing their stories, tending to them in what small ways I could—it seemed nice enough, but was it doing anything of real value, at least as I understood it then? My mind would drift to hypotheticals somewhere beyond the confines of that small, quiet refuge. Shouldn't I be saving children from starvation, protecting refugees from mortal danger, pulling this country out of poverty and into the 21st century? After all, I had come here to rescue people from their lot, to save helpless victims from suffering and injustice. This place seemed so stagnant, these people so quiet and inert. What was I doing here?

Early one morning, we found a frail old man had fallen and broken his hip in the middle of the night. His groans and whimpers suggested he had been without pain relief for hours, and he needed to get to the hospital. We placed him on a wooden board, loaded him into the church's van, and were off. I rode alongside him, anxious yet keenly aware of my inability to do much of anything for the poor man. Once there, it pained me to see him relegated to a corner of a busy emergency room where he simply had to wait his turn to be seen. Hours went by and I sat near him, wallowing in the helplessness that I now shared with him. What could I do? I felt that I had failed to be the protector, the helper, the healer—not for an entire country, but even for this one feeble man.

Our driver, a seasoned caretaker from the nursing home, came in with some bread and juice for the man, who silently accepted the gift and began nibbling away, partly concealed underneath the sheets draped over his stretcher. I sat and watched him intently with a mixture of exhaustion and pity as he littered himself with crumbs and peered out at me, eyes gleaming. It was then that something miraculous happened: the old man

223

broke his bread roll in half and stretched out his hand toward mine. An acute sense of surprise and embarrassment came over me, and at first I refused his offer, insisting that he eat it, for surely he needed it more than I. But my feeble attempts to decline the gift were wholeheartedly dismissed as he pushed the bread into my hand, motioning me to eat. And so I did, me looking bewildered and humbled, he looking quite pleased to share his meal with a near stranger.

Moments like these continue to deepen my understanding of what it means to embrace the non-doing. It's come to mean being brave enough to disarm myself, to set aside my intellectual firepower and self-protective shields, and to enter into another's chaos—not to do for them, but to simply be with them. It takes courage to sit in that silence, often empty-handed, and humbly accept the lesson that that feeble man so beautifully demonstrated that day: that I am as much the patient as he is the healer. That he is not a broken machine idly waiting to be fixed by the "non-broken," the "privileged," the "fortunate" among us. I believe that those we intend to serve have bread to offer us every day—humble reminders that we are co-creators in the promotion of life, gentle invitations to discard our pity and crawl down into the pit with another. In these precious moments, we're able to see our shared vulnerability as humans and to simply open ourselves to it, perhaps without much of any real hope of fixing anything in that moment or hour or day.

Beyond all of the things we do to act in service for the poor—delivering medical supplies, building health systems, strengthening human capacity—I've come to believe that there is something far more powerful in simply being in service with those in need. We might consider this other dimension of our work a ministry of presence—one that underlies and encapsulates all of our tangible efforts to console, to palliate, to rebuild in the face of disease and distress. I would argue that this is our strategic advantage among those in the vast arena of development work: that we do not walk away when things appear impractical, unfeasible, or futile. We stay, to perhaps accept defeat again and again, if only to show the world that the people we serve are worth more than the steps they may gain or lose on their path to a more dignified life. That we ourselves are worth more than our successes or failures on our path to building a more just world.

I see more clearly now how all my dissecting questions obscured the real meaning in those quiet gestures at the nursing home. Our collective attempts to concretize an abstract world—to understand the mechanics of material privation, to design interventions and harness resources that achieve a positive and quantifiable effect on the lives of the poor—can create the illusion that fixing is our only aim, that we must constantly be doing if we are to succeed. We can believe that if we can't show progress, then none has been made. And so we easily fall into the trap of making systems and machines out of countries, communities, and individuals—broken devices that only we can fix.

But real solidarity, true compassion, as I've come to discover through lived experience these past eight months, is grounded in something far deeper than our displays of technical prowess or standard notions of progress. It evades our attempts to capture its value with metrics and analytics, and perhaps for good reason. I believe it's revealed through an earnest and humble kind of love, one that neither feigns strength nor fears weakness. It can simply sit with another in the silence, not feeling frantic to fill it with words or deeds. It has the courage to look into the darkness of our finitude—both of our bodies and of our ambitions—which we all face, not just the sick. It can trust in the value of non-doing, of simply being present.

And so I say all of this as a hopeful reminder for each of us to restore a balance between what we do and who we are, being careful to not forget the unconditional value of the latter. Because at our core we are radical love, we are goodness, we are justice—a core that cannot be marred or diluted by all the apathy, cynicism, and resistance the world might throw at it, a world of practicality that tries to convince us that our efforts to transform it will inevitably fall short, that our gestures of good will are in vain, that we have not done enough today. It is from this core of being that we are able to infuse what we do with the goodness that we are—to make possible real healing, both visible and invisible, that often can't be measured.

I thank all of you for helping me to live out this truth and for being who you are, far beyond what you do.

For Reflection

1. What is the "something miraculous" that happens while Garrity waits with an old man with a broken hip in a Peruvian hospital? What dramatic elements and sensory details does he use to describe that scene?
2. How does Garrity define and/or exemplify "real solidarity" and "true compassion"? Describe your own examples and observations of this.
3. How does this narrative build empathy for Garrity and/or the injured man?
4. In what ways does Garrity appear to be a reliable narrator? In what ways does Garrity's story have relevance for you?

Student Reading

Student writer Geraldine Mukumbi comes from Ngezi, a small town in Zimbabwe. Her major was English with a minor in

Africana Studies. She will pursue any career that allows her to dream and create on a daily basis. Her narrative argument, "The Elephant Ear Memory," is a journey through the confusion of being new in a foreign place and coming to terms with the notion of difference. Despite being written out of sheer frustration, it offers a heartwarming perspective on how we grow into ourselves and ultimately takes the reader through one person's journey of becoming comfortable in her own hair.

Geraldine Mukumbi

The Elephant Ear Memory

I had my braids tied back the day I tasted my first elephant ear. This was a period of firsts: first year of college, first Texas State Fair on campus, and my first time breathing American air. I was a freshman in the true sense of the word. But, not everything was new. Small things made me forget that I was so far away from home. There was the sound of laughter that clung to the wind as it cooled down the summer night that reminded me of the streets of Harare. There was the sweet sugary smell that reminded me of local home-made sweets sold on street corners in my hometown. The Texas State Fair was abuzz with familiar energy but my heart was set on trying one new thing. Elephant ears.

A multitude of people stood between me and my first ever elephant ear. It seemed as though the clock was on a go-slow so I eavesdropped on as many conversations as my two ears could let me. Dorm parties, drunken madness, changing majors, and summer experiences. I heard it all. While I relished these stolen stories, I maintained that uninterested look of indifference. I was a casual spectator in a new world, experiencing everything anew. The night was just like any other, calm and uneventful. Till I felt a slight tug on my braids.

I had so many tiny braids spread across my scalp. They were the result of more than twelve hours of patience and adept twisting. Their size and number made people assume that it was impossible to feel any one of them. I could. I felt another tug. I ignored it. The quad was crowded so it had to be an accident. I felt it again and this time I heard the hushed tones behind me as a voice admonished her friend not to touch my braids or "hair" as she referred to it.

"I just want to see if it's her hair or they are extensions," a second voice responded.

"What if she feels it?" the first voice giggled.

A deep feeling of helplessness mixed with anger swept over me like a chill.

"She won't!" the second voice whispered loudly, tugging at yet another braid.

That night I got lost on my way back to my dorm. I also found out after my first bite that elephant ears were made with cinnamon. I hate cinnamon.

My braids were a little frayed at the roots when I realized I had a buffalo wing habit. Taco Bell was my favorite location on campus because they made the best buffalo wings. It was a long wait to get them. An entire eight minutes and thirty-five seconds on good days and two minutes more during weekends. The taste was worth the wait on any day. While I waited, my eyes always gazed right past the display with the cheese sticks and landed on an empty chair in the University Hair Stylists. The salon, with its huge square sign written in blue and white with a wooden trimming, reminded me of salons back home. Open. Airy. Spacious. Inviting.

Hair salons have always been synonymous with friendship and camaraderie. You enter the room and place your hair's fate in the hands of a stranger. It's a place in which you cannot help but make new friends. I always think of two sets of friends when I gaze into the salon. My new friend and my old friends. I met a girl who shares my name and my love for Azonto.[1] We bonded over hair, braids and the fact that English is neither our first nor second language. She never once asked to touch my braids. She had her own. Hers were thicker, longer, and had a dark black color that suited her skin tone and brought out the brown in her eyes. She laughed at me once when I told her that I would go to

---

[1] A popularized dance from Ghana.

229

the University Hair Stylists to get my hair braided. Her laugh had a sad ring to it.

"You need to go to the Multicultural Student Program and Services," she said. "They could give you directions to a place somewhere in South Bend where that could be done."

I wondered what such an important sounding department had to do with something as basic as hair.

I said nothing.

She had been here a year longer than me. She knew how the system worked. She accepted it in her own silent way.

My old friends on the other hand are all loud, budding activists. They believe in challenging anything that can be challenged. If they cannot change a situation they will talk about it relentlessly. They are the type of people who would probably walk over to the salon and demand that someone cornrow their hair just to highlight the injustice of it all. I sometimes wonder how they would respond when asked some of the questions that are constantly thrown at me.

"Can I touch your hair?"

"Do you have electricity in Africa?"

"Can you click for me?"

There is no universal formula or algorithm that can be used to determine how to answer such questions. It's a situation our parents skipped when they taught us about responding to bullies. So some of my friends choose to be passive-aggressive, others tend to be just aggressive. You cannot fault either one. I have a friend whose go-to response is, "Google is free. There is no excuse for your ignorance."

I imagine she raises a fit whenever anyone attempts to demolish her perfectly constructed afro. She believes that no one has a right to exoticize her and treat her in a manner fitting a subject in a petting zoo or a modern day Saartjie Baartman.[2] Like most of my old friends she is self-assured in the midst of uncomfortable conversations that are inspired by prejudice.

I remain a little unsure of how to act. On bad days this uncertainty makes me feel like a coward every time I quietly walk past the salon's blue and white entrance. On good days I believe my silence is a little loud.

My braids have snowflakes in them when I learn to appreciate the solidarity that friendship provides. Everything is white. It's the heart of a midwestern winter and snow covers the earth while the cold wind blows freezing air. I have a lot of friends now. Campus is warmer than it has ever been. The cold wind is taking its toll on my hair so I

---

[2]Baartman was a South African woman who was displayed for her physical features on stages in London and Ireland during the early nineteenth century.

plan a trip to the mall in search of the olive oil that my scalp is craving.

My friends come with me. I do not remember how we met but I recall how we bonded due to our love for real football which everyone calls soccer. We have an obsession with video games and we truly believe our basketball skills will one day take us to the NBA. One of us has a thick accent, another has been called the 'N' word in his dorm more than once, and the last is trying to figure out why everyone assumes she's Haitian. We argue about different things, what diversity does not mean, how to avoid being labeled as "the angry minority," and the thin line between ignorance and racism. Our friendship is strengthened by something bigger. We just get along. It also helps that we all love eating fast food in the early morning after long hours of studying.

The bus approaches. We hold our student ID's as a rite of passage, a demand for acceptance. We sit fairly close to the back of the bus. I would have liked to sit at the very back but there is a middle-aged man occupying the seat. He seems to know the woman sitting right behind us. There is a familiarity about him that I cannot place. He talks to the woman who just came back from visiting South Africa or just 'Africa' as he calls it.

"Did you see the children with the big bellies?" he asks and I place him immediately. He reminds me of a distant elephant ear memory.

I tug at my braids and try to stare out the window. The man continues a little louder, claiming he has a solution to the poverty problem in America, "Let's all chop up the homeless people and feed them to the hungry Africans."

A deep feeling of helplessness mixed with anger sweeps over me like a chill. This time there is a little less anger. After a while I cannot hear the man anymore. I block out the man and his words the same way I chose to ignore two girls at a Texas State Fair seven months ago. This has become a reflex action each time this country gets a little uncomfortable.

I turn to my friends and they seem not to hear him either. We play family feud. A little too loudly. We smile at each other. A little too hard.

I subconsciously tug at my braids. I think I will wear my braids in ponytails tonight. In the exact same way I did when I was younger. My head divided into two and the tails pulled back right under my ears. I think I will wear my braids in ponytails today.

There is something free about ponytails.

For Reflection

1. Describe Geraldine's narrative organization. How does it serve her purpose?
2. What sensory appeals does Geraldine use to show rather than tell readers about her experiences? To what extent are they successful?

3. What cultural aspects does Geraldine explore? Describe the inherent difference and/or conflict. Is that conflict resolved in any way by the end of the argument?
4. Identify the thesis statement or sentences that seem to share the main idea. What argument does Geraldine make? Is her argument reliable and relevant?

AUTOETHNOGRAPHY: THE WRITING PROCESS

In the following section, we use Geraldine's notes and drafts to examine her thinking about the writing process.

Analyze the Assignment

The title of this assignment, "Narrative Argument: Autoethnography," suggests four key aspects of this assignment:

1. How? The argument must use the *narrative* mode of storytelling.
2. That story must take a position on an issue through *argument*.
3. What? The story must be about or connected closely to the *author* ("auto" indicates the self).
4. The topic of the story and argument must be related to *culture* ("ethnography" indicates the study of specific cultures).

So the story has to have a purpose, a main point that is supported by narrative evidence. The definition of culture presented in the assignment description is broad, so many different types of groups or practices can be used. Good writers will explain how that group or practice constitutes a culture because readers might not be familiar with it. In addition, writers must define the culture being studied and move into narrative argument about the value (positive or negative) of that cultural practice to the author.

Geraldine created a new folder on her computer for this project, labeling the folder "Narrative Argument: Autoethnography." Next, she created a new document in that folder, named it "Assignment journal," and recorded her preliminary ideas and questions under the heading "Assignment analysis":

Assignment Analysis

- The action verbs in the assignment are
  1. "Understand when" to use narrative as a persuasive strategy
  2. "Select" events that suit the purpose
  3. "Employ" literary techniques
  4. "Develop descriptive writing" skills
  5. "Practice implicit writing style"

- The audience is my instructor and classmates as we do peer review. I want to be careful about how personal I get with this audience. The instructor made it clear that the goal is to write an argument, not just tell a shocking or sad story. It has to have a point.
- For this assignment, research might mean that I talk to people who were part of the experience I want to narrate.
- The description invites creativity, so I will take advantage of that opportunity.

Plan: Organizing the Process

Your instructor will set your deadlines and paper length for this assignment. Once you know those two critical pieces of information, you can map your schedule, giving yourself plenty of time to select an appropriate experience to narrate. Geraldine opened up her project folder and added the following text to the "Assignment analysis" section of her assignment journal:

Schedule

I have 3 weeks total from the day we were given the assignment to the day it's due. A "complete draft" is due in the second week for in-class peer review. I want to test my idea out on the instructor to make sure it works for this assignment and it's not too personal or too open-ended. My plan:

> WEEK 1: Meet with my instructor this week to test my idea. Make an appointment at the Writing Center for Week 2.
> WEEK 2: Take brainstorming ideas to session at the Writing Center to narrow my focus. Draft entire paper for peer review in class. Draft questions to ask my peers.
> WEEK 3: Revise based on peer review comments and advice from the instructor in class. Have instructor read my draft if possible to make sure the tone works. Submit assignment.

Question: Exploring Issues

This assignment does not require the use of outside sources, but you can still do two types of research: (1) research on the genre of narrative arguments and autoethnographies to see models that can inspire your work, and (2) research on the cultural practice you want to analyze.

Here are a few online sources for writing that could inspire your autoethnography. These might not follow the exact format and expectations of this assignment, but they give you a sense of the narrative tone and organization that works well in this genre:

- *StoryCorps*
- *This I Believe*
- *Humans of New York (and related "Humans of . . ." projects)*

After Geraldine explored these resources, she also searched for sources on braids and the trend for African American women to go natural in their hairstyles. She found many personal testimonies in blog posts and major news outlets about people asking—or just trying, without even asking first—to touch black women's hair. She added both her initial responses as well as ideas for how to proceed in her assignment journal:

- I looked at *This I Believe* and the *Humans of New York* projects, along with blogs on race and cultural identity. I am interested in stories about race and about international identities as both relate to my identity.
- I see a lot of anger in these stories and I know that my story will express anger and frustration as well. But I want my narrative to have a clear message so that people who haven't experienced what I describe can learn from it and start to notice those moments that happen all the time.

Read: Strategies for Reading in Research

In an assignment such as a narrative argument that does not require outside sources (other than the text of your experience that you are analyzing), support comes from relevant, specific examples from your experience. If you find yourself making claims without support from examples that demonstrate your point exactly, then you must return to the text to find supporting examples. If you cannot find worthy examples from the text, you must concede that your claim is unwarranted and must be revised. Good arguments are informed arguments. When no outside sources are required, it is that much more important that you inform yourself through critical reading and thinking about the primary text.

I did a lot of reading on websites that collect
different personal narratives. I saved the ones

I liked and started to note patterns in how many events they would include. I enjoyed reading them and it got me in the mood to write something that could be published someplace similar.

Invent: Take Note and Create

For this assignment, you'll draw on both creative and critical thinking to generate stories that could work for this assignment, as well as to consider how you might tell them for maximum impact on your audience. Stories can be high impact in many ways, from sharing a deeply spiritual practice (rituals of prayer or celebration) to sharing something odd, quirky, or just plain funny about your cultural practices (maybe your soccer team practices some odd rituals to ensure good luck before a game). However seemingly trivial the action, your goal is to make meaning out of a cultural practice, to explain its importance to readers and help them bridge that cultural gap.

- I have done freewriting before and decided to use that invention approach for this assignment. There are a couple related events swirling in my mind that I have talked to friends about that seem promising for this assignment. I think they are related but I don't know exactly how yet. I am going to set up at least two freewriting sessions where I focus on specific incidents and just write them out for about 10 minutes each. I will describe what happened and let my feelings flow, I won't censor anything. By freewriting about these incidents, I think I will start to make connections as I step back and review the freewriting.

Arrange: Prioritize, Organize, Outline

Now that these narrative scenes are captured in the freewrite, you can see thematic clusters to help determine your argument. Maybe one scene stands out as the perfect vehicle for your thesis. Maybe you see a group of scenes that would work together to make that point. (See Chapter 11, "Arrange: Prioritize, Organize, Outline" for more on creating an effective thesis statement.) Now you can start cutting scenes and ordering the ones that are left in a sequence that works with or against chronological order, depending on how you want to build your dramatic effect.

Geraldine opened her assignment journal and started a new section called "Outline ideas." She wrote:

Right now, these are the key ideas that stand out to me and can become an outline for the paper:

- Hair matters, it's very personal. That's not a small thing to notice as it has historical meaning about power and privilege.
- It's complicated when Americans read my race in a way that I don't necessarily feel or understand.
- I'm wrestling with racial and political identities given my international status; again, I seem to experience those identities in a different way than Americans sense those things about me.
- Those little everyday moments do matter, they are what snowball into larger cultural attitudes about race.

Draft: Introduction, Body, Conclusion

This assignment invites creativity in form and content, but that doesn't mean there's no organization. Quite the opposite. This means instead that you need to control the narrative in a way that takes readers through the journey of your story in a logical manner. (See Chapter 11, "Arrange: Prioritize, Organize, Outline.")

Introduction

Because this assignment can be fulfilled in many ways, the introduction is an important place to establish the tone, content, and purpose of your writing. You might need to define the cultural practice you intend to narrate for readers unfamiliar with it. You can take a traditional approach in which you announce the purpose of your argument, or you can begin more indirectly by starting in the middle of your action (in media res) to capture readers' attention first.

Many of my readers won't ever have experienced the kind of violation I experience with my hair, so I think it's important to take them inside that experience early on. That sets the stage for the other types of hostilities I want to narrate.

Body

The body of an autoethnographic argument will connect the personal narrative examples to the point you want to make about your larger cultural observation. In the "Outline ideas" section of her assignment journal, Geraldine jotted down some preliminary thoughts about the body of her analysis:

Voices are important for this story, so I want to include a few verbal exchanges to ground readers in some of the conversations I've had.

Conclusion

In this assignment, the goal is to help readers understand the cultural practice you present and respond to it as you have done. The conclusion does not require a call to action but should include an explicit or implicit call to understand given the scenes you have presented. Geraldine also recorded a possible approach to her conclusion:

I introduce several stories and people—my friends and others—so I think it's important to close by bringing it back to me and my hair. After showing so many other examples of racial and cultural conflict, I think the hair example will have added meaning when I mention it again at the end.

Revise: Strategies for Re-seeing

The autoethnography assignment can stir emotions and memories as you think about the significance of a personal experience. Plan to step away from your work several times and come back to it if your mind starts to wander into memories rather than focusing on the argument. Reading research about the cultural issue might snap you back into focusing on the argument and not just the incidents you narrate. Geraldine returned to her assignment journal to update her progress:

I had to take multiple breaks from writing this. I didn't want to rant, so I had to write what I felt, then come back and edit very carefully. In the end, it's almost more like poetry than prose because I chose each word so carefully, but that took setting this aside many times so that I could concentrate on the writing and not just the feelings.

Review: By Peers and Experts

Rethinking the authoethnography happens when you share your story with others. Try talking through the story with a friend or family member to gauge their reaction. Can they visualize your experience? Do they come to the same conclusions? Also, share the story with others in that cultural group. Do they feel that it represents them accurately? Are they comfortable with your representations and conclusions? Have them explain their reaction.

I talked to my instructor and she encouraged me to narrate these experiences, even if I didn't have it all figured out. I shared drafts of my writing at the Writing Center and with some of the friends who experienced these incidents with me. They confirmed most of what I observed, helped add some details, and generally made me glad that I was writing this. We talked about even more stories I could add, but I will stick with this.

Proofread and Submit

Your Autoethnography might represent different voices or perspectives that require clear punctuation and quotation for readers to follow. When Geraldine updated her assignment journal, she noted:

I wrote in a very careful, spare style. I had several friends read it to make sure it made sense, I hadn't cut too much, and to make sure the tone was forceful but not overwhelming for readers.

WHAT HAPPENS NEXT?

Narrative argument can be a highly persuasive rhetorical approach because reliable, relevant storytelling has the power to get an audience to understand experiences beyond their own. Narrative argument as a primary or secondary mode can spark awareness in readers who may not have previously recognized that other people were harmed by a particular policy or practice. Good narrative arguments help readers reflect on how their own actions contribute to the well-being or harm of the people described by those experiences.

For more active and activist uses of narrative argument in the civic domain, see the narratives used in political and nonprofit campaigns. Both use the stories of individuals to show how their candidate or cause addresses those needs and improves the lives of people like those depicted in that narrative. Sometimes, however, this telling of other people's stories seems to exploit the people depicted, reducing them to the "poster child" of a particular problem. As a good writer sensitive to the ethics of representing others, take care to ensure that when you use narratives to exemplify a problem or a cause, you do not do so at the expense of the people depicted. Instead, as a good writer, make sure those stories are reliable and representative in ways that protect the dignity of the people you represent.

OFFICE HOURS ➤ Setting Boundaries for Narrative Arguments with Personal Experience

Narrative arguments invite writers to draw from powerful personal experiences that have led them to new insights and/or concerns. The experiences you narrate might be comical or serious. Sometimes the word "personal" is interpreted only as meaning "private" or even "painful," and that might make you wonder what types of experience are appropriate to share in a personal narrative. Traumatic experiences often cause us to care deeply about particular issues and policies, and thus they often lead to powerful writing. But think carefully about what you chose to share. You are not required to share anything that makes you feel vulnerable.

When choosing experiences to narrate, consider the comfort level of three key stakeholders: you, your instructor, and your peers.

(continued)

Although writing can be a wonderful way to work through deep issues, remember that you are writing for the academic domain to an audience of peers and instructors. While you might draw from personal experience, you do so to create an academic argument.

If you are unsure whether your topic and experiences are appropriate for class, talk directly with your instructor before sharing a draft. Note that instructors are mandatory reporters, which means that they have to report anything you tell them—verbally or in writing—about physical or sexual abuse or discrimination. Your instructor can help you define expectations for what works in the academic domain so that you feel comfortable sharing your experience. Together you can determine an appropriate threshold for the rhetorical situation of your classroom.

CHAPTER eighteen

Causation: Making Connections

Causal arguments explore reasons why something has happened or could happen. They explain or predict cause and effect. Causal arguments ask, *why*? Or, *what if*? Working backwards (an approach called "past-oriented"), causal arguments try to show that one event (or series of events) caused another event or outcome. For example, a past-oriented causal argument might explain the most significant reasons leading up to an increase in childhood obesity in the United States. Looking forwards (a "future-oriented" approach), causal arguments might explain the likelihood of something happening based on past experience. For example, a future-oriented causal argument might claim that population growth will cause a crisis in access to fresh water in India. Causal arguments explore various reasons why something has or could happen, arguing that some of those reasons—also called factors or variables—are more significant or likely to be the source of change than others.

As curious human beings, we want to know why things happen so that we can intervene to create positive change. If we intervene without fully understanding the problem, then we might cause unintended negative consequences. The goal of understanding causes, then, is to help us make informed interventions that lead to positive change.

After we have sufficiently explored causes, we can use limited resources (time, money, etc.) to redirect the situation and create a better outcome. Cause and effect relationships, however, are rarely straightforward, and we are limited in how thorough we can be in researching causes. At some point, we have to decide to intervene based on the available evidence. Then, we must evaluate that intervention to see if we made a positive change, and we must keep checking to make sure that change lasts.

STRATEGIES FOR CAUSAL ARGUMENTS

To argue that one thing did or could cause another requires careful attention to all the factors in that cause and effect relationship. We often say that you have to collect the dots before you can connect the dots in analyzing factors in a causal argument. Some images used to describe causal arguments include a causal chain of events (where one link in the chain leads to the next), or the domino effect (where the last in a line of dominoes obviously falls because the first domino in the line was pushed).

In complicated problems, however, factors are rarely linked as obviously as a chain or lined up as neatly as dominoes. Instead, we might think of a *web* of causal factors that relate indirectly to the final outcome. A more accurate image of a causal argument might be a combination of the two: dominoes set up like a web in which a single cause (pushing the first domino) affects dominoes along many other strands of the web to topple.

In most cases, it is difficult to *prove* causation beyond a shadow of a doubt because there are so many factors to research in complicated issues. Causal arguments examine the most reliable information available at the time to make a compelling case for the connections between cause and effect. The following strategies will help you determine the best approach given the evidence and examples available to you.

Strategy 1: Find Common Threads

One way to establish causation is to show that whenever one particular factor is present, a specific outcome always happens. That factor is common to all incidents of that outcome, and as the common thread it is likely the common cause.

For example, some research shows that children who attend pre-school have better grades and fewer behavioral issues in elementary school. Furthermore, some longitudinal studies (studies that happen over a long period of time, typically many years) show that adults who attended pre-school as children make more money and are less likely to commit crime throughout their lives. The question, especially when we get many years past pre-school, is whether or not we can still point to pre-school as the common thread of positive influence when so many other factors come into play over those years.

Strategy 2: Explore Relevant Differences

In looking for a cause, you can compare two or more examples of incidents in which only one factor seems to change. If the only difference between those two examples happens when that different outcome occurs, then it is likely that the different factor caused the different outcome.

Here again, except in laboratory settings, it is difficult to find two completely identical incidents such that you know with certainty that one factor actually caused the different outcome. For example, in the nonfiction book *The Other Wes Moore: One Name, Two Fates*, author Wes Moore discovers another man named Wes Moore grew up only blocks away from him in their poor Baltimore neighborhood. Their neighborhood and home life share similarities beyond their name: both grew up with single mothers, struggled in school, and participated in illegal activity. However, they end up with very different lives: the author goes to military school, attends Johns Hopkins University, and becomes a Rhodes Scholar, a decorated combat veteran, a White House Fellow, and a business leader. The other Wes Moore is serving life in prison for the murder of a police officer during an armed robbery. What difference accounts for one's success and the other's distress? The author poses many possibilities: the time an officer gave him a warning rather than a criminal record when he was caught vandalizing property; the time his mother decided he had to go to military school and called on family members for financial support to send him; the time he was given a second chance to stay in school. Lives are filled with so many factors that it is difficult to isolate distinct factors as causes, but identifying key differences can help us narrow down potential causes in many situations.

Strategy 3: Consider Alternative Explanations

The key to constructing a strong causal argument is to make sure you have thoroughly considered alternative arguments. What else could be causing that to happen? Is the factor you are considering the most significant factor in that outcome, or are other factors more responsible?

This is where peer and other outside readers are so important. They can often see those other strands in the causal web that elude you as you focus on one thread. Find readers who will ask, "What about this? What about that?" If you can dismiss their alternate factors with relevant, reliable support, then you strengthen your position. If you can't, then it's time to rethink your argument.

In "The New Jim Crow: How the War on Drugs Gave Birth to a Permanent Undercaste," Michelle Alexander offers an alternative explanation for why so many black men are incarcerated: they are not inherently inclined to criminal activity, as some argued, they are instead pushed into it through systemic racism that limits their economic opportunities and targets them disproportionately in law enforcement and judicial sentencing.

Strategy 4: Avoid Anecdotal Evidence

Anecdotal evidence is based on a limited, unscientific sample of evidence rather than on multiple samples that make your research credible. When you construct a causal argument, choose an issue for which you can access or create many examples to consider cause and effect relationships thoroughly. While your personal experiences and observations are valid, they are limited. What appears to be the cause in one incident might prove to be different if you observe many more.

In the website "Global Climate Change: Vital Signs of the Planet," NASA offers centuries of data on global carbon dioxide levels to show that global warming since 1950 is far beyond the range of normal climate change. The depth of these data outweigh any one person's observation based on anecdotal evidence, for example, that winter in his/her town was colder than normal. While individual experiences might vary, overall data show a clear picture.

Strategy 5: Avoid Blame and Shame

A strong causal argument avoids the temptation to strike a tone of blame and shame in identifying causes. The primary impulse of a strong causal argument should be to show that you have compelling evidence to support your argument about the causes of an issue. Strong causal arguments are not driven by finding fault, blaming and shaming the cause of a problem. Rather, they are driven by the desire to articulate a logical rationale for why things are the way they are in order to increase our knowledge and improve our circumstances.

ELEMENTS OF CAUSAL ARGUMENTS

The core elements of strong causal arguments are that (1) the argument is based on causation, not correlation; (2) the factor you identify is both necessary and sufficient to explain the outcome observed; and (3) the causes of that issue are still actively debated.

Element 1: Causation, Not Correlation

Causation can be easily confused with correlation. Correlation means one event is associated with another event but does not directly cause it. The logical fallacy *post hoc, ergo propter hoc* is a Latin phrase that means "after this, therefore because of this" (see discussion in Chapter 4, "Argument"). This faulty reasoning suggests that if one event follows another, then the first event caused the second event.

But that is a big leap in logic. For example, you might observe that since the time your community saw a significant increase in immigrants, crime also increased. Could you then argue that the immigrants caused the crime? Not without showing evidence that the immigrants were the perpetrators of the crime, not the victims of it. And it would not mean much if the rate of crime perpetrated by immigrants was not significantly higher than that among non-immigrants—it is the comparison of these two groups, among many other factors, that would tell us something important about who or what is responsible for causing the increase in crime. Many alternative explanations, such as an increase in reporting crimes, would have to be explored before you can make such a claim with any confidence.

Element 2: Necessary and Sufficient Conditions

To establish a causal connection, the factor you intend to identify as the cause must be a necessary and sufficient condition of the effect. This means that the factor is both required by and compellingly relevant to the effect you are studying. Every time you see that effect, you know that the factor you identified as the cause is also present.

For example, if you wanted to argue that X [mental illness] causes Y [homelessness], you would have to provide evidence that in all verifiable cases, X [mental illness] is always present when Y [homelessness happens], indicating that mental illness is a necessary and sufficient condition of homelessness. In this example, you would surely find that there are many cases of people with mental illness who live in stable homes, and there are many people who are homeless who do not have mental illness. Mental illness does not, therefore, cause homelessness: mental illness is neither necessary nor sufficient by itself to cause homelessness. However, you would also find a significant correlation between homelessness and mental illness, meaning that the number of people who are homeless who have a mental illness is much greater statistically than in the population at large, suggesting a strong connection between the two. Mental illness does not automatically lead to homelessness, but this statistical difference indicates that people who have mental illness are more likely to be homeless.

Element 3: Debatability

Like all effective arguments, effective causal arguments focus on issues that are actively debated by reasonable people. Such arguments must explore causal connections that are not already common knowledge or resolved by experts in the field. As a student, you will therefore want to seek topics for causal arguments that either (1) have experts still debating about reasonable causes, thus allowing you to align your argument with some of those experts, or (2) are local and have not been fully explored or debated so that you can step into the conversation with some authority and expertise, possibly developing original data through archival or human subjects research that has not yet been done.

IN PROCESS: CAUSATION
Project: Arguing Why Something Happened or What
Will Happen

Objectives

- Discover a factor (or factors) within a complex issue in order to
  research how that one factor has a causal impact (an effect) on the
  larger issue.
- Identify scholarly and mainstream sources that provide reliable research on causal connections.
- Explain clearly how distinct factors relate to one another beyond
  correlation to become verifiable causes—clearly connecting the
  dots for readers to see a causal web.
- Acknowledge the high bar that must be met to establish logically
  sound causal claims.

Description

In this assignment, you will use reliable sources to write a causal argument explaining a cause (or causes) of a significant issue that is the
subject of current debate. You will first need to establish your definition of the issue and key terms so that your readers understand
your context. Next, establish that there is current, reasonable debate
about that issue. Then, explain why the factors you identify are causes,
meaning they are necessary and sufficient conditions, not just correlations, that account for the effect you are researching. Finally, explore
alternative explanations to show why they do not amount to necessary
and sufficient conditions.

Thesis Template

Here are templates that demonstrate two ways you might construct a
thesis statement for a causal argument:

Past-Oriented Causal Thesis: While [*opposing experts named x, y, and z*] argue that [*insert target factor*] [*is/is not*] a cause of [*insert effect*], I agree with [*experts named a, b, c*] who argue that it [*is not/is*] a cause because [*insert reason(s) why you are taking this stance about this cause*].

Future-Oriented Causal Thesis: While the causes of [*insert issue*] are complex and must be addressed on many levels in many ways, we [*indicating local, national, or international community in scope*] should consider how [*this new law, new program, recent event, etc.*] will impact [*insert effect you predict*]. It is clear based on [*insert key examples*] that [*insert predicted effect*] will happen if [*insert cause*] continues.

Model Thesis

Here is an example of a thesis informed by the future-oriented template:

> "While many people argue that the Confederate flag excites the kind of extreme racism that causes people to commit hate crimes against African Americans, I argue that the Confederate flag alone does not cause such acts. Therefore, calls for its removal only draw attention away from more important interventions, such as diversity training, that help us acknowledge and address racism in ourselves and others."

Published Reading

The New Jim Crow: How the War on Drugs Gave Birth to a Permanent Undercaste

Michelle Alexander

> *Michelle Alexander is a civil rights lawyer and Visiting Professor at Union Theological Seminary. Her book* The New Jim Crow: Mass Incarceration in the Age of Colorblindness *earned much*

critical acclaim and spent over a year on the New York Times Best Seller *list. She also writes freelance pieces concerning the mass incarceration of black Americans. The following argument explores the continued effects of racial discrimination caused by targeting black Americans as criminals.*

Ever since Barack Obama lifted his right hand and took his oath of office, pledging to serve the United States as its 44th president, ordinary people and their leaders around the globe have been celebrating our nation's "triumph over race." Obama's election has been touted as the final nail in the coffin of Jim Crow, the bookend placed on the history of racial caste in America.

Obama's mere presence in the Oval Office is offered as proof that "the land of the free" has finally made good on its promise of equality. There's an implicit yet undeniable message embedded in his appearance on the world stage: this is what freedom looks like; this is what democracy can do for you. If you are poor, marginalized, or relegated to an inferior caste, there is hope for you. Trust us. Trust our rules, laws, customs, and wars. You, too, can get to the promised land.

Perhaps greater lies have been told in the past century, but they can be counted on one hand. Racial caste is alive and well in America.

Most people don't like it when I say this. It makes them angry. In the "era of colorblindness" there's a nearly fanatical desire to cling to the myth that we as a nation have "moved beyond" race. Here are a few facts that run counter to that triumphant racial narrative:

*There are more African American adults under correctional control today—in prison or jail, on probation or parole—than were enslaved in 1850, a decade before the Civil War began.

*As of 2004, more African American men were disenfranchised (due to felon disenfranchisement laws) than in 1870, the year the Fifteenth Amendment was ratified, prohibiting laws that explicitly deny the right to vote on the basis of race.

*A black child born today is less likely to be raised by both parents than a black child born during slavery. The recent disintegration of the African American family is due in large part to the mass imprisonment of black fathers.

*If you take into account prisoners, a large majority of African American men in some urban areas have been labeled felons for life. (In the Chicago area, the figure is nearly 80%.) These men are part of a growing undercaste—not class, caste—permanently relegated, by law, to a second-class status. They can be denied the right to vote, automatically excluded from juries, and legally discriminated against in employment, housing, access to education, and public benefits, much as their grandparents and great-grandparents were during the Jim Crow era.

Excuses for the Lockdown

There is, of course, a colorblind explanation for all this: crime rates. Our prison population has exploded from about 300,000 to more than 2 million in a few short decades, it is said, because of rampant crime. We're told that the reason so many black and brown men find themselves behind bars and ushered into a permanent, second-class status is because they happen to be the bad guys.

The uncomfortable truth, however, is that crime rates do not explain the sudden and dramatic mass incarceration of African Americans during the past 30 years. Crime rates have fluctuated over the last few decades—they are currently at historical lows—but imprisonment rates have consistently soared.

Quintupled, in fact. A main driver has been the War on Drugs. Drug offenses alone accounted for about two-thirds of the increase in the federal inmate population, and more than half of the increase in the state prison population between 1985 and 2000, the period of our prison system's most dramatic expansion.

The drug war has been brutal—complete with SWAT teams, tanks, bazookas, grenade launchers, and sweeps of entire neighborhoods—but those who live in white communities have little clue to the devastation wrought. This war has been waged almost exclusively in poor communities of color, even though studies consistently show that people of all colors use and sell illegal drugs at remarkably similar rates. In fact, some studies indicate that white youth are significantly more likely to engage in illegal drug dealing than black youth. Any notion that drug use among African Americans is more severe or dangerous is belied by the data. White youth, for example, have about three times the number of drug-related visits to the emergency room as their African American counterparts.

That is not what you would guess, though, when entering our nation's prisons and jails, overflowing as they are with black and brown drug offenders. Human Rights Watch reported in 2000 that, in some states, African Americans comprised 80%–90% of all drug offenders sent to prison. Rates of black imprisonment have fallen since then, but not by much.

This is the point at which I am typically interrupted and reminded that black men have higher rates of violent crime. *That's* why the drug war is waged in poor communities of color and not middle-class suburbs. Drug warriors are trying to get rid of those drug kingpins and violent offenders who make ghetto communities a living hell. It has nothing to do with race; it's all about violent crime.

Again, not so. President Ronald Reagan officially declared the current drug war in 1982, when drug crime was declining, not rising. President Richard Nixon was the first to coin the term "a war on drugs," but it was President Reagan who turned the rhetorical war into a literal one. From the outset, the war had relatively little to do with drug crime and much to do with racial politics. The drug war was part of a grand and highly successful Republican Party strategy of using racially coded political appeals on issues of crime and welfare to attract poor and working class white voters who were resentful of, and threatened by, desegregation, busing, and affirmative action. In the words of H. R. Haldeman, President Richard Nixon's White House Chief of Staff: "[T]he whole problem is really the blacks. The key is to devise a system that recognizes this while not appearing to."

A few years after the drug war was announced, crack cocaine hit the streets of inner-city communities. The Reagan administration seized on this development with glee, hiring staff who were to be responsible for publicizing inner-city crack babies, crack mothers, crack whores, and drug-related violence. The goal was to make inner-city crack abuse and violence a media sensation, bolstering public support for the drug war which, it was hoped, would lead Congress to devote millions of dollars in additional funding to it.

The plan worked like a charm. For more than a decade, black drug dealers and users would be regulars in newspaper stories and would saturate the evening TV news. Congress and state legislatures nationwide would devote billions of dollars to the drug war and pass harsh mandatory minimum sentences for drug crimes—sentences longer than murderers receive in many countries.

Democrats began competing with Republicans to prove that they could be even tougher on the dark-skinned pariahs. In President Bill Clinton's boastful words, "I can be nicked a lot, but no one can say I'm soft on crime." The facts bear him out. Clinton's "tough on crime" policies resulted in the largest increase in federal and state prison inmates of any president in American history. But Clinton was not satisfied with exploding prison populations. He and the "New Democrats" championed legislation banning drug felons from public housing (no matter how minor the offense) and denying them basic public benefits, including food stamps, for life. Discrimination in virtually every aspect of political, economic, and social life is now perfectly legal, if you've been labeled a felon.

Facing Facts

But what about all those violent criminals and drug kingpins? Isn't the drug war waged in ghetto communities because that's where the violent offenders can be found? The answer is yes . . . in made-for-TV movies. In real life, the answer is no.

The drug war has never been focused on rooting out drug kingpins or violent offenders. Federal funding flows to those agencies that increase dramatically the volume of drug arrests, not the agencies most successful in bringing down the bosses. What has been rewarded in this war is sheer numbers of drug arrests. To make matters worse, federal drug forfeiture laws allow state and local law enforcement agencies to keep for their own use 80% of the cash, cars, and homes seized from drug suspects, thus granting law enforcement a direct monetary interest in the profitability of the drug market.

The results have been predictable: people of color rounded up en masse for relatively minor, non-violent drug offenses. In 2005, four out of five drug arrests were for possession, only one out of five for sales. Most people in state prison have no history of violence or even of significant selling activity. In fact, during the 1990s—the period of the most dramatic expansion of the drug war—nearly 80% of the increase in drug arrests was for marijuana possession, a drug generally considered less harmful than alcohol or tobacco and at least as prevalent in middle-class white communities as in the inner city.

In this way, a new racial undercaste has been created in an astonishingly short period of time—a new Jim Crow system. Millions of people of color are now saddled with criminal records and legally denied the very rights that their parents and grandparents fought for and, in some cases, died for.

Affirmative action, though, has put a happy face on this racial reality. Seeing black people graduate from Harvard and Yale and become CEOs or corporate lawyers—not to mention president of the United States—causes us all to marvel at what a long way we've come.

Recent data shows, though, that much of black progress is a myth. In many respects, African Americans are doing no better than they were when Martin Luther King, Jr. was assassinated and uprisings swept inner cities across America, particularly when it comes to the wealth gap and unemployment rates. Unemployment rates in many black communities rival those in Third World countries. And that's with affirmative action!

When we pull back the curtain and take a look at what our "colorblind" society creates without affirmative action, we see a familiar social, political, and economic structure: the structure of racial caste. The entrance into this new caste system can be found at the prison gate.

This is not Martin Luther King, Jr.'s dream. This is not the promised land. The cyclical rebirth of caste in America is a recurring racial nightmare.

For Reflection

1. What do the data tell us about how being black factors into incarceration rates? Compare that to public perceptions.
2. How does Alexander describe the purpose and plan of the war on drugs? Who might disagree with her description and why? What, in the end, does the war on drugs appear to cause?
3. If you wrote to Alexander, would you challenge and/or support her claim that we have a new Jim Crow? Research the original Jim Crow laws for support. What examples could you draw on from your own experience to support the presence or absence of colorblindness in the United States?

Student Reading

Allison Angeli is majoring in neuroscience and behavior and plans on attending medical school. She is particularly interested in body image and eating disorders, as well as other mental illnesses. The following essay is inspired by her personal experience of using fitspo while recovering from anorexia nervosa. She highlights the increasing prevalence and connection among eating disorders, body dissatisfaction, and media influence in order to address fitspo as a potential therapy to eating disorders.

Allison Angeli

The Effects of Fitspo Viewed on Social Media as a Therapy to Eating Disorders

"Every society has a way of torturing its women, whether by binding their feet or by sticking them into whalebone corsets. What contemporary American culture has come

260

up with is designer jeans," states Joel Yager, an M.D. psychiatrist who studies eating disorders. Eating disorders are becoming more prevalent and are occurring at younger ages. Some would argue this is caused by media influence, which aggressively advertises a thin yet toned female body. This manifests itself as "thinspo" or "thinspiration"—the inspiration to be thin—on social media sites (Angyal). Thinspo typically entails a mantra pasted over a photo of a woman's barely-clothed, malnourished body. Research supports a correlation of viewing images of thin models, or thinspo, and decreased body satisfaction, lowered self-esteem, and negative emotions, all of which contribute to the development of eating disorders (Polivy and Herman 2). However, the effects of viewing images of fit women, also called "fitspo" or "fitspiration," on eating disorders have not been thoroughly studied. Thus, this paper serves to study fitspo viewed by young women on social media sites as a potential therapy to eating disorders.

To understand how fitspo influences people, the social and cultural context must first be defined and analyzed. Today, body dissatisfaction, social media influence, and eating disorders are interconnected issues. Body dissatisfaction is the perception of one's body image in which one's ideal body size or shape differs from that of his or her current body. Many psychologists concur that body dissatisfaction is connected to the culturally defined ideal of beauty (Sivert and Sinanovic 55). This ideal of beauty is largely constructed and promoted via the media, whose hidden messages, particularly those containing ideals of physical appearance, can have negative psychological effects and lead to eating disorders. Eating disorders—anorexia nervosa, bulimia, and binge eating—are defined as extreme emotions, attitudes, or behaviors with food and/or one's weight (National Eating Disorders Association). The rates of eating disorders are increasing and beginning to occur at younger ages (Derenne and Beresin 4). However, before this rise in eating disorders is directly analyzed, we must first investigate the prominence of body dissatisfaction.

Studies show that the majority of women, particularly those in Western cultures, are dissatisfied with their body shape and size (Grogan 26). This poses serious concerns since body dissatisfaction is a risk factor for eating disorders (Homan et al. 50). In one study, women were presented with images of female silhouettes ranging in size from very thin to very large. The women were asked to identify which silhouette depicted their current body and which silhouette depicted their ideal body. Results showed a tendency for women to choose a thinner ideal body than their choice of their current body, supporting a dissatisfaction with their current figure (Grogan 26). Furthermore, a survey done by *Psychology Today* reported that 55% of women were dissatisfied with their weight and 45% of women were dissatisfied with their muscle tone (Grogan 29).

The currently idolized female body, particularly in Western cultures, is not only very thin, but also very fit (Homan et al. 50). In fact, in interviews conducted at Manchester Metropolitan University, many women reported a desire to be "skinny but shapely" (Grogan 38). This ideal body is even more taxing to achieve and creates a greater disconnect between the average woman's body and the idealized body often seen in the media.

What separates the modern, Western influences from the previously studied influences on the idolized female physique is a clearly more powerful presence of the media in today's society (Derenne and Beresin 4). A striking demonstration of the media's influence lies in a study comparing the rates of eating disorders in Fiji before and after the arrival of television in 1995. Previously in Fiji, a rotund body type was preferred because it signified wealth and the ability to care for one's family. Due to this cultural norm, only one case of an eating disorder had ever been reported in Fiji before the introduction of television. However, after television arrived in Fiji, the rates of eating disorders skyrocketed from 0 to 69%. Furthermore, young Fijians repeatedly cited their weight-loss inspirations to be the attractive, thin actors on TV shows such as "Beverly Hills 90210" and "Melrose Place" (Derenne and Beresin 258). This study supports a correlation between media influence and eating disorders.

The correlation among body dissatisfaction, social media influence, and eating disorders has been demonstrated. However, newer online communities that support and share "thinspo," defined as the inspiration to be thin, or "fitspo," defined as the inspiration to be fit, require further study. Thinspo users promote a lifestyle of "pro-ana," meaning pro-anorexic, or "pro-mia," meaning pro-bulimic. On social media thinspo sites, users post pictures of emaciated, skimpily clothed women with a mantra such as, "Nothing tastes as good as skinny feels." Due to the negative psychological effects associated with thinspo, some social media sites, such as Instagram and Facebook, have taken measures to ban online thinspo activity (Angyal). However, fitspo, a spin-off of thinspo that promotes a healthy lifestyle, has not been regulated by social media sites.

Fitspo motivates its viewers to be healthier by working out and eating nutritious foods. However, fitspo contains many similarities to thinspo, which has negative psychological effects. One apprehension is that fitspo can fuel an obsession, potentially leading to an eating disorder. In fact, Claire Mysko, who oversees teen outreach on behalf of the National Eating Disorders Association, stated, "We are, as a culture, so obsessed with 'health,' but there's a lot of stuff that comes under this umbrella of health obsession that actually is quite unhealthy" (Adams). With regard to fitspo, Mysko argues, "Most of this content [fitspo] is not promoting self-acceptance. It's saying, 'You're not good enough and you have to do this to get better'" (Adams). Her statement highlights fitspo's tendency to promote fitness at all costs, a mindset that can lead to an eating disorder.

This mentality of fitness at all costs is becoming more prevalent among adolescent boys as well as girls. Young males' unhealthy diet and exercise extremes have been driven by the media's advertisement of a muscular, fit body type. More specifically, this is found online in an intensified form as fitspo. Males use fitspo online in the same way females use thinspo. On bodybuilding forums, adolescent males share weight-lifting regimens and compare body fat percentages. On social media sites, young men post pictures of other men's lean, muscular bodies as inspiration and motivation (Quenqua). When extreme forms of fitness behaviors are examined in males instead of females, an increasing prevalence of a different risky behavior, namely the use of supplements and steroids, is observed (Eisenberg, Wall, and Neumark-Sztainer 1021). Supplements and steroids pose health issues, especially when taken in large amounts or to replace meals. Many supplements may contain anabolic steroids, which are often used individually or in addition to supplements. The primary health threat of anabolic steroids is that they stop testosterone production in men, resulting in serious withdrawal problems when still-growing males try to stop using them (Quenqua).

Although more males use supplements and steroids than females, these substances still have adverse effects on women's health (Grogan 48). Currently, 21% of women use supplements and 5% use steroids to aid in muscle growth and fat loss (Eisenberg, Wall, and Neumark-Sztainer 1021). Eisenberg explains, "The model of feminine beauty is now more toned and fit and sculpted than it was a generation ago.... It's not just being thin. It's being thin and toned" (Quenqua). Women who have previously undergone extreme methods, such as starvation or purging, to obtain a thin body type could be more likely to begin experimenting with supplements and steroids or forming an obsession with fitspo.

All of these methods are detrimental to a woman's physical and psychological health, and should be regarded as equally hazardous and risky.

While many studies have established a correlation between the viewing of media (such as thinspo) and body dissatisfaction in young adults (Homan et al. 50), to date little research has been conducted regarding exposure to images of fit physiques, or fitspo. However, the studies that have been performed suggest the complexity of the situation.

One such study analyzed the effects on body satisfaction after exposure to images of athletic models that were either thin or normal-weight. The study's results showed that viewers of the images of thin, athletic models reported an increase in body dissatisfaction. In contrast, viewers of the images of normal-weight, athletic models did not report any greater body dissatisfaction than the control group. This evidence supports that an ultra-fit physique alone does not cause body dissatisfaction. Instead, the thinness of the models is suggested to be the driving factor (Homan et al. 53–54). It would appear that fitspo using normal-weight models does not cause negative psychological effects. In contrast, fitspo using skinny yet athletic models could cause an increase in body dissatisfaction. However, the two types of images tested in this study were both of "athletic" women and merely differed in the level of adiposity [obesity], leaving a necessity for further testing.

A further study analyzed the effects regarding women's body satisfaction after viewing images of women's bodies varying in amounts of muscularity, as opposed to adiposity. Images were classified into three groups: thin, thin and muscular, and thin and hypermuscular. After viewing the thin and thin-muscular images, which are both representative of the modern ideal body types, women's body satisfaction decreased. In contrast, after viewing the thin-hypermuscular images, women's body satisfaction did not change (Benton and Karazsia 22). This study suggests that thinspo and fitspo, in the form of thin and toned bodies, are detrimental to women's body satisfaction and psychological health. Additionally, this study supports that fitspo, in the form of muscular, normal-weight women, is not detrimental to women's body satisfaction and psychological health.

Based on this research, fitspo was determined to be either negatively or positively influential based on particular factors, namely the type of fitspo being viewed and the individual viewer. Those who have previously taken drastic measures to achieve a particular body type may respond to fitspo in an unhealthy manner. However, those who are self-confident and have a healthy body image may respond to fitspo more positively. The response to fitspo is also based on the type of fitspo being viewed, namely whether the physique is thin or normal-weight. Fitspo of thin models will cause negative psychological effects, especially on those with eating disorders. However, fitspo of healthy and confident average-weight women will motivate viewers to lead a healthier lifestyle and holds the potential to be utilized as a therapy to eating disorders.

Furthermore, fitspo has the potential to shift our culture's view of the ideal female physique. Fitspo of healthy-weight women who are confident and have a positive body image could inspire others to be healthier too. This form of fitspo fits the true meaning of "fitness inspiration" by promoting health and body acceptance.

Works Cited

Adams, Rebecca. "Why 'Fitspo' Should Come With A Warning Label." *The Huffington Post*, 17 July 2014, www.TheHuffingtonPost.com. Accessed 15 Mar. 2015.

Angyal, Chloe. "The 'Thinspiration' Behind an Impossible Ideal of Beauty." *The Nation*, 23 Apr. 2013, www.thenation.com. Accessed 28 Feb. 2015.

Benton, Catherine, and Bryan T. Karazsia. "The Effect of Thin and Muscular Images on Women's Body Satisfaction." *Body Image*, vol. 13, 2015, pp. 22–27. Accessed 15 Mar. 2015.

Derenne, J. L., and E. V. Beresin. "Body Image, Media, and Eating Disorders." *Academic Psychiatry*, vol. 30, no. 3, 2006, pp. 257–61. Accessed 28 Feb. 2015.

Eisenberg, Maria E., Melanie Wall, and Dianne Neumark-Sztainer.
  "Muscle-enhancing Behaviors Among Adolescent Girls and
  Boys." *Pediatrics*, vol. 130, no. 6, 2012, pp. 1019–026. Accessed 10
  Apr. 2015.
Grogan, Sarah. *Body Image: Understanding Body Dissatisfaction in Men,
  Women and Children*. Routledge, 1999.
Homan, Kristin, Erin Mchugh, Daniel Wells, Corrinne Watson, and
  Carolyn King. "The Effect of Viewing Ultra-fit Images on College
  Women's Body Dissatisfaction." *Body Image*, vol. 9 , no. 1, 2012, pp.
  50–56. *Elsevier*. Accessed 15 Mar. 2015.
National Eating Disorders Association. "Types & Symptoms of Eating
  Disorders." *National Eating Disorders Association,* N.p., n.d. Ac-
  cessed 10 Apr. 2015.
Polivy, Janet and C. Peter Herman. "Sociocultural Idealization of
  Thin Female Body Shapes: an Introduction to the Special Issue on
  Body Image and Eating Disorders." *Journal of Social and Clinical
  Psychology*, vol. 23, no. 1, 2004, pp. 1-6. *ProQuest*. Accessed 4 Mar.
  2015.
Quenqua, Douglas. "Muscular Body Image Lures Boys Into Gym, and
  Obsession." *New York Times*, 19 Nov. 2012, www.nytimes.com. Ac-
  cessed 28 Feb. 2015.
Sivert, Sejla S., and Osman Sinanovic. "Body Dissatisfaction—Is Age a
  Factor?" *Philosophy, Sociology, Psychology and History*, vol. 7, 2008,
  pp. 55-61. Accessed 28 Feb. 2015.

For Reflection

1. Cite places in the text where the author defines key terms. Are those definitions clear enough for this argument?
2. Assess the strength of the sources cited. Are they recent, relevant, and reliable? How could the strength of sources cited be improved?
3. How successful is the author in making a causal connection between a single factor and a specific effect or outcome? Is the connection clear and compelling?

CAUSATION: THE WRITING PROCESS

In the following section, we use Allison Angeli's notes and drafts to examine her thinking about the writing process.

Analyze the Assignment

The Causal Argument assignment asks you make an argument based on a cause and effect relationship in a complicated issue. Your job is to focus on a key factor and explain why that factor, compared to others, is so significant to the outcome of that issue. Support from experts and relevant examples will strengthen your position.

To complete this assignment, use reliable sources to write a causal argument explaining a cause or causes of a significant issue in debate. You will first need to establish briefly your definition of the issue and key terms so that your readers understand your context. Next, you will need to establish that there is current, reasonable debate about that issue. Then, you will need to explain why the factors you identify are causes, not correlations, that account for the effect you are researching, exploring alternative explanations to show why they do not amount to necessary and sufficient conditions. Or, you will need to concede that you can only argue correlation, not causation.

Allison created a new folder on her computer for this project and labeled it "Causal Argument Assignment." She opened a new document, saved it as "Causal Argument assignment journal" and wrote down her preliminary ideas and questions:

Assignment Analysis

- The action verbs in the assignment are:
  1. "Explaining" a cause or causes
  2. "Establish" a definition

3. Help readers "understand"
4. "Establish" debate
5. "Explain" factors I "identify" as causes
6. Effect I am "researching"
7. "Exploring" alternative explanations
8. To "show" why

- From the assignment prompt, I see that my audience is my instructor and classmates.
- I have a lot of freedom to choose that debatable issue I want to research. That is so broad, though, that I will want to clarify with my instructor that I have chosen an acceptable issue when I think of something. We might have different definitions of "debatable issue."

Plan: Organizing the Process

Your instructor will set your deadlines and paper length for this assignment. Once you know those two critical pieces of information, you can map your schedule, giving yourself plenty of time to research support for your argument. Allison opened up her project folder and added the following text to her assignment journal:

I have 3 weeks total from the day we were given the assignment to the day it's due and I have another paper due during that writing window. I want to have most of my research done before we do the peer workshop in week two. If I have read my sources and I have an outline of the whole paper, I think I can get useful feedback in the workshop. I have never written a causal argument before, so I do want a lot of feedback. I want to visit the Writing Center after the workshop. My schedule:

WEEK 1: Make an appointment at the Writing Center for Week 2 after the peer workshop. Start brainstorming possible issues that I could write about—the issue has to be "debatable" by "reasonable" people, so that rules out a lot of what my friends talk about! I'm going to look at news headlines from newspapers because I want to write about something really current and interesting.

WEEK 2: Decide on issue. Find 3–5 solid sources and read them. Draft an outline and works cited page from the sources I find. Think of questions to ask my peer reviewers. Listen to their feedback and write as much of a first draft as I can before my Writing Center visit. Work with Writing Center tutor to get to full draft.

WEEK 3: Take my exam, then go back to this paper with fresh eyes to revise. Stop by my instructor's office hours to talk through draft.

Question: Exploring Issues

As the first step in this assignment is to find an issue, the initial resources you need are ones that will help you find appropriate topics. Watch headlines in reliable news outlets. What are people arguing about? Find arguments based on disagreements about causes and start listing them. Listen carefully in all your classes—potential topics are probably buzzing through many of your subjects. Review your list and decide which one seems to have that kairotic urgency that makes it important to address this issue right now.

Once you have your topic, search the library with carefully selected search terms and criteria for sources that meet your assignment requirements. Select many more sources than required as some of them might not be useful in the end. See Part Five: Doing Research for specific support on research methods that match your assignment requirements.

Allison listened carefully and explored sources for several days, writing this in her assignment journal:

- I've been looking at headlines from the *New York Times* and *Washington Post* and I've been looking at popular magazines. When I look at the pictures in those magazines, I see how we seem to idolize perfect bodies. My friends and I talk about how hard it is to see those images in the media. Several of us knew people who experienced eating disorders or experienced that ourselves. I might want to research my own experience with an eating disorder, but I want to talk to my instructor about that first.
- I used the library database to search the terms "eating disorder and media" and "eating disorder and body image." That search brought up some scholarly articles that mentioned cause and effect in the title, but I know people disagree about the reasons why this happens.

Read: Strategies for Reading in Research

The next step is to know those resources intimately through careful critical reading. Critical reading means trying to understand what the reader is attempting to communicate by paying close attention to every word, but then also asking hard questions about the text's weaknesses. What does it fail to say? Does it use the strongest reasons and evidence? Does it address opposing viewpoints adequately? You know you have done a good job of reading critically if you can agree with an author's thesis but still thoroughly critique the argument as it is written. Play the believing and the doubting game on each article: where does it convince you, where does it fall short? Critical reading is essential to finding reasonable alternative explanations you can address in your causal argument.

Allison did passive note-taking by highlighting key points in the articles she found, then she also did active note-taking by writing back to the published articles, responding to "Why?" "What if?" and "What about?" questions related to each article so that she could distinguish her thinking from the original author's thoughts. She also made a list of facts that could be useful.

I like to highlight and take notes on paper, so I printed out all the articles I thought would be most useful. I scanned them all first and a couple that came up in my search didn't seem useful, so I didn't even print them out. I also saved them all with their citation because I don't want to have to look for that later. To "explain" and be "compelling," I think it's important to have really strong sources back me up, so I want research from reputable sources that will build my ethos. It shouldn't be just what I think. It should be about what I can prove or at least show or suggest is true.

I highlighted strong quotes as I read the articles the first time, then I went back to pick out ones that would work as direct quotes in my paper, quotes that were clear on their own and short enough to include. I made a pull quote document because I like to start with a backbone of direct quotes for papers like this that need a lot of expert support to be convincing.

Invent: Take Note and Create

The next step is to explore what you think now that you are more informed on the issue. What did you learn? What facts or examples surprised you in your reading? Your answers to those questions might jump out right away or you might need to tease them out by doing an invention activity such as freewriting, concept mapping, or outlining.

Allison began to see what she thought by writing her answers to the Journalist Questions:

As I read about eating disorders, I realized that they are much more complicated than I thought. After I had done a lot of reading, I opened my computer and typed in the six Journalist Questions: Who? What? When? Where? Why? and How? I made myself answer each one based on what I learned through my reading and from my experience with people experiencing eating disorders. I had a lot to say about "why" related to why people start thinking negatively about their own bodies, so I think I will make that a key point in my argument.

Arrange: Prioritize, Organize, Outline

Causal arguments need strong organization to ensure that readers focus on the causal factors you want to highlight. An event can have many contributing factors, but your goal is to identify a key factor and explain why the audience should care about that particular one. They need to see a logical, linear connection between cause and effect to be convinced that your argument is sound, so arrangement is particularly important for causal arguments.

Allison opened her assignment journal and wrote:

I learned about many important factors that contribute to eating disorders, such as media images and even apps that are meant to encourage health. It's clear that no one factor is necessary and sufficient to cause eating disorders as there are people who have experienced those things but don't end up with an eating disorder. In the examples I have seen, one of the most common threads among people experiencing eating disorders is the use of apps that keep those idolized body images front and center. I think that is an important factor we should address because it's something we can change. I want that point to come out early in my paper to debunk other causes people might consider, so I will probably use the Arrangement by Order of Importance or Complexity approach.

Draft: Introduction, Body, Conclusion

Moving from an outline to a full draft you can see the strength of your argument and support. In narrative form, causal connections might become clear through a chronological arrangement, for example, that shows how a factor tends to predate an effect.

Introduction

In her writing journal, Allison noted the following:

I want readers to focus immediately on what I think is the key cause of eating disorders: the pervasive display of unrealistic body images. This is a serious topic, so I want a serious, direct tone. People have a lot of misconceptions about eating disorders, so I want to be straight with them from the beginning.

Body

Causal arguments need clear topic sentences that announce the movement of the argument, point by point. They might require heavy educating of readers on the history and opposing viewpoints of the issue, so clear topic sentences help readers keep track of the phases of the argument.

Allison jotted down some preliminary thoughts about the body of her analysis:

Because this is a complicated issue, I want to give readers a clear definition and some historical background early in the body of my argument. An example from research will help show the causal connection. I also want them to trust me on this issue, so I will acknowledge the opposing viewpoints of experts. But then I want to take a clear stand on what I think should be done.

Conclusion
In this assignment, clarity and consistency of message are key to convincing readers of a causal connection.

Allison also noted a possible approach to her conclusion:

I want to end by clarifying the definition of fitspo and offering a positive step readers can take. Keeping the conclusion simple will mirror my approach to the introduction.

Revise: Strategies for Re-seeing

To revise a causal argument, practice the distancing techniques that will allow you to look at the argument from your readers' perspective. Imagine that you are someone who thinks there is only a correlation, not a causation, between the factor you note and an outcome. Imagine you are a reader who thinks another factor is more key to causation. How would you want someone to convince you otherwise? What tone, reasons, and examples would change your mind?

Allison returned to her assignment journal to update her progress:

> I got so into this issue that I knew I needed to get an outside perspective to see if others would agree. I had a chance to test my ideas through an in-class peer workshop. I was right that people didn't know much about this issue, so defining terms was important at first. I had to give them all my reasons, and when I did, it seemed like the experts I read were pretty convincing to them. That confirmed that I need to spend plenty of time—maybe 2–3 paragraphs—summarizing the experts. My opinion alone isn't enough to get people to change their minds, but I can change minds if I lay out the reasons clearly enough.

Review: By Peers and Experts

Causal arguments are complex, so it is critical to test them on outside readers. By taking your writing to outside reviewers, you don't have to imagine alternative perspectives on causal connections, they are likely to come out naturally as you talk to more people. People prioritize how they will address a problem based on their own values and beliefs. The more information you give them the more likely they are to reconsider those priorities in ways you offer. Allison wrote in her journal:

> I want to make sure I am representing people who experience eating disorders fairly, so I

am taking this back to some of my friends to see if they think I represent this issue fairly. I also want to know if I'm teaching them something new.

Proofread and Submit

Your causal argument probably contains references to other sources. When doing your final review, make sure those sources are cited correctly to build your credibility. Know your common errors and target a reading directly on those errors. When Allison updated her assignment journal, she noted:

I used the Checklist: Proofreading Guide to go back over my draft to look for errors. I like to work from digital text, so I used the search function to look for problems with semicolons and apostrophes, which I sometimes need to correct. I am also worried about unnecessary repetition. I caught myself repeating some exact phrases as I was writing and I want to make sure I keep my style interesting throughout. Finally, I am going to read the paper aloud to make sure it all flows well.

WHAT HAPPENS NEXT?

Causal arguments are particularly critical in the civic domain, where leaders work with stakeholders to decide which interventions will cause their community to improve its well-being. To make the right intervention, we first have to understand causal relationships so that we address the right factors. Access to reliable, relevant data is key to having the right base of information from which to determine those causal relationships—informal observation might not be enough evidence to make a strong case. To make recommendations that help solve problems on the civic level—local, national, or global—it is critical to do due diligence in your research.

OFFICE HOURS ➤ Getting Past Correlation: Calling a Cause a Cause

One of the most challenging parts of writing a causal argument is knowing when you have enough evidence marshaled to call a cause a cause. A correlation means that although there is an association of some type between a factor and an outcome, that factor is not a necessary and sufficient condition for us to claim that it alone caused that outcome (see Figure 18.1). A causal factor means there is a direct, reliable, cause-and-effect relationship wherein a factor is directly responsible for an outcome: under the right conditions, where that factor exists, you can expect that outcome. It can be difficult to build that kind of certainty outside laboratory research conditions, and most people don't have a science lab at their disposal. Most people have to rely on the research of others and their own good reasoning informed by that research. So how much research is enough?

The threshold for claiming a causal connection varies by academic discipline and course. Contact your instructor when you have a draft and list of sources ready to see if your research meets the expectations of the course assignment. Your instructor can help you understand when you have met the threshold of expectations for this assignment to claim a causal relationship between a factor and an effect, and then confidently call a cause a cause.

Correlation ≠ Causation

1) Depression could cause poverty

OR

2) Poverty could cause depression

OR

3) Environmental and/or genetic factors could cause poverty
and depression (implying that poverty and depression have
correlation but not causation)

OR

Figure 18.1

Correlation Does Not Equal Causation

CHAPTER nineteen

Definition: Explaining the Nature of Something

Definition is both fundamental and powerful. We need shared definitions of words and concepts to communicate effectively. Yet sometimes those definitions create boundaries that limit, restrict, and even punish people through exclusion. Many of our most heated debates center on what we call "applied" definitions that require interpretation. For example, during much of its history, the United States defined "citizen" as white and male. Only people who met these criteria could vote and participate fully in American life. Americans fought hard to change that definition of "citizen," making incremental change towards greater inclusivity over decades of debate and action.

Providing clear definitions is especially important when laws and rights depend on the criteria outlined in a definition. Unfortunately, we often find vague or even competing definitions in legal documents. For example, the National Law Center on Homelessness & Poverty report titled "'Simply Unacceptable': Homelessness and the Human Right to Housing in the United States," highlights competing definitions of "homelessness" in government documents. Agencies disagree on whether or not people who are "doubling up" with others should be counted as homeless, for example. How are resources to be allocated fairly when we cannot identify potential recipients by consistent criteria?

In short, definition arguments outline criteria by which something does or does not count within a specific category. They rely on examples that show precisely what does and does not count for that definition, based on those criteria. Authors of definition arguments can use examples to help support a case for a preferred definition, or authors can select a definition and explain whether examples fit or do not fit that definition. There are two main approaches to a definition argument: differentiation and exemplification.

DEFINITIONS THAT DIFFERENTIATE AND EXEMPLIFY

Differentiation

In this approach, the author argues that the audience should adopt one particular definition among competing definitions. Authors can support someone else's definition or offer their own. Arguments that differentiate attempt to explain the concept itself in detail. For example, you could write a whole essay explaining what "social justice" means to you, as the student writer does later in this chapter.

Exemplification

In this approach, authors explain why something does or does not qualify as an example of something else based on specific criteria. Here authors are working from a specific definition of a complex concept and attempt to classify an example as counting or not counting as a valid representation of that concept. For example, in "The Real Rosa

Parks," Paul Rogat Loeb argues that Rosa Parks is not, as commonly believed, an example of the "lone hero" who stood up out of nowhere but was actually a well-seasoned activist trained in the techniques of non-violent resistance who acted on that training when she was told to give up her seat on a bus.

STRATEGIES FOR DEFINITION ARGUMENTS

Definition arguments are useful when a concept needs clarification because it has been misused or misunderstood in some way, or because new information and examples warrant our revisiting an old definition. The process for writing a definition argument includes choosing an appropriate concept to define, outlining specific criteria to help outline the concept, and then showing what does and does not count as an appropriate example of that concept through differentiation and/or exemplification. Following are some strategies to consider when writing a definition argument.

Strategy 1: Choose a Legitimately Contested Concept

A definition argument might be neither useful nor interesting if you choose a concept that is not contested in public discourse. Some terms represent functional definitions based on scientific or factual information that just do not require further attention unless there has been some new discovery. For example, there is not much to argue about what counts as an Africanized honey bee. We have a scientific definition for this species and can identify it with complete agreement. However, someone who claims that the Africanized honey bee is an invasive species in Michigan might encounter disagreement about what counts as an invasive species, or about whether or not the Africanized honey bee is a valid example of an invasive species.

Strategy 2: Outline Criteria

Criteria are the core elements that characterize something. If something has those elements, people universally know what it is and what it is not, as long as they agree on this set of criteria. In differentiation, you might compare and contrast the criteria used in differing definitions to show where they are the same and where they diverge. In exemplification, you might offer a detailed inventory of the criteria that define something. For example, you might ask: What is an American? What are the criteria by which we can measure and assess if someone is American? Is American synonymous with citizenship? If you were to ask others to list their criteria, you might find that you share many but not all criteria in common—enough to understand what others mean, but perhaps you would also find significant points of disagreement. If the criteria about which you disagree are part of a legal definition that gives or denies rights to resources or services, for example, then your different viewpoints have real world consequences.

Strategy 3: Acknowledge Competing Definitions

If your definition argument takes the approach of differentiation, which attempts to articulate the nature of a concept among competing definitions, it is important to name those competing definitions, even quoting those opposing viewpoints directly. This strategy builds your ethos by showing that you are considering all perspectives in this issue, not hiding anything. This also establishes the nature of the controversy, showing why it is important for you to define this term at this time. For example, after Hurricane Katrina hit the Gulf Coast, many in the media called people leaving the area "refugees" because they were seeking refuge after a natural disaster. However, others contested this use of the word as inaccurate, demeaning, and even racist because most of the people displaced were African American. They claimed that in practice, this term often suggests unwelcomed people who burden those who receive them, thus this application was both inaccurate and offensive.

Strategy 4: Use Examples: Ones That Count and Ones That Do Not

Exemplification is the process of using examples that count or do not count as representing the concept you seek to define. Examples put definitions into action and make definitions meaningful. Showing examples that should *not* be counted as part of a definition can be as instructive as showing what *should* count. Showing that "X is not a Y because . . ." can help you delineate the boundaries of your definition. For example, those who said the media should not use the word "refugee" when describing people leaving the Gulf Coast after Hurricane Katrina claimed that one criteria for the concept of a "refugee" is that they are from another country. The people leaving the flooded Gulf Coast were "Americans in America," thus invalidating the use of the term "refugee" by their definition.

Strategy 5: Appeal to Authority (and Define "Authority")

Citing authoritative sources will help bolster your argument, especially if you are arguing against other authorities in your definition. You might even need to explain why one type of authority can speak to a definition more accurately than others in a given situation. In other words, you might need to define for yourself who or what counts as an authority on this issue. For example, you might want to cite an economic expert to discuss how a living wage addresses actual needs while a minimum wage does not necessarily meet needs for survival in a particular area. But you might also want to cite a minimum wage worker who can vouch for the difference in her own struggle to meet daily needs. See Chapter 25, "Inclusive Writing," and Chapter 28, "Working with Human Sources," for more on how to identify and treat with respect people who you think meet your criteria for "authority."

ELEMENTS OF DEFINITION ARGUMENTS

Good writers attend to the following elements in both the differentiation and the exemplification approaches to definition argument.

Element 1: Deepen Meaning: Dictionary versus Applied

Effective definition arguments clearly show how the audience is either misunderstanding or simply missing key criteria of what something is or means. The author's goal is to help readers understand what that idea or thing is, so that readers can successfully apply that definition to new examples. A definition argument does not rewrite a definition but rather expands or interprets that definition to make its meaning clear in a specific context. Note, for example, how the student writer featured in this chapter makes this move in the last sentence of his definition argument. He reworks Paul Farmer's definition of social justice, that "the well should take care of the sick," to say in his own words that the well should take care of the "soon to be well."

Element 2: Examples

By using example criteria of what a thing or concept is or is not, authors seek to leave readers with a clear conceptual and practical picture. Readers are more likely to accept a writer's definition if they are given clear examples and shown exactly how each part of that example fits their definition. In "'Crack Babies' Talk Back" featured in the Published Reading section, Mariah Blake cites examples of the media identifying children as "crack babies" when scientists had not agreed upon criteria to make such a diagnosis.

IN PROCESS: DEFINITION
Project: Differentiation
Objectives

- Learn to recognize words or phrases that have contested definitions.
- Develop strategies to research definitions in sources other than the dictionary by using library databases and methods to find reliable sources.
- Outline specific criteria by which a definition can be applied consistently.
- Practice precise and nuanced use of keywords and phrases through extended discussion.

Description
In this assignment, you will develop an extended definition of a word or phrase contested in current discourse. You will use specific examples and scholarly sources to forward your preferred definition. First, choose a concept that people disagree about, such as the concept of "social justice." This is a rich subject for an extended definition because theologians, philosophers, economists, and media personalities have offered definitions and critiques of this concept since the nineteenth century. Your task is to find a similarly contested term, outline the criteria that form the basis of some of the competing definitions of that term (citing at least two authoritative sources), and position yourself in this debate by offering specific examples to show what you mean based on specific criteria.

You will be evaluated based on the strength of your argument, not the position you take. While you must include at least two reliable sources that offer competing definitions, additional sources may be used to offer more definitions or examples.

Part III   Arguing with Purpose

Thesis Template

Here is a template that demonstrates one way you might construct a thesis statement for a definition argument:

> While some argue that [*keyword or phrase*] means [*definition 1*] and others argue that it means [*definition 2*], I argue that [*keyword or phrase*] means [*insert your definition or endorse the definition given by someone else and cite that person thus constituting definition 3*].

Model Thesis

This example is informed by the template for differentiation definition arguments:

> "The Green Party platform suggests that social justice is present when people have equal access to resources. Media commentator Glenn Beck defines social justice as 'Forced redistribution of wealth with a hostility toward individual property rights, under the guise of charity and/or justice.' I believe that a society can only be called just when its people have their basic needs met. A society that allows anyone to go hungry or experience high food insecurity, as many do in our city, is not practicing social justice."

Published Reading

"Crack Babies" Talk Back

Mariah Blake

> *Mariah Blake is a former senior reporter for* Mother Jones, *and she is widely published in other sources such as* The Atlantic, The Nation, *and* The New Republic. *She published the following essay on Alternet, an online project of the Independent Media Institute, which aims to improve "the public's access to independent*

290

information sources." In it, Blake argues that the commonly accepted definition of "crack babies" is incorrect and belies a number of false myths that impact the treatment of infants and negatively affects their personal identities as they grow up.

Antwaun Garcia was a shy boy whose tattered clothes reeked of cat piss. Everyone knew his father peddled drugs and his mother smoked rock, so they called him a "crack baby."

It started in fourth grade when his teacher asked him to read aloud. Antwaun stammered, then went silent. "He can't read because he's a crack baby," jeered a classmate. In the cafeteria that day no one would sit near him. The kids pointed and chanted, "crack baby, crack baby." Antwaun sat sipping his milk and staring down at his tray. After that, the taunting never stopped. Unable to take it, Antwaun quit school and started hanging out at a local drug dealer's apartment, where at age nine he learned to cut cocaine and scoop it into little glass vials.

"Crack baby," he says. "Those two words almost cost me my education."

Antwaun finally returned to school and began learning to read a year later, after he was plucked from his parents' home and placed in foster care. Now 20, he's studying journalism at LaGuardia Community College in New York City and writing for *Represent*, a magazine for and by foster children. In a recent special issue he and other young writers, many of them born to crack addicts, took aim at a media myth built on wobbly, outdated science: crack babies. Their words are helping expose the myth and the damage it has done.

Crack hit the streets in 1984, and by 1987 the press had run more than 1,000 stories about it, many focusing on the plight of so-called crack babies. The handwringing over these children started in September 1985, when the media got hold of Dr. Ira

Chasnoff's *New England Journal of Medicine* article suggesting that prenatal cocaine exposure could have a devastating effect on infants.

Only 23 cocaine-using women participated in the study, and Chasnoff warned in the report that more research was needed. But the media paid no heed. Within days of the first story, CBS News found a social worker who claimed that an 18-month-old crack-exposed baby she was treating would grow up to have "an IQ of perhaps fifty" and be "barely able to dress herself."

Soon, images of the crack epidemic's "tiniest victims"—scrawny, trembling infants—were flooding television screens. Stories about their bleak future abounded. One psychologist told *The New York Times* that crack was "interfering with the central core of what it is to be human." Charles Krauthammer, a columnist for *The Washington Post*, wrote that crack babies were doomed to "a life of certain suffering, of probable deviance, of permanent inferiority." The public braced for the day when this "biological underclass" would cripple our schools, fill our jails, and drain our social programs.

But the day never came. Crack babies, it turns out, were a media myth, not a medical reality. This is not to say that crack is harmless. Infants exposed to cocaine in the womb, including the crystallized version known as crack, weigh an average of 200 grams below normal at birth, according to a massive, ongoing National Institutes of Health study. "For a healthy, ten-pound Gerber baby this is no big deal," explains Barry Lester, the principal investigator. But it can make things worse for small, sickly infants.

Lester has also found that the IQs of cocaine-exposed 7-year-olds are four and a half points lower on average, and some researchers have documented other subtle problems. Perhaps more damaging than being exposed to cocaine itself is growing up with addicts, who are often incapable of providing a stable, nurturing home. But so-called crack babies are by no means ruined. Most fare far better, in fact, than children whose mothers drink heavily while pregnant.

Nevertheless, in the midst of the drug war hysteria, crack babies became an emblem of the havoc drugs wreak and a pretext for draconian drug laws. Hospitals began secretly testing pregnant women for cocaine, and jailing them or taking their children. Tens of thousands of kids were swept into foster care, where many languish to this day.

Represent magazine was founded at the height of the crack epidemic to give voice to the swelling ranks of children trapped in the foster care system. Its editors knew that many of their writers were born to addicts. But it wasn't until late last year, when a handful expressed interest in writing about how crack ravaged their families, that the picture snapped into focus.

"I remember hearing about crack babies and how they were doomed,'" says editor Kendra Hurley. "I suddenly realized these were those kids."

Hurley and her co-editor, Nora McCarthy, had worked with many of the writers for years, and had nudged and coddled most through the process of writing about agonizing personal experiences. But nothing compared to the shame their young scribes expressed when discussing their mothers' crack use. Even the most talented believed it had left them "slow," "retarded" or "damaged."

The editors decided to publish a special crack issue to help break the stigma and asked the writers to appear on the cover, under the headline 'CRACK BABIES'—ALL GROWN UP. Initially, only Antwaun agreed. He eventually convinced three others to join him. "I said, 'Why shouldn't we stand up and show our faces?'" he recalls. "We rose above the labels. I wanted to reach other kids who had been labeled and let them know it doesn't mean you can't succeed."

As it happens, when the crack issue went to press, a group of doctors and scientists was already lobbying *The New York Times* to drop terms like "crack baby" from its pages. The group included the majority of American researchers investigating the effects of prenatal cocaine exposure or drug addiction. They were spurred to action by the paper's coverage of a New Jersey couple found to be starving their four foster children in late 2003. For years the couple had explained the children's stunted growth to neighbors and friends by saying, among other things, that they were "crack babies." *The Times* not only failed to inform readers that crack babies don't exist, but reinforced the myth by reporting, without attribution, that "the youngest [of the children] was born a crack baby."

Assistant Managing Editor Allan Siegal refused to meet with the researchers, saying via e-mail that the paper simply couldn't open a dialogue with all the "advocacy groups who wish to influence terminology." After some haggling, he did agree to publish a short letter to the editor from the researchers. While the paper hasn't used "crack baby" in the last several months, it has referred to babies being "addicted" to crack, which, as the researchers told the editors, is scientifically inaccurate, since babies cannot be born addicted to cocaine.

The researchers later circulated a more general letter urging all media to drop the term "crack baby." But the phrase continues to turn up. Of the more than 100 news stories that have used it in the last year, some 30 were published after the letter was distributed in late February.

Represent's writers made a more resounding splash. National Public Radio and AP both featured them in stories on crack's legacy. Inspired by their words, the columnist E.R. Shipp called on *New York Daily News* readers to consider the damage the crack baby myth has done. A July *Newsday* op-ed made a similar plea, and also urged readers to avoid rushing to judgment on the growing number of babies being born to mothers who use methamphetamines.

Still, a number of recent "meth baby" stories echo the early crack baby coverage. A July AP article cautioned, for instance, that an "epidemic" of meth-exposed children in Iowa is stunting infants' growth, damaging their brains, and leaving them predisposed to delinquency. In May, one Fox News station warned that meth babies "could make the crack baby look like a walk in the nursery." Research is stacking up against such claims. But, then, scientific evidence isn't always enough to kill a good story.

For Reflection

1. Describe the definition of "crack baby" that was commonly accepted in the 1980s. What criteria was that definition based on?
2. What claim does this article make about how we should understand and use the term "crack baby" today?
3. What does this article suggest about the importance of using clear, accurate definitions? What are potential consequences when we use imprecise or inaccurate criteria?

Student Reading

Ishmael Amegashie wrote the following definitional argument as a first-year student in a Community-Based Learning Writing and Rhetoric course. The course allowed him to serve at the Center for the Homeless and that experience influenced his choice of writing topics throughout the class, including this argument. He is now an engineer who notes this course as one of the most enriching in his undergraduate experience.

Ishmael Amegashie
Social Justice: More Than Meeting an Immediate Need

According to Paul Farmer, a Professor at Harvard University, for social justice to be achieved, "the well should take care of the sick," while Borlaug Borlaug, a 1970 Nobel Peace Prize Winner, posits that "the first essential component of social justice is adequate food for all mankind." I propose that social justice be viewed as more than simply providing for the needs of the weak and unfortunate, or supplying bowls of soup to the hungry; rather, social justice is what results, in my opinion, when we seek as a people to make every member of society capable of not only leveraging available resources, but also becoming independent of outside support as a result of those resources.

While I do agree that one manifestation of social justice is that it allows the "sick" to benefit from the "well," I refuse to accept that that is the only defining quality, or central pillar, of social justice. To be truly just involves more than simply helping individuals when they are at their lowest point of need; instead, true justice ensures that no one gets to that point of need, and that all have the opportunity and capacity to achieve for themselves a comfortable future. As John D. Rockefeller puts it, "charity is injurious unless it helps the recipient to become independent of it." It is in our interest, as a society, to put in place the structures that enable individuals to sustain themselves, such as an emphasis on education beyond high school, and the provision of jobs to accommodate individuals of all levels of expertise, with the ultimate aim of limiting the amount of "charity" and promoting self-sufficiency. The story of Shawn, a former guest at the Center for the Homeless, captures this point even more vividly. Shawn barely received his high school diploma when he fell in with the wrong crowd—drinking, smoking, drug abuse, and all sorts of social misconduct became the centerpiece of Shawn's life. Over ten years of poor choices landed him in jail and caused his parents to disown him, which is how he ended up at the Center for the Homeless. Through opportunities offered by the Center for the Homeless, Shawn was able to get rehabilitated, and today helps with adult education and mentoring at the homeless shelter. As opposed to committing simply to meeting Shawn's immediate need, the Center for the Homeless went a (necessary) step further: to bring him to a place of self-sustenance and even service—the ultimate expression of social justice.

Another misunderstanding or misinterpretation of social justice is that it is in some way connected to, or defined as, the provision of the basic needs (food, shelter, etc.) of the poor. I would argue that social justice is more than merely supplying "adequate food for all mankind," as suggested by Borlaug, because the reality is that anyone who does not have the capacity to satisfy her hunger is usually poor, whereas social justice, if it is to exist, would not only be for the poor but for all—the rich and otherwise. Consequently, the many challenges that society faces as it tries to establish social justice is mainly attributable to the fact that it is still a widely held view that social justice, if it were to exist, would solely benefit the poor. It is, thus, poisonous to view social justice as something that serves the interest of the underprivileged alone, as that would only equate it to radical ideas such as wealth redistribution or depict it as an instrument of class warfare. Rather, social justice should be seen as what it fundamentally is: a state in which all are treated equally, afforded the same opportunities, and allowed equal access to the safeguards that society has available. So that injustice whether it is suffered by a white or blue collar worker would mean the same thing, or as Martin Luther King Jr.

argues, "injustice anywhere is a threat to justice everywhere," and further that, "We are caught in an inescapable network of mutuality, tied in a single garment of destiny." Effectively, the goal in the end, as echoed by King, should be justice not because we want to be charitable to the poor but justice because we each have our future dependent upon it.

Ultimately, two ingredients suggest themselves as necessary for the attainment of social justice to its fullest extent: that we take a personal interest in the success of others, not through guilt-induced charity, but rather through a thoughtful effort to help every individual come to a place of self-sustenance, and that we view a threat to the success of others as a threat to our own success. For as Shawn's story shows us, a system committed to equipping individuals with the tools to go from being a cost to society to being an asset, is one that is not only efficient, as it transforms problems into solutions, but also sustainable in that it does not require too large an investment to run, and offers returns of logarithmic proportions on even the meager investments on which it operates. Overall, what a system of social justice that seeks not simply to meet the immediate need of the individual, but also to empower him, achieves is a dynamic in which it is not just the "well" caring for the "sick," but the "well" supporting the "soon to be well."

Works Cited

Borlaug, Norman. "Nobel Lecture: The Green Revolution, Peace and Humanity." *Prize Award Ceremony*, 11 Dec. 1970, Sweden, Stockholm, www.NobelPrize.org. Accessed 10 Oct. 2011.

Farmer, Paul. "HIV Through the Eyes of a Physician: Interview with Paul Farmer." *Satya*, Stealth Technologies, Inc., Apr. 2000. Accessed 9 Oct. 2011.

King, Martin L., Jr. "Martin Luther King's 'Letter From Birmingham Jail'" Received by C.C.J. Carpenter, Joseph A. Durick, Milton L. Grafman, Paul Hardin, Nolan Bailey Harmon, George M. Murray, Ed V. Rampage, Earl Stallings., *Atlantic Monthly*, 2nd ed., vol. 212, 16 Apr. 1963, Washington, D.C., pp. 78-88. *The Atlantic*, Atlantic Media Company, 16 Apr. 2013. Accessed 11 Oct. 2011.

"John D. Rockefeller." Gledhill Enterprises, 2011, www.1-Famous-Quotes.com. Accessed 11 Oct. 2011.

For Reflection

1. Which type of definition argument approach does the author take? Explain.
2. What strategies does the author employ? Give examples from the text.
3. What is at stake in exploring a definition for this particular concept?

DEFINITION: THE WRITING PROCESS

In the following section, we use student writer Ishmael Amegashie's notes and drafts to examine his thinking about the writing process.

Analyze the Assignment

The "Definition Argument" asks you to write an extended definition of a contested term supported by evidence from sources. You will be expected to go well beyond the dictionary definition of a concept to what it means more fully in theory and practice, using examples as support.

Ishmael created a new folder on his computer for this project, labeling the folder "Definition Argument." Next, he created a new document in that folder, named it "Definition argument assignment journal," and recorded his preliminary ideas and questions:

Assignment Analysis

- The action verbs and descriptive phrases in the assignment are:
  1. "develop" an "extended" definition
  2. "use" examples and sources
  3. "competing" definitions
  4. "firsthand observations"
  5. "citing" sources in works cited page
- The audience is my instructor and classmates as we do peer review. They probably read different types of media and might have very different perspectives on the concept I define. I don't want to make anybody mad, but I also want to take a stand that gets their attention.
- I haven't written a definition paper like this before, but the more I think about and look for it, the more I see how often people stop to define what they mean—especially in academics.

Plan: Organizing the Process

Your instructor will set your deadlines and paper length for this assignment. Once you know those two critical pieces of information, you can map your schedule. Ishmael opened up his project folder and added the following text to his assignment journal:

I have 2 weeks total from the day we were given the assignment to the day it's due. A rough draft is due at the end of this week for in-class peer review. I don't have time to go to the Writing Center before then, so I will try to go there when I have a complete draft done after the in-class peer review. My plan is:

> WEEK 1: Review media and decide what concept I will write about. Find 4–5 sources to bounce my definition off of—I might not use them all. If I hear somebody speaking about the issue on T.V. or see it on social media, I will search that person in the library's database to see what they have written on the topic. Write at least two pages for the in-class peer review so that they can give me more feedback.
>
> WEEK 2: Review draft based on peer review. Set up Writing Center appointment at least one day before the paper is due to get more feedback. Reread my draft and do more research if necessary. Upload paper to course website.

Question: Exploring Issues

The first step is to find a significant term about which people argue the meaning because they use a different set of criteria to define that term. You can get in touch with current debates through media outlets such as:

- International—Find English-language editions (or editions in other languages you understand) of national media from other countries, or read/watch the international sections of reliable American news sources.
- National—*New York Times*, *Washington Post*, National Public Radio, public television, network and cable news, and other media.
- Regional—Local newspapers, local television, local radio, and so on.
- Campus—Campus newspapers, campus magazines, campus television stations, and the like.

What word or phrase is causing confusion or conflict as people try to work through an argument? What word or phrase gets people on one "side" of an issue all worked up? Note all those words and phrases to consider as the subject of your definition argument. Ishmael wrote the following notes on the current debates he heard:

- I started watching CNN in the evening and put a news aggregator app on my phone to capture the headlines. I also flipped through the campus newspaper and was interested in debates people were having about what issues qualify students to start a club sponsored by the university. I took notes and thought I might focus on a specific issue until we had a good discussion in class one day about the nature of social justice. I had a different definition in mind than what some of my classmates said. I searched that term online and quickly saw that this is a "contested" concept. Some of the specific cases I wrote down might actually work as examples for my definition argument on "social justice."

Read: Strategies for Reading in Research

The next step is to read your sources critically. Critical reading means working to understand what a writer is trying to communicate by paying close attention to every word as well as asking questions that uncover potential weaknesses in the text. The sources you collect through your research for the definition argument might serve as voices articulating a competing or supporting definition of the word or phrase you are analyzing. They might also serve to provide examples for analysis that you test against the criteria that define your word or phrase. Ishmael found six possible sources by using "social justice" as a keyword search first in a general online search engine, then through his library's search engine. He downloaded and read each source critically, taking notes on where each author defined this term in his or her own words, and where they used examples to support that definition. Using a chart helped visualize those voices to compare and contrast the differing criteria. Ishmael noted the following in his assignment journal:

I started with a general online search using the phrase "social justice" to see what current conversations came up and what names seem most interesting. I was not sure if people were actively debating each other right now or if this was more of a long-time debate about the concept. I saw that there were a few times when it did come up as an active debate, such as when Glenn Beck gave his definition and many people responded. But I could also see that people have debated this concept for a long time. I chose some of the people who seemed to have the most interesting and different definitions and searched for them in our library's database to make sure I found the best writing sample on this topic. I knew it was important to use direct quotation in my essay to cite how at least two other authors defined the term "social justice," so I highlighted the place in each text where that happened. I noticed that sometimes authors define a term a couple times in their writing. That makes sense because I will probably do the same thing in my essay as I try to explain what I mean in different ways. I also made a list of examples they use to explain their definition. I might want to critique some of the examples used by people I disagree with.

Invent: Take Note and Create

Once you have chosen a key concept to define and have collected sources that both support and challenge your definition, you can start to develop your own definition. List the definitions from your sources. In what ways do they agree? What seems to be the motivation behind each different definition? What is at stake in the way the term is defined? How popular are particular definitions? Ishmael made a chart to help compare the different definitions.

- I made a chart to make sure I was looking at different sources in the same way. That helped me treat each one equally and fairly to hear what they were trying to say. It also helped me find the gaps in those sources so that I could insert my own thoughts and examples. [See Table 19.1, "Comparing Definitions of 'Social Justice'"].

Arrange: Prioritize, Organize, Outline

Begin your definition argument with an explanation of why a clear definition is needed for the word or phrase you have chosen. Describe the context of discussion and debate that make it necessary to do this definitional work at this time. Your thesis statement (see Chapter 12, "Draft: Introduction, Body, Conclusion") will situate your definition in relation to other definitions. You can then organize your essay in relation to other definitions and examples, possibly working through definitions you disagree with first, then stepping in to develop your definition (Chapter 11, "Arrange: Prioritize, Organize, Outline").

Table 19.1   COMPARING DEFINITIONS OF "SOCIAL JUSTICE"

Questions	Author #1: Borlaug, Norman. "Nobel Lecture: The Green Revolution, Peace and Humanity"	Author #2: Paul Farmer "HIV Through the Eyes of a Physician: Interview with Paul Farmer"	Author #3: John D. Rockefeller	Author #4: Martin Luther King, Jr. "Letter from a Birmingham Jail"	Me: Ishmael Amegashie
Definitions of "social justice"	"the first essential component of social justice is adequate food for all mankind."	"the well should take care of the sick"	"charity is injurious unless it helps the recipient to become independent of it."	"injustice anywhere is a threat to justice everywhere"; "We are caught in an inescapable network of mutuality, tied in a single garment of destiny."	Interest in the success of others and don't see others' success as a threat to our own success.
Positive examples that do represent social justice in action	All countries need food reserves in case of natural disaster, no matter how poor or rich they are. Increasing cereal grains in all countries, not just affluent ones. Export new seeds and technologies to other countries.	Equal standards of care regardless of whether patient can afford care.	Addressing the root causes of poverty.	Direct action that creates necessary nonviolent tension intense enough to demand change and negotiation.	Education beyond high school, jobs available to all levels of workers.

306

| Negative examples that do not count as social justice for this author | Dependence on international research groups alone will not substitute the need for national agricultural research organizations. Produce enough local food to feed the hungry rather than keep the situation from worsening. Producing food is not enough; must also be distributed to those who can't access it. | Different standards of care for people according to where they live. | Simply offering help by means of short-term material charities. | Obeying laws that are unjust. Disobeying just laws. Avoidance of extremism just to avoid extremism. Compromises to remove some artifacts of racism and delays in doing these. | Merely providing charity, food, and healthcare. Social justice that only aims to advance the interests of the underprivileged themselves. |

Ishmael opened his assignment journal and wrote:

Right now, these are the key ideas that stand
out to me and can become an outline for
the paper:

- Social justice has to do with hot button issues like race, gender, poverty, and religion. It has political implications.
- People who see or experience discrimination tend to be more in support of the idea of social justice. People who don't see or experience that tend to think social justice is about taking things away from rich and powerful people.
- Time is an important factor in thinking about social justice. Social justice can be about correcting immediate problems and/or about correcting long-term issues.
- Some people have strong views on this topic, but I'm guessing that people in my class might not have views on this topic yet, so I have a good chance to shape their thinking on this definition.

Draft: Introduction, Body, Conclusion

The purpose of the definition argument is to persuade your readers to accept your definition of a contested term among competing definitions. To do that, you will offer good reasons and clear examples to show what does and does not count as an example of that concept.

Introduction

The introduction to a definition argument should outline the context for dispute about the word or phrase you have chosen. Readers should quickly understand what word or phrase you have chosen and why you have chosen it. To do that, the introduction can either take readers through a quick summary of various viewpoints on this definition, or it can take readers into an example that either does or does not count as representing that concept. In his assignment journal, Ishmael noted:

People have wildly different ideas about what social justice means, so I think I need to represent some of those different viewpoints right up front in my introduction. Some of my readers might not have their own definition of social justice yet, and some might already align themselves strongly with one of these existing viewpoints. I need to be honest about the range of strongly differing views and get them on the table right away.

Body

The approach you take to the definition argument will help determine the structure of the essay. If you primarily want to *differentiate* your meaning of this word or phrase from how others define it, then it is important to use the body paragraphs to work through each of those alternate viewpoints, showing how your definition is the same or different from what others have said and giving good reasons to support your position. If you primarily want to *exemplify* your definition, showing why specific examples do or do not count as belonging to the concept you analyze, then you should introduce those examples early in your paper. You might choose to organize paragraphs around points related to one example. You could also draft new paragraphs for each example, explaining how those examples do or do not meet the criteria for the concept you are defining. In the "Outline ideas" section of his assignment journal, Ishmael jotted down some preliminary thoughts about the body of his analysis:

I want to differentiate my definition from what others have said. I narrowed down

sources to just a few that will be good to play
off. I will arrange my paragraphs to work
through each of those definitions by others
to show what I think does and does not work
in each.

Conclusion

In the conclusion of your definition argument, your goal is to leave
readers with a clear sense of why they should adopt your definition
of a word or phrase rather than the alternative options, or to show
how an example does or does not fit a particular definition. Ishmael
recorded a possible approach to his conclusion:

I want to end by emphasizing what I see as
the most important ingredients that must be
present to make social justice happen.

Revise: Strategies for Re-seeing

Rethinking the definition argument means stepping back to make
sure you have addressed opposing viewpoints and have chosen to analyze examples that make your point most clearly. Ishmael returned to
his assignment journal to update his progress:

To re-see my draft, I used the distancing
technique of setting the paper aside for a day
while I read two more relevant articles. I then
re-read the paper aloud to hear it anew before
starting to make revisions. I immediately noticed some places where I made assumptions
that had to be explained and where I left out
some important information that would help
readers. I added a citation from one of the
new articles I read to help fill that gap.

Review: By Peers and Experts

Careful review on the definition argument can help you confirm that you have considered all alternative definitions and presented yours with enough evidence to convince readers of your position. Ishmael noted this about his review process:

The in-class peer review was very helpful. They said they liked the sources I found but thought I was not representing the opposing viewpoints well enough, so I will summarize and explain those in more detail. They also wanted me to give more examples to explain my definition. I will revise based on their comments.

Proofread and Submit

Ensure that all the direct quotations are properly cited in text and in your Works Cited or References page. If you know of any style, mechanical, and formatting errors you frequently make, review your draft specifically to identify and correct those errors rather than trying to look at everything at once. When Ishmael updated his assignment journal, he noted:

I am most concerned that I make sure my points are clear and persuasive. I know that some of my readers won't initially agree with my point of view, so I don't want to offend them, but I also need to say what I believe in no uncertain terms. I want to look at word choice to make sure my tone is firm but not offensive. I also know that I need help with MLA style, so I will consult resources in my textbook and have a peer or Writing Center tutor look for those errors.

WHAT HAPPENS NEXT?

Paying attention to how stakeholders in the media, politics, popular culture, the community, and even the classroom define key terms is an important part of being an active listener in public discourse. Asking people to define what they mean—and formulating your own definitions based on meaningful criteria—can clarify points of disagreement as well as points of connection in an argument. Our words and actions spring from our basic concept of what something is, how it is defined. Leading with clear definitions shows your audience the foundation of your thinking, giving you a solid position from which to construct your message. Work on developing the habit of clarifying your definitions early in the process of talking or writing through an argument. The sooner you articulate a shared understanding of criteria or unearth differing expectations, the better able you are to offer the most persuasive claims and evidence to connect with your audience.

OFFICE HOURS ➤ Handling Controversial Topics

Definition arguments demand firm boundaries: you claim that something is *this* and it's not *that*. Such distinctions can cause people to choose sides, standing up for one definition and standing against another. Because of that tension, you might want to talk through your position with your instructor as you think about circulating your writing with other readers.

   For example, think of the recent debate about gay marriage. If society defines marriage as a contract between one man and one woman, then the law does not permit same-sex couples to marry. The law had to change—be redefined—in order to allow for new criteria. Even though the law has changed, some people still hold different working definitions of marriage.

As you write a definition argument on an issue being debated currently, as the definition argument requires you to do, you will likely discover that not all your readers agree with your definition. In fact, you should assume that they do not. As you share your writing with readers, they might express their disagreement with your position. How should you handle that feedback?

First, listen. By listening carefully, you learn about your audience and can appreciate their worldview a bit more. You might disagree on this issue but find common ground in a fuller discussion.

Second, remember that you are seeking feedback on your writing. Direct that attention back to the text so that your reader can point out where you are least and most convincing in the writing you shared. A good reader can disagree with your position but still be focused enough to help you strengthen your argument.

Talk with your instructor if you are nervous about sharing your position or if you encounter unproductive responses from your readers. You might not be alone in this regard and your instructor might want to discuss this challenge further with the class.

CHAPTER twenty

Evaluation: Considering Criteria

Evaluation arguments try to persuade readers that something is good or bad, right or wrong, based on specific criteria. We make evaluations every day, "liking" items posted online, choosing colleges, choosing classes, choosing careers, or supporting one candidate or cause over another. But the "like" button is not an argument. An evaluation argument includes not just your conclusion about what to do or not do but the reasons why you made that choice. Writing effective evaluation arguments requires you to articulate and assess your reasons for holding a certain position.

STRATEGIES FOR EVALUATION ARGUMENTS

You can approach an evaluation argument two ways: argue that something is (1) a good or bad example of a category, or (2) a right or wrong action, based on specific criteria. The following strategies will help you determine your approach and support that approach through an appropriate balance of ethical, practical, and aesthetic reasons.

Strategy 1: Claim Good or Bad Example of Category X

Evaluation arguments proceed from strong definitions. Once you establish the nature of something through definition, you can then argue that it counts as a good or bad example of that category based on specific criteria. If you were evaluating presidential candidates, for example, you might consider the following criteria: relevant leadership experience, record of ethical behavior, knowledge of domestic public policy, knowledge of foreign policy, personality and character, legal eligibility, and so forth. Legal eligibility is objective, but the rest require subjective interpretation supported by examples and evidence. If you were trying to select a presidential candidate, you would first outline the criteria that make for the ideal president, then you would evaluate specific candidates according to those criteria to see how well they meet your expectations. Your argument will explain why one candidate is the best and/or why other candidates are inferior or even bad examples of what a president should be.

Strategy 2: Claim Right or Wrong Action: Principles and Consequences

In addition to helping you define good and bad examples, evaluation arguments help you articulate right and wrong action based on specific criteria. That ethical assessment can be based on adhering to positive principles of what is right or avoiding negative consequences. We should do something because it meets the criteria of what has already been established as right, or we should not do that because it would cause an outcome that we have already determined to be ethically wrong. Evaluation is thus often an important component of proposal arguments as the careful attention to criteria helps establish the foundation of proposals for action.

For example, you might evaluate the U.S. War on Drugs to consider how we know if it has been effective and therefore whether or not we should continue with the policies, such as mandatory minimum sentences, that have defined this hardline approach. If your criteria for measuring what is right include fairness in application, you might consider how this approach has been unevenly applied across races as evidence that it is not the right course of action, evaluating it as a failure to equitably reduce crime and drug use.

Strategy 3: Balance Ethical, Practical, and Aesthetic Reasons

Writers of effective evaluations consider three types of reasons in their support: ethical, practical, and aesthetic. *Ethical* reasons address a moral perspective of whether something is right or wrong, just or unjust, fair or unfair based on a particular set of values. *Practical* reasons address outcomes based on logical factors such as economics, health, and efficiency. *Aesthetic* reasons address artistic qualities such as the subject's beauty; its success at provoking thought, laughter, pity or fear; or its originality. Most decisions benefit from considering all three perspectives, although a written argument may focus only on the most significant of those considerations.

When we interrogate our own values and reasons in the process of decision making, we become better equipped to apply and prioritize the lens that will help us make decisions we can stand by. People generally disagree not because they lack values, but because they have prioritized values in a different way. If we can understand how others apply those values in different situations, we can make a more persuasive appeal to them.

ELEMENTS OF EVALUATION ARGUMENTS

Good evaluation arguments attend to four different elements. They (1) compare and contrast examples, (2) construct and prioritize criteria, (3) use quantitative and qualitative methods, and (4) use powerful adjectives.

Element 1: Compare and Contrast Examples

Identifying something as good or bad requires comparison to other items in that category to establish a hierarchy of examples. If you only have one example, it's hard to say just how good or bad it is. By comparing and contrasting examples, you begin to see, for instance, that one presidential candidate, while not perfect, is better than another based on specific criteria. If you want to move from a claim of who is a good candidate to what is the right course of action in an election, then your final argument might rely on that comparison: vote for candidate x because she/he is the lesser of two evils or, preferably, the greater of two saints!

Element 2: Construct and Prioritize Criteria

To determine whether something is the best, worst, or mediocre version, you must first outline relevant criteria for measuring examples and then prioritize which of those criteria matter most and least. Your reasons for selecting those criteria could be ethical, practical, and/or aesthetic. See Table 20.1, "Defining Reasons for Evaluation," for lines of questions that help define categories. Depending on the rhetorical situation, you will weigh those categories differently. What we care about and how much we care can vary over time and place, so it's important to be clear with yourself and your audience about the framework you apply to reach your thesis stating your evaluation.

Element 3: Use Quantitative and Qualitative Methods

In addition to using ethical, practical, and aesthetic reasons to develop criteria for evaluation, consider both quantitative (numeric) and qualitative (quality) methods when constructing your evaluation. Adding these questions pushes you to ask: Can we measure how much better or worse (quantitative)? And can we describe in what ways it is better or worse (qualitative)? In *quantity*, can you provide

Table 20.1   DEFINING REASONS FOR EVALUATION

ETHICAL QUESTIONS	PRACTICAL QUESTIONS	AESTHETIC QUESTIONS
Will someone be physically, financially, or emotionally *hurt* by this?	Is this the most *efficient* response? Does it save time, energy, and/or money?	Will this advance *beauty* and *joy* in the world?
Will someone be physically, financially, or emotionally *uplifted* by this consistent with my principles and values?	Is this the most *effective* response? Will this complete the job/resolve the issue to the satisfaction of stakeholders?	Will this reduce *ugliness* in the world?
Will the benefit of this only be short term or can it be *sustained* long term?	Is there an *alternative* way to do this that would be more efficient or effective?	Does the way this is presented draw us into spending more time and *attention* on the issue?
Does the benefit of this extend beyond the individual to the local, national, or international *community*?	Is any harm caused by this a necessary or acceptable *consequence*?	Does the way this is presented advance our *understanding* of the issue?
What is at stake in *qualitative* terms—describe in words what could be better or worse. What is at stake in *quantitative* terms—offer statistical facts for comparison.	What is at stake in *qualitative* terms—describe in words what could be better or worse. What is at stake in *quantitative* terms—offer statistical facts for comparison.	Does this *move* people?
Would an alternative action or person produce a *greater good*?	Would an alternative action or person produce a *larger impact* using *fewer resources*?	Would an alternative action or person bring more *harmony*?

numbers that compare how much faster, how much less expensive, or how much less time something will be? In *quality*, can you provide evidence that something is a compassionate, fair, or successful expression of the issue? The most robust evaluation arguments will consider quantitative and qualitative methods when assessing the subject and will use both when constructing their own argument.

Element 4: Use Powerful Adjectives

Adjectives help you differentiate among multiple examples, showing that some are stronger than others. Vivid adjectives can provide nuance, adding an efficient persuasive punch in just one word. For example, you could describe a political candidate as "patriotic." That word evokes strong reactions. In a good evaluation argument, a writer would go on to define the word "patriotic," explain why he or she thinks that is a good or bad quality, and show how that candidate has performed patriotic acts.

Adjectives make great bumper stickers and campaign slogans, but they are only the beginning of an argument. Don't make the mistake of stringing together claims of good and bad, right and wrong, without evidence to support those assessments. Start with adjectives, but move beyond them into sound reasons and evidence.

IN PROCESS: EVALUATION
Project: Evaluate Policies, Programs, or People in Public Office

Objectives

- Identify policies or programs from government, business, non-profit, or academic institutions that should be evaluated.
- Articulate specific criteria to guide evaluation of a policy or program based on how good/bad or right/wrong it is.
- Locate scholarly and popular sources that provide sound research to construct an evaluation argument that considers ethical, practical, and aesthetic reasons.

Description

In this assignment, you will use reliable sources to write an evaluation argument assessing the effectiveness of a policy or program, especially one that addresses a social concern. The source of this policy or program could be a government, business, nonprofit, or academic institution. Be sure that the target of your inquiry is small enough that you can address it in this assignment, while you also have access to adequate data for a full and fair evaluation. You must have access to detailed information in order to make a solid assessment, and you must articulate specific criteria by which that assessment is made. For example, you could evaluate the success of a program for people who are homeless by the extent of its job skills course offerings or on the extent of its spiritual skills programming.

Evaluations are frequently assigned as capstone projects in community service courses, or undertaken as part of community-based internships. In the civic as well as the work domain, consultants, administrators, or board members who want to assess a policy or program to make recommendations about further action frequently write or commission evaluation arguments.

Thesis Template

Here are two templates that demonstrate ways you might construct a thesis statement for your evaluation argument:

> [*Name of program*] [*is/is not effective*] because it [*does/does not meet*] the most important criteria, [*name criteria 1, 2, and 3*], to achieve [*name the outcomes that would be evidence of success by your measure*].

> While [*opposing experts named x, y, and z*] argue that [*insert target social concern*] is [*effectively*] addressed through [*describe approaches that do not represent the criteria you most value*], I agree with [*name experts A, B, and C*] who argue that [*describe approach that you*

support] is most effective because it addresses *[name social concern]* by focusing on *[name activities that represent the criteria you do value]*.

Model Thesis

Following are two models of thesis statements for evaluation arguments that map roughly to the thesis templates presented:

> "Heifer Project International is an effective aid program for people experiencing poverty because it addresses immediate needs by providing livestock that offer nutrition such as milk, it addresses long term sustainability for the original family because their animals soon produce surplus food that can be sold for extra income, and it addresses community needs because the original family must share the offspring of their livestock with neighbors who will participate in the same way."

> "Although the Mayor's office fairly criticizes its limited capacity for residents, I agree with social workers who support the Delancey Street approach to homelessness as the most effective means of preventing recidivism because it emphasizes peer mentoring and career development without any time limit rather than pressuring people who are already distressed to get through programs within a strict time limit."

Published Reading

A Middle-Class Anti-Poverty Solution

Tressie McMillan Cottom

> *Lecturing and publishing widely on the subjects of inequality, education, race, and gender, Tressie McMillan Cottom is a sociologist and regular columnist for* Slate. *Her work appears in academic journals and in mainstream publications including*

The Atlantic, NPR, The Chronicle of Higher Education, and many more. McMillan Cottom served as a Fellow at the Center for Poverty Research at the University of California—Davis when she wrote this essay, originally published at Talking Points Memo, *an online political news organization. In this essay, McMillan Cottom analyzes the changing criteria by which the Higher Education Act of 1965 has been measured.*

Anxious middle-class families and students are struggling with rising tuition costs, growing inequality, and fewer clear paths for upward mobility. The prescription has long been to get a good education for a good job and good life. But what is "good," and how are you supposed to pay for it? The answer isn't as clear as it once was. With total student loan debt in the United States topping $1 trillion, it seems like a bad time to talk about how an anti-poverty program became a middle-class entitlement program. Designed as part of Lyndon Johnson's Great Society vision of a war on poverty, the Higher Education Act of 1965, which established financial aid assistance for students in need, had a clear goal: to give the poor an equal shot at college. Today, more than half of all students use federal financial aid to pay for college, but the program's anti-poverty focus has been replaced with a fuzzy affordability mission. More middle-class families are using programs designed as an anti-poverty solution, and poorer students are getting short shrift.

I made a pretty straightforward argument in the *New York Times* to this effect: If we are not clear as to what financial aid programs are supposed to do, they will work best and most for students with the resources to work the system. Commenters at the *Times* took issue with the idea that middle–class families do not deserve government assistance just because they have done all the right things and worked hard and prepared their kids well. They are right that tuition costs are outpacing the ability to pay, but we disagree on what financial aid is supposed to do—and that is not an accident. When financial aid went from addressing poverty to finding a fair way to help *all* students pay for college, it made strange bedfellows of students who have competing interests.

When I know what a thing is supposed to do, I know how to measure how well it is doing that thing. When financial aid was clearly about leveling the playing field for poor students by helping them do what wealthier families had for generations—pay for college—we had a good idea of how to gauge the success of financial aid. Ronald Reagan said of Johnson's war on poverty that "poverty won"—a dig at Johnson's social security and welfare programs. But Reagan never could have said federal financial aid had failed, because by almost any measure it was a success. With the means to pay for college, a record number of women, African-Americans, and low-income students changed the face of higher education in the 1970s.

How do you sell a successful program as a failure? Beginning with the Reagan administration, conservative rhetoric recast an anti-poverty mission as anti-equality. According to this line of thinking, by focusing on increased diversity in higher education, federal financial aid programs penalized wealthier families whose only crime had been playing by the rules and winning at life. By reducing Pell Grants, requiring tax forms for the poorest recipients, and reducing government subsidies of student loans, the government made the assumption that—as with the infamous "welfare queen" myth—the poor were prone to committing federal aid fraud.

While we think of "fair" as an absolute measure, in reality "fair" is awfully relative. Poorer students need financial aid to afford college, but are more likely to come from schools, families, and communities that cannot guide them through the process. At the same time, wealth advisers and elite media counsel wealthier families on how to leverage cheap financial aid money to protect family assets like investments and home equity. In practice, this is how inequality is reproduced. Financial aid reform largely focuses on making college more affordable. Like "fair," that sounds reasonable—until we ask, Whose measure of "affordable" are we using?

For wealthier students, achieving "affordability" may mean going to a more prestigious private or out-of-state college instead of taking the cheaper in-state option. For the poorest students, affordability may mean going to college instead of not going to college. Both are worthy goals, but when one program tries to serve them both, a muddled mission makes it hard to choose whose needs come first.

One example of this conflict is the requirement to submit your family's income information on the Free Application for Federal Student Aid, known as FAFSA. The process is designed to dole out grants and loans based on how much a family needs the help. But the form doesn't necessarily give an accurate reflection of a family's true wealth—it doesn't ask for home equity value, for example. Wealthier people tend to own homes with more equity. Homeownership is the primary form of wealth-building in this country—and it is primarily a concern that poor people don't have.

If relatively wealthy homeowners can withhold relevant data from the FAFSA, why do poor students with almost every other indicator of high financial need have to provide family income information to get financial aid? Poor students can be estranged from parents because of incarceration, illness, or countless other reasons. (On Twitter, one reader of my *Times* piece recounted losing a Pell Grant due to lack of information from an estranged parent.) But without providing their parents' income information, most cannot get financial aid; a lengthy, daunting appeals process often results. If we were clear about whom financial aid should serve most and best, then changing the form for poorer students would be a no-brainer.

But that hasn't happened, and neither have a host of other financial aid reforms that have been proposed over the years. The result is that even though financial aid was founded and expanded to stymie inequality, unequal experiences of what's fair have made a Great Society program just another entitlement for the wealthiest few who know how to game the system.

For Reflection

1. What criteria does McMillan Cottom argue should be used to measure the success of the Higher Education Act of 1965?
2. What criteria does McMillan Cottom claim that others use to measure the success of this program?
3. What is at stake when people have different criteria to evaluate this federal program?
4. What criteria would you use to evaluate this program? How would you measure its success?

Student Reading

Rebecca Van Handel wrote this evaluation argument as a first-year college student. She took a Community-Based Learning Writing and Rhetoric course partnered with the Center for the Homeless. As a graduate, she continues to work with people who are homeless as a result of that experience in her first year of college.

Rebecca Van Handel
So Efficient—Too Efficient: Evaluating SNAP

SNAP, the Supplemental Nutrition Assistance Program, began on May 16, 1939, the
brainchild of the Secretary of Agriculture
at the time, Henry Wallace. Twenty million individuals applied and were accepted
into the program within the first four years,
receiving blue and orange "stamps" that
could be used to purchase food items. The
program continued to evolve into the SNAP,
commonly known as food stamps, which
many are familiar with today. Eligibility has
expanded allowing approximately forty-five
million people a month to receive SNAP
benefits (United States Department of
Agriculture Food and Nutrition Service).
SNAP is extremely efficient; however, it
has essentially become too efficient to adequately regulate and audit the program for
abuse and corruption. Therefore, SNAP,
despite efficiency, needs to improve upon its
ability to assess what types of assistance are
provided by limiting the number of retailers
accepting the "stamps" and having tighter
controls on eligibility and retention within
the program.

An enormous government program such
as SNAP can be difficult to evaluate without
first determining specific criteria to assess.
A government assistance organization such

as SNAP can only be effective if it is able to reach a large percentage of its target population as well as control how its benefits are used. SNAP has made it extremely easy to apply for benefits. A simple visit to the organization's government website allows applicants to fill out all necessary forms online or print the form and mail the completed form to the SNAP processing center. The forms are quite easy to fill out, asking simple questions about household members' genders, ages, income, and expenses. Once information is verified and an individual or household is accepted into the program, a card with a monetary value based on provided information is mailed each month to the participant. The monetary value on the card is intended to be used to purchase nutritional food and other basic items at participating retailers (United States Department of Agriculture Food and Nutrition Service). This system has proved to be quite efficient with a simple mailing each month allowing participants to receive their benefits without delay; however, this is where corruption begins and adjustments need to be made to SNAP.

First, an audit needs to be conducted to determine what exactly qualifies under the clause of "nutritional food." Currently, carbonated beverages, potato chips, and even candy bars can be purchased in most states using SNAP benefits. It is ironic that these same foods have been ordered removed from government supplemented school lunch programs yet remain on the acceptable purchases with government SNAP benefits. In multiple states, under the "Restaurant Meals Program" portion of SNAP, food stamps can be used at various fast food locations, again targeted by the government for having unhealthy food offerings to children. Also because of the ease with which a card can be redeemed without identification a "black market" has emerged in which people sell their cards for pennies on the dollar. The cash received for the card can be used for any purchase including cigarettes, drugs, alcohol, and even online shopping (Cook). While the obvious consequence of this is federal tax dollars being improperly appropriated, upon further investigation other consequences become evident. According to an investigative report conducted by the University of South Carolina at Chapel Hill, more than 36% of food stamp recipients still rely heavily on local food pantries for goods. Through further investigations the study found instances of fraud in which food stamps were sold for cash that was used to purchase items not eligible to be bought with food stamps. The participants then merely went to their local food pantry to receive necessary food items (Paynter, Berner, and Anderson 31).

Reducing corruption will be difficult. Despite this, steps need to be taken to ensure the same efficiency currently enjoyed by the program, to provide for auditing, and to ensure benefits are properly used. Food stamp cards should specifically include the participant's name and address on the card. Retailers should then be instructed to check the identification of the person using the card. This would help to make it more difficult to sell food stamp cards for cash. In addition, reducing the amount of funds on the card, but in turn supplying each recipient with specific food items from a participating retailer within their region could allow the government more control over which items the participants receive. These simple adjustments to SNAP would do little to effect the high efficiency of the program, but would still attempt to put into effect some auditing control (Guthrie et al.).

Since 1939, The Supplemental Nutrition Assistance Program has provided individuals and households with food assistance. The goal of this program since its commencement was to provide nutritional food for food insecure households and individuals. Today, the program efficiently provides these benefits to forty-five million people each month. However, a cost of this efficiency is a lack of auditing and control within the program. Taking simple steps such as requiring identification to use food stamp cards and

reducing the monetary value of each card
and substituting it with specific food items
from retailers can drastically improve SNAP.

Works Cited

Cook, Katherine. "Feds: Portland Woman Brokered Food Stamps."
    Channel 8 News, 7 Apr. 2011, www.Kgw.com. Accessed 16 Oct. 2011.
Guthrie, Joanee et al. "Improving Food Choices – Can Food Stamps Do
    More?" United States Department of Agriculture, www.Ers.usda
    .gov. Accessed 16 Oct. 2011.
Paynter, Sharon, et al. "When Even the 'Dollar Value Meal' Costs Too
    Much: Food Insecurity and Long Term Dependence on Food Pantry
    Assistance." *Public Administration Quarterly,* vol. 35, no. 1, 2011, pp.
    26-58. *Business Source Complete*. EBSCO. Accessed 16 Oct. 2011.
United States Department of Agriculture Food and Nutrition Service. *Food
    Distribution Programs,* USDA, 14 Oct. 2011. Accessed 16 Oct. 2011.

For Reflection

1. Evaluate how successful Rebecca is in defining SNAP. Does her
   summary seem full and fair?
2. What criteria does Rebecca use to evaluate SNAP? If you were reviewing her work, how would you suggest she revise those criteria?
3. Does Rebecca adequately address opposing viewpoints or alternative options? Evaluate the success of her argument based on specific criteria.

EVALUATION ARGUMENTS: THE WRITING PROCESS

In the following section, we use student writer Rebecca Van
Handel's notes and drafts to examine her thinking about the writing
process.

Analyze the Assignment

This assignment challenges writers to identify something that can be evaluated well in the constraints of this assignment. The object of study must be limited so that writers can adequately research its qualities and respond by articulating specific criteria for assessment. Writers might need to draw from criteria outlined by experts but should also share their own standards.

Rebecca created a new folder on her computer for this project, labeling the folder "Evaluation Argument: Evaluate Policies, Programs, or People in Public Office." Next, she created a new document in that folder named "Assignment journal," and recorded her preliminary ideas and questions under the heading "Assignment Analysis":

Assignment Analysis

- I am used to evaluating artistic works but I have not evaluated public documents the way this assignment asks us to do. I will have to do a lot of research to make sure I can support my assessment.
- I am writing this for the class and instructor, so I will need to give them background on the issue.
- The hardest part might be balancing qualitative and quantitative information. We aren't required to do interviews but I can find some assessments by experts in my library research. The quantitative information will be important to convince people that this is a problem.

Plan: Organizing the Process

Your instructor will set your deadlines and paper length for this assignment. Once you know those two critical pieces of information, you can map your schedule, giving yourself plenty of time to read and annotate the text early in the process. Rebecca opened up her project folder and added the following text to the "Assignment Analysis" section of her assignment journal:

> We have 4 weeks to complete this project
> from the time we talked about it in class. I
> want to take plenty of time to choose the
> right issue to evaluate. I will take the first
> week to choose my topic, talking to my in-
> structor if I can make an appointment in
> that time. As soon as I have that, I will do re-
> search and then writing for about two weeks.
> Once my first draft is done, I will take it to
> the writing center and workshop it in class
> during the third week. I will do the final
> drafts based on that feedback in week four.

Question: Exploring Issues

Your instructor will give you guidelines on what types of policies, programs, and people in public office will work well as topics for this assignment. As always, listen carefully in your other classes, in your community engagement work, social media, and the news to discern what people are concerned about. Where do people question the usefulness of something? Where do they seem to have expectations that are too high or too low? Your evaluation can help provide a realistic expectation for how well that policy, program, or person is working.

Rebecca added the following to her assignment journal:

> My service at the Center for the Homeless has
> caused me to ask a lot of questions about public
> policy. I know it's hard to create effective pol-
> icies on the national level, but I am interested
> in politics and I would like to research a fed-
> eral policy so that I understand that better.

The guests at the Center talk about their food stamps a lot and I would like to know how that works. I've heard that people abuse that system so I want to ask about that carefully with some of the guests and administrators. I will schedule an appointment with my community site supervisor to talk through these ideas. Then I will do research on this program and fraud in the program.

Read: Strategies for Reading in Research

This assignment requires strong sources to ground the description and analysis of the subject. Good writers will quickly ask those big questions about the reliability and relevance of the sources they find to get right to the most useful documents. They will look for differing opinions across those readings and see where they seem to align with existing assessments. In active note-taking, writers will start to articulate how their assessment offers something new to the conversation.

In her journal, Rebecca wrote:

I need to read a lot to understand this program well enough to evaluate it. My instructor suggested I start my search with the CQ Researcher database, but it brought up more sources than I can possibly read. It's good to know that I can find those sources, but in my research process I will have to narrow down the pool of sources quickly. I am going to skim and scan for articles that address both SNAP and "fraud" or "cheating" to get to the most useful sources. I will highlight them first then go back and write notes to help me get a sense of my argument.

Invent: Take Note and Create

For this assignment, use concrete facts about your subject to ignite evaluation of its different components. For example, consider outlining the components of the program or policy and then offering a quick evaluation of each, such as three tiers: successful, moderately successful, unsuccessful. This will help you begin to formulate criteria.

I want to be organized in my writing so I don't get off track. I am going to generate ideas by freewriting from sources, then doing concept mapping.

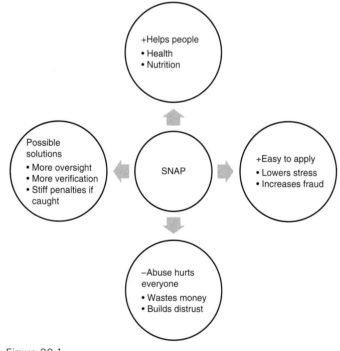

Figure 20.1

Model Concept Map

Arrange: Prioritize, Organize, Outline

With all those ideas from the sources in writing, it's now time to decide what does and doesn't belong in this argument. Categorize the points you've developed into four areas: essential, secondary, questionable, and unnecessary. This will help you identify your strongest points and eliminate the weaker or less relevant points. Draft a thesis statement after considering your main points and then consider which type of arrangement makes sense (see Chapter 11, "Arrange: Prioritize, Organize, Outline").

Rebecca started a new section in her journal called "Arrange: Prioritize, Organize, Outline" ideas and wrote:

The points that stick out to me right now are:

- SNAP serves an important purpose for the country so we want to make sure it operates efficiently
- It seems easy to apply for benefits, making it easy to commit fraud
- Adding a few more steps to the application and verification process could help reduce fraud

With these points in mind, I will create a full outline of the argument, showing where I will use some of the most reliable sources I found.

Draft: Introduction, Body, Conclusion

With key points and an outline in hand, you can begin to think about details of the full draft. Review the approaches to writing an introduction (Chapter 12, "Draft: Introduction, Body, Conclusion") to find an approach that suits your tone and content.

Introduction

The introduction of your evaluation argument should help contextualize the target text so that readers understand what you're analyzing. The thesis will then reveal your overall assessment of the target text.

Rebecca wrote:

SNAP is a complicated program. I will need to rely on my sources to establish my credibility in suggesting solutions and I should do that beginning in the introduction.

Body

The body of your evaluation argument should be organized for clear access to key points, moving from an outline of criteria to a discussion of how the policy, program, or person does or does not meet those criteria.

In her journal, Rebecca began to extend the points in her outline to create the body:

I need to spend some time explaining SNAP to readers who might not understand it, then I need to explain my criteria and define terms. Finally, I need to make a convincing case that there is corruption and that there are effective ways to reduce that corruption in the system.

Conclusion

The conclusion of the evaluation argument needs to drive home the key point about your assessment of this target text. Rebecca wrote:

I need to have a confident closing voice so that readers trust my evaluation and agree

with me that there is a problem with fraud
in SNAP benefits but we can do something
about it.

Revise: Strategies for Re-seeing

Re-seeing a draft of the evaluation argument should include thinking
carefully about opposing viewpoints. Who would challenge the criteria you've chosen or how you've then applied that to this case? Rebecca
returned to her assignment journal to update her progress:

As I look at this draft again, I wonder about
my tone. Am I being fair to suggest that
people who sell their SNAP cards, for example, only want to buy things that are bad for
them, like cigarettes and alcohol? They could
be buying other essential items. That makes
my case stronger but I wonder if it's fair.

Review: By Peers and Experts

The review process will give you a sense of how persuasive your argument is. Have you convinced the peer and expert readers you engage
that your criteria are sound and applied appropriately? Rebecca noted
in her journal:

My writing center tutor gave me helpful feedback on my tone and my citations. I wanted
to do some direct quotation and some paraphrasing and she helped me think about how
to choose when to do which. And my community partner supervisor challenged some
of my thinking about punishing people who

are already struggling when only a small percentage of people abuse the system.

Proofread and Submit

Your Evaluation Argument includes sources, which you will want to present with accurate citations and honest, fair introductions that are varied stylistically. Rebecca wrote:

> I will have my roommate read this and check the tone and citations. We read Chapter 5, "Writing Ethics, Responsibility, and Accountability," and Chapter 28, "Working with Human Sources" and I want to make sure I am being fair to the people I represent here. I got to know many people who use SNAP benefits during my community engagement and I would want them to approve of what I write. My roommate will be honest with me and I trust her judgment.

WHAT HAPPENS NEXT?

Evaluations mark an important point of clarity: you have looked at something carefully, measured its success by certain criteria, and assigned a qualitative and/or quantitative representation of your assessment. Your instructors do this when they grade, often offering you both narrative (qualitative) comments about your success and a letter and/or numeric grade (quantitative). But grading, as in most evaluations, is not the end goal. The broader goal in grading is to give you information you can use to be even more successful in that area when you write again. While it can be hard to hear a detailed critique of your work, by listening carefully to that evaluation you learn and grow, increasing your chances of success the next time. As a writer, you owe it to the authors of the works or ideas you evaluate to be as candid and thorough as possible in your assessment so that they can learn and grow from your response to their work.

OFFICE HOURS ➤ High Stakes Evaluations: When Claims on the Common Good Collide

Evaluation arguments challenge authors to take a stand and declare something right or wrong, good or bad, based on specific criteria. You might find, though, that your criteria contradict the criteria others outline for that same issue. You might find conflicting, even incompatible visions of the common good. How do we evaluate competing visions of the common good? What do we do when other people's visions for common resources don't seem at all good in our judgement? And what do we do in extreme cases when we see groups with radical worldviews driven by hate, violence, and intolerance for others? What do we do when lives are literally at stake if our arguments don't succeed?

You might not ever encounter those extremists personally, but you are a critical part of those life and death arguments when you vote and advocate on critical issues. Political diplomats represent you when they respond to international and domestic groups whose vision of the world harms others. What tools do diplomats use? They construct arguments out of the same strategies and elements of ethical argumentation you learned here —a balance of ethos, pathos, and logos; appeals to ethical, practical, and aesthetic reasons; and support through evidence and examples. These are the foundation of ethical argumentation. If you as a citizen continue to hold those high standards of argumentation when others offer false evidence and unsupported claims to justify unethical arguments, you help strengthen sound arguments and silence false arguments.

CHAPTER **twenty one**

Rebuttal: Negotiating Opposing Viewpoints

Citizens in a healthy society discuss and often disagree about many things, from public policies to keep people safe to plans for developing the economy. A healthy society not only allows but encourages people to make their ideas known so that others can consider the argument and evaluate its evidence. Civic debate happens through such venues as the media and town hall discussions. Academic debate happens through scholarly journals and conferences. Business debate happens at staff meetings, shareholder meetings, and conferences. Disagreement can lead to learning, growth, and a stronger society.

How we represent that disagreement, however, makes all the difference in how it is received. Every domain has standards that shape the etiquette or rules for response in that domain. And each source or site within those domains has its own specific expectations as well. A rebuttal argument is a response to a specific argument tendered by someone else. It can be a short, informal reaction or a formal, researched critique. This chapter will help you determine how to structure successful rebuttal arguments for rhetorical situations in which you need to engage at least one opposing viewpoint.

STRATEGIES FOR REBUTTAL ARGUMENTS

Strategy is extremely important to rebuttal. By definition, rebuttal involves writing for an audience that has a different position on an issue than you have. Your goal is to move them closer to what you think by dismantling their argument and/or presenting your own argument so robustly that it persuades them to think differently. Tone and organization are therefore critical to constructing a strong rebuttal argument. The following strategies will help you build a strong foundation for a successful rebuttal: (1) capitalize on kairos, (2) decide to refute or counterargue, (3) apply the Toulmin method and/or Rogerian rhetoric, (4) represent opposing viewpoints fairly, and (5) know where the author and the audience stands.

Strategy 1: Capitalize on Kairos: Rebut at the Right Time and Place

Capturing the kairos of the moment is essential—if someone has written a strong argument, you should respond quickly so that it does not take root as the seemingly correct or authoritative understanding of that issue. Take enough time to construct your rebuttal argument carefully lest your effort to respond backfire because it is poorly written, but don't wait so long that the other argument becomes established as the apparently correct or natural way to think about the issue. Plan to capture the same or larger audience (including the audience for the original argument) so that your rebuttal has a counterbalancing effect. Consider where that audience can be found and pitch your rebuttal to them in the same venue.

Strategy 2: Decide to Refute or Counterargue

Rebuttal arguments are organized either as refutations or counterarguments. In the *refutational* style, authors critique the opposing argument point-by-point, often moving sequentially through the original primary argument in order to challenge each of its points. The aim is less to offer a whole new position and more to show how the oppositional argument is deficient. In the *counterargument* style, authors point to a specific oppositional argument in the introduction but move forward with the aim of constructing their own position, not just tearing down the opposition.

Refutations are more tightly mapped to how someone else constructs the issue because you react point-by-point to what the original author decided is worth addressing. That might not give you much space to name and explore other aspects of the issue in depth, as the purpose is to identify errors in someone else's argument.

Counterarguments offer more room to include multiple perspectives on an issue, perhaps identifying multiple opposing viewpoints, as well as supporting ones, to situate your own position. Counterarguments might begin by summarizing those opposing viewpoints, turning next to the case you want to make for the bulk of the argument. The tone and organizational structure in counterargument highlights your viewpoint rather than using the opposing viewpoint as a constant touchstone, as in the refutational style.

Strategy 3: Apply the Toulmin Method and/or Rogerian Rhetoric

Two specific strategies for argumentation can help you structure your analysis and presentation of your rebuttal argument: the Toulmin approach and the Rogerian approach.

Named after the British philosopher Stephen Toulmin, the Toulmin method is a way of getting to the heart of an argument to see where people agree or disagree and why. See Figure 21.1 for a visualization of how the elements of the Toulmin method fit together.

Named after psychologist Carl Rogers, Rogerian arguments seek to find common ground on a heated subject and move participants toward compromise. Rogerian style arguments aren't about winning

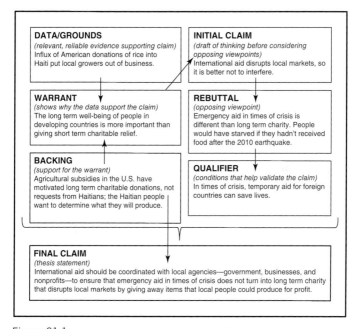

Figure 21.1

Visual Model of Toulmin Arguments

or dismantling opponents, they are about listening carefully to others, and finding solutions that work for everyone. Rogerian arguments are often more exploratory than definitive in their thesis and rebuttal.

Strategy 4: Represent Opposing Viewpoints Fairly

It might seem that rebuttal arguments are all about logos, and indeed reason and evidence are essential to strong rebuttal arguments. But, as always, ethos plays a major role as well, especially when you address an audience that could be resistant or even hostile to the position you want to present. To build trust in your readers, represent opposing viewpoints fully and fairly. If your representation of the opposing viewpoint omits key information, misrepresents their position, or belittles those who think differently, your readers might be so offended that they refuse to read your argument and you will have lost the opportunity to change minds. Imagine how someone might write a rebuttal to your rebuttal and treat other authors the way you would want to be treated.

Strategy 5: Know Where the Author and the Audience Stand

Do your research on the author and the audience before crafting a rebuttal for any rhetorical situation. What biases might the author have? What has he or she omitted or misrepresented? How representative are his or her views of the stakeholders he or she claims to represent? Figure 21.2 will help you assess the rhetorical situation for

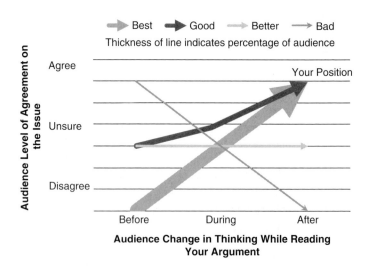

Figure 21.2

The Road to Rebuttal: Moving an Audience through Argument

rebuttal argument so that you can visualize where your audience is on the issue and how far they have to go to agree with you. The audience might be up and down throughout the reading in terms of agreeing with you, but by the end, reading your argument should have moved them in some way—ideally, toward agreement with you!

ELEMENTS OF REBUTTAL ARGUMENTS

After you consider the strategies for rebuttal arguments described above, apply the following elements of rebuttal arguments to strengthen your position: (1) challenge assumptions, evidence, and/or claims; (2) acknowledge agreement in disagreement; (3) call out logical fallacies; and (4) avoid ad hominem attacks.

Element 1: Challenge Assumptions, Evidence, and/or Claims

Successful rebuttal arguments locate the exact points of disagreement in opposing arguments, which could include any or all of the following: assumptions, evidence, and claims. For example, someone might claim that Senator Smith would not make a good president because he has been working in Washington, D.C., for too long. The underlying assumption (called a "warrant" in the Toulmin method of argumentation), not stated in this claim, is that lengthy experience in politics makes people less qualified for the presidency. The underlying assumption is that, instead, outsiders with different kinds of experience would be more appropriate for the role of president.

If you wanted to rebut this argument, you could focus on the aspect of the claim that says the number of years Senator Smith has been there is too many, or you could challenge the evidence by showing that Senator Smith actually spends most of his time working from his home in Alabama, or you could challenge the underlying assumption that experience working in Washington, D.C., is a disadvantage

Table 21.1   METHODS OF QUESTIONING EVIDENCE IN A REBUTTAL

METHOD	EXAMPLE
Rebut Representativeness (question whether the sample size of the data is *sufficient* to support the claims made)	Is anecdotal personal testimony from two white females who claim they received a strong education from their public school enough evidence to claim that American public schools are doing well?
Rebut Authority (question whether the experts cited have enough authority or *relevant expertise* for their testimony to count as sound evidence)	Can we trust a civil engineer with a Ph.D. to have the authority to make claims about the addictiveness of drugs?
Rebut Relevance (question if the data are *recent* enough to be valid, if the examples are from groups that are *similar* enough based on demographic information such as age, gender, race, geographic location, religious background, size of city, etc.)	If Chicago could reduce the diabetes rate in males over the age of 50 in the past decade, can we claim that Wyoming should be able to do the same in two years?
Rebut Reliability (question the *methodology* of the statistics or interviewing approach)	If I ask five children at the homeless center how they like the administrative staff, does that count as a valid program assessment?
Expand Evidence (include more examples, new statistics, new expert testimony, etc., that show a different way of looking at the issue)	If you only had data on how undocumented immigrants use social services, how would the argument change if you added how much they contribute in taxes and economic development?
Realign Reasoning (change the *frame* from focusing on practical reasons, for example, to ethical or aesthetic reasons that demand different types of evidence)	If you only had statistical data on how legalizing same-sex marriage effects the economy, how would the argument change by including personal testimony on the emotional effects of this change for gay couples?

on the record of a presidential candidate. Your argument will be significantly different depending on which aspect you choose to address. As you analyze the argument you intend to rebut, make sure you consider all three types of elements: assumptions, evidence, and claims.

Element 2: Acknowledge Agreement in Disagreement

Find common ground with people supporting other sides of the argument to humanize your discourse. Remember that the ultimate goal is to enlighten and strengthen the community through thoughtful exchange. By acknowledging others, you keep the audience attentive and in a more positive state of mind to receive your message. There are many ways to find common ground. For example, you might find that you agree with a writer's assessment of the causes of the problem but not her proposed solution, which you think emphasizes practical reasons while ignoring ethical reasons. Your rebuttal might begin by noting what works in the original argument before shifting into what does not seem to work. This move can be called "*yes, yet.*" In other words, you are saying, "*Yes,* I agree with you here, *yet* you have a logical fallacy here or have skipped something significant and I want to develop this argument further." This move suggests that you want to be part of reasonable dialogue on the subject and that you don't want to dismiss an argument entirely if it makes some valid points.

That turn to the "yet" requires a firm but sensitive rhetorical twist. You must shift from pointing out that while some part of the author's argument is true, likely, or plausible, you nonetheless need to direct our attention to a different or more compelling truth, likelihood, or plausibility. Polite transitional words such as "yet," "but," "however," or "in spite of" will cue and facilitate that redirection so that readers stay with you. Look for those cues in your reading so that you get a sense of how that shift happens.

Element 3: Call Out Logical Fallacies

Strong knowledge of common errors in logical reasoning can help writers explain in dispassionate language what troubles them about the original argument. When you familiarize yourself with the range of logical fallacies—that is, the range of common mistakes in logical reasoning—you are both better able to recognize the errors in other arguments and prevent them in your own. If someone claims, for example, "We can either protect Americans or protect the world," but you see other alternatives, call that claim a false either/or fallacy and outline the ways you think Americans can both protect themselves and others. See Chapter 4, "Argument," for a list and discussion of logical fallacies.

Element 4: Avoid Ad Hominem Attacks

One of the most common—or maybe the most tempting—logical fallacies in rebuttal arguments is the ad hominem attack, which focuses on the person (i.e., the author) not the argument. Since rebuttal arguments are designed to deconstruct, it's especially important to make sure you dismantle the argument, not the person making the argument. Your job as an author of a rebuttal argument is to critique the argument as it is presented, not to critique the author. Attacking an author rather than his or her argument is called an ad hominem logical fallacy, an attack against the person, not the argument. Although writers do build an ethos or sense of character through their writing, no one person is the sum of any one argument he or she writes, so it is important to separate the author from the argument.

Exceptions to this are if the writer's argument is based on his or her ethos. For example, if the author calls on her own credentials as an economist or a member of the clergy but those credentials do not align with the types of claims he or she makes, or the expertise itself is questionable, then you should address that in your rebuttal. An economist might be a credible expert on the financial implications of raising the minimum wage, for example, but might have less authority in making an ethical case about the necessity of creating a living wage to promote human dignity. In the case of relevant or reliable expertise, it would be acceptable to question the author's credentials. However, that questioning should be relevant and respectful so that you do not undercut your own ethos in the process. The strongest rebuttals still focus on the argument not the author.

IN PROCESS: REBUTTAL
Project: Rebut a Scholarly Argument
Objectives
- Identify the key elements of a specific scholarly argument with which you directly disagree.
- Determine whether refutation or counterargument is the appropriate organizational style for the response.
- Construct a response that pinpoints weaknesses in the opposing viewpoint while it also builds your position supported by strong evidence.

Description

In this assignment, you will identify a specific scholarly argument with which you disagree in part or in whole, and you will rebut that argument for an academic audience. You may either *refute* a single text or *counterargue* a position represented by multiple authors. You may choose a single reading from this book or elsewhere, according to your instructor's directions, to construct a direct refutation of a particular argument presented by an author. Or, you may choose a cluster of readings that collectively represent an opposing viewpoint you counterargue against. In both cases you may draw on scholarly sources you find through research to support your position. Rebuttal is an important feature of robust civic and academic discourse that considers reasonable opposing viewpoints. This assignment gives you an opportunity to join that robust discourse community.

Thesis Template

The following template suggests a useful construction for a rebuttal thesis statement:

> While some people [*you could insert specific names of individuals and/or titles of source you are refuting*] argue that [*insert fair, neutral summary of key points you intend to refute*], this [*misinterprets, misses, fails to acknowledge, etc.—insert polite active verb phrase that describes where that author(s) has gone wrong in your opinion*] evidence that [*insert your key points that counterargues that position*].

Model Thesis

This example models a rebuttal in which specific stakeholders are named on different sides of an argument:

> "While our student body president argued that students should be able to protect themselves by carrying guns on campus, I agree with our Chief of Security who argues that having more guns on campus will not reduce the likelihood of mass shootings and might in fact lead to more incidents of individual shootings."

Published Reading

Young, Black, and Buried in Debt
Kai Wright

> *Kai Wright is a professional writer and editor for* Colorlines *and* The Investigative Fund. *An investigative reporter and news commentator, he has also authored books and published in such periodicals as* The Nation *and* The American Prospect. *In the*

*following article, Wright argues that for-profit educational insti-
tutions often prey upon black students, crippling them with student loan debt.*

There are a few dictums that have enjoyed pride of place in black
American families alongside "Honor your parents" and "Do
unto others" since at least Emancipation. One of them is this:
The road to freedom passes through the schoolhouse doors.

After all, it was illegal even to teach an enslaved person to
read in many states; under Jim Crow, literacy tests were used
for decades to deny black voters their rights. So no surprise that
from Reconstruction to the first black president, the consensus has been clear. The key to "winning the future," in one of
President Obama's favorite phrases, is to get educated. "There
is no surer path to success in the middle class than a good education," the president declared in his much-discussed speech on
the roots of gun violence in black Chicago.

Rarely has that message resounded so much as now, with
nearly one in seven black workers still jobless. Those who've
found work have moved out of the manufacturing and public
sectors, where good jobs were once available without a higher
ed degree, and into the low-wage service sector, to which the
uncredentialed are now relegated. So while it has become fash-
ionable lately to speculate about middle-class kids abandoning
elite colleges for adventures in entrepreneurship, an entirely
different trend has been unfolding in black America—people
are going back to school in droves.

It's true at all levels of education. Yes, black college enrollment shot up by nearly 35% between 2003 and 2009, nearly
twice the rate at which white enrollment increased. But we're
getting all manner of schooling as we seek either an advantage in
or refuge from the collapsed job market. As I've reported on the

twin housing and unemployment crises in black neighborhoods in recent years, I've heard the same refrain from struggling strivers up and down the educational ladder: "I'm getting my papers, maybe that'll help." GEDs, associates degrees, trade licenses, certifications, you name it, we're getting it. Hell, I even went and got certified in selling wine; journalism's a shrinking trade, after all.

But this headlong rush of black Americans to get schooled has also led too many down a depressingly familiar path. As with the mortgage market of the pre-crash era, those who are just entering in the higher ed game have found themselves ripe for the con man's picking. They've landed, disproportionately, at for-profit schools, rather than at far less expensive public community colleges, or at public universities. And that means they've found themselves loaded with unimaginable debt, with little to show for it, while a small group of financial players have made a great deal of easy money. Sound familiar? Two points if you hear troublesome echoes of the subprime mortgage crisis.

Between 2004 and 2010, black enrollment in for-profit bachelor's programs grew by a whopping 264%, compared to a 24% increase in black enrollment in public four-year programs. The two top producers of black baccalaureates in the class of 2011 were University of Phoenix and Ashford University, both for-profits.

These numbers mirror a simultaneous trend in eroding security among ambitious black Americans with shrinking access to middle-class jobs. It's true that the country's middle class is collapsing for everyone, but that trend is most profound among African-Americans. In 2008, as black folks flocked into higher ed, the Economic Policy Institute found that 45% of African-Americans born into the middle class were living at or near poverty as adults.

For too many, school has greased the downward slide. Nearly every single graduate of a for-profit school—96%, according to a 2008 Department of Education survey—leaves with debt.

The industry ate 25% of federal student aid in the 2009–2010 school year. That's debt its students can't pay. The loan default rate among for-profit college students is more than double that of their peers in both public and nonprofit private schools, because the degrees and certificates the students are earning are trap doors to more poverty, not springboards to prosperity.

There's been growing, positive attention to this problem, and the Obama administration's ongoing efforts to rein in the excesses of for-profit schools are arguably among its most progressive policy goals. But few have understood the for-profit education boom as part of the larger economic challenge black America faces today. The black jobs crisis stretches way back to the 2001 recession, from which too many black neighborhoods never recovered. Workers and families have been scrambling ever since, trying to fix themselves such that they fit inside a broken economy. And it is that very effort at self-improvement, that same American spirit of personal re-creation and against-all-odds ambition that has so often led black people into the jaws of the 21st century's most predatory capitalists. From subprime credit cards through to subprime home loans and now on into subprime education, we've reached again and again for the trappings of middle-class life, only to find ourselves slipping further into debt and poverty.

Kiesha Whatley is an example. The 31-year-old mom in Queens, N.Y., has always done hair on the side to help make ends meet, so in 2006 she decided to go for her cosmetology certificate. She was in the city's welfare-to-work program, but was able to fill her work requirement by going to school. She figured what she needed most was to get a credential—to get legit. So she enrolled at a small, mom-and-pop for-profit in Brooklyn that her cousin had attended years before, but which had since changed ownership. Over what Whatley says was a seven-month program, she racked up more than $7,500 in debt, much of which she thought was actually a grant. She has still not passed the state cosmetology exam and she's back to doing hair on her own, now with debt she can't dream of paying back.

The subprime mortgage crisis was fueled by a similar mix of economic desperation, financial illiteracy and aspirational ideology. For a generation, working-class people who hoped to achieve more permanent economic stability were told, loudly and repeatedly, that buying a home would validate them as legitimate participants in American life, not just as people with an asset, but as true neighbors and community members and citizens. Prosperity preachers and presidents alike sung the praises of the "ownership society," as George W. Bush so often called it, in which "more Americans than ever will be able to open up their door where they live and say, welcome to my house, welcome to my piece of property." Homeownership was understood then—just as higher education is now—as good no matter what. Just don't read the fine print.

All it took was one devastating downturn for those doors to slam shut, forcing millions of Americans into foreclosure. That still unfolding crisis has been particularly devastating for African-Americans, who have lost more than half of their collective assets after being targeted with subprime mortgage products. The black-white wealth gap is larger today than it's been since economists began recording it in 1984. And according to a recent analysis from the Alliance for a Just Society, ZIP codes with majority people of color populations saw 60% more foreclosures than white neighborhoods and these homeowners lost 69% more wealth.

Now, to make matters worse, expensive, nearly useless degrees may be to the bust years what expensive, totally useless refinance loans were to the boom: too-good-to-be-true golden tickets to the American Dream, sold in an unregulated market and targeted at the people for whom that dream is most elusive.

Last year, Garvin Gittens became a literal poster child for why that market is so dangerous. For several months, his face was plastered all over the New York City subway system as part of a city-led campaign to warn would-be students about debt scams. When we met last summer, Gittens laid out for me how he racked up more than $57,000 in public and private debt in pursuit of a two-year associate's degree in graphic design at the for-profit Katharine Gibbs School, in Midtown Manhattan. Like subprime mortgages, the debt didn't appear so intimidating at first, but just as balloon payments capsized so many tenuous family finances, a cascading series of loans, a few thousand dollars at a time, eventually caught up with Gittens. In the end, his degree proved as meaningless as it was expensive. When he went to apply for bachelor's programs, no legitimate college would recognize his credits because the school's shoddy performance had finally led the state to sanction it.

So Gittens has started over from scratch—but with tens of thousands of dollars in loans hanging over his head. As I listened to him recount his tale, just as he was about to once again begin his freshman year of college, what struck me most was how insistently the 27-year-old was holding on to his goal of getting credentialed. Even without a degree, he'd built a modestly successful graphic design business of his own. He'd landed fancy internships with hip-hop clothing designers and made smart choices like offsetting his design work with more reliable income from printing jobs. Yet a college degree remained such a coveted treasure for him that, even having wasted tens of thousands of dollars and two years of his life, he was prepared to do it all again.

"It's more of an emotional thing," Gittens explained, citing a graduate degree as his ultimate goal. "I'd like to say, 'I have a master's in design.' That would make me feel good." And the sky's the limit when you're buying self-worth.

Of course, the industry that's been turning fast profit off of ambitions like Gittens' is finally seeing tough times of its own. Take Gittens' alma mater, the now-closed Katharine Gibbs School. It was owned by Illinois-based Career Education Corp., a publicly traded firm that still runs dozens of schools across the country and in Europe, and which is among the industry's largest players. Career Ed booked $1.49 billion in revenue in 2012, but it faces steadily declining stock values as a series of investigations and scandals have limited its ability to pull in new students. Its "student starts"—as enrollment is called in the for-profit sector—dropped 23% last year. That comes after attorneys general in both New York and Florida launched probes in 2011 of the company for falsifying job placement rates. Career Ed has also had to answer to two national accrediting bodies for its job placement reporting in the past two years.

The company responded to these probes by launching its own investigation and revealing that barely a quarter of its health and design schools actually placed enough graduates in jobs to maintain accreditation. So Chairman Steve Lesnik, who also runs a company that develops golf facilities and athletic clubs, took over as CEO and overhauled the way Career Ed reports job placements, adding independent verification. He stresses Career Ed's newfound compliance with regulators and called 2012 a "year of renewal." "It's a simple thought: students first," he said last February, as he addressed investors for the first time as CEO and sought to calm nerves over the regulatory probes. "That idea permeates every action we take."

But while the company reassures regulators and investors that its education is sound, it's failing starkly by another blunt measure. Nearly 28% of students at Career Ed's health services school in New York City, the Sanford Brown Institute, default on their loans after three years. That rate's outstanding even among for-profits, and it is a sure sign that these degrees aren't leading to jobs with decent salaries—if they're leading to jobs at all.

Big for-profits like Career Ed—often run by financiers, not educators—are eager to differentiate themselves from small, independent trade schools like the one Whatley attended, where they argue the bad behavior is concentrated. But what all of the industry's players have in common is a business model that targets desperate people who have been pushed out of the workforce in overwhelming numbers over the past decade.

You needn't look further than these schools' ad campaigns to discover who's in their target demographic. They're a model of diversity. It's tough to find a marketing image that doesn't picture a happy person of color or a young woman, or both. One Sanford Brown online ad features a verbal montage of emotional touchstones that seem tailor-made to speak to working-class frustrations. "Before I contacted Sanford Brown I was working second shift," says one woman's voice. "I needed a career for myself and my family," says another woman. "They empowered me to be a better person," another declares. Watching the ads reminds me of one Atlanta woman's explanation when I asked her why she signed off on such a bad deal as the subprime refinance that put her home at risk of foreclosure. She talked about the "nice young man" who came and sold it to her. He was well-dressed and clean cut and black. He seemed successful. He seemed to remind her of her ambitions for the young black men in her own life. Then he stole from her on behalf of his bank.

In this respect, for-profit schools function less like traditional educational institutions and more like payday lenders, rent-to-own businesses, pawn shops and the like—they all offer products that churn customers through debt for years on end. And, like the rest of the subprime market, selling for-profit degrees is especially good business in the worst of times. Career Ed's previous CEO left his post just as the New York attorney general's probe sent the company's stock into free fall; he departed with a reported $5.1 million parachute. According to a Senate report last July, which used data from 2009, three-quarters of students at for-profit schools attended institutions that were owned by publicly traded corporations or private equity firms. The former had an average profit margin of nearly 20%—and their CEOs made an average of $7.3 million.

Regulators at both the federal and state level have begun working furiously to rein all of this in. Among other things, the Obama administration has tightened rules for schools to participate in the federal student aid program upon which for-profits depend. Last year, the Department of Education instituted a rule that disqualifies any school at which 30% of students or more have defaulted on their loans within three years of graduation. The first sanctions under the new rule won't come until next fall, but according to the department's tally, for-profits accounted for nearly three-quarters of the schools that would have been forced out in 2012.

There is significant evidence that schools were gaming the feds' previous system for monitoring default rates. The Senate report from last July revealed aggressive machinations to push struggling graduates into forbearance—a costly way to escape delinquency—just long enough to push their defaults beyond the oversight window. At Career Ed, for instance, employees called students with delinquent loans an average 46 times to nudge them to file for forbearance, regardless of whether that was in the students' best interest financially.

Gittens, Whatley and thousands of other unemployed or underemployed African-American strivers have been told again and again—by elected officials, by community leaders, by their own optimistic families—that they hold their economic destiny in their own hands. That they must pick up new skills, get more training, earn more credentials, adapt or die. One day the jobs will come, we're told, and we'd all better be ready to fill them. They're earnestly heeding that message, but the only thing an awful lot of them are earning is another lesson in just how expensive it is to be both poor and ambitious in America.

For Reflection

1. Describe the argument Wright is responding to. Does he appear to represent it fully and fairly?
2. Wright indicates that different people are arguing for the same action, but they have different motivations. Who holds that opposing viewpoint and what are their motivations?
3. Wright uses analogy to sound the alarm about education debt: "From subprime credit cards through to subprime home loans and now on into subprime education, we've reached again and again for the trappings of middle-class life, only to find ourselves slipping further into debt and poverty." Is his analogy helpful and convincing? In what ways does it build his ethos?
4. Wright does a rhetorical analysis of the ad campaign for a for-profit school, analyzing how, for example, race and aspiration are represented in their pictures and dialogue. How might the producers of those media rebut Wright's critique?

Student Reading

Avani Agarwal did a double major in architecture and visual communications design. She is from Kolkata, India. Written as part of her Community-Based Learning Writing and Rhetoric class, Avani's essay is a rebuttal argument against the views expressed by Dr. Cornel West in his interview with "Democracy Now." It examines the validity of West's argument against Obama on the basis of faulty assumptions, false analogy, and West's overlooking many key factors.

Avani Agarwal
Revisiting Moral Authority

What connotations does moral authority
hold in the 21st century? Is it fair to say that
moral authority is immutable because the
truth never changes? Or is it affected by sit-
uated and role identities of an individual? Is
it justified to engage in immoral activities
to maintain peace and goodwill? Different
people have different ways of looking at a situation, and their thought process generally
determines their stance on a particular issue.
In an interview with "Democracy Now,"
Dr. Cornel West expressed his derision for
what he perceived as President Obama's hyp-
ocritical response to the killing of Trayvon
Martin and the acquittal of George Zimmerman. West speaks of the ineffective criminal
justice system prevalent in the United States
that still practices laws like stop and frisk and
stand your ground. He refers to the social
set up of America as "Obama's plantation"
(27:22) where instances of Wall Street criminality and "re-niggerising of the black" (27:15)
abound. West questions Obama's priorities as
president and draws the reader's attention to
the fact that in his five-year term as president,
Obama has achieved very little in terms of
the issues he promised to tackle, having only
talked the talk and not achieved much in reality. Giving concrete examples, West points
to the discrepancies that exist in the United

States administration, where commissioners are rewarded for their discriminating acts.

West introduces his main claim at the beginning of the interview: "Obama has very little moral authority" (24:52). West uses two main subclaims to establish and support his view. First, he vehemently calls Obama the "drone killing president" (36:28); subsequently, he attacks Obama for not being progressive enough to stand against and repeal past policies that are unjust. As much as I agree with West, some of his arguments are based on faulty reasoning and incorrect assumptions. Moreover, West overlooks many important aspects to the discussion and oversimplifies the situation to suit his needs.

Speaking to the show's host, Amy Goodman, West calls Obama "a global George Zimmerman" (25:05), comparing the collateral killing of 221 innocent children through the military's use of drone strikes to Zimmerman's killing of Martin, an unarmed minor. West's claim rests on making a faulty analogy as the rationale behind Obama's actions are justified, whereas those behind Zimmerman's hold no basis. As Leonard Pitts argues in his article, "Perceptions of race and criminality," Trayvon Martin's suspicious behavior could have been the consequence of his having "turned around in an unfamiliar neighborhood," or having a conversation on his phone that he didn't want his dad to overhear. On the other hand, President Obama uses targeted killing only when he is assured that the target is a haven for terrorists. While West correctly states that the death of innocent people is a global concern, I believe that drone killing can be seen as a major humanitarian advancement in that it is less damaging than sending the military to end terrorist activities and more discriminating than opening fire on a large expanse of land which might end up involving more people than required. Targeted killing helps keep American service personnel out of necessary risk of death in a war field and prevents loss of livelihood for many families.

Furthermore, West's claim that instead of identifying himself as Trayvon Martin, Obama should say that he could have been "Anwar al-Awlaki" or the 221 other "precious children, who are as precious as the white brothers and sisters in Newtown" (31:11) rests upon the questionable assumption that President Obama functions according to the same value system as his. However, West should note that it is not the responsibility of the President of the United States to take care of every human being on the planet equally as he feels it should be. While Obama's value system might tell him to keep in mind the pain caused to victims of drone strikes, he acts in keeping with his duties as President. These duties require him to put the well-being of the United States and its citizens before his own moral values. In today's world, characterized by political unrest and hostility between nations, we need to eliminate all possible threats, even if that means using weapons that result in the unintended death of innocent people.

Moreover, West is mistaken in his aversion towards drone strikes as he overlooks the consequences of not using them. As Sasha-Dominik Bachmann points out in "Targeted Killings: Contemporary Challenges, Risks and Opportunities," targeted killing provides a military benefit as a holistic counterstrategy against "hybrid threats" (272). She defines hybrid threats as technological, ecological, economical and scientific threats including cyber-attacks against strategic infrastructures" (273). These threats, which can surface anytime and anywhere, make it important for countries to possess sufficient kinetic options of suppressing the threats to protect their own homes. Thus, it is highly imperative for the United States administration to develop and employ these weapons for use when needed. The only reason West can sit in a studio safely while giving an interview on national television is that there are intelligence experts working day and night to identify potential terrorist attacks and put an end to them using drones before they strike America.

Not only does West fail to delve deeply into the pros and cons of drone killing, he oversimplifies the issue of Obama not having dealt appropriately with oppressive policies of the past. West questions why the administration shuts its eyes to the misdoings of previous presidents. West claims that Bush was the "capture and torture president" (36:25), as he decided to keep Guantanamo Bay open and continued the torture of detainees. West goes further to say that presidents do not comment on or try to change policies followed by their predecessors as they "don't want [a] subsequent administration to take them to jail" (35:38). West is right that certain issues have not been looked into; however, his assertion that President Obama is not undoing the horrors of the policies advocated by President Bush stand contrary to evidence. On May 22, 2009 President Barack Obama said the "U.S. has suffered a setback to its moral authority, which is its 'strongest currency' in the world, by running the controversial Guantanamo Bay prison and vowed to stick to his decision to close the Bush-era anti-terror jail facility." Furthermore, throughout his term, Obama has tried time and again to make this promise of his come true, but has always met with some unforeseen opposition in the form of missing files of detainees or a negative vote from the senate.

Although West makes valid arguments against Obama's priorities, he fails to examine the nitty-gritty details of the problem at hand. Unlike what West did, it is important that citizens weigh President Obama's actions on a deeper level than what appears to be true at the surface since most of Obama's decisions are taken keeping in mind the common good of the United States. How people react to Obama's decisions is highly subjective in that what one perceives as the right thing to do in a situation differs from one individual to another. What might be right according to Obama acting as the President of the United States may or may not be accepted as a reasonable decision by the common person, who looks at his decisions with a narrower perspective. Can we say that Obama is wrong in approving drone strikes when all he intends to do is safeguard his country and reduce the loss of military men? Is it right to blame Obama for the opposition he faced despite his sincere efforts to close Guantanamo? As president, Obama has a lot of commitments and some of his decisions and statements might not appeal to certain sections of society.

However, that doesn't mean that they are baseless. Under the pressures of globalization and increasing security threats as well as maintaining diplomacy with other nations, any president would earn a few negative criticisms. In the 21st century, it is natural for the leader of a superpower like the United States to buckle under pressure from different fronts, nationally and internationally.

Works Cited

Bachmann, Sascha-Dominik. "Targeted Killings: Contemporary
  Challenges, Risks and Opportunities." *Journal of Conflict Security
  Law,* vol. 18, no. 2, 31 May 2013. Accessed 5 October 2014.
Pitts, Leonard. "Perceptions of Race and Criminality." *South Bend
  Tribune,* 6 May 2012.
"US 'Moral Authority' Suffered Setback Due to Guantanamo:
  Obama." *Business Insights: Essentials,* The Press Trust of India, 2009.
  Accessed 5 October 2014.
West, Cornel. "Cornel West: Obama's Response to Trayvon Martin
  Case Belies Failure to Challenge New Jim Crow." *Democracy Now,*
  By Amy Goodman, 22 July 2013. Accessed 4 October. 2014.

For Reflection

1. Does Avani refute or counterargue her response to Cornell West?
2. Where does Avani identify places of agreement?
3. What logical fallacies does Avani call out? Does she commit any logical fallacies herself?
4. Does Avani challenge assumptions, evidence, and/or claims in the primary argument?

REBUTTAL: THE WRITING PROCESS

In the following section, we use student writer Avani Agarwal's notes and drafts to examine her thinking about the writing process.

Analyze the Assignment

For this assignment, identify a specific source with which you disagree in part or in whole. Imagine having a public conversation about the specifics of the argument, a cordial but critical back and forth about its core points.

Avani created a new folder on her computer for this project, labeling the folder "Rebuttal: Negotiating Opposing Viewpoints." Next, she created a new document in that folder, named it "Assignment journal," and recorded her preliminary ideas and questions:

Assignment Analysis

- I love to debate so I am looking forward to this assignment. We have to find our own source and choose to rebut or counterargue its main points using sources to support our position.
- The audience is the class, but it seems like the kind of letter to the editor I like to read in newspapers where people catch an error or logical fallacy in someone else's writing and they write in about it.

Plan: Organizing the Process

Your instructor will set your deadlines and paper length for this assignment. Once you know those two critical pieces of information, you can map your schedule, giving yourself plenty of time to read and annotate the text thoroughly early in the process as that primary text is the engine for your work in this assignment. Review the submission guidelines of the publication you are writing to or determine with your instructor's approval an appropriate form of response. Allocate time for library research that will help you strengthen your points.

Avani opened up her project folder and added the following text to her assignment journal:

This assignment is due in 2 weeks. I need to choose a text in the next couple days so I can start finding sources that will support my side of the argument. I want to draft my response by the end of this week, keep working in sources next week, and do peer review after that.

Question: Exploring Issues

Your instructor will either give you a text to rebut or guide you toward sources that would work for this assignment, possibly even readings from this book. Most important is that you work from a text that takes a clear stance on a current issue in such a way that you can challenge it point-by-point.

After Avani explored the recommended resources, she added both her initial responses as well as ideas for how to proceed to her assignment journal:

The exploration style that worked for me was first finding the right text, then reverse outlining its main points, then freewriting my position off each point. I could see quickly which points I agreed and disagreed with the most and that will help me organize and prioritize my points.

Read: Strategies for Reading in Research

Once you have chosen a target text, do a close rhetorical analysis to identify each claim and type of support. If you have questions about the reliability or relevance of that support, read additional sources to deepen your understanding of the issue and this author's take on it.

Avani used her reverse outline of the primary text to help her see how the sources she found would fit in:

The reverse outline was really helpful in
seeing what points I needed to rebut. Some
points I could handle on my own, but for
others I needed an expert source as back up.
This helped me find the keywords I used in
searching for my sources.

Invent: Take Note and Create

Your creative and critical thinking will be most needed in this assignment to help you understand the other author's worldview, which has
led the two of you to come to different conclusions. By understanding
that opposing worldview you will be better able to refute the argument in such a way that you might actually gain a hearing and even
agreement from those who seem to oppose you.

Avani chose to freewrite from some sections of the primary text
she highlighted in her reading that had the strongest claims:

I pulled out sections of the primary text to
get my ideas going. I did freewriting from
those key sections so that I could work on re-
futing specific points and that worked really
well. I could see where I had more to say and
where I needed help from other sources.

Arrange: Prioritize, Organize, Outline

Write a thesis statement that responds directly to the primary text.
Define your terms early in the essay, particularly if your definitions
are different from those of the original text. You may take the exact
order of the original argument in order to refute it point-by-point or
consider other logical ordering of responses.

Avani opened her assignment journal and started a new section:

Right now, these are the key ideas that stand
out to me and can become an outline for the
paper:

- I need to get into the definition of "moral
  authority" early on—how does West
  define that? How do I define that?
- I need to present West's main claims early
  in the paper as well, letting him speak
  first but also telling readers that I agree
  with some but not all of what he says.
- West's connection between individual
  shootings and drones is complicated, so
  I need to try to present his point of view
  clearly and succinctly so that I can explain my position in much more detail.
  That's probably about as far as I can get
  because this is a short paper and I want to
  use most of the paper making my case as
  strong as possible.

Draft: Introduction, Body, Conclusion

You may well be writing for a doubting, even hostile, audience, so
keeping an engaging and conciliatory tone is essential to keep readers
reading. Support for this assignment should be guided by the target
publication, but feel free to err on the side of using more scholarly
sources to build your case.

Introduction
The introduction of a rebuttal refutation argument should directly
state the name of the article and author to which it is responding and
explain clearly how you differ from that stance.

In her assignment journal, Avani noted:

The introduction is pretty straightforward—
state the information in the primary text and
write a thesis that shows how I disagree.

Body
The body of a rebuttal refutation argument can follow at least two different organizing structures: point-by-point following the chronological order of claims made in the primary text or more thematic by areas of general disagreement (and, perhaps, some agreement).

Avani thought through her organizing structure this way:

I am going to focus on just a few of West's
points because they are loaded and I don't
have a lot of room to go into everything he
said in the interview. I want to focus on doing
a good job of rebutting those few key points.

Conclusion
In this assignment, it is important to help readers differentiate between the primary text and your rebuttal as well as see where you have the strength of mind and character to find points of agreement. Use your conclusion to emphasize your goodwill to find common ground even though you see much to disagree with in the argument you rebutted.

Avani recorded this possible approach to her conclusion:

I have so much to cover that I think my
conclusion is going to have to keep moving
through my main argument. I know I need
to help persuade people who agree with
West's position that I respect him but disagree with some of his statements, so I will
make sure the tone is firm but scholarly.

371

Revise: Strategies for Re-seeing

You are responding to an article that has been published and there-fore represents the viewpoint of some faction of the audience of that publication, so it's clear that some in your audience disagree with the position you are taking. That means you have to be exceptionally per-suasive and polite. You won't change minds without a respectful tone; reliable, relevant evidence; and good reasons the audience hasn't yet heard. That's a tall order, but it can be done. Sometimes the very format of a rebuttal forces writers to be specific in ways that make for a com-pelling argument. You have to be disciplined when you know that nay-sayers are reading. Imagine having a conversation, face-to-face, with the author of the primary text. What would you say to him or her? How would he or she respond? What would it take for you to move that person on this issue? Make sure you cover that in your writing.

Avani returned to her assignment journal to track her progress:

I did a reverse outline to see how my argument looks. Now that I see it, I think my draft makes strong claims but it doesn't have enough sup-port. I'm not going to change anybody's mind if I don't back up my position, so I am going to try some new keywords to expand my search for solid sources to back up my position. I will check my terms with my instructor.

Review: By Peers and Experts

Seek out as many reviewers as you can to help keep you on track in the tone of your rebuttal. While the purpose of a rebuttal is to disagree, try not to be disagreeable in how you construct that response. You have to do more than say the opposite of the original rebuttal, you have to construct a compelling counter-narrative that honors the primary text author but explains clearly how you see things differently. External readers can tell you where word choices or assumptions seem to impede that aim.

When Avani updated her assignment journal, she noted:

I looked at the Reader Response sheet and decided to take that to my session at the Writing Center so that I got feedback mapped to
our assignment goals. I told the tutor to play
the doubting game with me, pushing back on
all my claims so that I can see if they hold up.

Proofread and Submit

Follow the Strategies for Proofreading and use the "Checklist: Proofreading Guide" in Chapter 15, to make sure no lower-order concerns
impede the message you want to send.

When Avani updated her assignment journal, she noted:

Apostrophes don't like me. I'm going to visit
the Writing Center to have them look at
everything but also focus on those. I don't
want any distractions in my writing.

WHAT HAPPENS NEXT?

Growth and learning happen when we listen to viewpoints we don't think
we agree with yet we consider carefully. Sometimes listening to those opposing viewpoints causes us to strengthen our stance. Sometimes listening
to a strong opposing viewpoint causes us to concede points and change our
minds. A change in thinking based on new information is the definition
of education. Your goal is both to become more educated and to educate
others. Through rebuttal argument, you have the chance to educate others,
to give them new information or to frame it in a way that makes the audience see the issue anew. Rebuttals constructed with a respectful tone,
logical evidence and reasons, and a fresh framing of the issues are vital to
democratic discourse in all domains. This chapter gives you tools to continue participating in constructive dialogue on important current issues.

OFFICE HOURS ➤ Toning Down, Yet Dialing Up:
Balancing How You Rebut

Tone can be tricky to manage in rebuttal arguments. You are addressing an audience with a different viewpoint—they could be resistant or even hostile to other viewpoints, or at least protective of
their own. So you want to be polite enough to keep them listening
but firm enough to convince them to consider changing their minds.
The key is to strike the right balance between the two, and to know
what kind of audience you're dealing with.

Is it possible that some people are so set in their ways that they
aren't worth approaching? Are some people so hostile that it isn't
worth engaging them? We tend to think that an audience that listens
can learn. If you are challenging someone's deeply held values or
beliefs, treading on their religious or moral ground, you aren't likely
to move them, and that's probably not what you mean to do anyway.
If you know an audience holds particular values that appear to conflict with your position on an issue, consider ways to honor those
core values but reframe the issue to show how a particular position
does not actually conflict with those values. For example, American
attitudes about legalizing gay marriage seemed to shift when the conversation began to focus on gay marriage as respect for the institution
of marriage and the values of lifelong commitment. People who might
follow different religious teachings on homosexuality or have different
understandings of the nature of homosexuality found some common
ground in the idea that marriage represents love and unity.

It is important to lead (and conclude) by establishing common
ground. By doing so, you build your ethos as one who is trying
to listen, thereby modeling what you want your audience to do. Use
clear but polite rhetorical phrases to shift into your points, then
close with another nod to how your position works for everyone.

Test your tone on readers who have a sensitive ear on this issue,
ideally on people who genuinely oppose you on the issue. They will
be the best at pointing to the words or phrases that hurt instead of
heal and enlighten.

CHAPTER **twenty two**

Proposal: Advocating for Change

Proposal arguments are common in all domains because they allow us to engage others in making change. Proposal arguments ask others to consider taking action based on support the author provides so that the audience can make an informed decision on what to do or think based on that proposal. Such arguments bridge personal and public interest. For example, in the work domain, bids are proposal arguments that claim your organization is qualified to do a job. In the public domain, policy proposals claim there is a better way to achieve a stated societal outcome or goal. In the academic domain, research proposals claim that if given the requested resources (e.g., time, access to materials, money) you will be able to produce writing and/or conduct experiments that will advance knowledge in your field. Proposal arguments ask the audience to trust your claim and invest in your idea.

Proposal arguments make three general moves: (1) identify a problem, question, or opportunity; (2) inform the audience about its significance; and (3) use support to recommend a specific action. Authors of proposal arguments want their readers to take action based on what they share. Thus, it is critical for authors to understand what

375

the audience already knows and what they need to know to be moved to take the recommended action.

Be mindful that proposal arguments negotiate power: an author is asking an audience to act, and the audience can accept, reject, or ignore that plea. Good writers don't aim for action at any cost, they value ethically informed, justified action above all else. Good writers only propose a course of action to others after researching it fully and fairly and presenting their conclusion with equal care. Good writers do not manipulate emotions or rely on false claims or false reasoning. Good writers believe that their recommendations will have the predicted outcome and that the outcome will contribute to the common good. At their core, proposal arguments not only propose action, but imagine and advance a better future.

STRATEGIES FOR PROPOSAL ARGUMENTS

Strategies for proposal arguments focus on positive action. While they address an issue, they do so to inform the audience in order to move forward, not to dwell on past pain. To motivate an audience to action, good proposal arguments (1) establish the stakes, (2) scale the scope, (3) aim for common ground, and (4) avoid appeals to fear.

Strategy 1: Establish the Stakes: Explain Urgency and Relevance

To convince your audience to act, you must first inform them fully and fairly of the problem, question, or opportunity. They need to understand the kairos—the urgency of addressing this issue from your well-researched perspective, and why it's significant for them to address this now. Let them know what's at stake if things change or if they stay the same. Why should this particular audience care? How is this relevant to them directly or indirectly? What are the most compelling practical, ethical, and/or aesthetic reasons to act?

Strategy 2: Scale the Scope: Make it Doable

You probably see a lot you want to change in the world, but a successful proposal argument addresses one specific issue with an audience who has the ability to respond as recommended—if you successfully convince them to do so. Scale down the scope of your proposal argument to increase the odds of success. Consider the timetable needed to complete the action and the resources needed to do so. Is your request reasonable under those conditions? If not, scale back. An old saying advises: "Pick battles big enough to matter and small enough to win." (See Chapter 4, "Argument": Figures 4.1 "Measuring Issue Impact," and 4.2, "Investment in the Ask.")

Strategy 3: Aim for the Common Good: Avoid Unintended Consequences

Good writers aim for the common good, showing what's at stake for the immediate audience and the larger world. They show how practical reasons for change are often aligned with ethical reasons for change. They assure readers that they have gone beyond good intentions to recommend action that does its best to avoid unintended negative consequences. While the ultimate goal might be a solution to fix a problem, good writers temper expectations and acknowledge their own limitations. They provide a clear justification for this course of action that is based not on retribution but on constructive forward movement

Strategy 4: Avoid Appeals to Fear Based on Pathos

Good writers avoid appeals to fear that are based solely on pathos, working people up about something without evidence that it is likely to happen. Concerns should be grounded in evidence and examples should have a direct relevance to the issue.

377

ELEMENTS OF PROPOSAL ARGUMENTS

The core elements of a proposal argument are (1) give full disclosure, (2) establish ethos and show evidence, and (3) show a clear vision of change.

Element 1: Give Full Disclosure: Explore Alternative Viewpoints, Costs, and Risks

Good proposal arguments focus on urgent issues that reasonable people want to address. Research competing voices (including naysayers and doubters), and address those positions so that the audience knows you have considered this issue from many viewpoints. Your job is to acknowledge the most reasonable and/or popular opposing viewpoints and explain how your recommendation is more effective and efficient. Furthermore, acknowledge the costs and risks of your proposal. What might we have to sacrifice to implement this proposal? What could go wrong? Proposals are future-oriented, so there is no guarantee that the proposal you suggest will have the outcome you desire. Acknowledge that uncertainty while you reduce that fear.

Element 2: Establish Ethos and Show Evidence

To move people from agreement to action takes a significant amount of trust in your ethos (credentials) and recommendations. The audience needs both to trust you as an individual and to trust that your recommendation is right. If they don't trust you, then you have a long way to go in getting them to accept and act on your recommendation. If they trust you but don't see sufficient evidence for your proposal, they still might not be moved to act. Always make your case with varied types of evidence. These days, we are all bombarded by calls for action. Only the most effective proposals will cut through all the pleas for our limited resources.

Element 3: Show a Clear Vision of Change

Audiences are more likely to be moved to action when they can see the future as you imagine it. While you might be writing about something you have cared about for a long time, it could be a new issue to your audience. It's your job to help them imagine what's possible if they perform the recommended action. But keep it realistic. Show intellectual humility: you don't have all the answers and all the solutions, but you have researched this issue and are confident that your recommendation will improve the situation.

IN PROCESS: PROPOSAL
Project: Advocating for an Issue

Objectives

- Identify an issue you care about and want others to help you address
- Identify an audience who could help you address this issue if convinced to do so
- Determine the most effective method of reaching this audience
- Consider how best to balance informing and advocating for this rhetorical situation
- Research sources to acknowledge opposing viewpoints and provide evidence of supporting viewpoints

- Scale the scope of the proposal so that it seems doable to the target audience, moving them not just to agree but to act as you recommend

Description

For this proposal argument, you will recommend that your audience think or do something that will contribute to the common good based on evidence and reasons supporting your claim. Successful proposal arguments inspire action. Your argument should make the following moves: (1) establish that the issue you address is currently debated by reasonable people and needs attention now, (2) outline the sources that oppose and support your viewpoint on how to address the issue, and (3) make a recommendation that moves the audience to agree and act as directed.

Thesis Template

The following template suggests one way you can construct the moves of your proposal argument:

> In order to achieve [*goal for change*], [*subject/actor*] should [*or should/not*] [*describe course of action you are proposing*].

Model Thesis

The following thesis proposes a specific change enacted by specific stakeholders to achieve a desired goal:

> "To improve the health of people living in low income communities, the city government should require corner stores to stock healthy food such as fresh fruit and vegetables."

Published Reading

End the School-to-Prison Pipeline by Addressing Racial Bias
Karen Howard

> *Karen Howard is vice president of early childhood policy at First Focus, a bipartisan advocacy organization whose mission is to make children and families a priority in federal budgetary decisions. A lawyer, Howard has more than 20 years of experience in legal, policy, and advocacy work focused on health and education policy. Howard published this commentary in 2014 on the website* Spotlight on Poverty and Opportunity, *a nonpartisan initiative that provides a platform for people with wide expertise to propose solutions to reduce poverty and increase opportunity in the United States.*

Long a pillar of our democracy, quality public education can serve as a pathway for millions of poor children of color to achieve economic and social mobility. So it is startling that for many African American and Hispanic students, school has become a fast-track to prison that starts as early as preschool and ends in increased school drop-out rates, unemployment, poverty, crime, and often incarceration.

The school-to-prison pipeline is the product of draconian school disciplinary policies that require suspensions, expulsions, school-based arrests, and referrals to law enforcement for relatively minor, non-violent infractions, such as tardiness and insubordination. These rules are disproportionately enforced against students of color, and their impacts are devastating. If we're serious about addressing this "school-to-prison pipeline," it's imperative that we acknowledge and confront the subtle racial biases that give rise to these gaping social inequities.

The statistics are alarming. From suspensions and expulsions to in-school arrests and referrals to the juvenile justice system, African Americans students are overwhelmingly subject to disparate disciplinary actions. African American students constitute 34% of the 3 million students expelled from school annually, but only 16% of public school enrollment. And African American and Latino students represent 55% of students involved in "school-related arrests and 51% of "referrals to law enforcement."

These disparities begin as early as preschool. According to the Department of Education's Office of Civil Rights, African American children are just 18% of public preschoolers, yet nearly half of preschool children with more than one suspension are African American.

Education advocates have known about the school-to-prison pipeline for decades. While its causes involve many complex factors, policymakers have been reluctant to address racial bias as one of the causes of the disparate discipline. Recently, however, the science behind implicit bias is being used to explain the disproportionality of school discipline.

Implicit biases are subconsciously held beliefs that influence the way we view, treat, and make decisions about other people based on race, ethnicity, age, religion and appearance. Simply put, implicit biases are imprints on our brains that reinforce negative stereotypes or beliefs about certain groups, even when we desire to be fair and view our decisions as impartial.

Researchers believe that implicit bias is influenced by our societal culture and norms about who in our society is viewed as powerful, privileged, and beautiful, and the groups or populations who are not. Implicit bias has received greater national attention in the wake of the Trayvon Martin shooting and the Michael Brown police shooting as a way to understand the biases that influence conduct, particularly conduct by the police and others in authority, toward African American youth.

But implicit bias is not fait accompli. It can be corrected. Social scientists believe that just as implicit biases are acquired associations, they can be replaced with new mental associations. This corrective action is known as debiasing. It involves acknowledging the presence of implicit biases and consciously forging links between oneself and members of the disfavored group to reduce prejudice and stereotypes, promoting interpersonal connections across racial and ethnic groups and priming multiculturalism.

In January the U.S. Department of Education and Department of Justice jointly released federal policy guidelines to help schools administer discipline without discriminating on the basis of race. Recently, the Supportive School Discipline Initiative, a collaborative effort among the Department of Education, the Department of Justice, experts in education and behavioral health, law enforcement, parents, youth, and advocates, issued extensive recommendations, integrating the best and most innovative thinking around strategies to reduce the school-to-prison pipeline. Both the guidelines and recommendations briefly acknowledge implicit bias as a factor in the school-to-prison pipeline.

Although the guidelines and recommendations are important first steps, more needs to be done to address implicit racial bias in our schools. As of this school year, more than half of all K–12 students are now students of color. That trend, which is projected to increase, makes schools a natural place to begin decreasing racial bias. It also makes debiasing schools imperative for our future educational and economic success.

We should start by acknowledging that teachers and administrators may hold unconscious negative views and stereotypes about students of color that cause them to view their conduct and treat them differently. The Department of Education and the Department of Justice should issue additional guidance that incorporates recommendations based on the emerging social science on debiasing, including requiring cultural responsiveness training for educators, increasing the diversity of the educational workforce to better reflect the student population, and training educators to effectively teach diverse learners, including working with parents, guardians, and colleagues to improve their own practice and the success of students.

Dismantling the school-to-prison pipeline is more important now than ever before. The preceding recommendations will help debias our schools, end the school-to-prison pipeline, and increase educational and economic equity.

For Reflection

1. To what extent does Howard convince you that this is an urgent issue that needs to be addressed now? Which parts of her argument are most convincing about the urgency and stakes of this issue?
2. Does Howard's proposal seem doable? Is the scale and scope of the issue something her audience can address?
3. To what extent does the author offer a clear vision of how the world will improve if the audience responds favorably to her proposal?

Student Reading

Fauvé Liggans-Hubbard majored in Anthropology and minored in Poverty Studies. She wrote the following op-ed for the Daily Southtown, *a publication related to* The Chicago Tribune, *after taking a community-based course that engaged her with people in a local prison.*

Fauvé Liggans-Hubbard
Providing Higher Education within the Prison System Is Beneficial for All

People who have access to college courses while they are incarcerated are less likely to return to prison. Higher education not only gives them a purpose while serving their sentence but also a purpose and skillset to use upon release. Education within the penal system as a means of rehabilitation better prepares a formerly incarcerated person to be a more productive and faster adapting member of society. Therefore, their time spent in prison is not a loss of X amount of years but a preparation for their future contribution to society. The Obama administration attempted to tackle this issue and while the Trump administration has commented on the high rates of incarceration and the need to decrease it there has been no answer to how this will be done. I propose that providing people who are incarcerated with access to higher education is a long-term solution to decreasing incarceration rates in general but also significantly decreasing reincarceration rates.

A study conducted by the RAND Corporation found that providing educational programs to those who are incarcerated decreased the overall recidivism rate by 13% and the individuals who were a part of these programs had a 43% lower chance of recidivating than their peers. However, leaving incarceration with this new set of knowledge and skills does not automatically ensure employment. The label of felon still carries a high stigmatization and along with that a society's unwillingness to accept their change in the form of employers refusing to hire them. However, even though this is an added barrier, according to the RAND Corporation study, those who had received education while incarcerated had a 13% higher chance of finding employment upon release.

Many argue that providing these educational programs to those in prison wastes funds on those who need it the least. This sentiment was made concrete in the 1994 Violent Crime Control and Law Enforcement Act, which stripped persons in prison of their access to the Pell grant, federal awards for undergraduates that do not have to be repaid; without this funding, people who are incarcerated cannot obtain higher education. However, maintaining a person in prison is expensive but the return on investment with education is even greater. The formerly incarcerated person is able to better contribute to the economy by having a greater chance of joining the workforce, having money to spend to support the economy, and having a lower chance of returning to prison. So, ultimately, providing educational programs in prison would actually decrease the amount that taxpayers give to the penal system.

Programs such as the Bard Prison Initiative and the Prison University Project of San Quentin have built successful models that support the findings of the RAND Corporation Study. The Second Chance Pell Pilot Program partnered 67 colleges and 100 plus federal and state correctional institutions to serve approximately 12,000 incarcerated students. It was estimated that taxpayers would save four to five dollars for every one dollar spent on the educational programs. So with this knowledge and that of the reduced recidivism rates this pilot program was enacted. The pilot students entered their first educational year (2016-17), and there are high hopes for the outcome of this pilot program. If you want to decrease incarceration and reincarceration rates, support federal legislation as well as local and/or private initiatives to reinstate higher education in prison.

For Reflection

1. What does Fauvé say is at stake in this issue?
2. What reasons does Fauvé give for saying this should matter to her audience?
3. In what ways does Fauvé establish her ethos and provide evidence? How would you suggest she improve in this area?

PROPOSAL: THE WRITING PROCESS

In the following section, we use student writer Fauvé Liggans-Hubbard's notes and drafts to examine her thinking about the writing process.

Analyze the Assignment

The proposal argument invites you to inform an audience about a current issue and ask for their support based on the evidence and reasons you provide.

Fauvé created a new folder, labeled "Proposal Argument," on her computer. Next she created a new document in that folder, named it "Assignment Journal" and recorded her preliminary ideas and questions under the heading "Assignment Analysis."

Assignment Analysis

I have a lot of issues on my mind right now that I care about and want other people to care about, so I have to write a list of potential issues and see which one makes me feel the most but also seems like it fits this assignment. Because I have to "inform" the audience, it also needs to be something I have researched, maybe something from one of my classes.

Plan: Organizing the Process

Your instructor will set your deadlines and paper length for this assignment. Once you know those two critical pieces of information, you can map your schedule, giving yourself plenty of time to read and annotate the text thoroughly early in the process as that primary text is the engine for your work in this assignment. Fauvé opened her project folder and added the following text to the "Assignment Analysis" section of her assignment journal:

The instructor gave us about three weeks to complete this assignment. I want to choose a topic in the next couple days and start researching it before we talk about potential topics in class. I want to use the writing center at least two times, so I will schedule appointments with them now: one early, one later. I will have a full draft done in one week, second draft four days later, and final draft before the deadline.

Question: Exploring Issues

Urgency (kairos) is key to choosing a strong topic for the proposal argument. The audience needs to feel that you're writing about something that matters today, that matters to them, and that they can do something about it. Scan the headlines and listen carefully to what seems to frustrate the people around you. List everything then start to prioritize according to your passion on those topics.

Fauvé spent some time formulating her list and wrote the following in her journal:

There's no shortage of issues that matter to me and the people around me. With this assignment in mind, I have been listening in a different way at my social concerns club meetings, in my classes, and even at the dining hall. The student monologues on campus have opened up the most issues—they are written anonymously and performed by actors. So many issues are raised there. The issue I keep coming back to, though, is inequality and incarceration. I am taking an Inside/Out course with inmates at the local prison and I realize how important that educational experience is to them. That's top on my list right now. I'm also thinking about my format and I think that writing an op-ed would give me the best possible rhetorical situation—I need to reach a wide audience of people who haven't thought about this issue or who think differently about it than I do. A news outlet would do that.

Read: Strategies for Reading in Research

Proposals have to convince an audience to agree and to act. That's a high bar. Good writers will research the issue fully and will understand where their audience stands on this issue already. They will target their research to understand the issue from as many perspectives as possible and will even cite those opposing viewpoints in their writing in order to analyze and address them.

Fauvé had strong feelings about her issue, so she knew she needed to consider alternative viewpoints through her research.

I am surprised to find that I like reading opposing viewpoints on this issue because I really don't find them convincing. From a practical standpoint, it is expensive to provide higher education in prison, but you can't argue with the return on investment. From an ethical standpoint, I think our society believes that education is a right not a privilege.

twenty two   Proposal: Advocating for Change

So the more I read, the stronger I feel and the
easier it seems to present and refute opposing
viewpoints.

Invent: Take Note and Create

Taking notes in the proposal argument process means listening carefully to all sides of an issue, brainstorming the strongest counterarguments for those positions. You can create a cluster map of those
different viewpoints to capture the breadth and depth of the issue.

I am freewriting from sources, both sources
from my research and some of the quotes
from my inmate peers in the Inside/Out class.
Then I am outlining based on that freewriting. Op-eds are short, so I have to highlight
my best points and let go of ones that aren't as
persuasive or relevant for this audience.

Arrange: Prioritize, Organize, Outline

A key move of an effective proposal argument is making the shift between informing the audience on the issue and then convincing them
to act in the way you recommend. You have to understand your audience well enough to know how much time to spend on informing
compared to how much time you spend on convincing. (See Chapter
11, "Arrange: Prioritize, Organize, Outline.")

Fauvé started a new section in her Assignment Journal called
"Outline Ideas." She wrote the following:

The most important idea I see from my notes
is that education matters to people in prison.
It also matters to people not in prison because it helps people re-enter society and live

a stable life after incarceration. There's all kinds of debate about what type of education should happen there—more professional or humanities—but I'm not sure I can get into all of that in this op-ed. I'm afraid that the more specific I am about what people should study in prison, the more people will reject what I have to say. I just need a baseline agreement that we should support higher education in prison right now.

Draft: Introduction, Body, Conclusion

The introduction, body, and conclusion of the proposal argument rely on your knowledge of the audience and the genre in which you've chosen to write (i.e., an Op-Ed, a bid for business, or a scholarly grant). Keep your specific audience in mind as you consider the rhetorical purpose of each of these elements. (See Chapter 12, "Draft: Introduction, Body, Conclusion.")

Introduction

Think about what your audience knows and needs as you design the introduction. Can you safely assert your proposal in the introduction, or do you need to lead up to that by informing them about the issue first? Know how favorable or unfavorable they might be and craft your tone and content accordingly.

Fauvé captured her thoughts in her journal:

I think a lot of my audience will be hostile to the idea of higher education in prison because they will see it as a luxury or privilege, not as a right. They just aren't informed, so I have to present the factual support that

shows the practical side of this argument as
it relates to everyone in my audience.

Body
The body will balance informing the audience about the issue and opposing viewpoints with pitching your solution to the issue that calls
for their action. If your audience likely knows about the problem, you
can shift to solutions more quickly. If they haven't thought about it,
then you have to take time to inform them about the urgency of this
issue first. Get them to care the way you care.

Op-eds are short, so I have to use the body to
provide supporting evidence.

Conclusion
In this assignment, the conclusion has to drive home the importance
of your audience taking the specific action you recommend. In some
proposal arguments, writers hold that call for action until the conclusion, working up to it throughout. Others introduce the call up front
and reinforce it in the conclusion. Either way, the call to think or do
something needs to be feasible for your audience. You want them to
take action because they are moved, convinced, and informed enough
by your argument to follow through on what you've proposed.

Fauvé wrote:

My issue is big and complicated and I am
writing in a newspaper format that only lets
me write a little bit. I'm not sure how much I
can expect of my audience. At the very least, I
want them to think about higher education in
prisons if they have never thought about it. On
the high end of my expectations, I want them
to be so moved that they support local/private

393

efforts like the Bard Prison Initiative and I want them only to support political candidates who support progressive prison reform.

Revise: Strategies for Re-seeing

Rethinking the proposal argument requires real effort to consider how people with opposing views or no views on this issue will be able to absorb and respond to the information and call to action you offer. Think of specific people or generalize about groups of people who might see this differently. What would it take to get them to listen, to agree, and to act? Revise with those people in mind.

Fauvé wrote in her assignment journal:

I keep thinking about the people who are hard-line about prison and think people shouldn't have any "luxuries" there. I know they will have a hard time understanding how education benefits all of society, not just that individual. If I can get them to see their own self-interest, I will have a better shot at convincing them of this solution to reducing the recidivism rates. You really have to see the big picture and think long term to buy into this approach. If they can only imagine prisoners sitting around reading Shakespeare, then I leave them with the wrong impression of what this is all about.

Review: By Peers and Experts

Review by peers and experts will help you test your argument to see if you can sufficiently inform those readers to act on your proposal. Tell your readers to be honest with you and test their reaction over time, if possible. If this is a new issue, it might take some time for them to process what you're saying and move forward as recommended.

I have some friends who questioned why I wanted to take the Inside/Out course. To many people, prison is just a mystery and it's scary. Honestly, I was scared at first as well—maybe I still am—but I have a totally new understanding of what it means to be imprisoned and it makes me question the intentions of our criminal justice system. What we tell the public it does and what it actually does seem to be two different things. I need to test my writing on people who have and haven't experienced the Inside/Out course and who think differently about this issue so that I can see if my argument is convincing to people on all sides.

Proofread and Submit

Make sure your peer and expert reviewers know the expectations of your assignment and the expectations of the venue you're writing to so the formatting aligns.

Fauvé wrote.

I shared the submission guidelines for the newspaper I am writing this for with my peer and writing center readers so they could make sure I followed everything right, especially my reference to sources and facts.

WHAT HAPPENS NEXT?

The answer to the question "what happens next?" says a lot about the success of your proposal argument. If the audience acts on your recommendation, then you know your message was effective. If the audience accepts your bid, votes in favor of your policy, or awards you a grant, then you know that your proposal argument succeeded.

But how do you build on that success? If you've connected with the audience so successfully, they might expect more from you. Not everyone can get an audience to both agree with a proposed course of action *and* act on it. If you achieve that kind of response, consider what ethical implications you have in monitoring that movement and taking it forward. Are you now the leader of a group that's taking action? What do they and you do after this step is taken? What is the end goal and how can you maintain that level of care in all your subsequent recommendations? Good writing leads to good action. Continue to consider what you have to write and to do to contribute to the common good.

OFFICE HOURS ➤   Going Public: Writing an Op-Ed

Proposal arguments require a reaching out to ask others—people you might not know—to listen to you and follow your recommendations. Going public with a proposal can be daunting because you don't know how people will react. When you write an op-ed and you submit it for publication, you have the potential to reach a wide audience (note that op-eds are longer arguments on an issue as compared to letters to the editor, which are often short rebuttals to other news stories). That audience is unknown to you, so it is important to follow the guidelines of proposal writing outlined here to help ensure that you get a full and fair hearing of your proposal. If you don't, you risk adding to the apathy or even hostility surrounding the issue. If your proposal is well-crafted, you have a chance to gain allies who will address an issue you care about.

If you gain confidence in writing for the public, the op-ed is a venue you can engage throughout your life. Op-eds can address public policy, historical events, popular culture—anything about which reasonable people can hold different opinions. Different publications will, of course, prefer different topics, catering to the perceived interests of their readers. As a genre, though, the op-ed is an effective tool for addressing and even swaying public opinion. A well-written op-ed has the potential to change the thinking that changes action. You don't have to hold a special position to use this tool—you are qualified to submit something right now. To get past the editors and get to the readers, though, you have to have a clear sense of insight, strong support, and an engaging, trustworthy voice that's worth the print (or pixels).

A useful strategy is to think locally, writing to sway opinion through your local media where you might encourage people to do something that addresses community issues in front of you, such as: support a school funding initiative to improve education, support programs that reduce juvenile offender recidivism rates, advocate for increased public transportation routes so that low-income residents can get to and from work safely and on time. Those local changes can have a significant impact and contribute to the common good by modeling solutions that can be transferred to other cities or even scaled up to the state or federal level.

CHAPTER twenty three

Multimodal Composition

As we discussed in Chapter 1, "Why Write?", we have three general reasons to write: to inform, to entertain, and to argue. To achieve your purpose, plan, as Aristotle recommended, to draw from "all available means of persuasion." Good writing uses multiple means or modes of persuasion, not just one. In classical rhetoric, we talk about modes as types of writing, and in modern rhetoric we talk about modes more as the sensory pathways through which the message is conveyed. What is most important to understand is that all writing is multimodal, reaching readers through multiple persuasive pathways. Good writers understand those options and control the balance and delivery style to suit their purpose. This chapter defines and bridges both categories of modes.

A DEFINITION OF CLASSICAL MODES

A mode describes the way writing is produced, the way writing works. In classical rhetoric, the overall effect of a single text, such as an essay or email, is its primary mode. Secondary modes work within the text in individual paragraphs or clusters of paragraphs to advance the primary purpose of the writing, which could be to inform, entertain, or argue.

The four classic modes of discourse included narration, description, exposition (explanation), and argumentation. In writing for the common good, it's helpful to consider an expanded list of types of modes: argumentation, narration, description, explication (exposition), classification, compare/contrast, pro/con and rebuttal, definition, and common ground. Good writers know a range of modes and use them deliberately to achieve their purpose.

For example, you might submit an op-ed to your local newspaper's website to persuade citizens to vote against an ordinance that would fine residents who let their grass grow taller than nine inches high. In your op-ed, you explain that people who cannot afford to cut their lawn or have physical disabilities would be unfairly penalized and still could not cut their grass.

In this example, the primary mode is argumentation—you want to persuade readers to oppose this ordinance. However, you also need to outline your reasons through explication, showing how financial or physical difficulty might prevent people from mowing in the first place. If you describe an example of a specific person who does not have the means to cut her lawn, then you are using the modes of narration and description. In this case, narration and description serve as secondary modes supporting the primary mode of argumentation.

Finally, note that the genre of the text does not dictate its mode. You could also write an op-ed in which your primary purpose is explication. For example, you could explain how fines for breaking local ordinances are collected and used in local government and how they affect those who are fined. Included in that explanation might be an argument for or against using fines to manage citizens' behavior (i.e., encouraging them to keep their lawns cut). But the primary purpose is to help readers understand a process better. Therefore, the primary mode in this example is explication.

TYPES OF CLASSICAL MODES

The purpose of a text is advanced through careful application of a wide range of modes. For example, a few paragraphs in a longer argumentative essay could turn to explication to represent a process readers need to understand in order to accept your argument. A paragraph that narrates a specific anecdote might provide evidence. Following are some common types of modes.

Argumentation

This entire book is about argumentation, persuading an audience to think or act differently based on what you communicate. In this chapter, we also talk about argumentation as a mode that can be used in writing whose purpose is to inform or persuade.

Example of Argumentation

In this excerpt from a feature article in the journal *Scientific American* titled "How Diversity Makes Us Smarter," professor of leadership and ethics Katherine W. Phillips argues that her position on the value of diversity in organizations is supported by research in many areas:

> The fact is that if you want to build teams or organizations capable of innovating, you need diversity. Diversity enhances creativity. It encourages the search for novel information and perspectives, leading to better decision making and problem solving. Diversity can improve the bottom line of companies and lead to unfettered discoveries and breakthrough innovations. Even simply being exposed to diversity can change the way you think. This is not just wishful thinking: it is the conclusion I draw from decades of research from organizational scientists, psychologists, sociologists, economists and demographers.

Narration

As a mode, narration tells a story. Narration can move in chronological order, or it can move back and forth between past and present. Narration can include voices other than the narrator or author, sometimes through direct quotation of dialogue. Narration can be used to represent an example from personal experience, something witnessed, or a hypothetical scenario.

Example of Narration

In his novel *The Absolutely True Diary of a Part-Time Indian*, writer Sherman Alexie uses narration to describe an incident that shows the pain of poverty in a visceral, vivid way. In this scene, the narrator's father does the only thing he has the power to do when the family cannot afford the vet bills they would need to pay to heal their dog:

> It sucks to be poor, and it sucks to feel that you somehow *deserve* to be poor. You start believing that you're poor because you're stupid and ugly. And then you start believing that you're stupid and ugly because you're Indian. And because you're Indian you start believing you're destined to be poor. It's an ugly circle and *there's nothing you can do about it.*
>
> Poverty doesn't give you strength or teach you lessons about perseverance. No, poverty only teaches you how to be poor.
>
> So, poor and small and weak, I picked up Oscar. He licked my face because he loved and trusted me. And I carried him out to the lawn, and I laid him down beneath our green apple tree.
>
> "I love you, Oscar." I said.
>
> He looked at me and I swear to you that he understood what was happening. He knew what Dad was going to do. But Oscar wasn't scared. He was relieved.
>
> But not me.

401

I ran away from there as fast as I could.

I wanted to run faster than the speed of sound, but nobody, no matter how much pain they're in, can run that fast. So I heard the boom of my father's rifle when he shot my best friend.

A bullet only costs about two cents, and anybody can afford that.

Description

Description is writing that appeals to the senses in order to help an audience imagine or feel an experience. Description is commonly used with narration in order to illustrate the narration in more detail, using vivid verbs and adjectives that engage the senses.

Example of Description

In *The Immortal Life of Henrietta Lacks*, writer Rebecca Skloot helps readers get to know the African-American woman behind the HeLa cells that continue to populate medical labs long after their source, Henrietta Lacks, has died. Because Skloot also wants readers to understand the science of this story, she describes a cell and its functions for a general audience that might not have a strong science background:

> Under the microscope, a cell looks a lot like a fried egg: It has a white (the *cytoplasm*) that's full of water and proteins to keep it fed, and a yolk (the *nucleus*) that holds all the genetic information that makes you you. The cytoplasm buzzes like a New York City street. It's crammed full of molecules and vessels endlessly shuttling enzymes and sugars from one part of the cell to another, pumping water, nutrients, and oxygen in and out of the cell. All the while, little cytoplasmic factories work 24/7, cranking out sugars, fats, proteins, and energy to keep the whole thing running and feed the nucleus—the brains of the operation. Inside every nucleus

within each cell in your body, there's an identical copy of your entire genome. That genome tells cells when to grow and divide and makes sure they do their jobs, whether that's controlling your heartbeat or helping your brain understand the words on this page.

Explication

Explication is the act of explaining something, typically addressing why or how something is the way it is. Writing that explicates how a process happens step-by-step so that others can understand how it works and perhaps replicate the process themselves is known as process analysis. Explication can also address concepts and theories, explaining why something might be the way it is, as we see in the following example.

Example of Explication

In his examination of the disproportionate enrollment of African Americans in for-profit higher education programs, Kai Wright explains, step-by-step, the debt problems they face in his *Salon* article "Young, Black, and Buried in Debt: How For-Profit Colleges Prey on African American Ambition":

> But this headlong rush of black Americans to get schooled has also led too many down a depressingly familiar path. As with the mortgage market of the pre-crash era, those who are just entering in the higher ed game have found themselves ripe for the con man's picking. They've landed, disproportionately, at for-profit schools, rather than at far less expensive public community colleges, or at public universities. And that means they've found themselves loaded with unimaginable debt, with little to show for it, while a small group of financial players have made a great deal of easy money. Sound familiar? Two points if you hear troublesome echoes of the subprime mortgage crisis.

Classification

Classification puts things into categories to show what they do and do not resemble. As such, classification is related to the modes of definition and compare/contrast. Classification is useful when presenting something that might be new to an audience or when trying to redefine a concept or term. This chapter, for example, classifies the concept of modes by highlighting connections and differences across various types of modes and by using examples to help make those differences clear.

Example of Classification

In his essay, "Measuring the Unmeasurable," Partners in Health (PIH) medical volunteer Phil Garrity reflects on what he calls the work of "doing" and "non-doing." In the following passage, Garrity lists service activities that typically count as active "doing." Later he lists critical activities often overlooked that count as "non-doing," such as listening to people tell stories and just being present during their suffering. He thus classifies different activities as the "doing" and the "non-doing" of service with people who are poor:

> [M]uch of our work and my role here at PIH continues to place particular emphasis (as it rightly should) on an intrinsic part of serving the poor: the doing. My mind is often focused on what protocols our staff are implementing, how many home visits our community health workers have completed this month, how often our HIV patients have been seen in clinic. You may preoccupy yourself with such questions as how many letters have been sent, web pages designed, meetings scheduled, donors courted, supplies procured, services delivered, money raised

Compare/Contrast

Compare/contrast focuses on comparison between two or more items in order to either classify or assess them. As such, compare/contrast is related to definition and classification, and it is a particularly useful strategy for argumentation if the author claims that one of the items is better than or preferable to the other. In contrasting items or ideas, the author might try to show that one thing does *not* belong in a particular class or should not be defined in a particular way.

Example of Compare/Contrast

In the article "'Crack Babies' Talk Back," journalist Mariah Blake reports on adults whom the media sensationally labeled "crack babies" as children, comparing that to the more recent label of "meth babies":

> Still, a number of recent "meth baby" stories echo the early crack baby coverage. A July AP article cautioned, for instance, that an "epidemic" of meth-exposed children in Iowa is stunting infants' growth, damaging their brains, and leaving them predisposed to delinquency. In May, one Fox News station warned that meth babies "could make the crack baby look like a walk in the nursery." Research is stacking up against such claims. But, then, scientific evidence isn't always enough to kill a good story.

Pro/Con and Rebuttal

In a pro/con argument, you write detailed reasons for and against something for an audience, typically taking a side and persuading the audience to agree with your assessment (thus making this a form of argumentation).

Rebuttal is a form of pro/con in which the author has a firm position on an issue but wishes to clearly state and respond to someone who has articulated an opposing viewpoint. The opposing viewpoint is typically outlined first, either in full or point-by-point; the author then responds to that position by rebutting it with evidence, reasons, and examples that support his or her position.

Example of Rebuttal

Teju Cole's article in *The Atlantic*, "The White-Savior Industrial Complex," is an extended rebuttal argument. Cole opens by reprinting tweets he sent that triggered heated responses from many people, including Pulitzer Prize winning journalist Nicholas Kristof, whom Cole claims is well-meaning but misguided in his efforts to assist struggling Africans. In the article, Cole rebuts those critiques of his original claims:

> But I disagree with the approach taken by Invisible Children in particular, and by the White Savior Industrial Complex in general, because there is much more to doing good work than "making a difference." There is the principle of first do no harm. There is the idea that those who are being helped ought to be consulted over the matters that concern them.

Definition

With definition, a writer offers an extended or even new definition of a term or concept. While definition can be a primary mode (see Chapter 19, "Definition: Explaining the Nature of Something"), as a secondary mode it usually takes the form of a few sentences or a paragraph in which a writer explains how she defines a term or concept within the larger context of her argument. Such paragraphs or sentences usually appear early in a text, in order to ensure that the audience understands how a writer is using key terms.

Example of Definition

In this section of a paragraph in Martin Luther King, Jr.'s "Letter from a Birmingham Jail," King succinctly defines just and unjust laws (and then goes on to classify segregation laws as unjust laws, thus justifying his actions to resist them):

> Any law that uplifts human personality is just. Any law that degrades human personality is unjust.

Common Ground

Finding common ground is an important mode for ethical argumentation. Finding common ground means you name the places where you and people who might take a different position than you actually agree on something. By naming points of agreement, you draw your audience in and increase the likelihood that they will listen to your position. It shows that you are digging deep into the argument to see exactly where your thinking diverges and converges with what others think.

Example of Common Ground

In "The White-Savior Industrial Complex" in *The Atlantic*, Teju Cole uses what he calls "direct speech" to rebut well-meaning but, he says, misguided efforts by white Americans including journalist Nicholas Kristof who want to improve well-being in places such as Africa. Offsetting that direct critical approach, Cole also takes time to name multiple points of agreement:

> Kristof and I are in profound agreement about one thing: there is much happening in many parts of the African continent that is not as it ought to be. I have been fortunate in life, but that doesn't mean I haven't seen or experienced African poverty first-hand. I grew up in a land of military coups and economically devastating, IMF-imposed "structural adjustment" programs. The genuine hurt of Africa is no fiction.
>
> And we also agree on something else: that there is an internal ethical urge that demands that each of us serve justice as much as he or she can.

A DEFINITION OF MODERN MODES

Today we increasingly also use the term *mode* in reference to the five pathways through which we compose and convey communications: linguistic, visual, aural, spatial, and gestural. All communication is multimodal, meaning that it uses more than one pathway. For example, a traditional academic essay printed on paper uses the linguistic mode of words and the visual mode of layout in black ink on white paper formatted with MLA design in spacing. The explosion of digital media has heightened our awareness and expanded our options for multimodality because it is now so common to read and so easy to produce digital media that use an array of aural, visual, spatial, and gestural modes in addition to the linguistic. A typical blog, for example, might contain short articles on a specific topic, photos to show readers an example or case, and a video interview with an expert. Good writers consider all five of these modes when composing and they are able to re-mediate or remix texts, transforming their modes and media for platforms and/or audiences that have different needs, abilities, and affordances or opportunities. See Chapter 26, "Design and Delivery: Print, Digital, and Oral Presentations" for discussion of some of those affordances and limitations in design and delivery.

TYPES OF MODERN MODES

Compositions take many different forms and mix many different media to convey messages today. The formats and tools for such composing change quickly, so it is most important that you understand the underlying principles of multimodal composition (you can learn how to use specific production tools in class and/or online). Good writers know how to mix modes for the greatest persuasive impact in any given rhetorical situation.

Linguistic

Linguistic refers to the use of words, sentences, paragraphs, and structured language in written alphabetic text or speech. Linguistic considers such elements as vocabulary, genre, and grammar. This mode of conveying meaning is particularly critical for human communication because we use language to convey everything from practical instructions to expressions of love and injustice.

Visual

Visual refers to the use of still and moving images. Those images might include photos, videos, drawings, charts, graphs, and tables. Visuals consider such elements as the use of color, shape, page layout, and camera movement to convey meaning. See Chapter 26, "Design and Delivery: Print, Digital, and Oral Presentations" for a detailed discussion of common visuals.

Aural

Aural refers to the use of sound. Sound includes voice, music, sound effects, noise, ambient sounds of the environment, and other acoustic considerations. Sound considers such elements as volume, silence, pitch, emphasis, accent, and rhythm.

Spatial

Spatial refers to the physical arrangement or spacing of the text, how its pieces relate to one another and to the audience. Space includes distance between images and the general outline/architecture of the composition. Space considers such elements as proximity, layout, and direction.

Gestural

Gestural refers to body, hand, and facial movement. Gestures can come from people in live or recorded contexts, or they can come from other living or animated figures. Gestures are conveyed through such venues as live presentations or performances, recorded videos, or animated drawings or photos. Gestures consider such elements as speed, stillness, angles, and rhythm.

STRATEGIES FOR MULTIMODAL COMPOSING
Consider Classical and Modern Modes

All compositions benefit from considering classical types of modes that define the purpose and modern types of modes that consider how the messages reach their audience: all modes matter. Continue to ask: What am I trying to do (purpose)? How am I going to do that (strategy)? Multimodal analysis will help you respond to those questions.

Know Affordances and Limitations

Every type of mode can do some things well (affordances) and yet falls short in other areas (limitations). Carefully consider how each mode can advance your argument in a particular rhetorical situation. See Chapter 26, "Design and Delivery: Print, Digital, and Oral Presentations" for further exploration of some affordances and limitations.

Compose Inclusively

Know your audience and compose accordingly, particularly when making media design choices. Does your audience have the right kind of computer access to get the full effect of your multimodal composition? Does your audience have physical limitations, such as vision or hearing loss, that would make it difficult for them to receive your full message? Using multiple modes often creates an emphasis or productive redundancy that expands access to more people.

Remix, Remediate

In the revising process or even in designing the final delivery of your message, push yourself to remix or remediate your text using different modes. Think of yourself as a maker trying out different styles of production, remixing a printed academic researched argument into a series of blog posts, then into an animated slideshow for kids, then into a gallery of protest signs, then into a song. By trying different modes, you can stretch yourself in ways that make for interesting and sometimes even more powerful and persuasive delivery of your message.

OFFICE HOURS ➤ Moving Modes: Working with Reviewers to Select, Order, and Balance Modes

Modes are structural building blocks of an argument, so you should think about them early in the writing process. As you analyze the assignment, ask your instructor, peers, and/or writing center tutors about how modes could operate to meet the assignment goals. Ask your reviewers how the selection, order, and balance of certain modes can advance the tone and purpose you seek. With reviewers, work through each type of mode listed in this chapter to explore: (1) whether or not it could be useful for this assignment, (2) if so, where in the project it might be effective, and (3) how much of that mode seems appropriate; that is, should it be a primary or secondary mode?

You should also consider the rhetorical moves you will make to transition between modes. For example, you might consider what difference it would make to open with definition, then move to narration, or vice versa. The former might set a more analytical tone than the latter. Or you might consider whether a video would deliver your argument to an intended audience of teenagers more effectively than a web-based report. Your reviewers can help you consider options for effective arrangement of modes for your project.

Critical Questions

1. Describe the primary and secondary classical modes you used in a recent writing assignment. Why did you choose those modes?
2. Which classical modes do you prefer to read and write? Why?
3. Which types of modern multimodal texts do you prefer to read/hear/watch and compose? Why?

CHAPTER twenty four

Style

Writing style refers to how writers convey their meaning. Good writers control, develop, and adapt their writing style to fit the rhetorical situation. They know how to use style to maximize effectiveness in four areas: clarity, simplicity, voice, and visualization. Within those areas, writers make choices about *how* to say what they want to say. In this chapter, we explore techniques that help writers succeed in each of the four core elements of style.

FOUR CORE ELEMENTS OF STYLE

Developing writing style is about knowing the rules that guide an audience's expectations. It's about developing a genuine ethos of credibility so that your audience listens attentively. Finally, writing style is about knowing the rules and expectations so that you can occasionally break those rules for effect.

In this section, we describe four core elements of style: simplicity, voice, and visualization. Within each core element we outline techniques that writers can employ to adapt their style to fit the rhetorical situation.

Clarity

Sometimes writers who want to develop their academic style write long, complicated sentences with "big" words to impress their audience. Remember, though, that readers want to understand what you have to say. Readers get frustrated if they have to work too hard to follow your argument. It's important to know your audience and pitch your writing at an appropriate level of sentence length, word choice, and paragraph construction.

Paragraph Structure
Good writers see paragraphs as discrete units with a specific purpose, and they make that purpose clear to readers. They open with topic sentences stating the purpose of that paragraph, then follow with relevant reasons, evidence, and examples to support that idea. Their paragraphs are animated by a specific mode that helps further its purpose (see Chapter 23, "Multimodal Composition").

Sentence Structure
Good writers build effective sentence structure by varying grammatical organization and length to keep the audience interested. For example, they use parallel structure to compare like items or ideas within or across sentences, creating a pleasing rhythm for readers. For example, in his "Letter From a Birmingham Jail," Martin Luther King, Jr., writing to white religious leaders who have asked him to "wait" for change, writes a litany of parallel clauses in a single long sentence beginning with the phrase "when you . . ." followed by example after example of intolerable discrimination. This parallelism concludes with a clause beginning, "then you will understand..." While the sentence is extraordinarily long, the repetition of that key phrase makes it easy to follow: readers can tally injustice after injustice.

> Perhaps it is easy for those who have never felt the stinging darts of segregation to say, "Wait." But when you have seen vicious mobs

lynch your mothers and fathers at will and drown your sisters and brothers at whim; when you have seen hate filled policemen curse, kick and even kill your black brothers and sisters; when you see the vast majority of your twenty million Negro brothers smothering in an airtight cage of poverty in the midst of an affluent society; when you suddenly find your tongue twisted and your speech stammering as you seek to explain to your six year old daughter why she can't go to the public amusement park that has just been advertised on television, and see tears welling up in her eyes when she is told that Funtown is closed to colored children, and see ominous clouds of inferiority beginning to form in her little mental sky, and see her beginning to distort her personality by developing an unconscious bitterness toward white people; when you have to concoct an answer for a five year old son who is asking: "Daddy, why do white people treat colored people so mean?"; when you take a cross county drive and find it necessary to sleep night after night in the uncomfortable corners of your automobile because no motel will accept you; when you are humiliated day in and day out by nagging signs reading "white" and "colored"; when your first name becomes "nigger," your middle name becomes "boy" (however old you are) and your last name becomes "John," and your wife and mother are never given the respected title "Mrs."; when you are harried by day and haunted by night by the fact that you are a Negro, living constantly at tiptoe stance, never quite knowing what to expect next, and are plagued with inner fears and outer resentments; when you are forever fighting a degenerating sense of "nobodiness"— then you will understand why we find it difficult to wait.

Word Choice

Good writers choose words carefully to establish a credible voice and tone for the essay. They choose words that are appropriate for the domain (level of formality) and precise, using varied, vivid verbs. Some of the more powerful verbs King uses in the preceding passage include "lynch," "kick," "kill," "drown," and "concoct." Good writers also use lively adverbs and adjectives, but only sparingly. For example, King describes African Americans as "*harried* by day and *haunted* by night," using alliteration—repetition of an initial sound—to further emphasize and connect these sharp adjectives. Finally, good writers make sure their pronoun references point clearly to a subject named earlier. In King's passage, "you" clearly refers back to "those who have never felt the stinging darts of segregation."

Emphasis

Good writers use points of emphasis, such as beginnings and endings of sentences and essays, to highlight key points where an audience is most likely to tune in to the message. Good writers repeat words or phrases occasionally to highlight key words or concepts and make them stick with the audience. For example, in the preceding passage, King's repetition of the direct call to the reader—"when you"—at the beginning of each clause reminds readers that they personally are called to reflect and act.

Format

Good writers use features of format such as headings to announce new points and provide an accessible visual outline of the text. Heading style—capitalization, bold, italics, and so forth—should follow an appropriate guide such as Modern Language Association (MLA) or the American Psychological Association (APA) (see Chapter 27, "Working with Published Sources" for key components of MLA style).

Good writers also use formatting features such as italics, bold, all capitals, and dashes to set off words or ideas that need extra attention. But they limit their use of these features, so that it is significant to the audience when they do appear.

Simplicity

Simplicity in writing means saying what you have to say with precise words in as few words as possible. It also means using transitions within and across sentences that help show the relationship between ideas. The goal of simplicity is to allow readers to understand your message quickly and clearly.

Sentence Structure

Simplicity means using sentences that are clear and concise, even when presenting complex ideas. When good writers use compound sentences, they show the relationship of ideas through appropriate use of punctuation, coordinating conjunctions, *and* words that transition and subordinate ideas. In "The New Jim Crow: How the War on Drugs Gave Birth to a Permanent Undercaste," Michelle Alexander succinctly rebuts critics who claim, falsely, that African Americans are imprisoned more because they use drugs more: "This war has been waged almost exclusively in poor communities of color, even though studies consistently show that people of all colors use and sell illegal drugs at remarkably similar rates." Here, the transitional phrase "even though" signals a critical contrast to readers: our actions contradict the evidence.

Effective Words

Good writers use adjectives and adverbs sparingly. Instead, they use vivid verbs and specific nouns to tell the story concisely. In *Soul of a Citizen*, writer Paul Rogat Loeb demonstrates this:

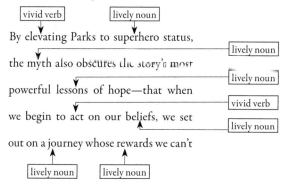

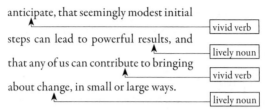

anticipate, that seemingly modest initial
— vivid verb

steps can lead to powerful results, and
— lively noun

that any of us can contribute to bringing
— vivid verb

about change, in small or large ways.
— lively noun

Note as well how the dash signals that the lessons of hope will be outlined next.

Good writers minimize nominalizations, in which a verb or adjective has been used as a noun, for example, "performance" (for the verb "to perform") or "analysis" (for the verb "to analyze"). When they do use nominalizations, they make sure not to obscure who is doing the action described in the sentence. The following sentence, for example, nominalizes and obscures who is doing what to whom: "There was a discussion about the new policy." An effective revision that succinctly identifies the actors and the action would be: "The events committee discussed the new policy."

Unnecessary Words

In their revision process, good writers look for and cut unnecessary words, ideas, and information that distract readers from the main idea. Good writers also cut filler words and phrases that do not advance the message (see Table 24.1, "Cut Unnecessary Words"). Note that phrases such as "there are"/"there is" and "person who" often signal places to cut words.

Voice

Voice refers to the presence of the author in a text. Authors might be highly present, using the first person and personal examples, or they might use the third person and a more objective tone that conveys distance and anonymity. Authors have to assess the rhetorical situation as well as the genre to decide how best to adjust their voice to audience expectations. The following features describe voice in good writing.

Table 24.1 CUT UNNECESSARY WORDS

	Unnecessary Words	Concise Version
Redundancy *Redundancy is unnecessary repetition, repetition that does not add important emphasis or say anything new. Good writers cut all such instances.*	5:00 a.m. in the morning	5:00 a.m.
	a person who is caring	a caring person
	biography of her life	biography
	circular/square/rectangular in shape	circular/square/rectangular
	cooperate together	cooperate
	end result	result
	exactly the same	the same
	final outcome	outcome
	free gift	gift
	future plans	plans
	he/she is a person who	he/she
	important essentials	essentials
	in a confused state	confused
	in light of the fact that	because
	in spite of the fact that	although
	in the event that	if
	in the field of chemistry	in chemistry
	longer/shorter in length	longer/shorter
	of expensive quality	expensive
	of particular interest	of interest
	one and the same	the same
	past memories	memories
	period in time	time
	period of two weeks	two weeks
	personally, I think that	I think
	puzzling in nature	puzzling

(Continued)

Table 24.1   CUT UNNECESSARY WORDS *(Continued)*

	refer back	refer
	repeat again	repeat
	revert back	revert
	summarize briefly	summarize
	surrounded on all sides	surrounded
	terrible tragedy	tragedy
	the future to come	the future
	there is no doubt but that	no doubt
	true facts	facts
	unusual in nature	unusual
	various differences	differences
	we are in receipt of	we received
Intensifiers *Intensifying words such as "very," "really," "extremely," or "too" elevate or add force to the quality of the word that follows. In most cases, good writers eliminate the need for intensifiers by using an adjective or adverb that fully conveys the level of that quality.*	Extremely dangerous	dangerous
	really astounding	astounding
	very cold	frigid
Clauses *Good writers see that they can often rewrite clauses beginning with the words "that," "which," and "who" by using adjectives to describe or modify the noun more concisely.*	The energy source that is most accessible and renewable (9 words)	the most accessible and renewable energy source (7 words)

Formality

Good writers select their language to fit the occasion. Technical words, third person (he/she/they/it), and an objective tone signal higher formality, which is often preferred in academic, civic, and work domains. For example, in her essay "The New Jim Crow: How the War on Drugs Gave Birth to a Permanent American Undercaste," Michelle Alexander uses technical, precise language to make one of her central claims: "The uncomfortable truth, however, is that crime rates do not explain the sudden and dramatic mass incarceration of African Americans during the past 30 years." Conversely, common words, contractions, first person (I/we), and a familiar tone signal an informal language level often preferred in the home domain or in less structured exchanges in academics or work. In his reflective essay "Measuring the Immeasurable," Phil Garrity uses contractions and the personal pronoun "I" to discuss the life lessons he learned through various forms of service, drawing readers close in this heart-to-heart sharing: "But real solidarity, true compassion, as I've come to discover through lived experience these past eight months, is grounded in something far deeper than our displays of technical prowess or standard notions of progress."

Ethos

Good writers engage their audience as guests they respect and want to entertain and inform. They use a respectful tone (with inclusive language), educate at an appropriate level (defining terms and explaining context), and show passion and interest in the issue (see Chapter 25, "Inclusive Writing"). Good writers take the ethical high road, divulging relevant information and acknowledging opposing viewpoints without using logical fallacies (see Chapter 4, "Argument" and Chapter 5, "Writing Ethics, Responsibility, and Accountability").

Tone

Good writers express an attitude, or tone, that suits both the topic and the author's character. They use pathos in balance with appeals to logos, not unfairly animating irrelevant fear or anger, but calling on an emotional connection to advance logical arguments. They consider if humor can be used appropriately to connect with readers. See Chapter 4, "Argument," for more on logos and pathos.

Active and Passive Voice

Good writers determine whether active or passive voice is appropriate for the rhetorical situation and genre. Active voice refers to sentences in which the subject clearly does the action of the verb: "Medicare paid for her prescriptions." In passive voice, the verb acts upon the subject: "Her prescriptions were paid [by Medicare]." Active voice typically uses fewer words and is more direct, often making it a preferred style to achieve clarity and simplicity. In our examples, the active voice emphasizes the fact that Medicare is doing the paying. However, some academic disciplines, such as chemistry and biology, prefer passive voice, where the author is an observer of the action, not an actor who should be emphasized. See Table 24.2, "Active and Passive Voice Analysis," for annotated examples of active and passive construction.

Positivity/Kindness

Good writers keep a positive attitude, even when addressing opposing viewpoints or examining fault in others. They can be direct, firm, and critical, but stay professional and dignified in critique. Good writers respect the dignity of others as well by avoiding ad hominem attacks and name-calling, and sticking to information relevant to the issue. In his article "I am the Person You Hurt When You Say the R-Word," John Franklin Stephens shows kindness in the face of pain: "How shall we respond to those of you who still use the r-word? Well, like Van Helsing and Buffy, we are going to aim at your heart. The only difference is that we are determined to drive a smile, not a stake, through your heart."

Table 24.2   ACTIVE AND PASSIVE VOICE ANALYSIS

Voice	Comments
Active Voice "The city council passed an ordinance to fine people caught asking for money in a ten-block section of downtown."	We see clearly who (the city council) has done what (voted to fine) to whom (people caught asking for money). In this sentence we know that members of the city council—real people we could name—did the action of voting to prohibit others, probably people who are homeless, from asking for money in a certain area of town. Such transparency shows ethical writing—good writing. (19 words)
Passive Voice "An ordinance was passed by the city council to fine people caught asking for money in a ten-block section of downtown."	In this example, you have all the same details except the sentence leads with a reference to the ordinance—that's a point of emphasis—thus minimizing the role of the city council. It also takes two more words to say the same thing, thus cluttering the message. (21 words)
Passive Voice "An ordinance was passed to fine people caught asking for money in a ten-block section of downtown."	In this construction, one important detail is left out: the fact that the city council is responsible for making this decision. If you were reading this in the newspaper, it would not be immediately clear whom you should praise or blame for this decision. This is shorter, but it omits important information. (17 words)

Visualization

Visualization refers to writing that allows the audience to engage the idea or experience what you are trying to share. It means more than just visual imagery—it includes all writing that activates the five senses to simulate an experience. Yet good writers do not get carried away with such techniques, undermining the goal of simplicity by distracting readers with too many competing images. See Table 24.3, "Avoid Clichés and Euphemisms," for a list of ineffective imagery that is over-used and/or misleading.

Analogy

Analogies compare two things, typically one thing the audience already understands well and something else the writer is trying to explain. Good writers use analogies to create a sense of story and vivid imagery that activates the senses for the audience, helping them experience the issue more fully. For example, in his article "I am the Person You Hurt When You Say the R-Word," John Franklin Stevens writes, "Like Dracula, the r-word just sucks the life out of those of us who fall in its path."

Metaphors

Metaphor is a literary device in which an author claims that one thing is another thing in order to draw a comparison. Good writers choose the subject for comparison carefully, knowing that an audience has to be able to see how the comparison works. For example, President Lyndon B. Johnson declared a "war on poverty" in 1964. Was it an actual war fought with military weapons? No. The metaphor was meant to underscore the seriousness of the issue and the level of resources and attention that would be given to it. Critics would later use this metaphor against Johnson, saying he fought the war on poverty and poverty won.

Similes

Similes use the words "like" or "as" to signal an imaginative comparison. For example: "She's as poor as dirt," or "On New Year's Eve, the city buzzes like a beehive." Rather than relying on overused images like these that have become clichés, good writers craft original similes so that the audience actually summons the image rather than reading past it.

The more you write, the more you will develop your own personal sense of writing style—or, really, styles. Different occasions call for you to try different writing styles to appeal to the audience.

And there's no opting-out of style—you are communicating a sense of formality, complexity, voice, and vision whether you think about it carefully or not. See Table 15.1, "Checklist: Proofreading Guide," for a checklist that will help you address style. By attending to these elements consciously and carefully, writers can improve their writing style dramatically.

Table 24.3   AVOID CLICHÉS AND EUPHEMISMS

Clichés *Replace overused phrases that have become clichés with fresh imagery.*	better late than never brought back to reality blind as a bat busy as a bee/beaver cool as a cucumber calm, cool, and collected crack of dawn dead as a doornail dog-eat-dog world easier said than done easy as pie face the music flat as a pancake gentle as a lamb good time was had by all happy as a lark head over heels	heavy as lead last but not least needle in a haystack open-and-shut case pretty as a picture rat race ripe old age sad but true sick as a dog slow as molasses smart as a whip spread like wildfire strong as an ox thin as a rail to make a long story short work like a dog
Euphemisms *Replace euphemisms that say something sensitive indirectly, hiding the meaning, with more direct language.*	certified pre-owned (used) collateral damage (civilian deaths) courtesy call (survey) economical with the truth (lying) economically disadvantaged (poor) enhanced interrogation methods (torture) leveraging up (spending money you don't have) passed away (died) temporary negative cash flow (broke) thin on top (bald) underperforming assets (debts)	

OFFICE HOURS ➤ Breaking the Rules with Style

Just as people have different styles or patterns of speech, we also have different styles of writing. We develop that style based on the patterns of speech and writing we are exposed to through our family, our community, and outside influences such as the media. And yet, despite those influences, we also develop our own unique style of voice.

All language is controlled by rules of grammar, some of which have remained fixed for centuries. Yet English has been described as a "living language," meaning that it adapts and grows to include new words ("neologisms") and new forms of expression to allow for changes in our social, political, technological, and geographic contexts. Some argue that the rules of grammar should *prescribe* or firmly fix how a language works so that it never changes. Others argue that those rules should evolve to *describe* that growth, not prevent it.

What does that mean to you, one of the more than 800 million speakers of English worldwide? It means the more you know about the rules of English grammar, the better able you are to navigate those rules as you develop your style. And the rules change. Many question the grammar rules that people once followed strictly. People now "break" some of those rules so routinely that it's considered more of a style choice than a crime against the grammar police.

Talk with your instructor about how such choices are perceived in different rhetorical situations. What might be an acceptable pattern in one domain—or even part of the world—might be perceived differently elsewhere. Once you know the rules or the norms, you can control how you work within those expectations or how you might push against those boundaries to express your own style.

Critical Questions

1. Which of these elements of style are strongest in your writing? Which do you think you should work on? Describe your sense of writing style.
2. Name a few writers whose style you admire. Using the descriptions above, name the elements of style they use that make their writing appeal to you.
3. How do you think style could draw readers in or push them away? Give real or hypothetical examples of how writing style could make a difference in how an audience receives a message.

CHAPTER twenty five

Inclusive Writing

Good writing is inclusive writing. When you write inclusively, you seek to treat people and groups with respect. That respect includes all areas of personal identity, including (but not limited to) gender, race, ethnicity, religion, class, age, citizenship, mental and physical ability, and family formation. In both practical and ethical terms, it makes sense for writers to respect their readers. Readers might reject your argument if the ethos you construct seems to deny or insult their identity or the identity of others, or if your writing appears oblivious to the ways in which individuals and groups prefer to be described.

If you want your argument to reach a diverse audience, it is important to know and respect all aspects of that diversity. Respectful acknowledgement of diversity demonstrates your "cultural competency," which is your ability to interact effectively with people of varying races, ethnicities, religions, economic backgrounds, and so forth, as well as your understanding of your own cultural identity.

Some language offends people because it demeans a part of who they are—or demeans people they care about. Whether or not you think they *should* feel offended by certain language or whether or not you *intended* to offend someone is irrelevant. Set a tone in which you treat readers as guests welcomed into the rhetorical space you construct. Treat those guests with care while they are in that rhetorical space, and they are more likely to return your generosity by listening carefully to what you say.

PRINCIPLES FOR INCLUSIVE WRITING

It is hard to be aware of and sensitive to every evolution in language that could be considered offensive. But we can follow some basic principles of inclusive writing to reduce the risk of harm to others. Table 25.1 shows some common examples of exclusive language (words or phrases that negate or deny an aspect of someone's identity) and some suggested corrections to make them inclusive. This list is not comprehensive. If you are unsure about word choice, ask your instructor, writing center tutors, class peers, or others —to make sure your choices are respectful and inclusive (see Chapter 15, "Proofread and Submit").

Respect Your Audience

Expect the best of your audience. Expect them to be professional, intelligent, and kind people who want you to educate, inform, or entertain them in ways that do no harm. Target your writing to their most generous selves as a sign of respect for their intelligence and good nature. Respect your audience and they are more likely to respect you.

Be Kind to Your Audience

Good writers make sure that messages reach the intended audience— an audience they presumably care about. Ad hominem attacks (attacks that insult the person instead of critiquing the issue) or more subtle forms of belittling distract readers from useful information. Assume your readers are intelligent people who want to learn from you. Avoid anything that detracts from that purpose.

Note that this does not mean you can't make controversial points. You most certainly should say what you need to say with clarity and force. However, the tone of your argument should not alienate your audience. Confront ideas, not people.

Do Not Assume You Know Your Audience

Never assume you know all there is to know about your audience. Never assume they agree with you in every way just because they seem to be like you in some ways. People can share the same political party, religion, or race, for example, and have very different experiences and views. Some writers think they can use negative language when writing to a group they assume they know only to find out that those views are not shared or appreciated. If you would not say what you have written to anyone face-to-face, do not write it either.

Furthermore, do not assume your experience as the default perspective of your readers. Good writers have an intended audience in mind, but they also think about the many ways their audience could differ and they avoid generalizing, projecting their own experience as representative of their audience's experience.

Diversity is increasing in every domain as our global society enables more intercultural interactions that lead to diverse workplaces, neighborhoods, and even marriages. You can expect to write with and for diverse audiences throughout your life because civic and workplace leaders intentionally seek diverse teams. Practicing inclusive language now will make you a more valued and respected colleague and citizen later.

Be Positive

Use language that focuses on what people can do, not on what they cannot do. Emphasize abilities and assets, not limitations and weaknesses. For example, calling people "AIDs victims," "wheelchair bound," or "poverty stricken" frames people as having little control and suggests judgment about their circumstances. Instead, state their situation in a more factual frame: "people diagnosed with AIDs," "people who use wheelchairs," "people with income below the federal poverty line."

Use Person-Centered Language

Use language that humanizes. Avoid focusing primarily on one aspect of someone's identity—such as their race, ability, or class—especially if it isn't essential to make your point. Focus instead on personhood. For example, use "people with mental illness" rather than "the mentally ill" as the latter phrase subtly emphasizes the disease over the person who happens to experience it, making the disease seem like the most important aspect of that person's identity. If you are not sure what to call or how to describe people, *ask them* (if possible), and honor their preference.

Trust Your Feedback

If, despite your best efforts to write inclusively, you receive feedback that something you have written is exclusive and/or offensive, honor that feedback. Try to understand it. Adapt. If people feel excluded or offended, you have likely lost them as readers. You can always find a way to write inclusively. Inclusive writing creates a healthy, productive environment for dialogue.

Table 25.1   ALTERNATIVES TO EXCLUSIVE LANGUAGE

This table shows examples of exclusive language and alternatives to make them inclusive. These revisions attempt to be more factual, positive, and people-centered.

	Exclusive Language	Inclusive Language
Age *Avoid language that suggests fragility, dependence, or being out of touch. Correct by focusing on precise age and ability, not stereotypes.*	• Golden age • Old • Old folks • Over the hill • Senior citizens • The aged • The elderly	• Over 65 • Retirement age
Citizenship *Avoid language that equates U.S. citizenship with full humanity and dignity and belonging. Correct by using exact citizenship status, and only mention that status when it has direct relevance.*	• Illegal alien • Illegal immigrant • Illegals	• Person who is undocumented • Undocumented worker
Class & Economic Status *Avoid language that equates financial status with intelligence, drive to work hard, particular political parties, honesty, integrity, or general character. Correct by mentioning class or economic status only when it is directly relevant and by avoiding the suggestion that happiness and goodness are not the norm for people with low income.*	• The poor • Ghetto • Poverty stricken • Poor but honest • Redneck • White trash • The disadvantaged	• People who are poor • People who are low income • People who are below the poverty line • People experiencing poverty

Family Formation *Avoid the assumption that all families have a married mother and father living in the home with children. Correct by acknowledging parents and caregivers if you are unsure of family structure.*	• Parents, mother, or father	• Caregivers
Gender and Sexual Orientation *Avoid language that uses one gender pronoun or that defaults to male pronouns for powerful positions. Avoid language that equates sex with gender. Correct by using gender-neutral pronouns and acknowledging a range of sexual orientations.*	• Sexual preference • "That's gay" • Men and women, boys and girls, ladies and gentlemen, brothers and sisters • Cameraman, policeman, man-made, manpower, etc. • His or her (when gender is uncertain)	• Sexual orientation • "That's silly/ strange/odd/ unexpected/ awesome" • Everyone, the group • Camera operator, police officer, human-made/ artificial • Their (or other gender-neutral pronoun)
Physical & Mental Ability *Avoid focusing on disability or suggesting weakness. Correct by emphasizing personhood and ability and stating a precise condition.*	• The mentally ill • Crazy, nuts • AIDS victims • Wheelchair bound • Retard(ed) • Handicapped	• People with (or experiencing) a disability • People with (or experiencing) mental illness • People with (or experiencing) bipolar disease • People using a wheelchair • Person with (or experiencing) Down syndrome

(Continued)

Table 25.1   ALTERNATIVES TO EXCLUSIVE LANGUAGE *(Continued)*

Race & Ethnicity *Avoid using colloquial language to identify these categories, even if people in those categories use such terms. Avoid equating race or ethnicity with stereotypical expectations about preferences, intelligence, and character. Correct by naming race or ethnicity only when it is directly relevant. Consult experts who can confirm appropriate terms.*	• Racial and ethnic slurs abound, so we won't attempt to list them all here • Non-white	• A person from [country name] • Mexican American (remove hyphen)

BEYOND WORDS: VISUAL INCLUSIVITY

Inclusive visuals are just as important as inclusive language. Because visual evidence can be such a powerful component of an argument, learn to identify (or create) and incorporate visuals in your work in a respectful and representative manner.

For example, consider visual representations of poverty. Research shows that, compared to actual statistical data, adult black men have historically been overrepresented in visuals used to illustrate texts about poverty in the U.S. You may be surprised, then, to learn that whites are and always have been the largest racial demographic in poverty, while women are the largest group by sex, and children are the largest group by age. When an audience is constantly shown images that do not reflect reality, they cannot engage accurately or thoughtfully in dialogue. As a writer, therefore, you have to think carefully and ethically about visual inclusivity when using visuals to support your evidence or emphasize your points.

Published Reading

I Am the Person You Hurt When You Say the R-Word

John Franklin Stephens

> *John Franklin Stephens is a Special Olympics athlete and global messenger. He has been described as "an actor, author and advocate who happens to have an extra chromosome in every cell of his body." Frank is proud to be a man with Down syndrome whose life is worth living.*

Sometimes I feel like Professor Van Helsing, or maybe Buffy the Vampire Slayer. I keep trying to kill this thing and it just won't die. Of course, my nemesis is the "r-word," not a vampire.

Like Dracula, the r-word just sucks the life out of those of us who fall in its path. It spreads like an infection from person to person. It seems as though perfectly nice people who "mean no harm" get bitten by hearing others using the term while "meaning no harm." And so it goes, from person to person, until it becomes so common that even Presidential Chiefs of Staff, radio talk show hosts, movie characters and famous political pundits use the nasty slur—then say they "meant no harm."

To all of you who use it, let me say it one more time, THE R-WORD HURTS. You don't have to aim the word directly at me to hurt me and millions of others like me who live with an intellectual disability. Every time a person uses the r-word, no matter who it is aimed at, it says to those who hear it that it is okay to use it. That's how a slur becomes more and more common. That's how people like me get to hear it over and over, even when you think we aren't listening.

So, why am I hurt when I hear "retard." Let's face it, nobody uses the word as a term of praise. At best, it is used as another way of saying "stupid" or "loser." At worst, it is aimed directly at me as a way to label me as an outcast—a thing, not a person. I am not stupid. I am not a loser. I am not a thing. I am a person.

It hurts me to think that people assume that I am less than a whole person. That is what is so awful about slurs. They are intended to make their target seem smaller, less of a person. People who live with an intellectual disability do not have an easy life. We have to fight to understand what the rest of you take for granted. We fight for education. We fight to live among the rest of you. We struggle to make friends. We often are ignored, even when we have something to say. We fight so hard to be seen as whole people. It hurts so much, after all that struggle, to hear you casually use a term that means that you assume we are less than whole.

How shall we respond to those of you who still use the r-word? Well, like Van Helsing and Buffy, we are going to aim at your heart. The only difference is that we are determined to drive a smile, not a stake, through your heart. Come join me on the side of the good guys. I promise you will feel better about yourself—and no other people will have to feel bad about themselves.

For Reflection

1. Analyze the ethos, or character and credibility, of the speaker in this article. What if any difference does it make that the author himself has been called the r-word?
2. Is Stephens acting as what some call "the word police," and/or is he being "politically correct"? Define those terms and give reasons why Stephens' argument does or does not count as an example of this.
3. In a *New York Times* article on the issue of the r-word, journalist Lawrence Downes reports that the earnestness of the "Spread the Word to End the Word" campaign is not well-received by some who argue that "banishing the R-word for another clinical-sounding

term is like linguistic Febreze: masking unpleasantries with cloying euphemisms." Explain. How do you think Stephens would respond to this?

4. Quite often a word that offends is replaced with a new word that eventually comes to offend the same population. Does that mean it's futile to advocate for changing exclusive or offensive language? Explain.

Writing inclusively requires a careful ear and a heart willing to acknowledge and respond constructively to language and images that can cause harm to others. While we might not ever fully understand the depth of the pain caused by some words and phrases, we do not have to fully understand that pain in order to know that we should try to prevent it. Good writers choose to write inclusively to keep their audience feeling interested, engaged, and respected.

OFFICE HOURS ➤ Learning Inclusive Language

If you are unsure which words and phrases might offend others, ask your instructor. College is often a time when students encounter people who are very different from themselves. While it is natural to be unsure about how to talk both with and about types of people you have never met before, your classroom is an excellent opportunity to learn how to do that well.

If possible, talk with your instructor or a writing center tutor to explain your uncertainty before sharing your writing with peers. If you cannot do that, it might be helpful to let your peers know about your questions before sharing a draft with them. Announcing your uncertainty up front will help them understand that you do not mean to offend and are trying to learn how to write inclusively.

Critical Questions

1. Have you or your family ever been harmed by the type of exclusive language discussed in this chapter? Explain.
2. What does freedom of speech have to do with the type of word choices we argue for and against in this chapter?
3. What do you think is the most effective way to convince people to change their use of exclusive language? What wouldn't work and why?

CHAPTER twenty six

Design and Delivery: Print, Digital, and Oral Presentations

Design is a fundamental element to consider at the planning stage, not just at the end of your composition process. Form and content are the foundations of good writing and they are inextricably linked – especially in today's highly multimodal culture. Design—the choices you make in the delivery of your ideas to your audience—profoundly affects how the audience receives your argument. When we talk about multimodal design, we mean how messages draw on classical mode types and the five modern modes of communication: linguistic, visual, aural, spatial, and gestural (see Chapter 23, "Multimodal Composition"). Good design furthermore considers the diversity of its audience and how design can help everyone access messages equally, including people with disabilities and people who speak multiple languages. In this chapter, we explain why design matters, outline types of visuals because visuals are such a pervasive and powerful mode, explore the elements and principles of design, and discuss design in the delivery of print, digital, and oral presentations.

WHY DESIGN MATTERS

Design matters for practical, ethical, and aesthetic reasons that affect how an audience receives a message. The practical reasons for attending to design are closely related to ethical reasons for doing so. On the practical level, a well-designed text is one that an audience can understand quickly and easily. It is user-friendly, meaning that an audience can quickly locate the most important ideas, the supporting ideas, and the sources that validate all those ideas.

Information design is so important that the United States Department of Health and Human Services (HHS) devotes a website to this purpose: usability.gov. HHS is responsible for helping all people access critical government resources (such as the Center for Disease Control), so clear, user-friendly communication is essential. The usability.gov website helps government employees create content that is easy for users to understand and access. It promotes "plain writing"—writing that uses simple, clear words and sentences (linguistic mode)—and provides templates and principles that help people create effective visual designs. The easier it is for HHS users to understand what is being asked of them, the more likely they are to submit the right information quickly and clearly. This makes communication more efficient, expediting services and reducing the time spent on each case—a financial and time savings for clients and the government. That provides a strong practical reason for attending to design.

The business case for effective design just described—clear communication saves money—is connected to the ethical reasons for this attention. If your message is important, then time matters. The sooner your audience understands, the sooner they can act. Think of Americans who need to apply for Medicare benefits to treat illnesses, or people seeking critical treatment through the Substance Abuse and Mental Health Services Administration, all of whom need information from HHS. Their needs are urgent, so they might already feel stressed: clear design helps deliver information quickly to meet vital needs. Moreover, clear communication promotes an ethos of credibility and transparency. In government agencies, those qualities are highly sought. People can feel that the government gives them "the run around" when communication is unclear, when important details are buried in "fine print"—small type that technically delivers the information but does so in a way that manipulatively hides it from readers. Effective design helps communicate a tone of service and assistance to citizens in need. The actual and perceived improvement to services provides a compelling ethical reason for attending to design. If your message is important, then you should use all available means of persuasion—including design—to send that message.

About 8 percent of online users have some type of disability that interferes with their ability to access a traditional website. Researchers and developers have created design guidelines and digital tools to help people who are blind, deaf, or physically challenged access that information. Compliance with the guidelines for accessible design is required for websites created for or by the United States government through Section 508 of the Rehabilitation Act. Furthermore, it's just good business and good sense for everyone who wants to reach a wide audience to follow those guidelines voluntarily. Again, the ethical value of inclusion aligns with the practical value of reaching an audience. You can find the complete guidelines online, but note that one general principle is to make sure that information online is accessible through as many sensory pathways as possible. For example, include text-equivalents for all non-text images so that computer software can read the image description aloud to users with visual loss. Likewise, do not use color alone to convey meaning; instead, reinforce that meaning with shapes and alphabetic text so that someone who is colorblind can still understand your message. Incorporating this kind of sensitivity and redundancy helps clarify your message for all readers. As you determine your audience and genre, plan to design according to those guidelines of accessibility for all.

Financial accessibility is another ethical concern. If you design texts that require advanced computers, large screen, or expensive applications, then you limit access to your texts to a more privileged audience. While the text might be impressive, it will only impress a limited audience.

Good writers also consider the audience's primary language. If you have an important message, your audience will not be able to access it unless they speak and/or read your language well enough to understand all the nuances of your message. If members of your intended audience might not share the same language, consider asking a careful translator(s) to translate your work as needed. Many local governments and businesses with large populations of people who speak other languages publish messages in multiple languages based on the ethical value of inclusion and the practical value of clear communication for public service and safety.

Finally, design is directly related to aesthetics. Good design can make your message more appealing so that it stands out among the clutter of competing messages that surround us. Pleasing design invites an audience to linger with your message. Furthermore, aesthetics set the tone. HHS uses bright blocks of color coded to each branch of the organization, simple images that convey what the organization does to appeal to various levels of literacy, and parallel organization within each area to make content convey a tone of order, structure, and stability. Good design helps that message stick with the audience because key points are highlighted and emphasized effectively through the types of design techniques described below.

TYPES OF VISUALS

Almost all texts have some type of visual interface, so it is important to consider visual rhetoric in analysis and production of texts. Here we briefly describe several types of supporting visuals you might use in various domains. To consider what types of visuals might be appropriate for a text, consider the rhetorical analysis framework, asking: Who? What? When? Where? Why? and How? Remember three key areas as you decide if and how to incorporate visuals: tone, support, and display.

First, visuals contribute to the tone of your message. Make sure the tone of your visuals is consistent with the tone of your writing. For example, an academic paper that includes relevant charts to display statistical information reinforces an ethos of professional research. Second, visuals should support and extend an idea or information offered in the body of your text. Supporting visuals should not say something entirely new or repeat exactly what has already been said in the text unless your visual helps readers digest that information. Use a visual when a verbal discussion of an idea or information (especially numerical or quantitative data) would take longer or be less clear. Third, design your visuals with a sense of how they will be displayed to the audience. For example, if you compose texts that will be delivered online, you might be able to include interactive charts or videos. If you do so, consider whether or not your audience will have the technological resources (such as a high-speed internet connection) to view those visuals as intended, and attend to accessibility as described earlier.

Following are descriptions of some commonly used visuals.

Tables

Tables display series of numeric and/or alphabetic text so that you can easily see trends or make comparisons of data. If you have just two or three numbers or concepts to share, you can explain them in the body of your written text. If you have much more than that, and all those numbers and ideas are relevant and necessary to make your point, a table can help you organize the data into user-friendly units of information.

Table 26.1 EXAMPLE OF A TABLE: KEY INDICATORS BY RACE AND HISPANIC ORIGIN

		NATIONAL AVERAGE	AFRICAN AMERICAN	AMERICAN INDIAN	ASIAN AND PACIFIC ISLANDER	HISPANIC	NON-HISPANIC WHITE	TWO OR MORE RACES
ECONOMIC WELL-BEING								
Children in Poverty	2015	21%	36%	34%	13%	31%	12%	21%
Children Whose Parents Lack Secure Employment	2015	29%	45%	47%	21%	34%	23%	33%
Children Living in Households With a High Housing Cost Burden	2015	33%	47%	32%	32%	45%	24%	35%
Teens Not in School and Not Working	2015	7%	10%	13%	3%	9%	6%	7%
EDUCATION								
Young Children Not in School#	2011-15	53%	49%	56%	46%	60%	51%	52%
Fourth Graders Not Proficient in Reading	2015	65%	82%+	76%+	47%+	79%	54%	62%+
Eight Graders Not Proficient in Math	2015	68%	88%+	81%+	42%*	81%	58%	65%+
High School Students Not Graduating on Time	2014/15	17%	25%*	28%*	10%*	22%	12%	N.A.

444

		HEALTH						
Low-Birthweight Babies	2015	8.1%	13.0%	7.5%	8.4%	7.2%	6.9%	N.A.
Children Without Health Insurance	2015	5%	4%	13%	4%	8%	4%	4%
Child and Teen Deaths per 100,000	2015	25	36	28	15	20	24	N.A.
Teens Who Abuse Alcohol or Drugs	2014^	5%	4%+	5%+	2%*+	6%	5%	3%*
		FAMILY AND COMMUNITY						
Children in Single-Parent Families	2015	35%	66%	52%	16%	42%	25%	41%
Children in Families Where the Household Head Lacks a High School Diploma	2015	14%	12%	19%	10%	33%	6%	9%
Children Living in High-Poverty Areas	2011-15	14%	32%	31%	7%	23%	5%	12%
Teen Births per 1,000	2015	22	32	26	7	35	16	N.A.

#Data are from 5-year American Community Survey (ACS) data and are not comparable to the national average using 3 years of pooled I-year ACS data.

*Data are for non-Hispanics.

^These are single-year race data for 2014. Data in index are 2013-14 multiyear estimates.

+Data results do not include Native Hawaiins/Pacific Islanders.

N.A. = Data not available.

445

Charts

Charts combine graphic and numeric and/or alphabetic information to show how numbers or concepts are trending and relate to one another. There are many different styles of charts—you might learn to create advanced charts as you study research methods in your field. Below is a table of chart types showing some of the different options. Base your choice on the nature of the information you want to show and the rhetorical context of delivering that information. Those factors will help you determine which chart type will display your information most clearly.

Table 26.2   TYPES OF CHARTS

TYPE	STRENGTHS	LIMITATIONS
CHARTS FOR NUMBERS		
Column Graph (Stacked)	Compares 2 or more examples across multiple factors, shows distribution. Stacking shows trends.	Common type because it is easy to read, but therefore might not show creativity.
Bar Graph (Stacked)	Horizontal orientation emphasizes greatest element, shows comparison and distribution. Stacking shows trends.	Can show so many factors that it might overwhelm an audience.
Line Graph	Useful to show how one or more factors progress over time (trends).	Straight lines do not cue readers to the nature of the subject studied.
Pie Graph	Shows proportion of a whole to compare individual shares.	Hard to compare factors over time in a single pie graph.
Scatter	Shows correlation between variables.	Can only show 2–3 variables.
Doughnut	Shows proportion of a whole to compare individual shares.	Hard to compare factors over time.

Bubble	Useful to compare and show relationships among variables, similar to scatter.	Most useful at showing 3–4 variables.
CHARTS FOR IDEAS		
Flowchart	Shows process, steps, and if/then decision options for different causal outcomes.	Hard to show numerical information such as statistics.
Organizational Chart	Emphasizes hierarchy of relationships and/or categories.	Hard to show change over time.

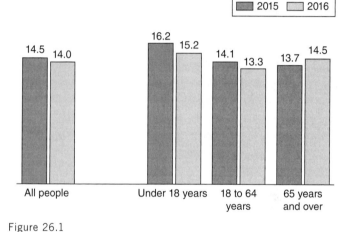

Figure 26.1

Model Chart: Supplemental Poverty Measures

Art

The art category covers a broad range of other types of images you can use to inform your audience and/or explain something more vividly.

Diagrams

Diagrams are visuals that explain how something is related or connected. One useful type is the Venn diagram, which shows how areas are separate from and overlapping or connected to other areas through a series of circles. The area in the middle represents the ideal or target, where all the separate areas come together. In Figure 26.2, we see that sustainable development occurs at the intersection of viable environmental, economic, and social conditions.

Infographics

Infographics are static or dynamic visual graphics that often use multiple images to narrate a data-based story, making them robust enough to make an argument or inform readers about a complex topic.

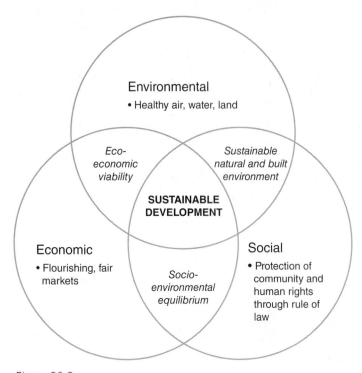

Figure 26.2

Example of Venn Diagram: Defining Sustainable Development

448

Infographics have surged in popularity as people exchange ideas online in forums that favor brief, highly visual representations of ideas and arguments.

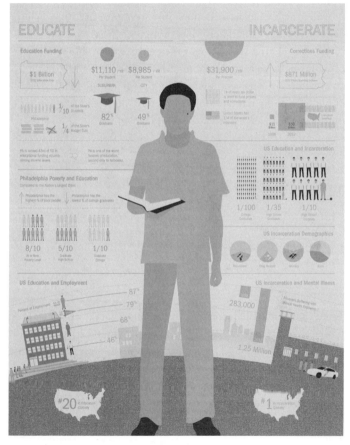

Figure 26.3

Example of Infographic: Costs of Education Compared to Incarceration in Philadelphia

Photos

Photos often suggest authenticity and realism, even though they can be edited to misrepresent their subject just as other visuals can. Photos can function as the object of study in a rhetorical analysis, or they can provide visual evidence, for example, in narration of an ethnography or definitional argument. Photo voice projects often ask someone to capture a sense of place by looking at their environment through the lens of a camera. If you take the photos, they can add to your credibility as an eyewitness to an event. Remember, though, to consider the ethics of photographing human subjects the way you would consider writing about them: ask whether the photo would harm the subject and seek permission through an informed consent form (see Chapter 28, "Working with Human Subjects").

Drawings

Drawings are useful to depict hypotheticals or situations that were not otherwise recorded. They can be designed to show exactly what you want to show, making them extremely relevant. Drawings are often a component of infographics.

Word Clouds

Word clouds are visuals created by programs that take a text and then produce a visual showing the key words used in that text, sized according to frequency of usage: the larger the word, the more often it comes up in the original text. Frequency can be taken as a sign of importance, so the word cloud has the effect of suggesting a reverse outline of key words and phrases.

Videos

Videos, which of course also often include sound and gestures, can help explain, support, or demonstrate the vision of your argument. For example, they can be the object of study in a rhetorical analysis,

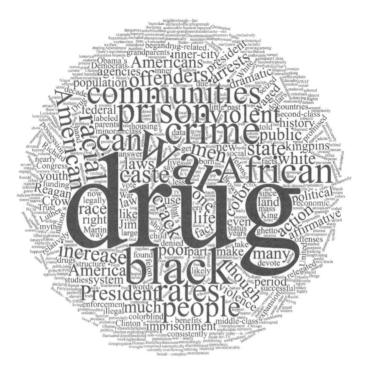

Figure 26.4

Example of a Word Cloud: Text of Michelle Alexander's "The New Jim Crow: How the War on Drugs Gave Birth to a Permanent Undercaste" (Chapter 18)

or they can provide visual evidence in the form of recorded interviews, focus groups, or explorations of place and environment. Like any visual, videos should be relevant, they should extend your argument in a way nothing else could do, and they should adhere to ethical standards of inclusive design (outlined above) and representation of human subjects (outlined in Chapter 28, "Working with Human Subjects"). For example, videos can be designed to use captioning to assist people who have hearing loss or who need translation, which has the added practical benefit of making it easier to access the video without playing sound aloud.

ELEMENTS OF DESIGN

Here we provide an overview of complex elements and principles from art and design theory that will help you consider visual rhetoric. These are foundations you can explore in more detail for projects that rely heavily on visual design, such as a research poster, a webpage, or a digital slide presentation.

Proximity

Proximity refers to how near or far pieces of the document are from one another. Nearness invites comparison—either to show that items are similar or different. Distance shows separation, perhaps to suggest different units of meaning that should not be compared.

Alignment

Alignment relates to the order and sequencing of proximate items to suggest an order for reading or interpretation. Alignment can run horizontal, vertical, diagonal, or circular. The absence of alignment—i.e., random or scattered order—also conveys meaning about the nature of the content.

Color

Color immediately conveys emotion, tone, formality, and other layers of meaning. Because of its impact, it should be given careful attention. Colors can mean different things in different cultures, so it is important to think about your rhetorical situation to make sure you convey the intended meaning (see "Office Hours: The Color of Culture: Researching Visual Norms Across Contexts" at the end of this chapter). Saturation refers to the density of color used; a transparency effect, for example, reduces the saturation so that you can "see through" an image to what is behind it. Value is the lightness or darkness of a color (also called tone).

Size and Scale

The largest items in a document tend to get our attention first. Size suggests importance in document design because our attention is drawn to and lingers on larger objects. A sense of scale is created when a document contains both large and small items, thus inviting a comparison that can convey difference in importance or meaning.

Shape and Space

Shapes communicate tone—playful to serious—before we can even read a word in the document. They also help communicate priorities and organization of data. All documents produce shapes. Shapes can be familiar geometric outlines or more organic originals produced by drawings or other patterns. The shapes you produce intentionally are called the positive shape. Each positive shape then creates a negative shape in the surrounding space. Good designers pay attention to both.

Line

Lines can be created by hand, by computer, or by joining different objects. They can be thick, thin, dotted, or created through a sequence of images. Lines divide and organize by creating chunks of information to be read together or separately, like punctuation. Lines can organize and prioritize information in tables or in different sections of an alphabetic text.

Texture

Texture refers to how smooth or rough the surface of the document is. In digital documents, texture is simulated to create a two- or three-dimensional effect. Texture can create patterns and a sense of movement, so it should be used carefully to highlight meaning rather than drawing attention away from other units of meaning.

Typography

Typography is the style of your type. Different styles of type affect the tone and readability of the text. More serious, academic styles include such fonts as Times New Roman. More casual, playful fonts include **Comic Sans**. Fonts classified as serif type have small lines embellishing each letter, such as in Times New Roman and Georgia. Many consider serif style easier to read in print. Sans-serif fonts such as **Helvetica** and **Arial** have cleaner lettering without the extra flair, making them easier to read in digital formats that have much lower resolution than print. Google moved from a serif to a san-serif font in 2015 so that its logo would be easier to read on mobile devices. Good designers tend to use no more than two different fonts in one document, often using a serif font for the main body of a lengthy text and a sans-serif font for headings.

PRINCIPLES OF DESIGN

The principles of design explain how those elements of design can be used to communicate the desired message. These foundations of design thinking will help you consider how your texts function to help you say what you want to say clearly.

Balance, Scale, and Proportion

Texts should be arranged in a way that creates an overall sense of balance, appropriate scale, and proportion. For example, visuals can be dispersed at regular intervals throughout a text to create ongoing visual interest, rather than being bunched up on top of each other in one place, overloading the audience with a sensory experience. Good designers consider symmetrical (perfect equity top to bottom and/or side to side) and asymmetrical design. Asymmetry often creates more visual interest and a sense of movement through different sizes, colors, and shapes. Overall, though, those creative pieces should be balanced to create a user-friendly, accessible, clear narrative experience for the audience. Balance means finding the right pace of delivering those visual experiences within and across a text.

Perspective

Visual perspective refers to the point of view an audience is invited into. They might see a long-view covering a lot of geographic distance, for example, that creates a coherent, identifiable visual scene. Or, their experience might be framed as a close-up on something that seems disconnected, even disembodied from its environment and/or background. Close-ups force a specific focus. Long-views often invite more open interpretation or a sense of mood. Good designers use perspective to help control the tone and focus.

Direction

Documents comprised only of alphabetic text have an obvious direction: start at the top of the first page, then read left to right (in cultures where this is the direction for reading written texts). Visuals have no pre-determined starting point, so designers have to cue readers through elements that attract attention to suggest a starting point. Good designers use elements such as bright color and large size to signal starting points that cascade into subsequent points, leading the viewer along in a meaningful sequence.

Repetition

Repetition highlights and therefore emphasizes the importance of the key subject. Repetition is particularly important for texts that include multiple visuals. To create a sense of coherence, good designers repeat elements such as colors and/or shapes to easily identify and organize different pieces of the text.

Contrast

Contrast in such elements as color, size, location, type, and texture invite comparison of the contrasting elements. They sharpen the focus visually and say something new by attracting our attention through dissonance or tension.

Unity and Harmony

Unity and harmony are created when designers align such elements as colors and shapes to indicate a connection of ideas or themes. Harmony also relates to the design goal of creating a pleasing and consistent tone to the design. Colors should not clash with one another on the color wheel or shift randomly from a family of earth tones to neon, for example, unless you are using that clash by design to draw attention and create tension. And the tone of the elements—colors and shapes and lines—should reinforce the content of the message. If the alphabetic text conveys a serious message, then the visuals should have a more professional, academic, somber tone as well. The audience should have a sense of the tone and content of the alphabetic text just by looking at the visuals first.

Dominance, Hierarchy, and Emphasis

Good designers stack their visual messaging so that audiences can easily see what is most important and what is secondary to the message. Something stands out. They use strategies for emphasis, such as using bright, highly-saturated colors and large, dominant shapes to flag importance and signal order. They consider the rule of thirds in planning the visual architecture that will guide an audience toward understanding. The rule of thirds guides designers to segment the visual area into nine equal parts, then position the most important elements on the intersection of the invisible lines marking those segments. When objects are placed at these points, the image tends to have more tension and interest for readers than when the focal object is positioned in the center.

DELIVERING VISUALS

Where and how visuals are created and delivered determines the affordances—the actual and perceived characteristics of the medium—available for design. In the academic domain, alphabetic texts printed on paper or delivered as digital documents produced on a word processor are common. In the workplace and civic domains, a variety of texts are produced, often as multimedia texts that combine alphabetic and highly visual texts available online. In all three of these domains, you might be asked to do a presentation that requires you to interact with various texts, so your design must account for both visual and oral presentation. Good writers consider delivery as an aspect of design when they compose visuals integrated with alphabetic text. Table 26.3 outlines some common types of communications by their delivery modes and media, along with some of their affordances and limitations.

Table 26.3   VISUAL DELIVERY: MODES, MEDIA, AFFORDANCES, LIMITATIONS

DELIVERY	MODES	MEDIUM	AFFORDANCES	LIMITATIONS
On Paper *Academic Essay, Brochure, Letter*	Linguistic Visual	Paper and Ink	Permanence of paper so audience can re-read anytime, can be any length; text is stable, so every audience member engages what author created	Cannot hear inflection of author's voice to add nuance, need access to printer
On Posters *Research Poster, Conference Poster*	Linguistic Visual Spatial	Posterboard, Ink on Paper, Digital PDF	Can increase size for clear visuals, such as charts and graphs; text is stable, so every audience member engages what author created	Difficult to convey detail of full argument, so narrative appeal can be lost
Online *Website, Blog, Public Service Announcement, Podcast, Video*	Linguistic Visual Spatial Aural	Digital Webtext, Video Channel, Podcast Channel, Blog Network	Many modes available, potentially reaches large audience	Easily shared out of original context in ways that disrupt or change meaning, viewing on different platforms or devices can alter features

Email *Many providers with similar features for producing text and attaching materials*	Linguistic Visual Spatial	Digital Text	Reaches individuals or large groups, shares simple text or embedded or attached multimodal texts	Get ignored as spam if they don't seem relevant, body of email not conducive for long text, viewing on different platforms or devices can alter features
In Person *Oral presentation, Research Report, Job Talk, Division Report*	Linguistic Visual Aural Spatial Gestural	Voice, Digital Slides (e.g., PowerPoint), Prezi, Posterboard	Human interaction and connection, can adjust live to the rhetorical situation	Presenter could forget or accidentally misrepresent information, acoustics/surroundings could distract audience

DELIVERING ORAL PRESENTATIONS

A good oral presentation can stick with an audience for a lifetime. The very human exchange of one person standing in front of an audience—vulnerable, honest, and sincere—to share something they think we should know can be powerful. While many people get nervous about speaking in public, they also crave that moment when their message hits the mark and makes a difference to their audience. We offer some guidelines here to help ignite your presentations.

Presentations have a variety of purposes across domains—to explain research you have conducted; to introduce a new idea, service, or product; or to convey important information to peers, colleagues, or neighbors. Here we offer some guidelines for preparing and delivering a successful oral presentation.

1. Know your audience. Analyze the rhetorical situation so that you have a strong sense of the Who? What? When? Where? Why? How? of your presentation context. Find out who will be seated in that audience—just your classmates? Community partners with whom you work? Faculty members and administrators? Knowing exactly who will attend helps you determine what they know and what they need to know so that you can pitch your content and tone accordingly.

It is important to understand the expectations of the audience in context before crafting your presentation. For example, at an academic conference, some people write out a paper as if for publication in a journal, then read that paper, possibly using a few presentation slides to emphasize key points or show examples. Some people appreciate such high-level thinking and content development. Others find written, scripted prose hard to follow in a presentation—they want something more casual, interactive, and designed for delivering in person. You should determine the best format based on knowledge of your audience's expectations and knowledge of your own strengths and limitations. If you tend to freeze or ramble when you don't have a script and are just working from notes, then writing out your talk might be a good idea. If you practice your talk enough, you can move off the script and keep notes there just as a safety net. You don't want to deliver a mechanically memorized speech, but if you rehearse the material well, you can deliver the content in a polished but natural tone.

2. Explore your presentation space. Get to know the physical space where you will present. Test the equipment so that you know how everything works. Pay attention to sound—if your presentation uses audio and/or video, test it out. Make sure updates are installed on the computer and that you know how to adjust the volume. Before the presentation begins, pull up multimedia elements to the right starting point (e.g., bypassing commercials) so they are ready to go when you are. Practice projecting your voice to the back of the room. Explore your presentation space—get your hands on the equipment and walk the room—to help calm your nerves. By feeling out the space, it becomes familiar and you can visualize yourself giving a successful talk there.

3. Design for *this* audience in *this* place. As you explore the space where you will give your presentation, think carefully about your modes and media of delivery and test them out. For visuals, you can ask: What font size can be seen clearly from the back of the room? What colors project well? Is the color and saturation contrast sharp enough for the audience to distinguish all your elements? Are you using visuals that are familiar to this audience such that you can move through them quickly? Or should you break down your visuals into smaller chunks of information your audience can digest more easily?

4. Keep it simple. Studies show that people cannot absorb what they hear as quickly as they absorb what they read. Depending on how much time you have, plan to make 3-5 key points. If you are presenting research that is also written in a paper, trust that the fine details will be delivered in the paper. Segment your talk so that the audience gets a preview of your points (tell them how many points will be made and number them as you go so they can follow along). Let them know where they are in your talk, and give a recap of what they should take away at the end. Use visuals—numbered lists with key phrases, for example— to cue the audience visually and reinforce what you tell them.

5. Use stories and stats. Good presentations strike a balance between telling stories and sharing statistical information ("stats"). While we all like to hear people tell good stories, these tend to be anecdotal, representing a limited experience. Strong statistics convince us of validity, but they rarely motivate us to care and act. Good presentations *inform* us with data (not overwhelming us with too many numbers) that appeal to logos and *motivate* us through emotional appeals to pathos. They reel us in close with an intimate, relevant story, then they bolster our belief that the story is valid through relevant evidence, examples, and reasons.

6. Practice, practice, practice. Although you might have watched some presentations that seem relaxed and unrehearsed, it often takes a lot of practice to achieve that effect! Comfort and confidence are developed through rigorous practice. Practice first by yourself, so that you can revise obvious flaws. Then, practice for a real audience—invite people from your class or elsewhere to do a trial run. Practice in the actual room you will use if possible. Most importantly, use your presentation voice, time yourself, and take it seriously. Project so that the person in the back of the room you will use can hear you clearly. If available, use presentation software features for notes and time keeping, or have clear printed notes on hand so that you don't have to worry about "blanking"—forgetting what you were going to say, a temporary state that soon fades but can be unnerving. Get feedback from your practice audience and try it again.

7. Work the room. During the presentation, take advantage of the affordances of sharing the same space with your audience. Connect with them directly by making eye contact and gesturing to include everyone. Having a live audience can backfire if some in the audience feel that you are ignoring them, favoring certain people through your eye contact and gestures. In class presentations, speakers sometimes favor the instructor—try to avoid that as instructors want to see you work the room, and you want to maintain the interest of your peers as well. Make sure *everyone* in the room can see and hear you clearly. Position your body so that you aren't blocking the view of your visuals. Never turn your back to the audience—gesture toward your visuals from the side. And walk around—people snap to attention when you get close to them. They also tune in when you use their name. If you can reference an earlier presentation, for example, you build your ethos by showing that you listened carefully to others. Never use your public podium to belittle others—that's how you lose credibility.

8. Do not read from the visuals *or* let them speak entirely for themselves. There are different schools of thought on this. Some people say that you should never read any text from a slide during a presentation. However, this can be done well if you do it sparingly, only as a technique to emphasize a particularly important point or a direct quotation that you want to say exactly.

9. Use techniques for emphasis. An audience cannot process what they hear as quickly as what they see. They will immediately read text behind you, so use that to your advantage by giving them the key points or examples to illuminate what you are saying at that time. Do preview and recap slides so that your key takeaways stick. Repeat words and visuals to show categories of concepts and to highlight key points. Practice modulating sound so you have louder, quicker moments, and slower, more dramatic moments that cue the audience to pay attention. Practice the pause: intentional silence can be a powerful way to let a point sink in. Finally, control motion of your arms, body, and face to underscore what you say. Stepping closer to the audience, using hand gestures, making eye contact, and even smiling are all ways to connect with a physical audience and make your message clear.

10. Pace yourself. Don't put yourself in a position to rush. Practice so that you set the right pace to get through all your material without being penalized for going past your allotted time, then watch the clock as you present. Use question time to pull in points you missed.

11. Look presentable. You are on stage. This is your moment. Dress professionally—it shows preparation and builds your ethos immediately.

12. Control Q&A. If you have time for a question and answer session, consider that an extension of your presentation, an opportunity to clarify points, offer new evidence, and explain points that were unclear. If someone challenges your ideas, thank them for their point of view. Be polite. Have a response ready for questions you can't or don't want to answer, such as, "That's an interesting perspective. I appreciate your comment. I will have to keep thinking about that." Or, "That wasn't part of the scope of this project, but it's an interesting question that deserves attention."

We live in a highly visual culture where people convey messages through videos and images combined with alphabetic text on websites, on television, in academic papers, and in oral presentations. Good writers understand how to make good choices about document design and the use of visuals so that they add value to the written text. Your use of design and choice of visuals should appeal to the audience on aesthetic, practical, and ethical levels. Visuals should be aesthetically pleasing, attracting readers to the information and making it clearer through the design. Visuals should be practical, extending information beyond what is in the alphabetic or verbal text in a way that only a visual could do effectively and efficiently. And the design of your document should follow ethical guidelines, making images and text accessible to your audience, which might include people who have disabilities or speak other languages. Finally, remember that if you use a visual someone else created—whether it is a photo, drawing, a chart or any other visual—you must cite the source.

MLA STYLE: FORMATTING DELIVERY

Traditional academic writing requires a style format that guides writers to create visually uniform documents. Many writers are required to use Modern Language Association (MLA) format so that readers familiar with the style know exactly how to find the information they expect to see. We list some of the core elements for MLA style in Table 26.4. We then show what those look like visually in Figures 26.5, 26.6, and 26.7. The marginal notes in those figures provide the exact specifications you should follow.

The complete guide to MLA format is online. For MLA format of in-text citations of direct quotations and paraphrases, see Chapter 27, "Working with Published Sources."

Table 26.4   QUICK GUIDE: MLA STYLE (8TH ED.) FOR CORE ELEMENTS

ELEMENT	RULES
Margins	1 inch all around, except for the running head and page number, which are at 1/2 inch
Text Format	• 12 point font • Standard font (e.g., Times New Roman) • Justify margins flush left only • Do not auto-hyphenate • Double-space the entire paper, including long quotations, notes, and Works Cited page • Indent first line of paragraphs 1/2 inch more than 1 inch margin • Indent every line of long quotations (four or more lines of direct quotation) 1/2 inch more than 1 inch margin • Use one space after a period or other end punctuation

(*continued*)

Table 26.4   QUICK GUIDE: MLA STYLE (8TH ED.) FOR CORE
ELEMENTS (*continued*)

Headings and Title	• On the first page, top left, justified, double-spaced, write: Your Name Your Instructor's Name Your Course Name The Date • On the next line, center your title using normal type, capitalize first word and all words except articles and prepositions; follow formatting rules such as italicizing titles of long works • On the next line, begin your first sentence by indenting 1/2 inch from the 1 inch margin for a new paragraph
Title Page	• Only use a separate title page for group projects and then begin the first paragraph at 1 inch from the top of the next page
Running Head and Page Numbers	• Insert a header in the top right corner 1/2 inch from the top that includes your last name, one space, then the page number—nothing else (your instructor might want you to omit this on the first page) • Continue numbering uninterrupted through the Works Cited page
Works Cited Layout	• Begin on a new page, after any endnotes • Title this Works Cited, first letters capitalized and centered at 1 inch from top—no special formatting
Works Cited Entries	• After the Works Cited title, double-space and begin justifying flush left at 1 inch margin • Alphabetize by last name • Use a hanging indent feature on your word processor--the first line of each entry is at 1 inch, then following lines from that entry are at 1.5 inches • Use regular double-spacing between entries, no extra space • *Note: See Chapter 27, Table 27.4 in "Working with Published Sources" for common Works Cited entries in MLA style*

Tables	• Insert the table close to the text describing its content, flush left, using capitalization for titles (each major word, not articles or prepositions) • Number the tables in order followed by a title • Cite the source immediately below the table if you did not create it
Figures	• All visual material that is not a table (e.g., drawings, photos, charts) are labeled Figure and given a number and a caption
Short Quotations	• Four or fewer lines of typed prose, three or fewer lines of poetry quoted exactly and put in quotation marks • Put parenthetical citation between the closing quotation mark and your sentence-ending punctuation • Put sentence-ending punctuation outside the closing quotation mark
Long Quotations	• Five or more lines of typed prose, four or more lines of poetry quoted exactly • End signal phrase with colon, then return and indent so that all of the quotation is 1.5 inches from the margin, flush left • Do not use quotation marks • Put citation (author's last name and page number) in parentheses after the sentence-ending punctuation of the last sentence if it is not already in the signal phrase • Maintain double-spacing
Paper, Printing, Binding	• Use white paper, 8½ x 11 inches • Print double-sided unless your instructor requests single-sided • Reprint if you see significant errors • Staple the upper left corner unless directed otherwise
Electronic Submission	• See the assignment description for digital document delivery; follow directions on format type (e.g., Word, PDF, GoogleDoc) and file naming conventions which might include your last name, title of the assignment, draft number, and date

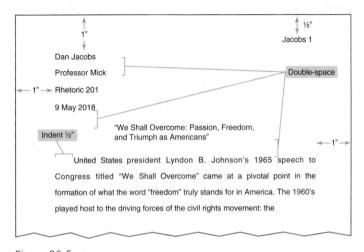

Figure 26.5

Margins, Text Formatting, Heading and Title

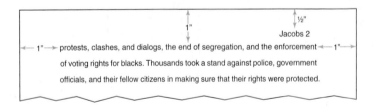

Figure 26.6

Running Head and Page Numbers

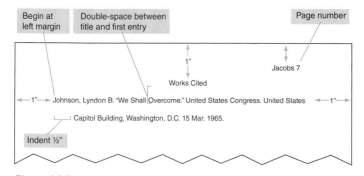

Figure 26.7

Works Cited Layout

OFFICE HOURS ➤ The Color of Culture: Researching Visual Norms Across Contexts

Keep in mind that some elements of visual texts, like some elements of alphabetic text, differ across various cultures. An American audience can claim some general agreement about the psychological connection between certain colors and concepts. If you have spent much time immersed in American culture, for example, you won't be surprised to hear that research shows that Americans connect the color red with the idea of love and romance (and you won't be surprised to hear that American marketers and politicians are known for reinforcing those psychological shortcuts to make it easier for them to sell us products and ideas). But that color association is not universal. In South Africa, the color red is associated with mourning; in China, red is associated with prosperity and luck.

(continued)

As you analyze your audience, you might find yourself writing to people with a different cultural background. That different background could mean that they bring different associations about visual design elements such as colors and shapes. Talk to your instructor about this and research those potential differences. Test your visuals on someone with that cultural background, if possible, asking specifically about these visual elements. Many of us aren't even aware of these associations, making them seem universal when they are really the product of constant cues from our cultural context.

Critical Questions

1. How might visuals enhance an academic argument? How might they detract from it? Give examples.
2. Describe a multimodal text you encountered recently that was well designed or poorly designed. Explain how that design and use of the five modern modes of communication impacted your interaction with the text.
3. Using the guidelines for delivering oral presentations, describe and evaluate an oral presentation you heard recently. Where did it succeed, where did it fall short? What advice would you offer that presenter to improve?

twenty seven

Working with Published Sources

An ethical approach to writing informs *what* you do and *how* you do it. In this chapter, we add practical information—*what* it means to work with published sources—to complement the ethical discussion of *how* to do that offered in Chapter 5, "Writing Ethics, Responsibility, and Accountability." The guidelines for writing with integrity discussed in that chapter emphasize the importance of finding and representing sources in ways that respect the source and the argument. In this chapter, we explore the steps needed to find, evaluate, and argue from published sources. We focus on what steps to take when working with published sources in an ethical approach to argumentation.

FINDING SOURCES

When you analyze your assignment, you will see what types of sources are required or recommended. Your assignment description and discussions in class will help you shape your research accordingly. Begin your search for sources when you have clear answers to three questions: (1) What type of sources should you use?

(2) Where can you find good sources? and (3) How many sources should you include? The following section helps you answer those questions.

What Types of Sources Should You Use?

In this section, we explain two types of published sources: scholarly and popular. If your assignment asks you to generate original sources, such as interviews, see Chapter 28: "Working with Human Sources."

Scholarly Sources

Much of the writing you do in the academic domain will require you to use scholarly sources. Scholarly sources are generally written by academics, based on substantial research, for the benefit of other academics and to contribute to a field of knowledge. Academic disciplines have their own scholarly conventions. Ask your instructor or librarians to help you make sure you have the right type of source for that discipline. Scholarly sources are defined by the general characteristics described in Table 27.1 "Characteristics of Scholarly versus Popular Sources."

Popular Sources

Popular sources include all non-scholarly publications, such as newspapers, magazines, and opinion-based blogs. Popular sources cover a wide range of writing, some of it more reliable and useful for academic arguments than others. In some introductory courses, your instructor might allow you to use popular sources, such as credible newspapers that can provide reliable facts and thoughtful opinions. Popular sources are defined by the general characteristics described in Table 27.1 "Characteristics of Scholarly versus Popular Sources."

Table 27.1   CHARACTERISTICS OF SCHOLARLY VERSUS POPULAR SOURCES

	SCHOLARLY SOURCE	POPULAR SOURCE
Author's credentials	The author has an advanced degree and is considered by other scholars to be an expert in the field.	Authors are generalists and journalists with varying credentials. Their expertise may not be scholarly, but rather based on professional or other experience.
Target audience	The text is written for an academic audience who has interest and some expertise on the issue themselves.	Expertise in the audience is not always expected; the author might hope to spark new interest in the topic.
Role of peer review	The text was peer-reviewed, meaning that other experts agreed that the argument was sound and an audience would find it worth reading. If accepted for publication, peer review typically includes a significant revision process in which the author addresses comments and critiques from other experts.	The text might have little or no peer review; an editor might review work but might not have expertise on the issue.
Use of sources	The text uses in-text citation and bibliographic conventions specific to the academic discipline. Footnotes with additional citations might be included to highlight works that are related but not directly relevant.	The text might use a variety of sources and evidence, and there is no standard expectation for how many, what type, or if/ how those sources are cited; there might not be any in-text citation or reference list.

(*continued*)

Table 27.1   CHARACTERISTICS OF SCHOLARLY VERSUS POPULAR SOURCES (*continued*)

Publisher's credentials	The text is published by an academic press or professional scholarly association.	The text is not published by an academic press; authority of credentials vary widely.
Circulation of text	The text is often only available through a library or direct subscription.	The text circulates in general publication outlets, sometimes through subscription; generally widely accessible to the public.
Format	The format usually includes an abstract, literature review, methods, results, and discussion.	Format varies depending on the publication; disclosure of research methods is not standard practice.

Primary and Secondary Sources

Sources can also be divided into two categories that represent the nature of the information and how it will be used by the author: primary and secondary sources. Primary sources include original artifacts such as first-hand accounts of events written by witnesses or subjects when the event happened, and original creative productions. Examples of primary texts include diaries, artwork, films, results of experiments, and legal documents.

Secondary sources are commentaries on or interpretations of such primary texts. Secondary texts include academic articles, reviews, and various types of criticism.

Use a primary text as the object of your own original analysis, such as rhetorical analysis of a speech. Use a secondary text to provide support or represent opposing viewpoints within your own argument.

Books and Journal Articles

Another consideration regarding the type of published source is whether to use books and/or articles. Academic books (other than anthologies) represent the sustained work of an expert or team of experts, and thus provide in-depth analysis of an issue. Articles have to be more focused because they are shorter. The advantage of books is the depth of study, but the trade-off is that they take so long to write and publish that they often cannot cover the most current events and findings. Articles come out more quickly and can thus respond to current developments, but they are limited by how much they can cover. An article might only be able to include a brief history or context on the issue. Find and cite both types of sources to draw from both of their strengths.

How Can You Find Good Sources?

When you think about finding good sources, you might be most familiar with online searches in popular search engines. With the right search methods, you can use those search engines to find strong sources to research many day-to-day questions related to purchases, health, education, and so much more. However, when you do academic research, your search must target scholarly sources (in addition to popular sources if your instructor allows you to use them). Here, we describe how different research portals can improve your search for scholarly and sound popular sources.

Library Catalog

As a university student, you have the privilege of accessing hundreds of thousands of sources through your campus library. Academic libraries invest in collections of print and digital sources that will advance the scholarship of faculty and students, so you have special access to a wealth of sources while you are a student. Every library is a little different, so you should schedule an orientation at your library as quickly as possible. But all libraries share the goal of helping you advance your understanding by accessing reliable publications, and all librarians welcome your questions.

To sort through all those publications, you need to have a clear sense of what you're researching and you need to understand how to use the library's catalog. Your library's catalog is specific to its holdings, meaning that a search in your catalog will show you the print and digital sources you are entitled to access quickly. You can see what books your library owns and if they are checked out, and you can find relevant articles and often download full text through a "Find Text" button.

Your catalog search portal allows you to do a quick search by keywords or phrases and it allows you to do an expanded search to narrow down results and increase relevance. Your library's main portal likely searches multiple databases as well as its own book catalog simultaneously. In addition, your library's catalog likely does some or all of the following: returns results with information on how to find the text, cites those sources in various styles, allows you to send those results to a citation generator, and tells you how to request that source from another library through interlibrary loan if your library does not own it.

Databases

Your library's website will give you access to the individual databases it owns to help you do research in any field. You can start at its main search portal, which likely searches multiple databases at once, or you can target your search by searching in a particular database. Here is a description of some common databases:

- Academic Search Premier—This database searches many disciplines at once, which makes it broad but not always deep on particular topics.
- JSTOR—This database holds a selected collection of some core academic titles but does not always have the last 3–5 years of those journals. Thus, it might lack currency.

- Web of Science—This database focuses about 70% of its sources on hard science and the rest on social science and humanities. It allows you to search by number of "times cited" to show how useful a source is in the field.
- LexisNexis Academic—This database searches thousands of domestic and some international news sources as well as some business and legal documents.
- CQ Researcher—This is not a database but is a source that itself aggregates reliable summaries and analysis of current issues. This resource is helpful in generating ideas but could also provide scholarly sources.
- WorldCat—This database searches the collections of more than 10,000 libraries worldwide; with interlibrary loan, you might be able to request delivery of sources found here.

Web-Based Sources

Online search engines can help you navigate millions of sources around the world, but to get relevant and reliable results, you need to choose accurate keywords and scan results efficiently. The web has many valuable, free sources from public and private researchers, but it also has so much inaccurate information and "fake news" that you have to be extremely careful in checking your results. Furthermore, some popular search engines allow people and organizations to pay to have their sites appear at the top of a search results page. This skews the scholarly approach to searching for sources, which is founded on relevance and reliability, not commercial factors.

One reliable popular online search engine is Google Scholar (*not* the regular Google search), which searches for academic work available on the web and which functions more like a library catalog. Google Scholar also tracks citations of those works and integrates its search with many libraries.

Librarians

Visit your librarian! Don't forget the human beings who will talk to you in person or chat online. They can guide you through the catalog and databases, answering questions specific to your search. They might have print handouts and web guides to reinforce those techniques, and as you start to specialize your interests, you can work with a librarian who specializes in your field for even more insight on finding the best sources efficiently. Many campus libraries offer free tutorials and orientations—be sure to take advantage of this critical human resource.

By Foot

If your library gives you direct access to its books, go there. Look up a book that seems on target, go find it yourself, and scan the books near the book you found as their content will be related. Flip through the table of contents of a few books and see if they offer new insight on your issue. Sometimes a good walk and a little curiosity lead you to interesting avenues in your research.

How Many Sources Should You Use?

Your analysis of the assignment description will reveal what type of sources and how many sources your instructor expects. You might be given a minimum and maximum. That seems like a simple answer to this question, but remember that those numbers represent the sources you cite in your final draft. As you conduct research, plan to consult many more sources than the maximum number. Read widely so that you understand the issue well and cite the sources that are most useful. Return to finding sources as you write if the sources you have do not provide sufficient support. You don't want to cite sources so often that your own voice is lost, but you do want to show that you've done the research and know your issue well.

EVALUATING SOURCES

Now that you know how to find sources, it's time to think carefully about selecting the best sources to cite in your work. Your initial search results will likely return many more sources than you can read or would want to use. Your next step is to scan those sources efficiently to see which ones hold the most promise.

Many scholarly sources include abstracts to expedite your search. Abstracts are typically a brief summary of an article in which authors outline the argument, methods, and findings. An abstract will give you a clear sense of whether you should read the full article.

Whether reading the abstract or full text of the source, test the source according to the following categories to see if it appears to hold up as worthy of your citation. Remember, the sources you cite contribute to your ethos, so you want to surround your words with strong arguments and information from others.

Many librarians recommend the PARC test (also known by the more colorful reversal of those letters, the CRAP test!): *p*urpose, *ac*curacy, *r*elevance, *c*urrency.

Purpose

Why was this source written—to inform, entertain, and/or persuade? Is that the most helpful purpose given the type of voice you need in your argument? Is the point of view of this author the most effective for your purpose, or do you need to find a source on this issue that fills a different kind of voice? Are the author and/or the site trying to sell you something, indicating a commercial interest that could compromise the authenticity of the message?

Accuracy

Is this source reliable? Do you trust the publisher and the person? Is the source in a more authoritative domain, such as the U.S. government (.gov) or an educational institution (.edu), or is it commercial

(.com or .net) or nonprofit (.org)? Does the author have the appropriate credentials and authority to write about this particular issue? Does the source cite its own sources? Does the information here seem consistent with what you already know and are reading elsewhere? Does that difference indicate innovation or inaccuracy? Does the publisher have a bias or agenda that might skew the information?

Relevance

Will this particular source advance your argument or take you off track? Not all good sources are on point enough to be included, so don't stretch your argument just to include an interesting source—save it for a future project.

Currency

What we understand about issues evolves as new arguments and information are added to the conversation, so it is important to use sources that represent current thinking. Some databases will let you select a date range for sources; consider limiting your search to articles published in the past five years. If a lot has been written on a topic, you might want to make that range even shorter. If less has been written, you might want to go back further.

ARGUING FROM SOURCES

Citing sources puts you in conversation with others who have something important to say about an issue. Good writers honor that opportunity by representing those sources fully and fairly. They edit direct quotations and paraphrase in ways that acknowledge the true intent of the original source and do not misrepresent the original text or idea by taking it out of context. In the academic domain, those sources are always given credit for their contribution to your argument through formal citation.

Quoting

Direct quotation, using the exact words of a source in quotation marks, is a powerful way to build your ethos. It shows you are willing to enter into a conversation with the intellectual humility to cite supporting viewpoints that extend your argument and opposing viewpoints that test it. Readers respect such openness.

Use direct quotation when you could not have made that point any clearer on your own. Set up quotations with a signal phrase that situates the quote meaningfully, announcing significant information, such as the author/speaker, source, and date. The signal phrase can also cue the audience on whether you are using that quotation to support your argument or represent opposing viewpoints. See Table 27.2, "Constructing Signal Phrases for Direct Quotation" for examples of signal phrases and Table 27.3 "Verbs and Adverbs for Signal Phrases" for a bank of words to help you do that work.

Paraphrasing

Paraphrasing is putting someone else's idea in your own words. Paraphrase when you can be more concise or clear than what was in the original text. In the academic domain, you must still parenthetically cite (according to the assigned style guide) the original author whose ideas you are using even if you do not use a direct quotation. Take care not to commit inadvertent plagiarism by including phrases that resemble the original text but are not put in quotation marks. Paraphrase means you are fully translating the original text into your own voice. See Table 27.4, "Direct Quotation versus Paraphrase: MLA Style" for examples of direct quotation and acceptable paraphrasing.

Table 27.2   CONSTRUCTING SIGNAL PHRASES FOR DIRECT QUOTATION

Example: In his book *Just Mercy: A Story of Justice and Redemption*, Bryan Stevenson argues incisively from experience: "My work with the poor and the incarcerated has persuaded me that the opposite of poverty is not wealth; the opposite of poverty is justice" (18).

AUTHOR (Bryan Stevenson)	SOURCE *Just Mercy: A Story of Justice and Redemption*	{adverb} incisively	{verb} argues	{punctuation} :	{quote} "My work…"	{citation} (18)
Name the author in the signal phrase or in parentheses at the end of the sentence.	Name the source if the title provides useful context; omit it if it is vague or disruptively long.	Optional: insert an adverb or phrase that indicates whether the quote supports your argument or presents an opposing viewpoint.	Use verbs that stage the quote.	Follow grammatical rules: use no punctuation if your signal phrase runs into the direct quote, use a comma or colon if the signal phrase sets up a full sentence.	Quotes can be single words, phrases, or full sentences. Use a block quote if the quote runs more than four lines.	Consult the style guide your instructor requires for correct format on citing sources.

Table 27.3   VERBS AND ADVERBS FOR SIGNAL PHRASES

	Verbs and Adverbs for Signal Phrases
Verbs	acknowledges, agrees, argues, asserts, believes, claims, concludes, concurs, confirms, criticizes, details, disagrees, discusses, disputes, emphasizes, explains, expresses, highlights, hypothesizes, illuminates, interprets, objects, observes, offers, omits, opposes, points out, remarks, reveals, says, states, succeeds, suggests, writes
Adverbs	*Neutral*—briefly, broadly, comprehensively
	Supportive—accurately, correctly, fittingly, incisively, perfectly, properly, rightly
	Opposing—erroneously, falsely, inappropriately, incorrectly, mistakenly

Citing

In all domains, good writers show respect for the conversation they enter by acknowledging their sources. In the academic domain, writers are required to cite sources in an approved style format such as MLA, APA, or Chicago. We discuss the ethical reasons why such citation is expected in academic arguments in Chapter 5, "Writing Ethics, Responsibility, and Accountability."

Analyze the assignment description to find out which style to use. Ask your instructor if the assignment description does not indicate the preferred style. You can find complete guides for common style formats in print and online sources. You can also access citation generators through your library or online. Consult the style guide before, during, and after you write to make sure you meet those expectations.

Table 27.4 DIRECT QUOTATION VERSUS PARAPHRASE: MLA STYLE

Direct Quotation	Unacceptable Paraphrase	Acceptable Paraphrase
In his book *Just Mercy: A Story of Justice and Redemption*, Bryan Stevenson explains, "The closer we get to mass incarceration and extreme levels of punishment, the more I believe it's necessary to recognize that we all need mercy, we all need justice, and—perhaps we all need some measure of unmerited grace" (18).	As we continue to send people to prison, we have to remember that everyone deserves mercy, justice, and unearned grace. **Problems:** *Stevenson is not cited but the three needs reflect his observation of attitudinal changes needed to disrupt incarceration trends.*	While some people argue that the sole purpose of prison is punishment, Bryan Stevenson asks us to consider the role of mercy in criminal justice (18).
Michael F. Maniates claims: "When responsibility for environmental problems is individualized, there is little room to ponder institutions, the nature and exercise of political power, or ways of collectively changing the distribution of power and influence in society—to, in other words, 'think institutionally.' Instead, the serious work of confronting the threatening socio-environmental processes that The Lorax so ably illuminates falls to individuals, acting alone, usually as consumers" (33).	If we do not consider how institutions perpetuate environmental problems through political power, then the environmental problem falls to individuals, who must act alone, usually as consumers, and individuals, Maniates argues, never have as much power as institutions. **Problems:** *While Maniates is named, he is not given credit for all the ideas that are his. Furthermore, some exact phrases are used without quotation and a change in tense does not adequately change wording.*	In his article "Individualization: Plant a Tree, Buy a Bike, Save the World?," Michael F. Maniates claims that Americans have generally responded to the environmental crisis as if it were a problem caused by individuals, but he argues that we should really look at institutions for causes and solutions (33).

The three most common academic styles are:

- MLA (Modern Language Association)—This style is preferred in the humanities.
- APA (American Psychological Association)—This style is preferred by the social sciences.
- Chicago (Chicago Manual of Style or CMS)—This style is often used in academic and professional publishing.

Citation formats guide you on in-text citations (the way you reference a source in the body of your writing) and on the Works Cited/References page (the list of full citations following the body of the academic argument naming all the sources actually referenced in the body of the text).

In-text citation is the way authors tell their audience how to find the sources they used. In-text citation allows readers to easily find the full citation in the Works Cited or References page at the end of the text. The in-text citation minimal requirement in MLA style is that in the sentence where a writer uses source information, the writer identifies the source author's last name and the page number (if available) where that specific information can be found. The author's last name leads readers to the list of Works Cited, which is organized alphabetically by authors' last names. See Table 27.4, "Direct Quotation versus Paraphrase: MLA Style," for examples of in-text citation of quoted and paraphrased references.

The in-text citation points readers to the Works Cited for the complete source information of all sources directly quoted or paraphrased in the argument. A complete style guide will tell you exactly how to format each source you use based on three factors: (1) the number of authors (zero to many), (2) the type of source (book to performance), and (3) how you accessed that source (online database to personal interview). Given all the style guides and all the factors within each guide, we recommend you consult an official style guide to make sure you have every detail correct—from punctuation to capitalization. Table 27.5, "Works Cited: Common Examples in MLA Format," shows how to cite three common sources in MLA style: a book, a journal article, and a website.

Table 27.5   WORKS CITED: COMMON EXAMPLES IN MLA FORMAT

SOURCE TYPE	MODELS BASED ON *MLA HANDBOOK* (8TH ED.)
Book (one author, print)	**Format**: Last Name, First Name. *Title of Book*. Publisher, Publication year.
	Example: Butler, Paul. *Chokehold: Policing Black Men*. The New Press, 2017.
Scholarly Journal Article (two authors, print)	**Format**: Last Name, First Name and First Name Last Name. "Title of Article." *Title of Journal*, volume, issue, date, pages.
	Example: Anque, Don, and Christopher Doval. "Latinos Seek Environmental Justice and Public Discourse for Underserved Communities in the United States." *Harvard Journal of Hispanic Policy*, vol. 26, 2013, pp. 13–20.
Website (one page, example has no author, publishing organization and title of site are the same, no version available)	**Format**: Last Name, First Name. "Title of Page." *Title of Website*, version number, publishing organization, date of site creation, URL/DOI/permalink. Date of access.
	Example: "The Facts: Criminal Justice Facts." *The Sentencing Project*, 2017, www.sentencingproject.org/criminal-justice-facts. Accessed 26 Mar. 2018.
Personal Interview (original interview you conduct yourself in person, by phone, or electronically)	**Format**: Last Name, First Name. Personal Interview. Date.
	Example: Tran, Cindy. Personal Interview. 26 February 2018.
Speech, Lecture, Oral Presentation	**Format**: Speaker's Last Name, First Name. "Title." Name of event, name of sponsoring organization, date, name of venue, city, state. Descriptor [Speech, Lecture, Reading, Conference Presentation, Keynote Address, etc.].
	Example: Yousafzai, Malala. Nobel Lecture, Nobel Peace Prize 2014, 10 December 2014, Oslo, Sweden. Lecture.

This table shows the exact order and format for three common types of sources. If your source does not have an element of this information, omit that item from your reference.

See Chapter 5, "Office Hours: Understanding Common Knowledge" for a discussion of ideas and facts that are considered such common knowledge that they do not need to be cited.

Academic arguments rely on the citation of sound sources. Good writers pursue sources through reliable academic methods that help them find sources that will expand all sides of an issue by locating the strongest evidence and arguments. They wrestle with other ideas and challenging facts in order to strengthen their own positon. Good writers write the kind of arguments that others would want to cite in their arguments.

OFFICE HOURS ➤ Who Thought That? Claiming Claims While Citing Sources

Good writers wade into the world of existing knowledge through sources and create arguments that add value to the world of ideas. You don't have to create something entirely new—although you might. Good writers aim to offer arguments with what we might call informed originality—they add something new to what we already know.

All that wading into ideas, though, can saturate your mind so much that it becomes hard to distinguish the source of ideas. You might find yourself asking, "Whose idea is that?" You might even find yourself channeling the voice of some of your sources, wondering, "Whose voice is that—theirs, mine, or ours?" Doing careful note-taking through the research process will help you track the origin of those ideas so you do not plagiarize unintentionally. See Chapter 9, "Read: Strategies for Reading in Research," for guidance.

So the goal is to expand knowledge. Advance the conversation on this issue and cite the people who helped you make that progress. Take questions of citations to experts—your instructor, librarians, writing tutors—so that they can help you disentangle that wonderful web of ideas to give credit where credit it is due: to your sources and to you.

CHAPTER twenty eight

Working with Human Sources

In Chapter 27, "Working with Published Sources," we address the process of doing research with published sources in the form of writing for both scholarly and general audiences. You might also find that your writing requires other types of sources, such as fieldwork or conversations with people whose expertise supports your argument or illustrates your research. When you create this new data using research methods such as interviews or focus groups, you must ensure that your information is accurate, that no one is harmed by your interaction, and that benefits increase. This chapter defines human subjects research, explains common types of human subjects research, and explores the ethical considerations of using this type of research in your writing.

HUMAN SUBJECTS RESEARCH: A DEFINITION

Increasingly, undergraduates are encouraged to participate in research. Depending on the discipline, that research might have you looking at archival texts in the library, using microscopes in a lab, uncovering artifacts at an archeological dig, or many other types of activities. All these activities require training on research methods and ethical conduct for that discipline so that your research is reliable and respectful to the objects and subjects you study. When those research activities require you to work with human beings, specific federal and academic institutional guidelines are in place to help you understand how to do that effectively and ethically.

This chapter provides an introduction to some methods and principles of human subjects research. If you study a field that requires research, you will take courses that give you a full overview of research methods and ethical conduct specific to your discipline. This chapter gives you a foundation in just a few of those research areas that might be relevant to your study of writing.

What Is Human Subjects Research?

When we talk about "human subjects" in research, we mean the type of research that takes human beings as its focus and/or as a source—in the form of observation, interaction, intervention, or the use of private and identifiable information.

The U.S. Department of Health and Human Service's foundational definition of ethical research appears in a section of the Belmont Report (1979) titled "Ethical Principles and Guidelines for the Protection of Human Subjects of Research." This definition is specified further in a federal policy known as the "Common Rule." In the Belmont Report, research is defined as a formal, organized activity with the purpose of expanding knowledge through rigorous methods of experimentation, then sharing those findings as "generalizable knowledge" (a representation of research that others could rely on as sound knowledge) in forums such as publications and conferences. This level of research requires students and faculty to submit a plan, or protocol, for their research to a committee at their university typically called the Institutional Review Board (IRB). The IRB decides if the research plan meets the required level of ethical conduct for research. Students and faculty who intend to publish their findings or present them widely must get *prior* approval from this board to do so and check in with them as research progresses.

Expectations vary across institutions, but generally, human subjects research (such as interviews and focus groups) conducted for a class assignment that is not shared beyond that class does not have to be submitted to an IRB (if you are working with vulnerable populations, such as children or prisoners, you and your instructor should still check with your school's IRB). This coursework would not have to go through IRB because you do not intend to publish or present the results of your research to an external audience as "generalizable knowledge." Your instructor will confirm your research status. However, you are still held to high standards for ethical conduct with human subjects. In fact, your instructor might ask you to complete the student version of the national Collaborative Institutional Training Initiative (CITI), a short web-based training that prepares you to conduct human subjects research.

Working with human subjects is an effective, rewarding, and innovative way to advance your thinking and your writing. Authors who capture unique voices of experience and expertise through original human subjects research raise the level of ethos and logos in their project to a level difficult to match by other methods.

How Do You Plan for Human Subjects Research?

Unlike library and archival documents, which are logistically easy to locate and retrieve, working with human subjects can be much more complicated. Human subjects can be hard to connect with and unpredictable when you do.

To address those challenges, a key recommendation for working with human subjects is to start early. The process of locating and confirming the participation of human subjects can be time-consuming. The more time you allow, the better chance you have of getting this completed on time for your writing process (see Chapter 7, "Plan: Organizing the Process").

Here are some of the steps in the process of working with human subjects:

- Identify the human subjects who would be best for your research (who has the background, experience, and expertise you want to investigate)
- Determine the most appropriate recruiting method: face-to-face, flyers, hyperlinks to online sites, and so forth
- Locate the appropriate approval and documents from your instructor and campus administrators
- Secure the best contact information for the intended human subjects
- Prepare a compelling request for their participation in your research
- Confirm the time, place, and length of interview or focus group in an appropriate setting
- Conduct the interview or focus group

The second recommendation for planning to work with human subjects is to plan for success but prepare for failure. When interviews, focus groups, and observations go well, they often become the highlight of the research. Those new voices and ideas are tailored to your project, and that often captures and retains readers.

However, *getting* an interview, for example, does not automatically mean you will get a *strong* interview. You might interview someone who wanders in ways that do not advance your research, or your subjects might not say as much as you want due to nervousness, lack of trust, or inexperience. People might give you conflicting information either because they do not remember or have not fully processed what they think.

To account for the possibility that you might not get the information you need from your human subjects, plan to schedule multiple opportunities to gather original data. In the following sections, we review strategies for planning, scheduling, and gathering useful data from human subjects.

What Ethical Issues Should You Consider When Doing Human Subjects Research?

Even as an undergraduate researcher whose work does not go through the IRB, you must still meet ethical standards. The following table outlines the professional research standards outlined in the Belmont Report, which set the national standards *required* for professional research on human subjects. It compares those professional expectations to typical classroom expectations for meeting the same goals of ethical research even if they do not have to go through the formal review process of documentation and proposals in the IRB.

Table 28.1   GUIDELINES FOR RESEARCH WITH HUMAN SUBJECTS

The Belmont Report: Ethical Guidelines for Professional Research with Human Subjects Considered for IRB Approval	Ethical Guidelines for Classes that Conduct Research with Human Subjects Without a Formal IRB
Principle 1: **Respect for Persons** People should be treated as autonomous agents; people with diminished capacity should be protected *Action*: Use an informed consent form to help explain the research goals, risks, and benefits. Do so in a clear form in person in a manner that does not confuse or pressure the subject to participate. Have the person confirm with signatures that they agree to participate voluntarily under the conditions described in the informed consent form.	*Principle 1 Questions* Are the people you want to interview *free* to say yes or no without consequences? Do they have the mental ability to understand if there are consequences? Prisoners, minors under the age of 18, and people with physical and mental disabilities might not be able to participate freely and fairly, so they require extra protection as potential human subjects. *Action*: Discuss the need for an informed consent form with your instructor. Your institution might already have a template for undergraduate research; alternatively, your instructor can work with you to create such a form. Make sure subjects understand the research goals, risks, and benefits. Do not pressure people to participate.

Principle 2: **Beneficence** First, do no harm to the human subjects or people affected by this research. Second, maximize possible benefits and minimize possible harms related to this research.	*Principle 2 Questions* Do the benefits of conducting this research outweigh potential harms? Have you done everything possible to determine potential harm and increase potential benefit?
Action: Systematically assess the probability and scale of risks and benefits. Do due diligence to make sure your research design and methods are sound by con-sidering all risks and benefits.	*Action:* Write a research proposal in which you explain why it is necessary to conduct this interview or focus group. Discuss potential risks and harms to people who choose to participate. Do this even if this is not a required part of a class assignment so that you can explain the rationale to your human subjects when you meet them.
Principle 3: **Justice** Consider who should receive benefits and who should bear burdens of the research process and its results. *Action:* Design fair procedures and outcomes for selecting human subjects.	*Principle 3 Questions* Is distribution of research benefits and burdens fair? Are research subjects chosen based on relevance or random purposes? Are they chosen in a way that makes some bear more of the burden and less of the benefit?
	Action: Design a fair way to select human subjects for your project, perhaps randomly selecting from among eligible participants. When the research is complete, and possibly along the way, share it with the participants so that they benefit from the results of their participation, and they learn what you learn.

COMMON TYPES OF HUMAN SUBJECTS RESEARCH

Following are some of the common types of human subjects research used in undergraduate writing courses, many that require engaging experts in the community.

Interviews

Many researched writing projects benefit from personal interviews with people who have expertise and/or experience directly related to your research questions. If you can get the right person (or people) to agree to an interview, and if you ask the right questions and draw out complete answers, your research can offer original insight on the topic.

Some possible disadvantages to pursuing interviews include that you might not be able to interview the ideal subject for your topic due to such barriers as their status as a vulnerable person who cannot consent to research, or their availability compared with your availability and deadlines. You might also find that you set up an interview that does not go as planned. The measures outlined in this chapter will help you increase the likelihood of having a successful interview with an expert. Once you determine that you do have permission to pursue an interview with someone who could advance your writing and research, carefully consider the following:

Logistics

To help make sure your interview is successful, be organized in how it will happen and be clear about expectations. Following are some questions your interviewee might have before agreeing to an interview:

- Where and how is the content of this interview being used? (Consider: Is this just for class or will you submit it for publication somewhere? State all possibilities and let the interviewee know if plans change later and you want to share it with a wider audience.)

- Will the interview be conducted face-to-face or by phone, email, or video conferencing? Will the interview be audio or video recorded?
- How long will the interview last?
- Will there be follow-up questions or interviews at a later date? (Ask if it's okay to follow-up with points of clarification or with new questions.)
- Will you give the interviewee a copy of the final write-up and/or share drafts for his/her approval?
- Will there be an incentive, such as a gift card, for participation? What will it be specifically? How much will it be? When/how will it be delivered?

Principles

1. Persistence and Polite, Professional Persuasion. Once you identify someone whose expertise and/or experience could make a significant contribution to your research and whom your instructor approves, contact that person to request an interview. Use a polite, professional tone to persuade the person to accept your invitation. Explain how this interview would benefit both you and, to some degree, the person being interviewed (either directly or because you are addressing an issue that person cares about). Outline the timeline, research goals, intended audience, and any other details the person might want to know before consenting to the interview. If that person is busy, it might take both persuasion and persistence to get your invitation delivered and accepted. Start this process early so that your deadlines do not pressure the interviewee.

2. Prepare and Plan. Once your interviewee agrees to the interview, it is time to plan your questions. Write out more questions than you think you will have time for so that you have plenty to draw from. Begin with ice-breaker questions to help build rapport with the interviewee, but do not ask basic questions easily answered through existing data, as the interviewee might feel that you are wasting his or her time. For example, you could say, "I know that you have an M.D. and a master's degree in public health. As a primary care physician, how do you think your background in public health affects the way you practice medicine for low income patients?" Move from ice-breaker questions to priority questions when you both start to feel at ease. Keep track of time and purpose, moving to your priority questions quickly enough to allow your interviewee to give full answers. How quickly you shift might depend on how well you know the person already and the sensitivity of the questions you ask.

3. Connect and Care. The mutual benefit you describe in your request for an interview should be sincere. Take care that your interviewee senses that you care as much about *his or her* experience in the interview as you do about getting what *you* need out of it. That initial exchange in which you build rapport is essential in helping the interviewee trust you with his or her story—whether that story is more objective or more personal. The interviewee wants to know that you are listening carefully and will represent what is said accurately and with respect. In addition to what you say, your tone and body language go a long way in establishing that relationship.

4. Focus, with Flexibility. Enter your interview with a specific research project and direction in mind and know how this interview fits into your research intentions. Stay focused and do not let the conversation wander away from the topic you came to discuss. However, it is also important to listen well enough to let the interviewee steer you into a better story and research plan.

5. Don't Dodge Difficulty. You might have some tough questions on your research question script. They might be hard for you to ask and hard for your interviewees to answer. However, if you need to have those questions answered for your research, and if you were clear that you would ask this type of question, persist gently until you either get an answer or a firm refusal. If interviewees refuse to answer a question or follow your line of inquiry, they might have changed their mind about telling the story or do not feel comfortable telling that story to you. If that happens, be polite and gracious, but give them every opportunity to share if they want to by repeating your question in new ways and asking follow-up questions to make sure they know what you want them to address.

6. Wait and Watch. The most challenging task for you as an interviewer is absorbing your subject's answers. Your recording device will capture what is *said*, but your job as an interviewer is to absorb and respond to what is *meant*. That means paying attention not just to words but to the silences and body language that reveal *how* someone is feeling about what they are saying. Stay alert and attentive right to the end—the wrap-up is often when people disclose the clearest, deepest comments. The most important question you might ask is a sincere closing invitation, "Do you want to tell me anything else?"

To become more confident and comfortable with interviewing, workshop your questions with peers and your instructor to make sure the tone and sequence move from ice-breaking and relationship-building to more focused curiosity. Get a feel for tone, timing, and sequence, and then revise accordingly.

Checklist ➤ Interviews and Focus Groups

Before the Interview

☐ Write a rationale for how and who you will interview based on the guidelines for ethical research on human subjects in Table 28.1.

☐ Get a copy of your institution's informed consent form, or create one with the support of your instructor; interviewees must complete the form before you begin.

☐ Contact your potential interviewees in a polite, professional exchange. Explain the nature of your research, how

(Continued)

the interviewee might contribute to and benefit from the research, and when and where it would be ideal to conduct the interview. Share an informed consent form so that your expectations are clear.

☐ Reserve recording equipment if necessary and test to make sure it is working properly and you know how to use all relevant functions.

☐ Consider whether your questions could prompt your interviewees to divulge sensitive or even traumatic information. Prepare your response.

During the Interview

☐ Arrive on time, rested and alert.

☐ Bring two copies of your informed consent form for each interviewee (one copy for you, one copy for the interviewee). Both copies should be signed by both parties.

☐ Bring all recording equipment, fully powered.

☐ Ensure that the room is and remains appropriately private.

☐ Take handwritten notes throughout the interview in case the recording equipment fails and to note additional body language and cues about meaning that would not be picked up by the recording device.

☐ Maintain eye contact and make sure the interviewee is comfortable, especially if talking about difficult topics.

☐ Monitor the recording equipment to make sure it continues to work properly.

☐ Monitor the clock to make sure you are moving through your questions at an appropriate pace given the length of time you reserved with the interviewee.

After the Interview

☐ Thank the interviewees immediately in person for sharing their time and insight. Follow up within a week with a handwritten thank you card or email.

☐ If you promised compensation in your informed consent form, deliver it promptly.

☐ Contact the interviewees with limited follow-up questions if you reserved the right to do so.

☐ Share drafts of the research in progress if you agreed to do so.

☐ Deliver a copy of the completed research to the interviewees so that they benefit from what they shared with you.

☐ If you feel unsettled by anything your interviewee shared, talk with your instructor.

Focus Groups

A focus group is a small group of people whom you gather to address questions related to your research. A focus group is useful if it is important to hear conversation about the issue you are researching among people with relevant backgrounds. In a group, you hear multiple perspectives at once, and you can observe whether or not someone can be easily persuaded by others to think differently on that issue. Carefully consider what points of view or backgrounds you want represented in the group.

Disadvantages of focus groups include the fact that you might hear less from each individual because the time is divided, and some individuals might not feel comfortable dissenting from the group. You can reduce those possibilities by actively attending to the flow of the conversation and adjusting questions to increase trust and equal participation.

Although the same logistics and principles outlined for individual interviews apply to working with a focus group, it is more challenging to negotiate those details with a group of people. You need to be sure you have addressed all their expectations, are probing deeper based on their silences and body language, and they all have room to disclose what they most deeply want to share.

Observations

Observation is useful when you have a research question that can be answered through deliberate observation of human activity that you have permission to watch.

Address two key aspects of your methodology when designing observations:

1. Consider whether the observation will be obtrusive or unobtrusive. If the observation is obtrusive, your presence is known to those being observed; you might also participate actively with those being observed thus potentially affecting the action. If it is unobtrusive, you do not notify those being observed about the research and you stay detached from the action.
2. Consider whether anonymity of identity can be protected for human subjects based on the scale and demographics of people being observed.

Work with your instructor to explore these elements of the observation you want to design.

How you conduct your observation and how you report on it should be guided by ethical standards outlined in the Belmont Report and enforced by IRBs. For example, policies differ for public versus private locations because people have different rights and expectations in those environments.

Surveys

Surveys help academic researchers contact a large number of people to yield a significant number of responses (the "sample size") to a consistent set of questions. If gathered accurately, the larger sample size can yield more reliable data. Online survey tools have made this process both efficient and inexpensive, and therefore accessible to undergraduate researchers. Surveys can be used to gather a broad and diverse sample of responses to research questions so that you can begin to see trends in attitudes and experiences that will inform your study.

Whether or not a survey is considered human subjects research depends on what you ask. Gathering personal information that could be used to identify specific individuals along with questions about what that person thinks or has experienced which could put them at risk if their identifying information is revealed, could be considered sensitive data. Being "at risk" could mean that you stir up traumatic experiences that cause emotional pain, jeopardize someone's employment or standing at school, or make their location known to abusers. If you must gather sensitive data for your research, then your project should be guided by the ethical code of conduct outlined by the Belmont Report (Table 28.1) to protect the people who are taking that survey to advance your research.

The guidelines for professional research on human subjects outlined in this chapter serve as the foundation for ethical conduct in any academic research project. The principles and reasons for protecting human subjects are the same, whether an IRB is involved or not: respect the dignity of human beings, and use procedures that increase the likelihood of accurate, reliable data. The challenge of meeting those high expectations is rewarded with an irreplaceable exchange of information that advances what we know about the human experience.

OFFICE HOURS ➤ When What You Hear Is Heavy

For some research projects, you might know that you are asking questions about sensitive information that could lead your interviewees to share deeply personal and sometimes painful information. In other cases, you might not have any idea that what you ask will lead your interviewee to reveal something sensitive, even traumatic. When you connect with people through conversation, particularly people on the margins of society who are not often invited to speak, it is hard to predict what they will share. They might not know themselves until it happens.

If you anticipate that the topic of your interview could stir up difficult memories for interviewees, work with your instructor and peers before the interview to make sure you are prepared to accommodate and alleviate their discomfort. Here are some ways to prepare for this ethical challenge:

- When you request the interview, be clear about the topic of your research and the nature of your questions. This gives your interviewees time to prepare mentally and emotionally, if necessary, and decline if desired.
- Practice asking the questions with a peer before the interview. Ask your peer to give some answers that include sensitive information.
- Practice what you will say if the conversation does get heavy.
- Have interviewees sign an informed consent form that states clearly how information from the interview will be used so that they have a sense of the audience and can choose to share at their own comfort level.
- At the start of the interview, remind interviewees that they can stop the interview anytime or refuse to answer any questions.

If you are in an interview and the conversation does turn to serious matters, such as physical abuse, addiction, death, or criminal activity, think first about the person or people in front of you and second about the research. Ask if your interviewees are comfortable sharing that information. Ask if they are okay. Say they can stop anytime. Ask if there is someone else they would like to share this with as well. If the information is relevant to your research, confirm that they are still comfortable with you including that in your writing. Remind them of the informed consent form they gave you regarding anonymity and make sure they are still comfortable with their choice given how this will be shared. You have an ethical obligation to reduce risk to your human subjects by making sure they are comfortable with what goes into your research.

When someone tells you about a traumatic experience, it can be traumatic for you as well. Talk to your instructor about your experience. If you heard something that troubles you, your instructor can help you find support yourself and, if necessary, for the person you interviewed.

credits

Index

Figures and tables are indicated by f and t following the page number.